CLOCKWORK PLANET

III

STORY BY YUU KAMIYA & TSUBAKI HIMANA
MANGA BY KURO
CHARACTER DESIGN BY SINO

ClockWork Planet
CONTENTS

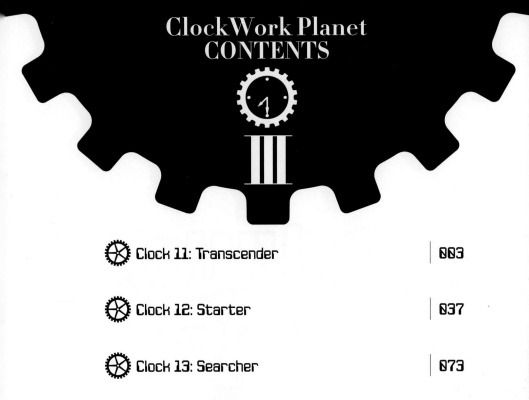

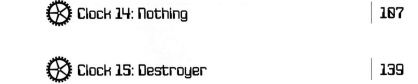 Clock 11: Transcender | 003

 Clock 12: Starter | 037

Clock 13: Searcher | 073

Clock 14: Nothing | 107

Clock 15: Destroyer | 139

Afterword | 170

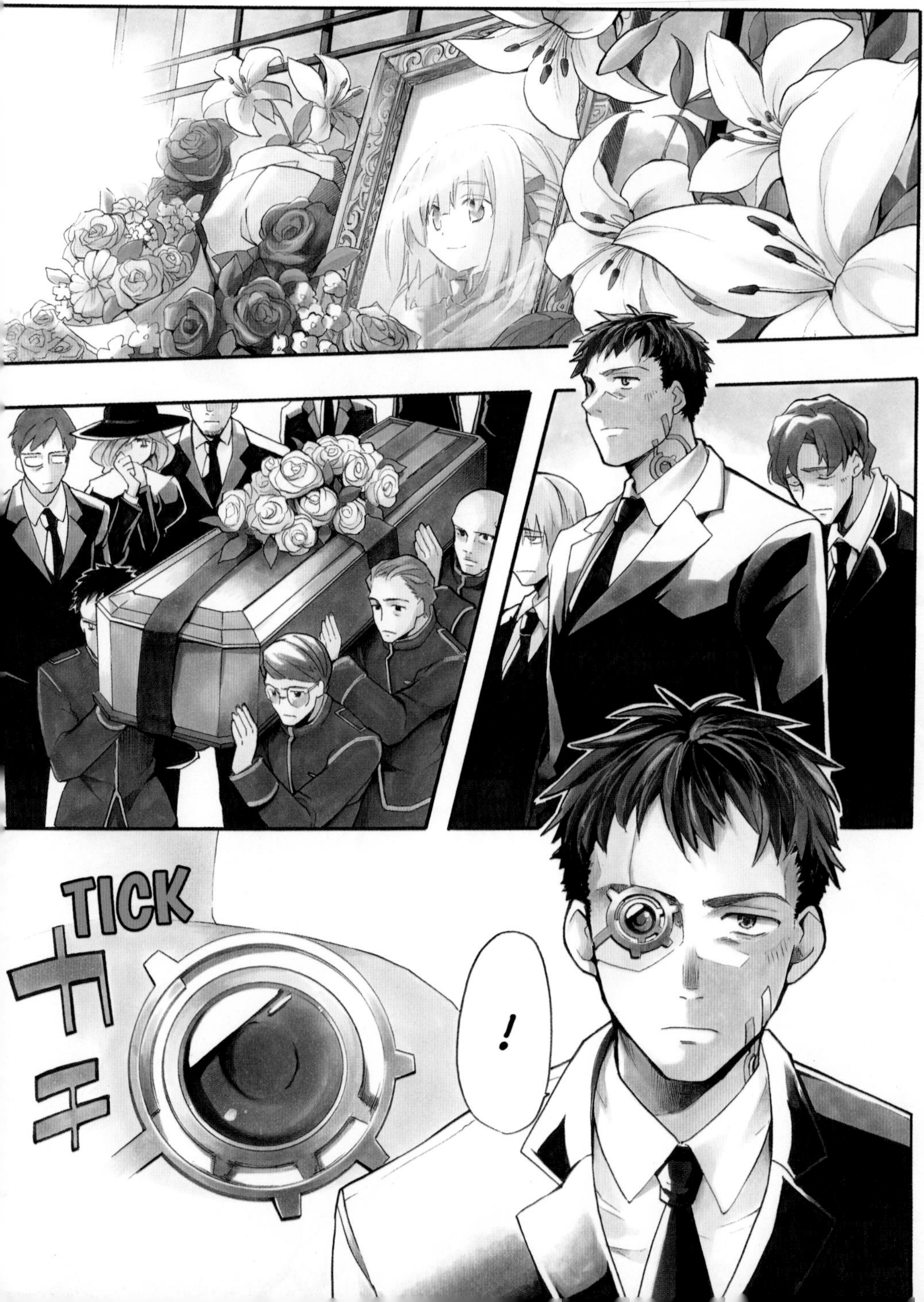
TICK
!

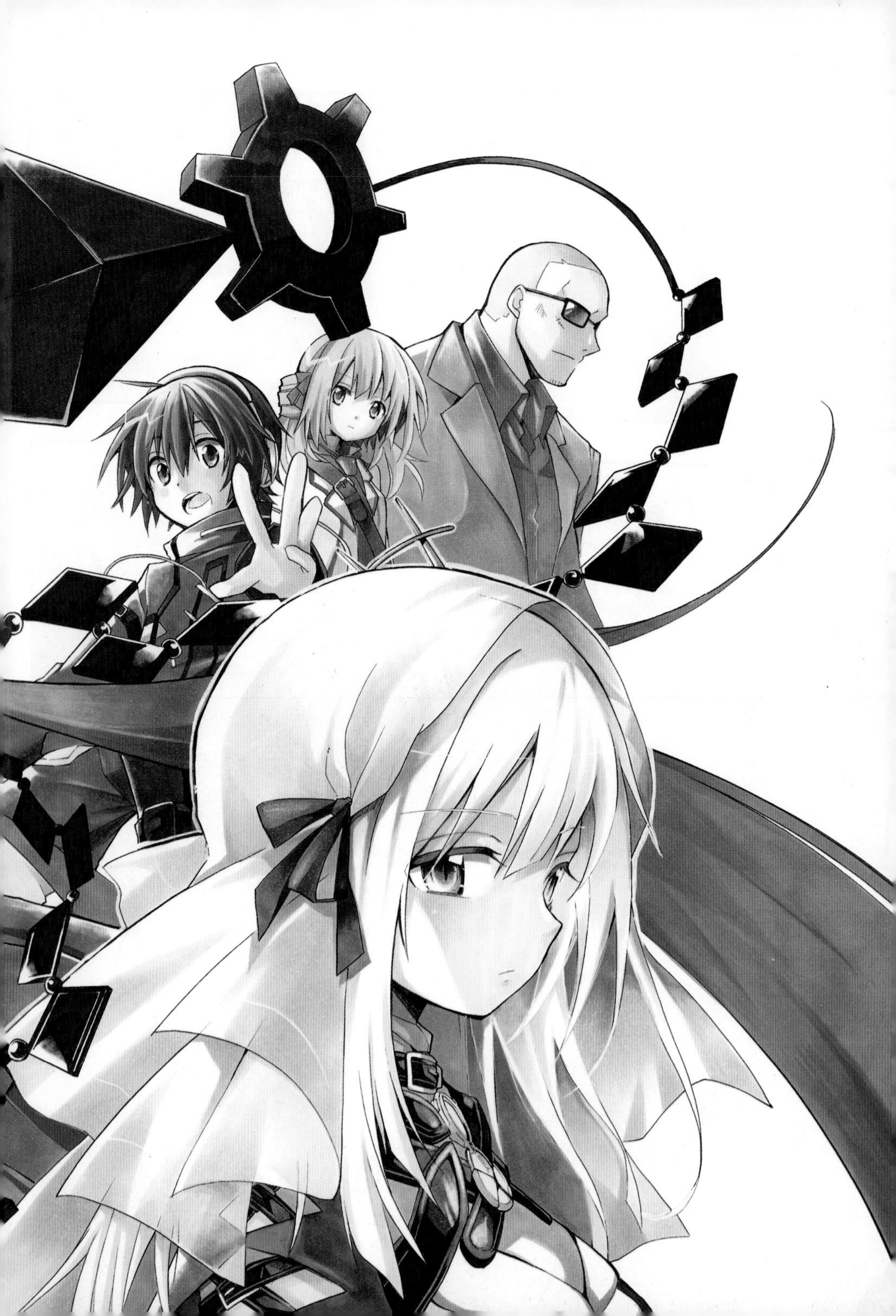

Clock 11: Transcender

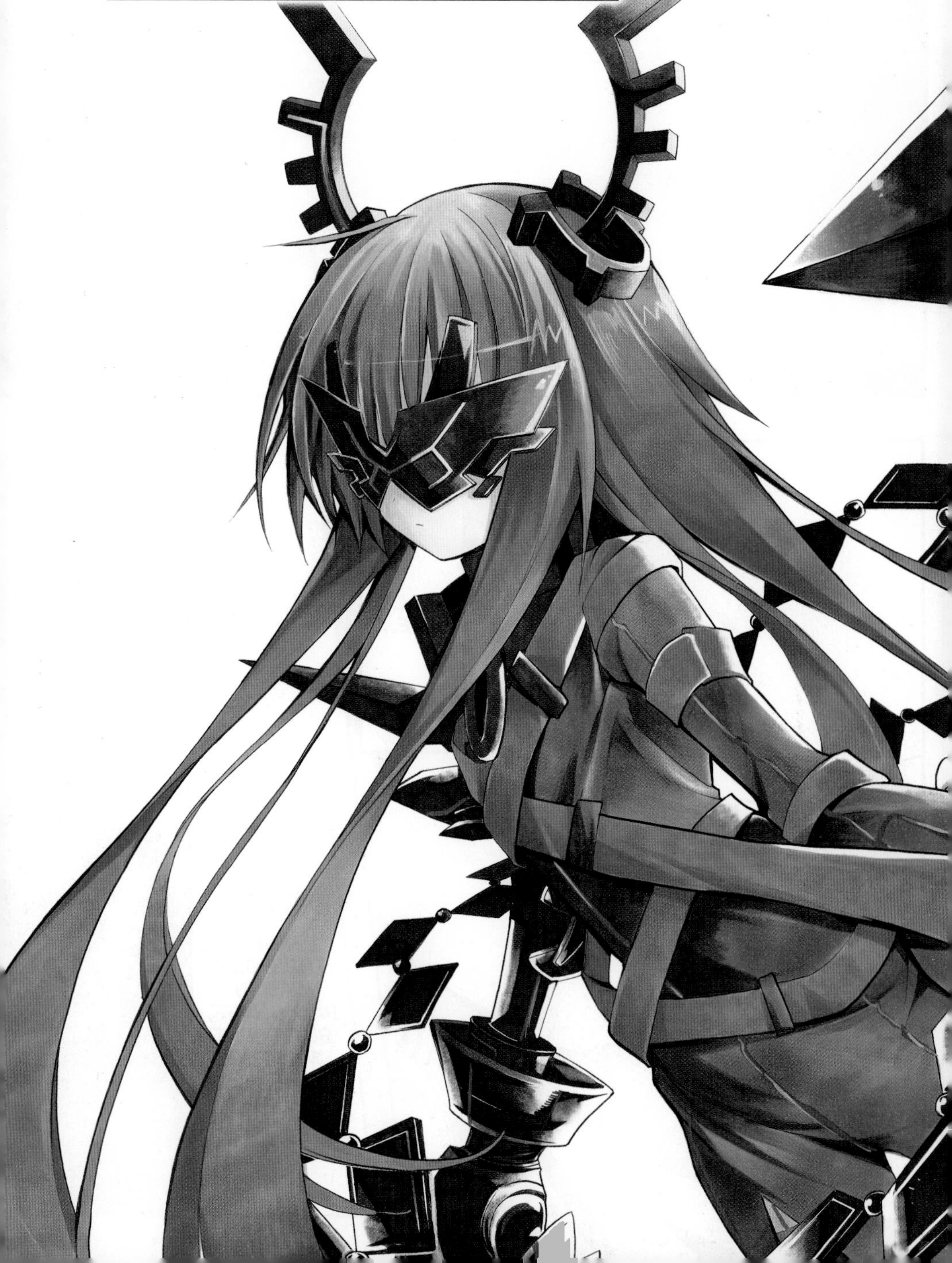

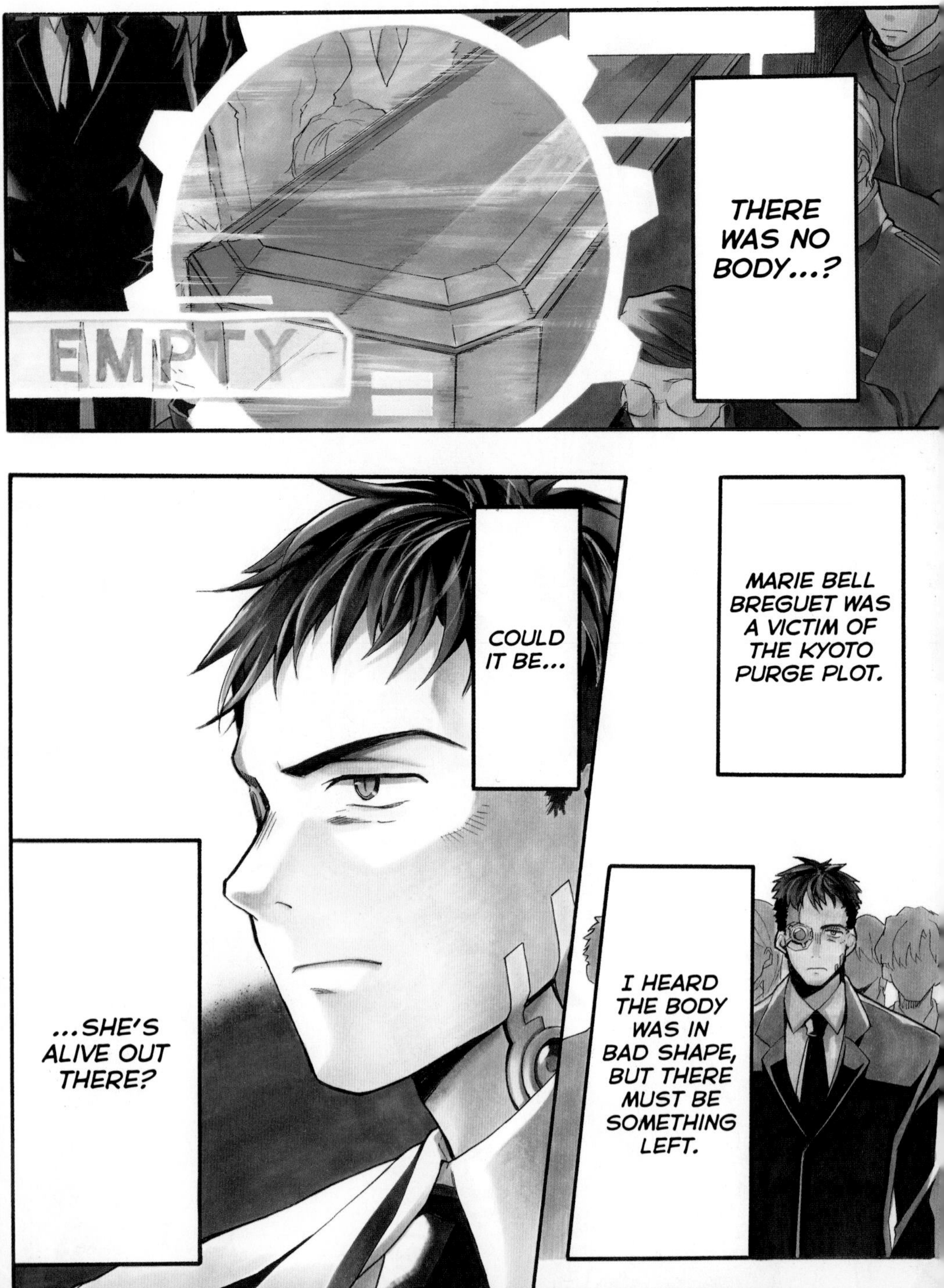
THERE WAS NO BODY...?
EMPTY
MARIE BELL BREGUET WAS A VICTIM OF THE KYOTO PURGE PLOT.
I HEARD THE BODY WAS IN BAD SHAPE, BUT THERE MUST BE SOMETHING LEFT.
COULD IT BE...
...SHE'S ALIVE OUT THERE?

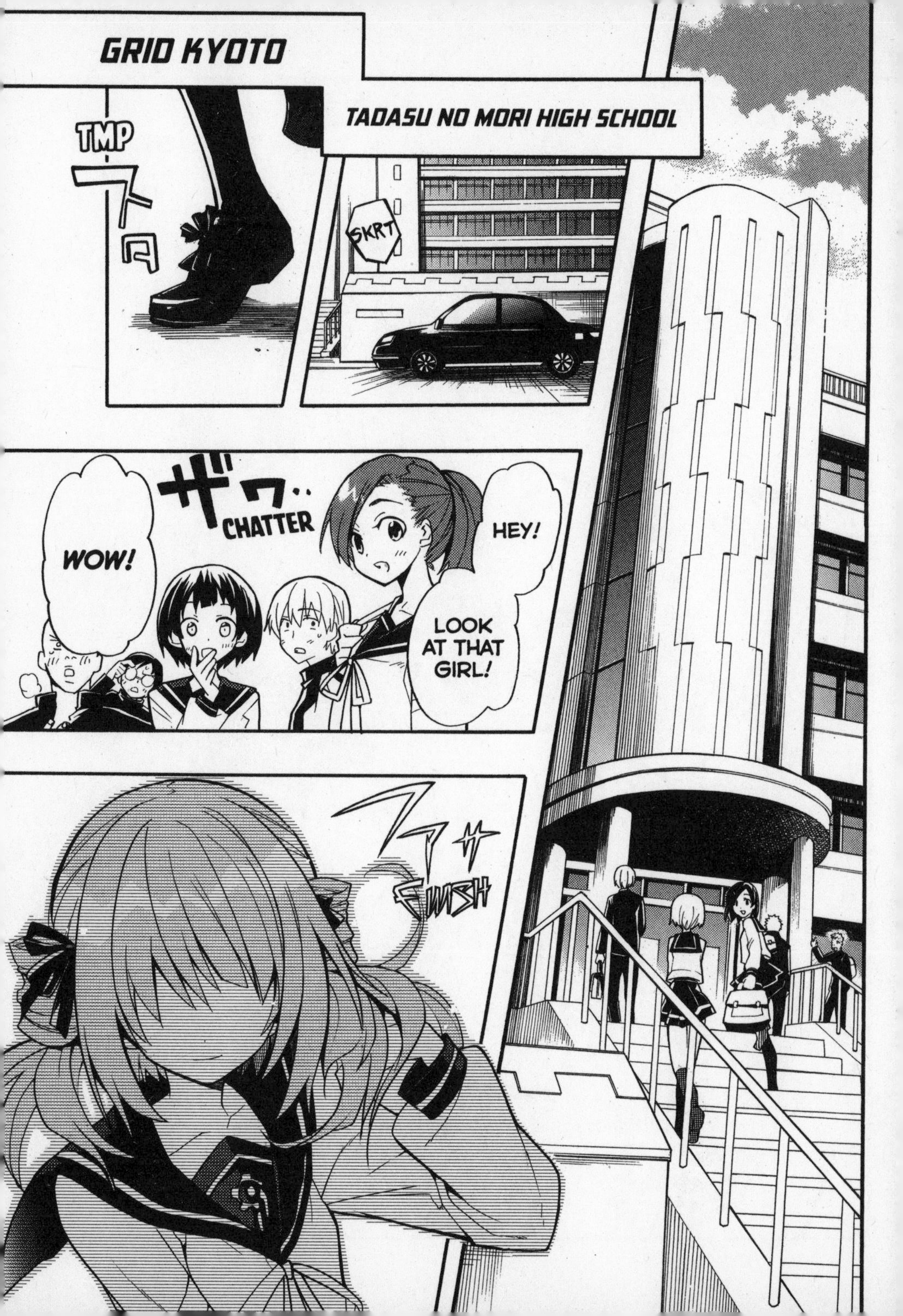
GRID KYOTO
TADASU NO MORI HIGH SCHOOL
SKRT
TMP
HEY!
LOOK AT THAT GIRL!
CHATTER
WOW!
FWISH

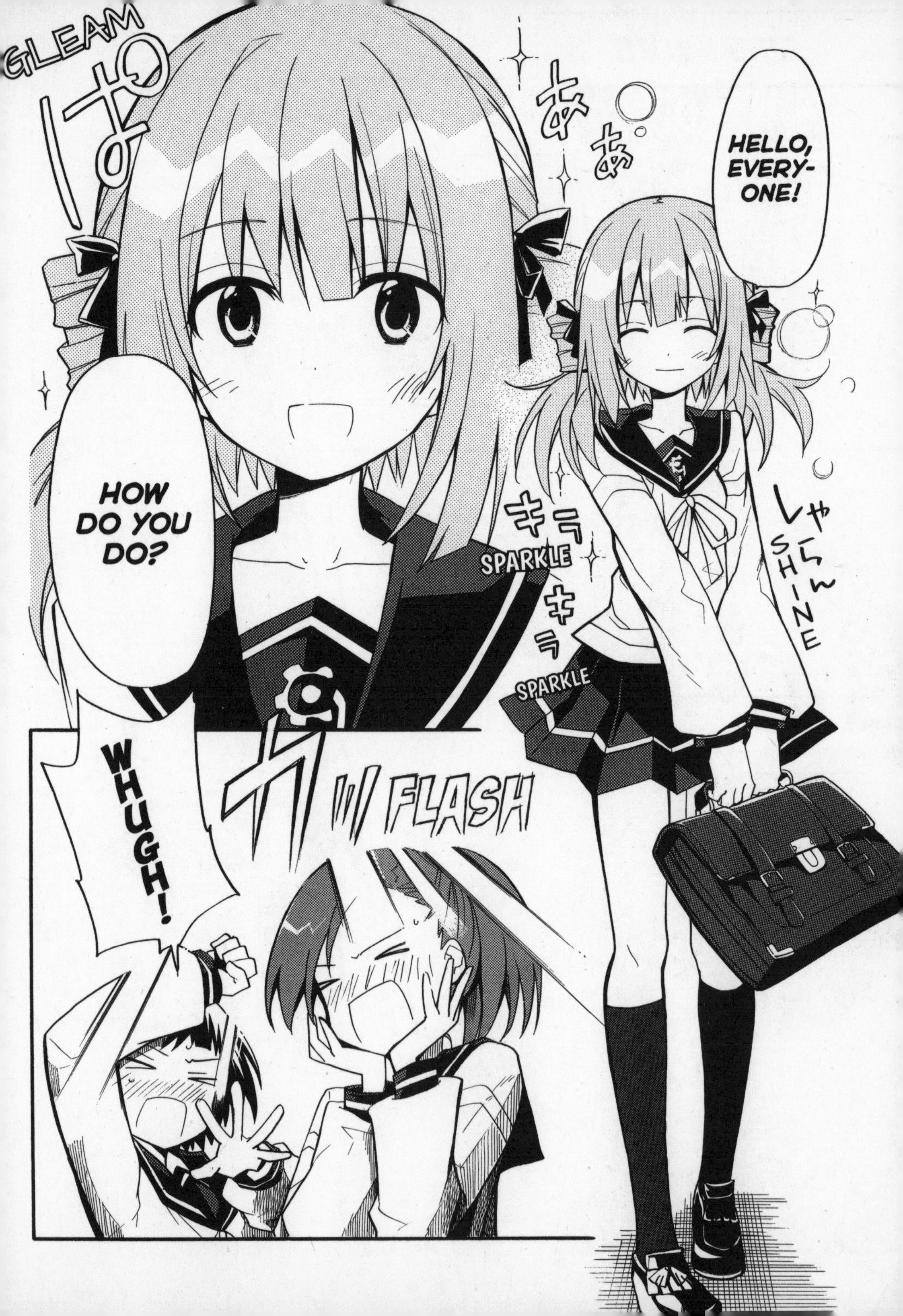
HELLO, EVERY-ONE!
しゃらん
SHINE
キラ
SPARKLE
キラ
SPARKLE
あぁ
ぱー
GLEAM
HOW DO YOU DO?
ガッ
FLASH
WHUGH!

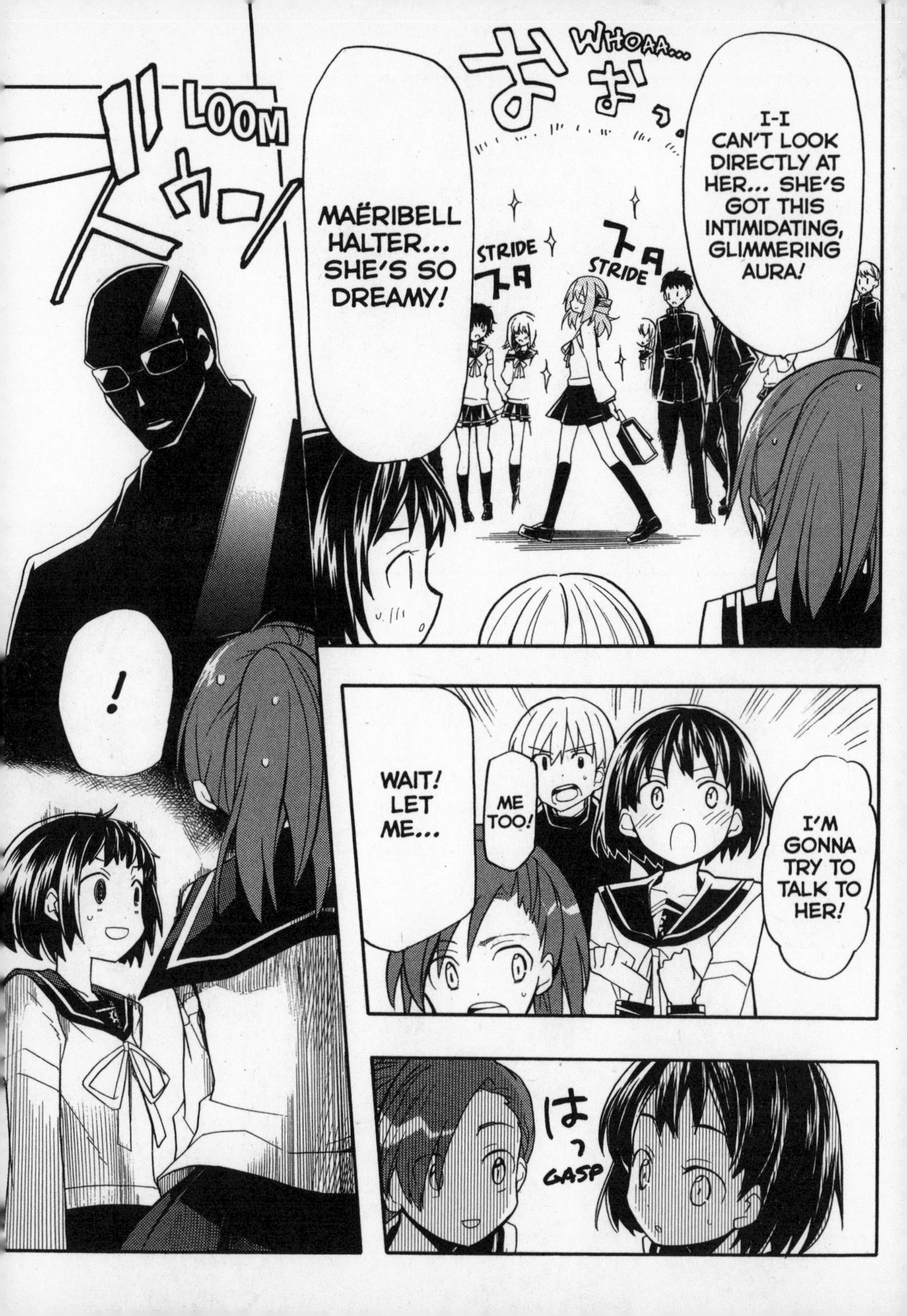
I-I CAN'T LOOK DIRECTLY AT HER... SHE'S GOT THIS INTIMIDATING, GLIMMERING AURA!
WHOAA...
STRIDE
STRIDE
MAËRIBELL HALTER... SHE'S SO DREAMY!
LOOM
I'M GONNA TRY TO TALK TO HER!
ME TOO!
WAIT! LET ME...
GASP
!

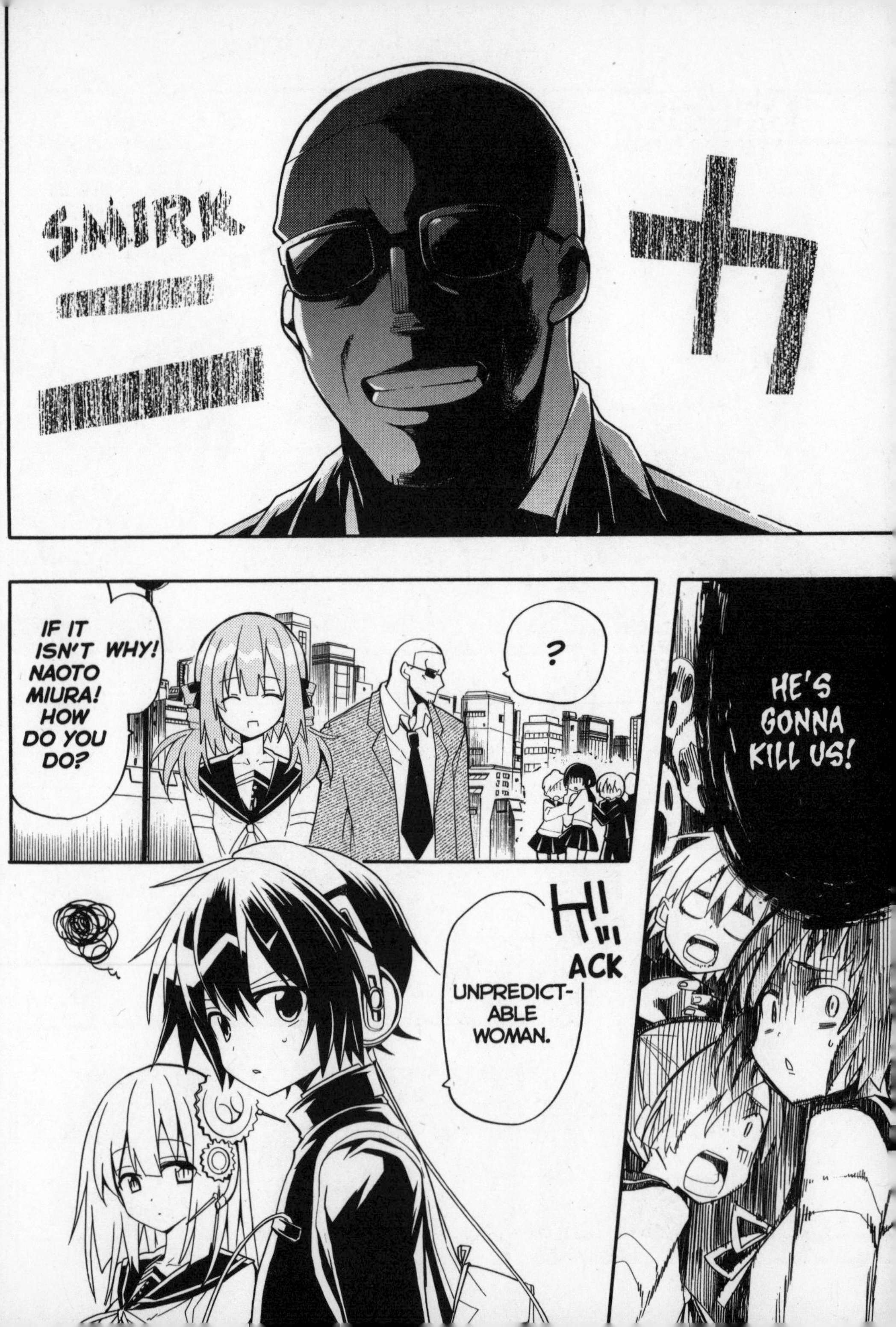
SMIRK
HE'S GONNA KILL US!
IF IT ISN'T WHY! NAOTO MIURA! HOW DO YOU DO?
?
ACK
UNPREDICT-ABLE WOMAN.

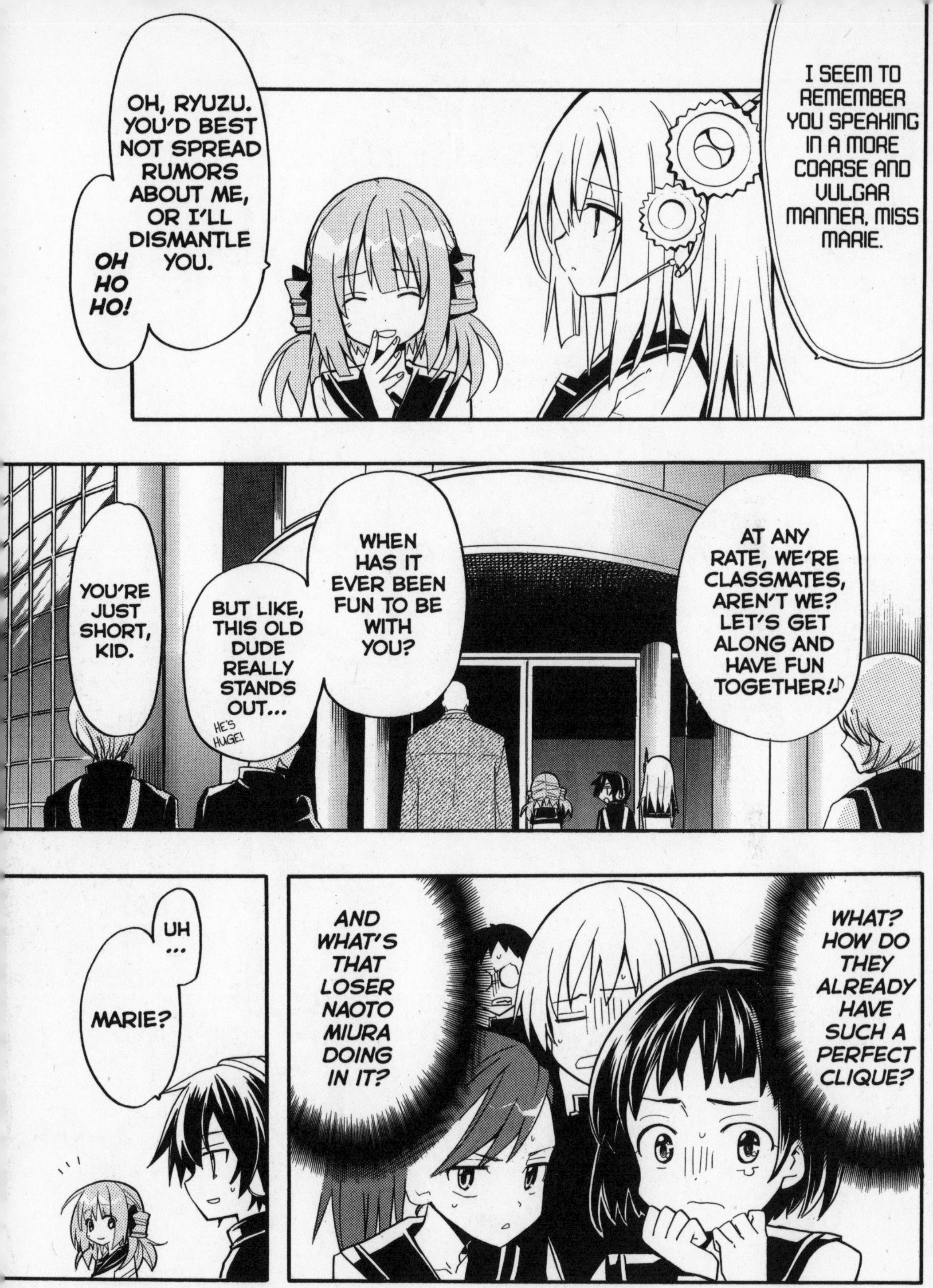
I SEEM TO REMEMBER YOU SPEAKING IN A MORE COARSE AND VULGAR MANNER, MISS MARIE.
OH, RYUZU. YOU'D BEST NOT SPREAD RUMORS ABOUT ME, OR I'LL DISMANTLE YOU.
OH HO HO!
AT ANY RATE, WE'RE CLASSMATES, AREN'T WE? LET'S GET ALONG AND HAVE FUN TOGETHER!♪
WHEN HAS IT EVER BEEN FUN TO BE WITH YOU?
BUT LIKE, THIS OLD DUDE REALLY STANDS OUT...
HE'S HUGE!
YOU'RE JUST SHORT, KID.
WHAT? HOW DO THEY ALREADY HAVE SUCH A PERFECT CLIQUE?
AND WHAT'S THAT LOSER NAOTO MIURA DOING IN IT?
UH ...
MARIE?

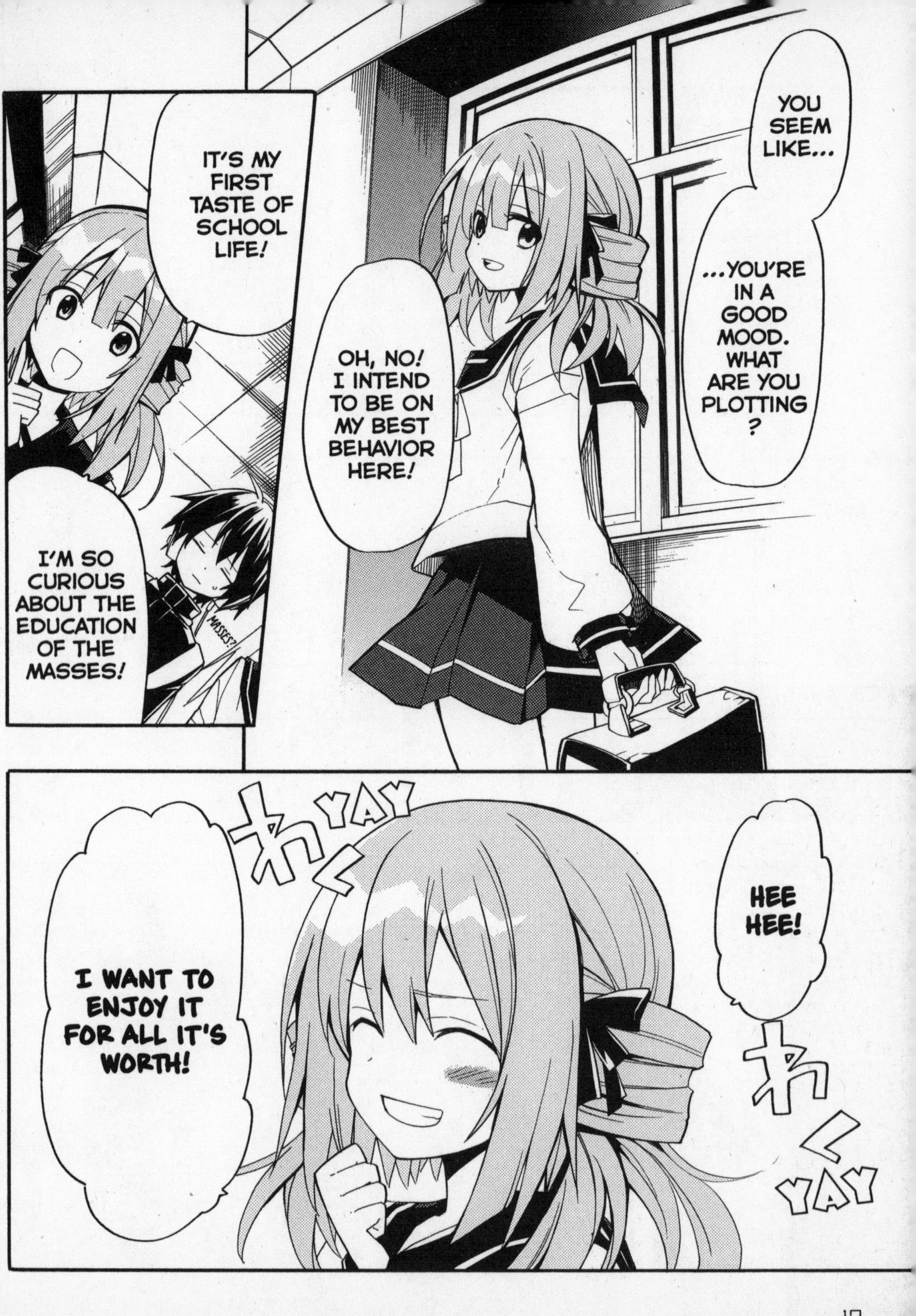
YOU SEEM LIKE...
...YOU'RE IN A GOOD MOOD. WHAT ARE YOU PLOTTING?
OH, NO! I INTEND TO BE ON MY BEST BEHAVIOR HERE!
IT'S MY FIRST TASTE OF SCHOOL LIFE!
I'M SO CURIOUS ABOUT THE EDUCATION OF THE MASSES!
MASSES?
HEE HEE!
わく YAY
わく YAY
I WANT TO ENJOY IT FOR ALL IT'S WORTH!

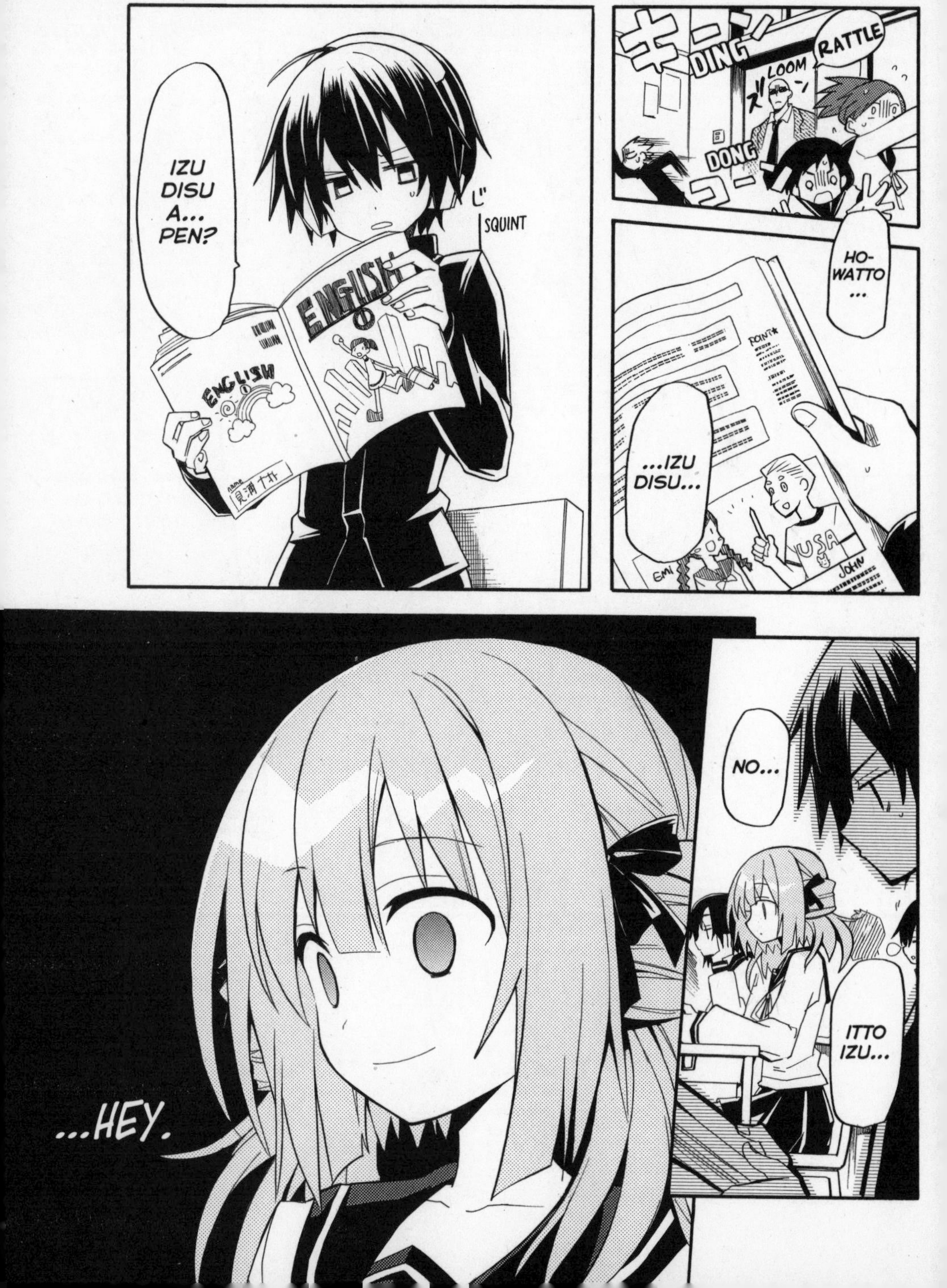
DING
RATTLE
LOOM
DONG
HO-WATTO...
...IZU DISU...
IZU DISU A... PEN?
SQUINT
NO...
ITTO IZU...
...HEY.

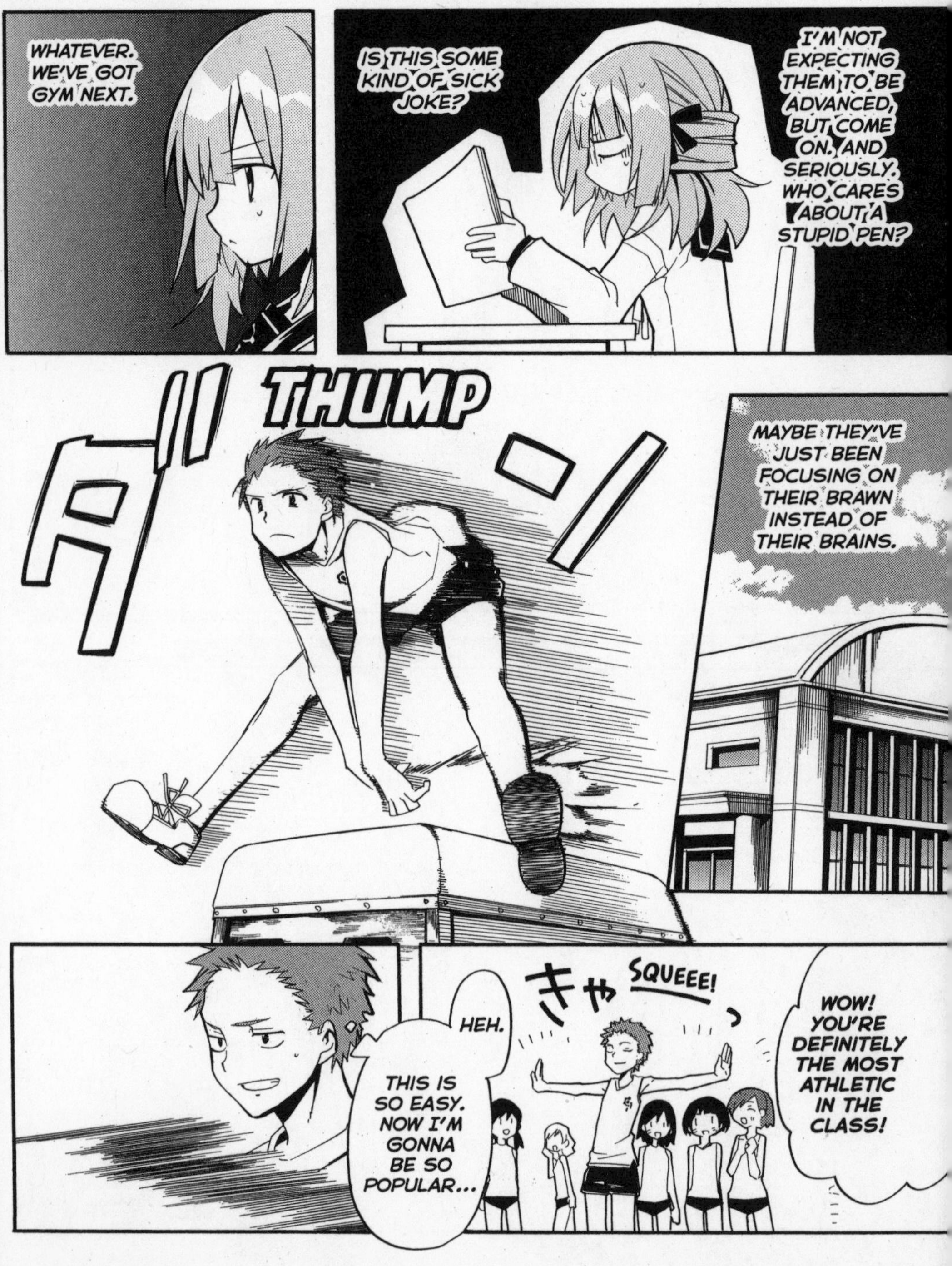
I'M NOT EXPECTING THEM TO BE ADVANCED, BUT COME ON. AND SERIOUSLY. WHO CARES ABOUT A STUPID PEN?
IS THIS SOME KIND OF SICK JOKE?
WHATEVER. WE'VE GOT GYM NEXT.
MAYBE THEY'VE JUST BEEN FOCUSING ON THEIR BRAWN INSTEAD OF THEIR BRAINS.
THUMP
ダン
WOW! YOU'RE DEFINITELY THE MOST ATHLETIC IN THE CLASS!
きゃっ
SQUEEE!
HEH.
THIS IS SO EASY. NOW I'M GONNA BE SO POPULAR...

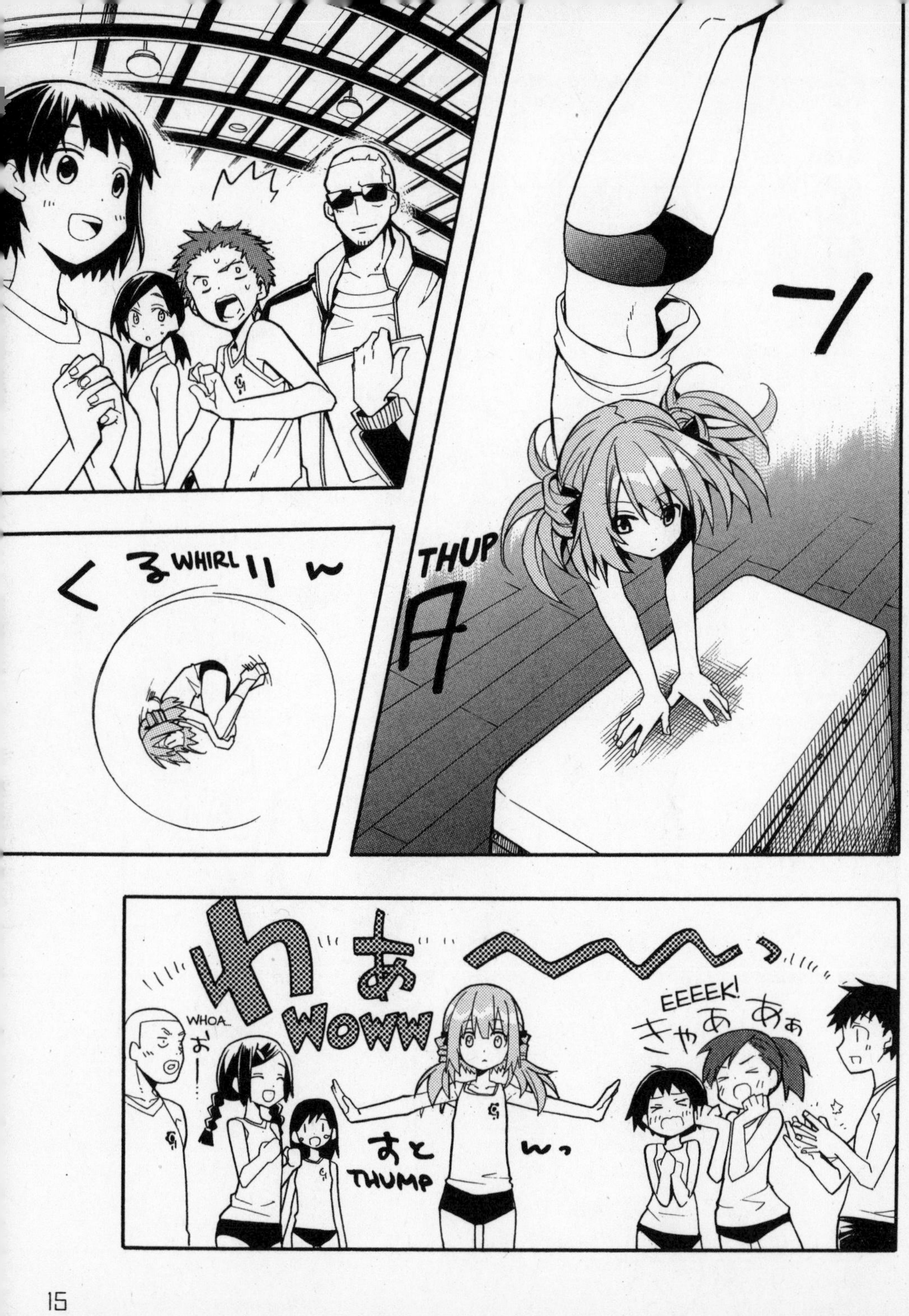
THUP
くる WHIRL りん
わあ〜〜〜っ
WOWW
EEEEK!
きゃあ あぁ
WHOA...
おー…
おと
THUMP
んっ

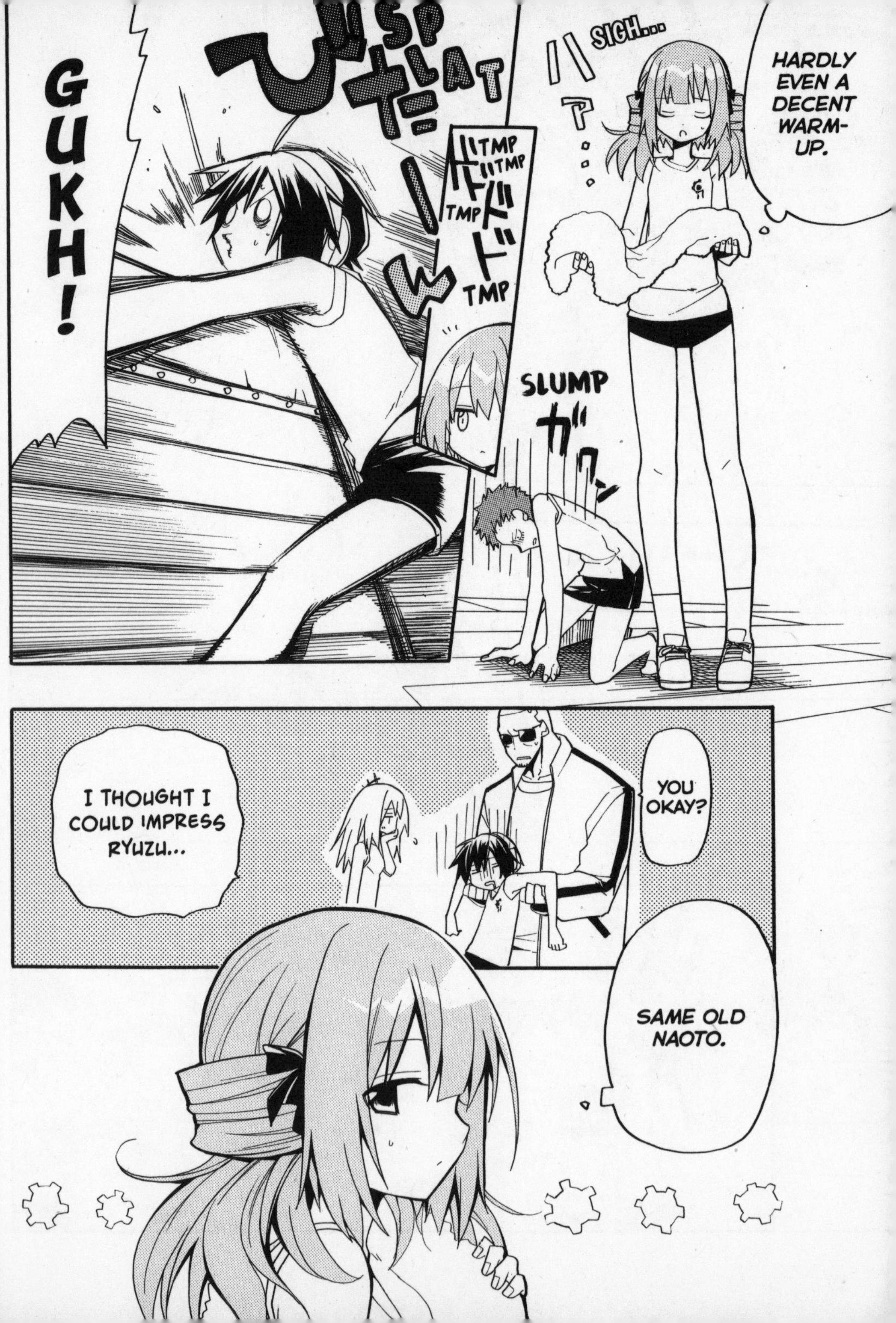
SIGH...
HARDLY EVEN A DECENT WARM-UP.
SLUMP
SPLAT
TMP TMP TMP TMP
GUKH!
YOU OKAY?
I THOUGHT I COULD IMPRESS RYUZU...
SAME OLD NAOTO.

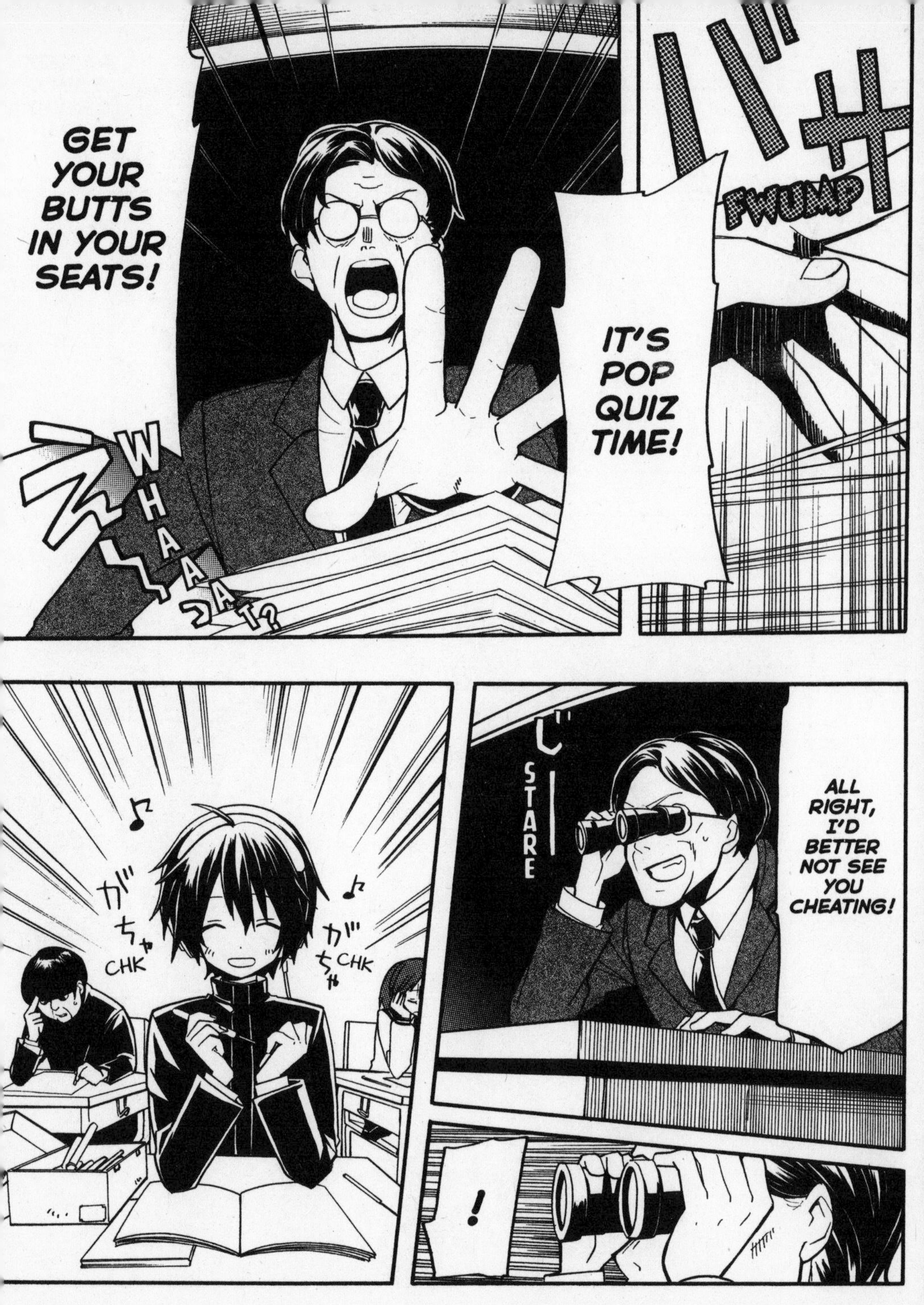

バサ
FWUMP
IT'S POP QUIZ TIME!
GET YOUR BUTTS IN YOUR SEATS!
WHAAAAT?
ALL RIGHT, I'D BETTER NOT SEE YOU CHEATING!
じー
STARE
!
ガちゃ
CHK
ガちゃ
CHK

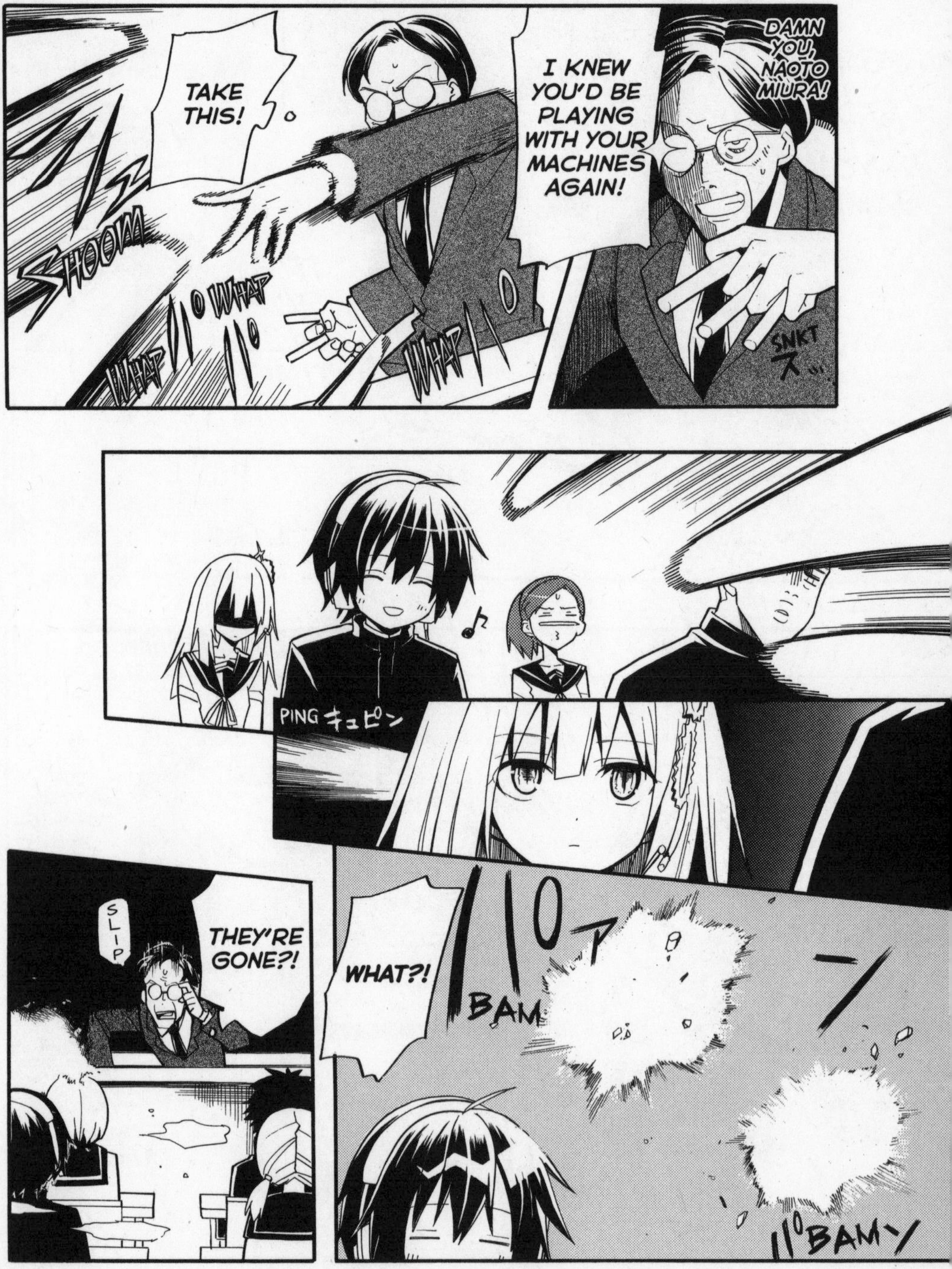
DAMN YOU, NAOTO MIURA!
I KNEW YOU'D BE PLAYING WITH YOUR MACHINES AGAIN!
SNKT
TAKE THIS!
SHOOM
WHAP
WHAP
WHAP
PING キュピン
BAM
BAM
WHAT?!
THEY'RE GONE?!
SLIP

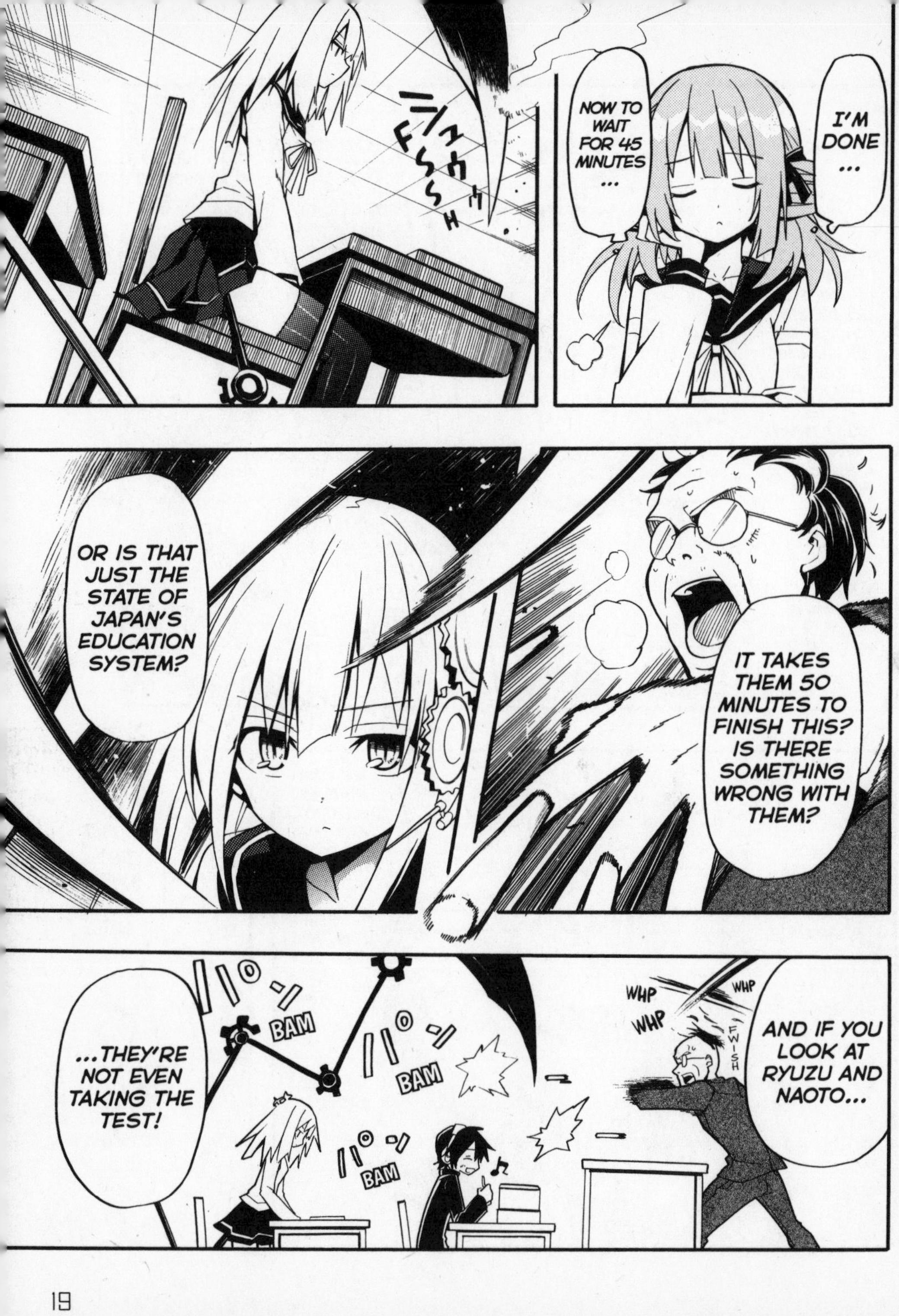
I'M DONE ...
NOW TO WAIT FOR 45 MINUTES ...
FSSSH
IT TAKES THEM 50 MINUTES TO FINISH THIS? IS THERE SOMETHING WRONG WITH THEM?
OR IS THAT JUST THE STATE OF JAPAN'S EDUCATION SYSTEM?
AND IF YOU LOOK AT RYUZU AND NAOTO...
WHP
WHP
WHP
FWISH
BAM
BAM
BAM
...THEY'RE NOT EVEN TAKING THE TEST!

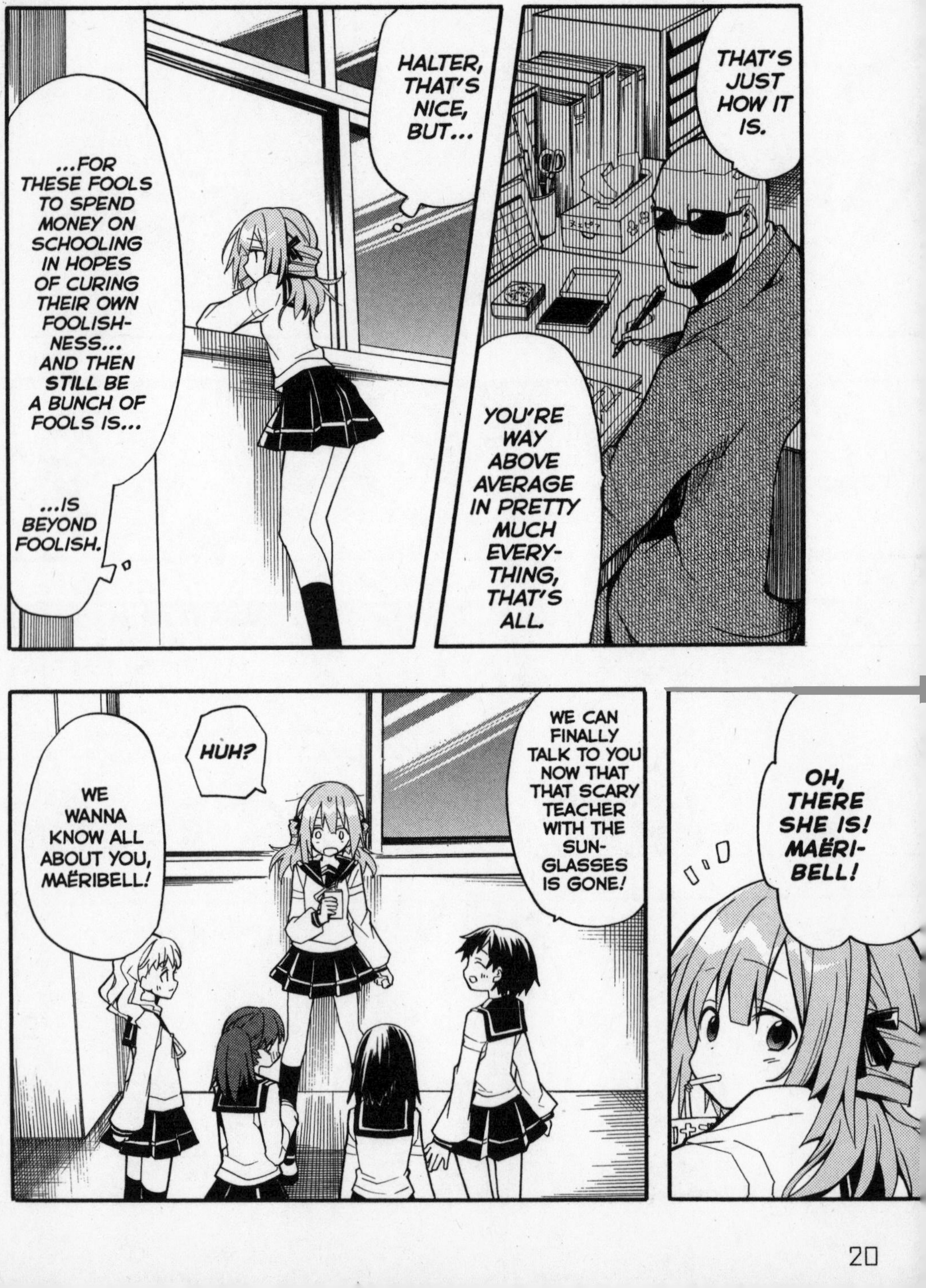
THAT'S JUST HOW IT IS.
YOU'RE WAY ABOVE AVERAGE IN PRETTY MUCH EVERY-THING, THAT'S ALL.
HALTER, THAT'S NICE, BUT...
...FOR THESE FOOLS TO SPEND MONEY ON SCHOOLING IN HOPES OF CURING THEIR OWN FOOLISH-NESS... AND THEN STILL BE A BUNCH OF FOOLS IS...
...IS BEYOND FOOLISH.
OH, THERE SHE IS! MAËRI-BELL!
WE CAN FINALLY TALK TO YOU NOW THAT THAT SCARY TEACHER WITH THE SUN-GLASSES IS GONE!
HUH?
WE WANNA KNOW ALL ABOUT YOU, MAËRIBELL!

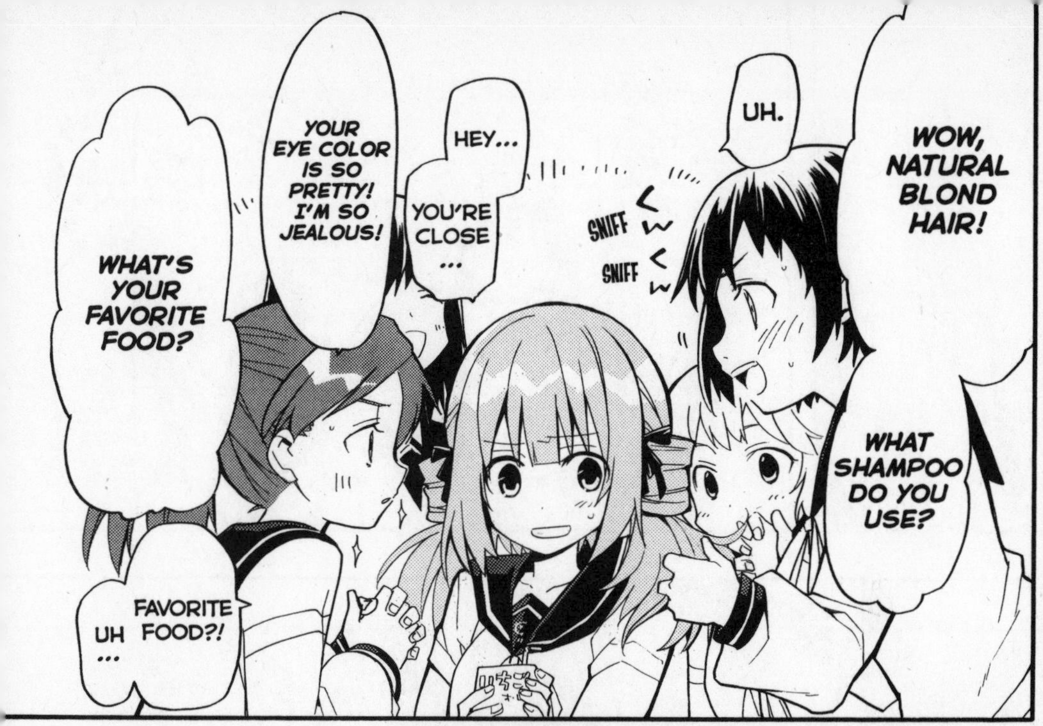
WOW, NATURAL BLOND HAIR!
UH.
WHAT SHAMPOO DO YOU USE?
SNIFF
SNIFF
HEY...
YOU'RE CLOSE...
YOUR EYE COLOR IS SO PRETTY! I'M SO JEALOUS!
WHAT'S YOUR FAVORITE FOOD?
FAVORITE FOOD?!
UH...

Carton: Strawberry Au Lait!

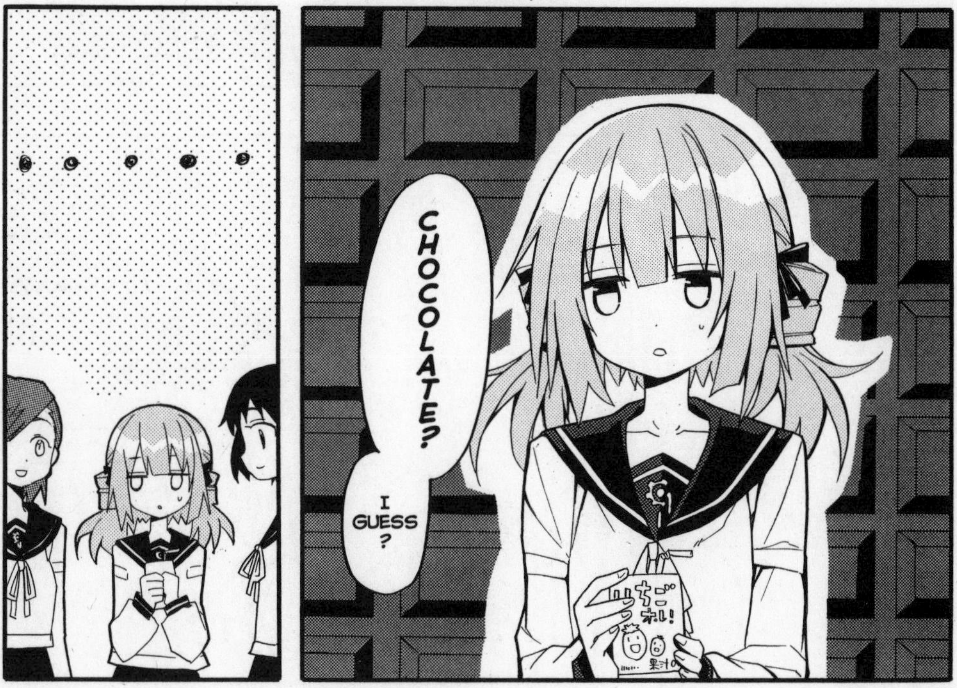
CHOCOLATE?
I GUESS?
.....

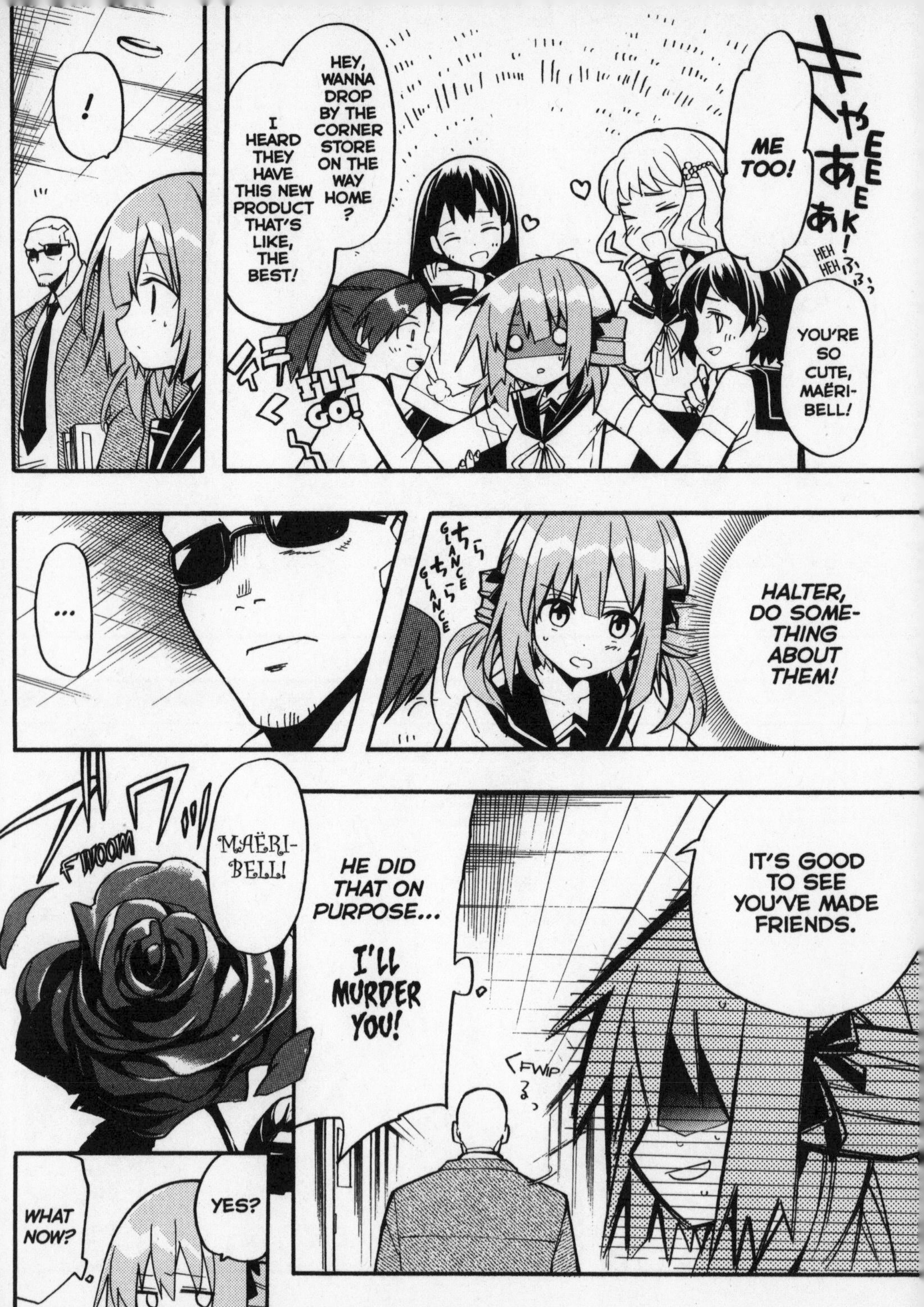
EEEK!
ME TOO!
HEY, WANNA DROP BY THE CORNER STORE ON THE WAY HOME?
I HEARD THEY HAVE THIS NEW PRODUCT THAT'S LIKE, THE BEST!
HEH HEH
YOU'RE SO CUTE, MAËRI-BELL!
I'LL GO!
!
HALTER, DO SOME-THING ABOUT THEM!
GLANCE GLANCE
...
IT'S GOOD TO SEE YOU'VE MADE FRIENDS.
FWIP
HE DID THAT ON PURPOSE...
I'LL MURDER YOU!
MAËRI-BELL!
FWOOM
YES?
WHAT NOW?

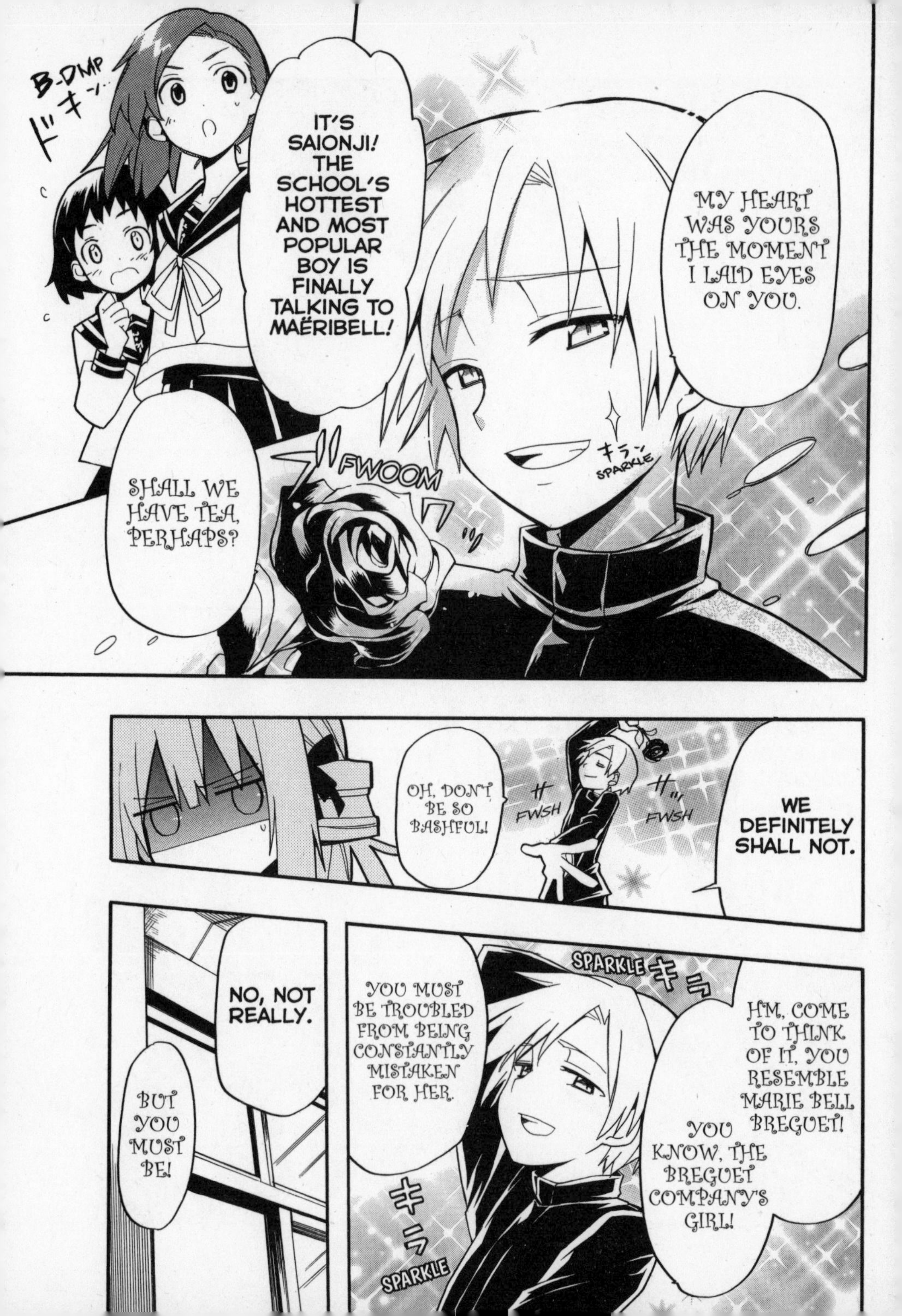
MY HEART WAS YOURS THE MOMENT I LAID EYES ON YOU.
キラン SPARKLE
IT'S SAIONJI! THE SCHOOL'S HOTTEST AND MOST POPULAR BOY IS FINALLY TALKING TO MAËRIBELL!
B-DMP ドキーッ
FWOOM
SHALL WE HAVE TEA, PERHAPS?
WE DEFINITELY SHALL NOT.
FWSH
FWSH
OH, DON'T BE SO BASHFUL!
SPARKLE キラ
HM, COME TO THINK OF IT, YOU RESEMBLE MARIE BELL BREGUET!
YOU KNOW, THE BREGUET COMPANY'S GIRL!
YOU MUST BE TROUBLED FROM BEING CONSTANTLY MISTAKEN FOR HER.
キラ SPARKLE
NO, NOT REALLY.
BUT YOU MUST BE!

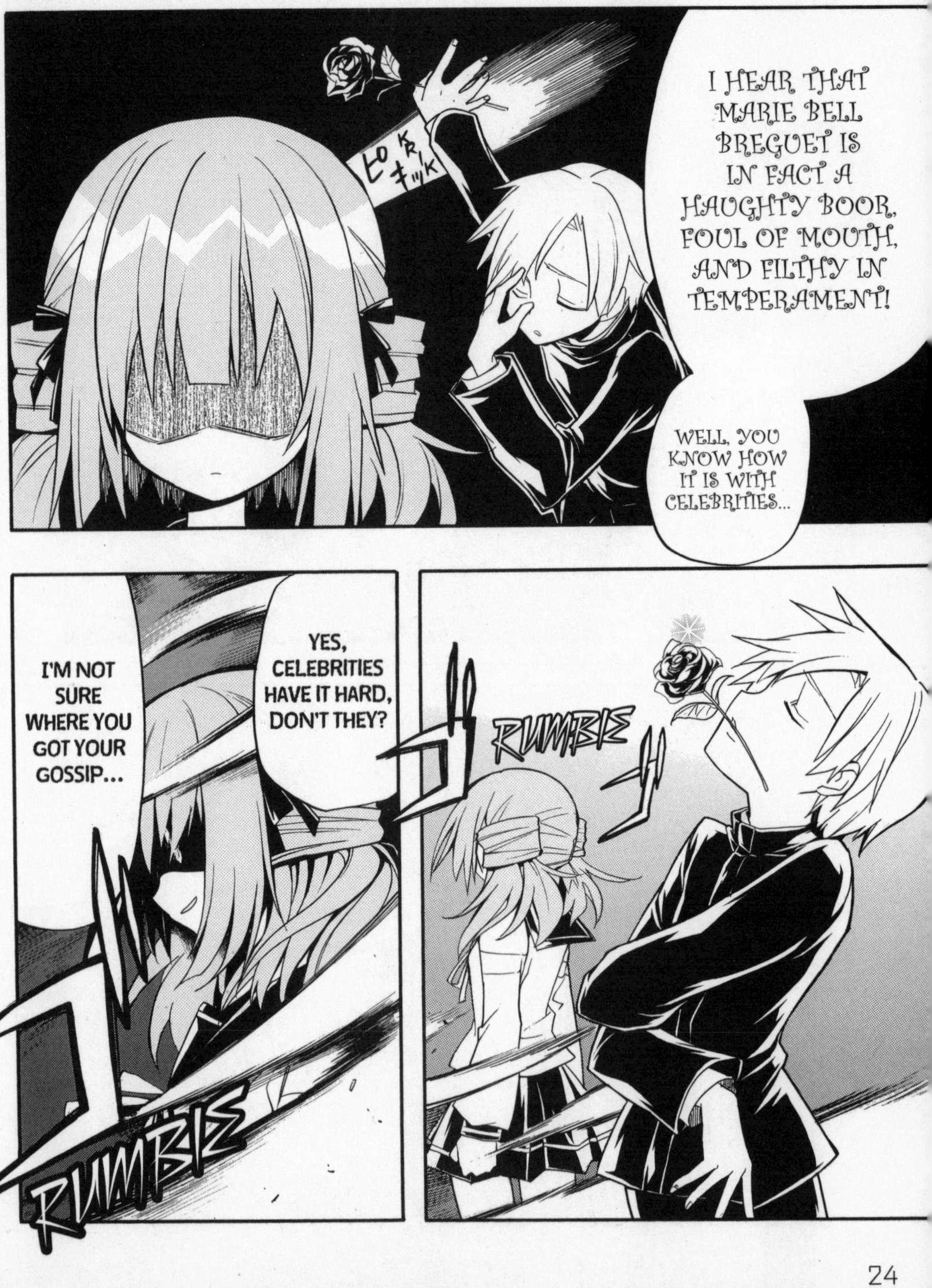
I HEAR THAT MARIE BELL BREGUET IS IN FACT A HAUGHTY BOOR, FOUL OF MOUTH, AND FILTHY IN TEMPERAMENT!
KRIK
WELL, YOU KNOW HOW IT IS WITH CELEBRITIES...
RUMBLE
YES, CELEBRITIES HAVE IT HARD, DON'T THEY?
I'M NOT SURE WHERE YOU GOT YOUR GOSSIP...
RUMBLE

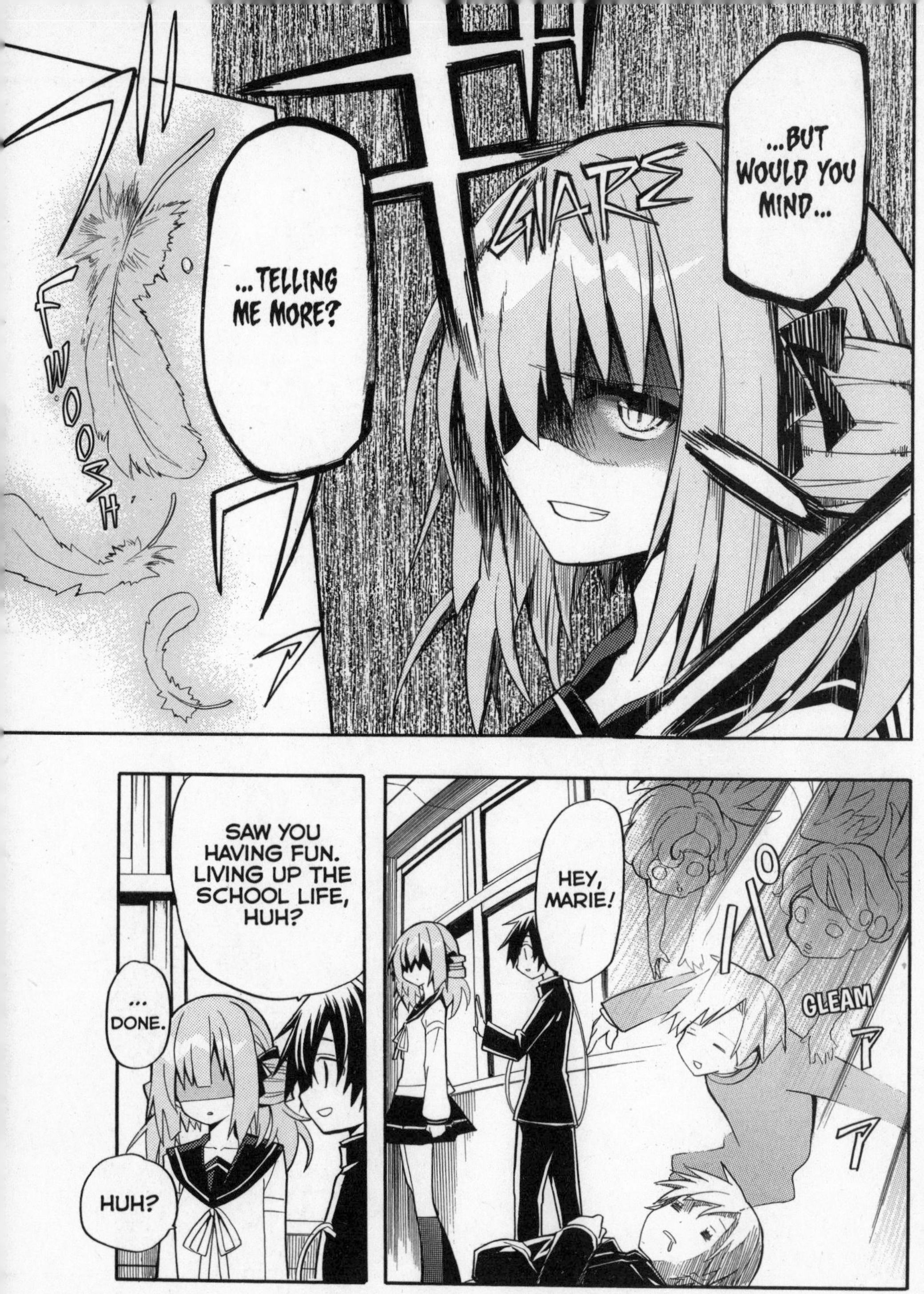
...BUT WOULD YOU MIND...
GLARE
...TELLING ME MORE?
FWOOSH
HEY, MARIE!
GLEAM
SAW YOU HAVING FUN. LIVING UP THE SCHOOL LIFE, HUH?
... DONE.
HUH?

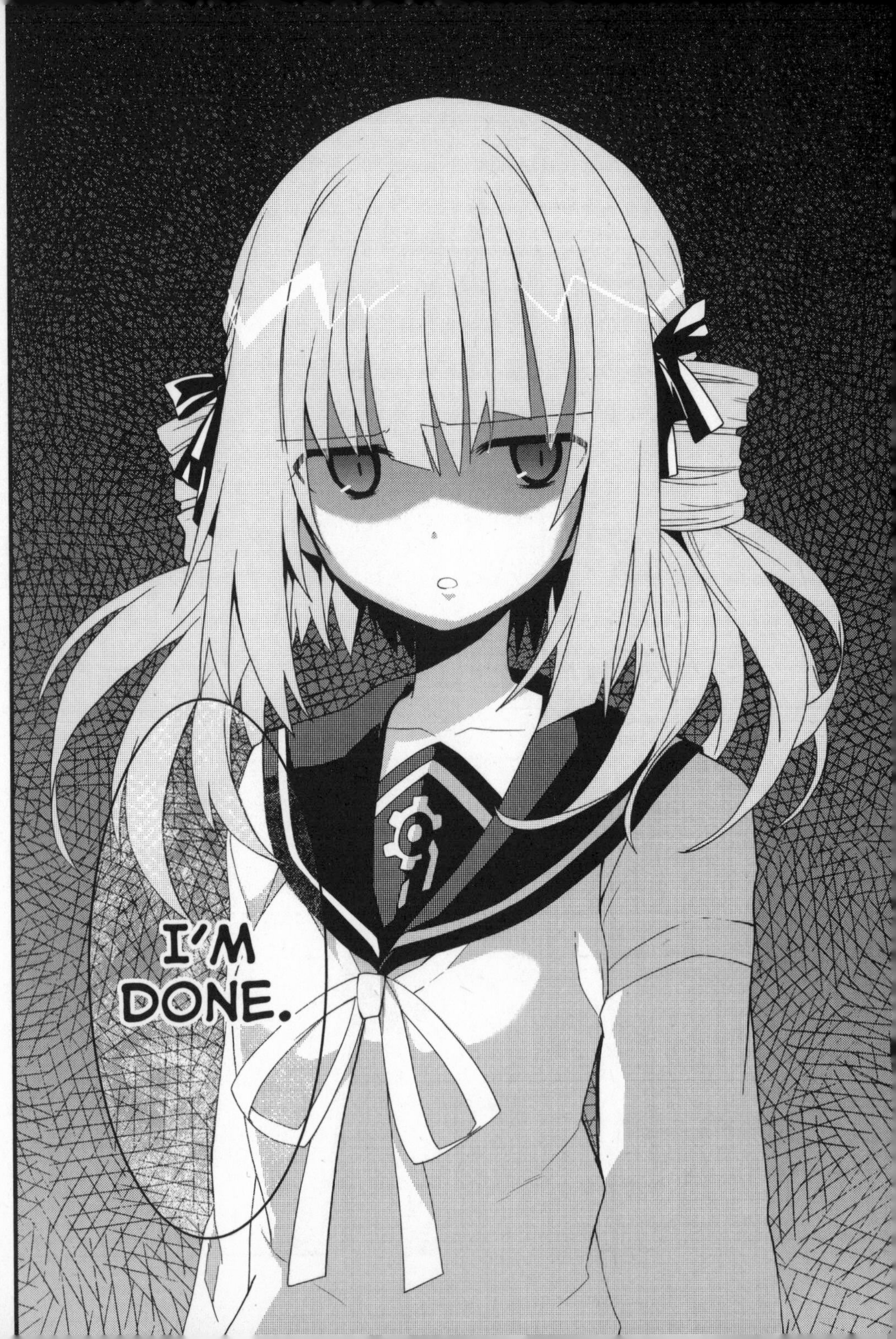
I'M DONE.

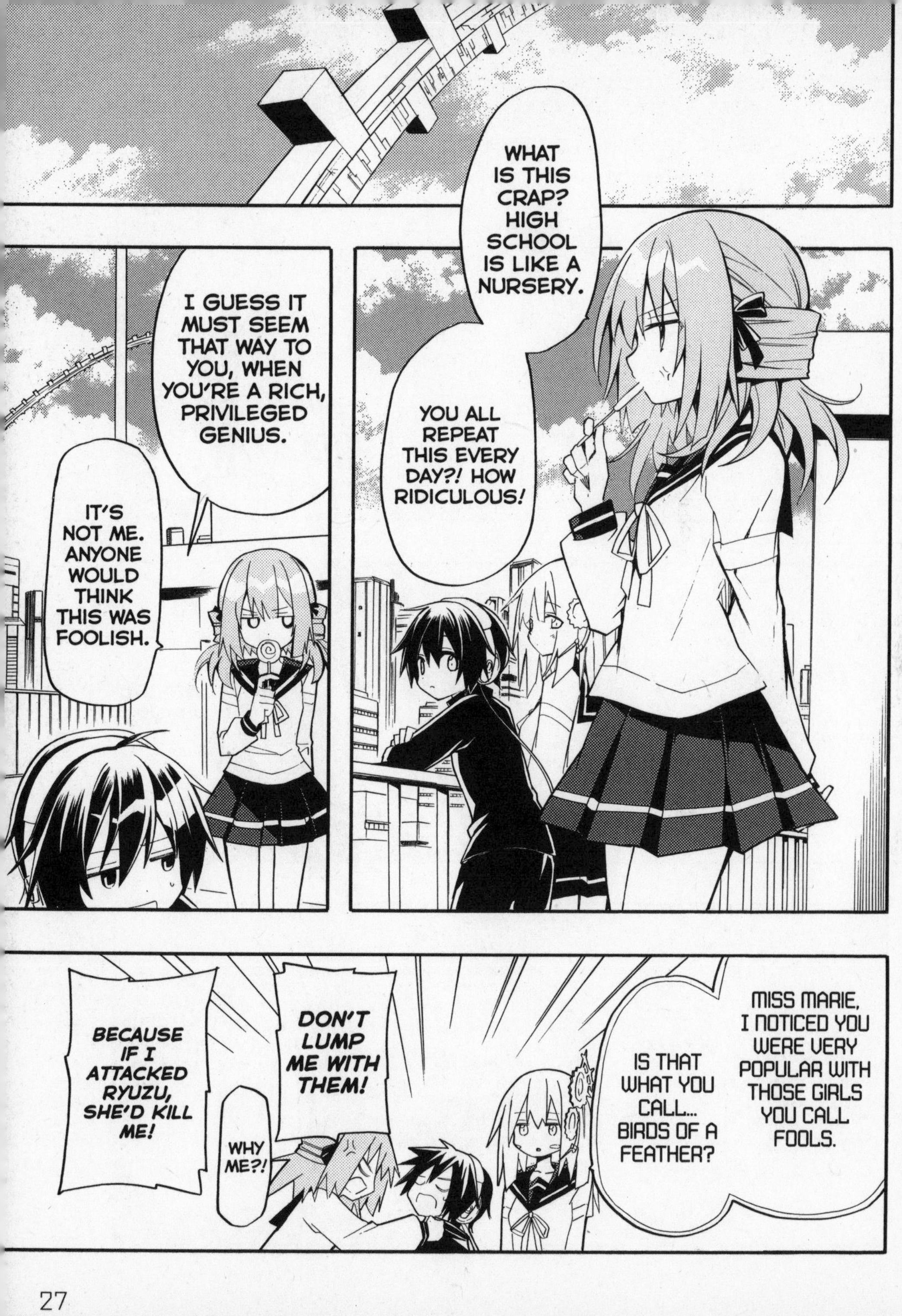
WHAT IS THIS CRAP? HIGH SCHOOL IS LIKE A NURSERY.
YOU ALL REPEAT THIS EVERY DAY?! HOW RIDICULOUS!
I GUESS IT MUST SEEM THAT WAY TO YOU, WHEN YOU'RE A RICH, PRIVILEGED GENIUS.
IT'S NOT ME. ANYONE WOULD THINK THIS WAS FOOLISH.
MISS MARIE, I NOTICED YOU WERE VERY POPULAR WITH THOSE GIRLS YOU CALL FOOLS.
IS THAT WHAT YOU CALL... BIRDS OF A FEATHER?
DON'T LUMP ME WITH THEM!
WHY ME?!
BECAUSE IF I ATTACKED RYUZU, SHE'D KILL ME!

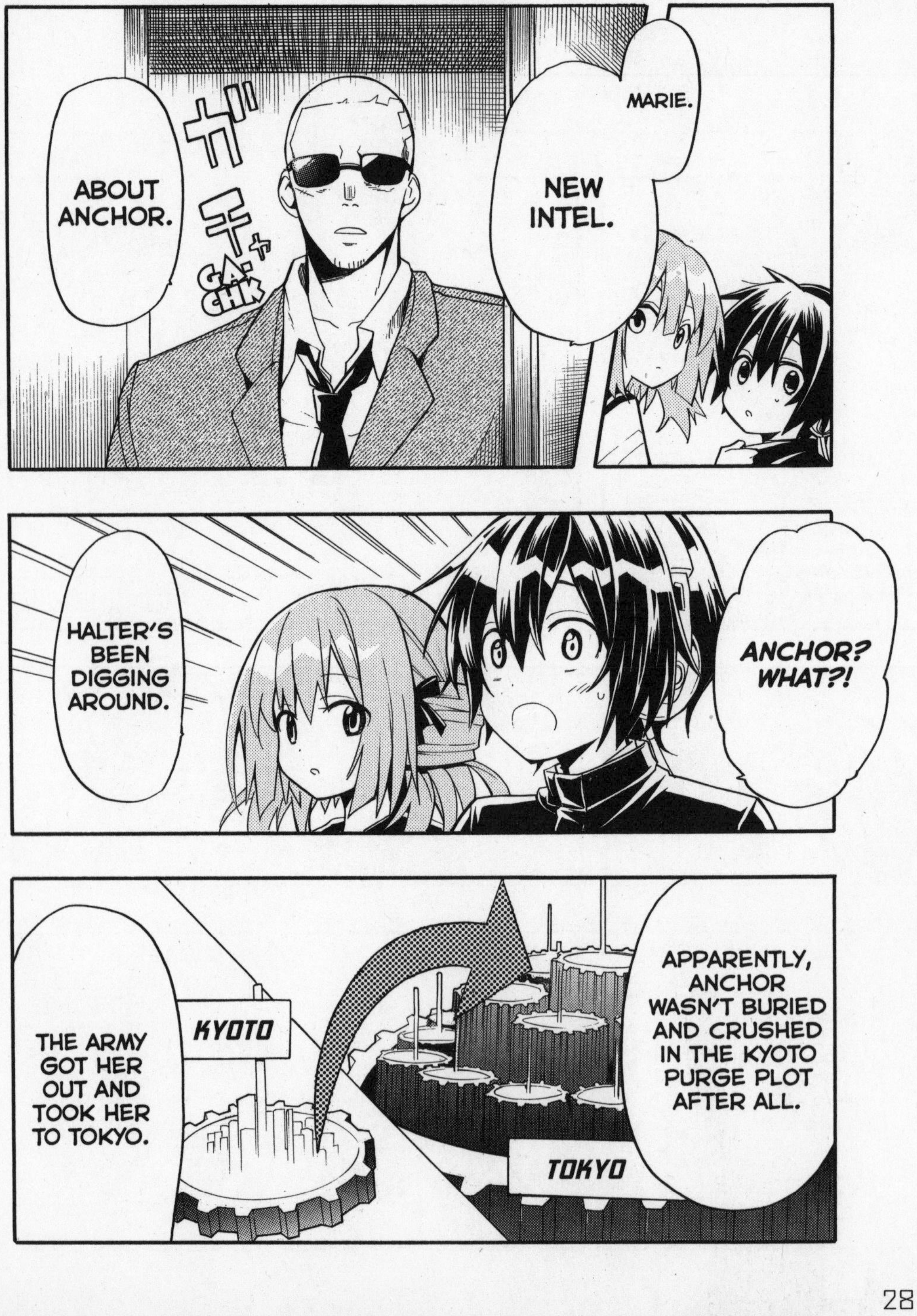
MARIE.
NEW INTEL.
ガチャ
GA-CHK
ABOUT ANCHOR.
ANCHOR? WHAT?!
HALTER'S BEEN DIGGING AROUND.
APPARENTLY, ANCHOR WASN'T BURIED AND CRUSHED IN THE KYOTO PURGE PLOT AFTER ALL.
TOKYO
KYOTO
THE ARMY GOT HER OUT AND TOOK HER TO TOKYO.

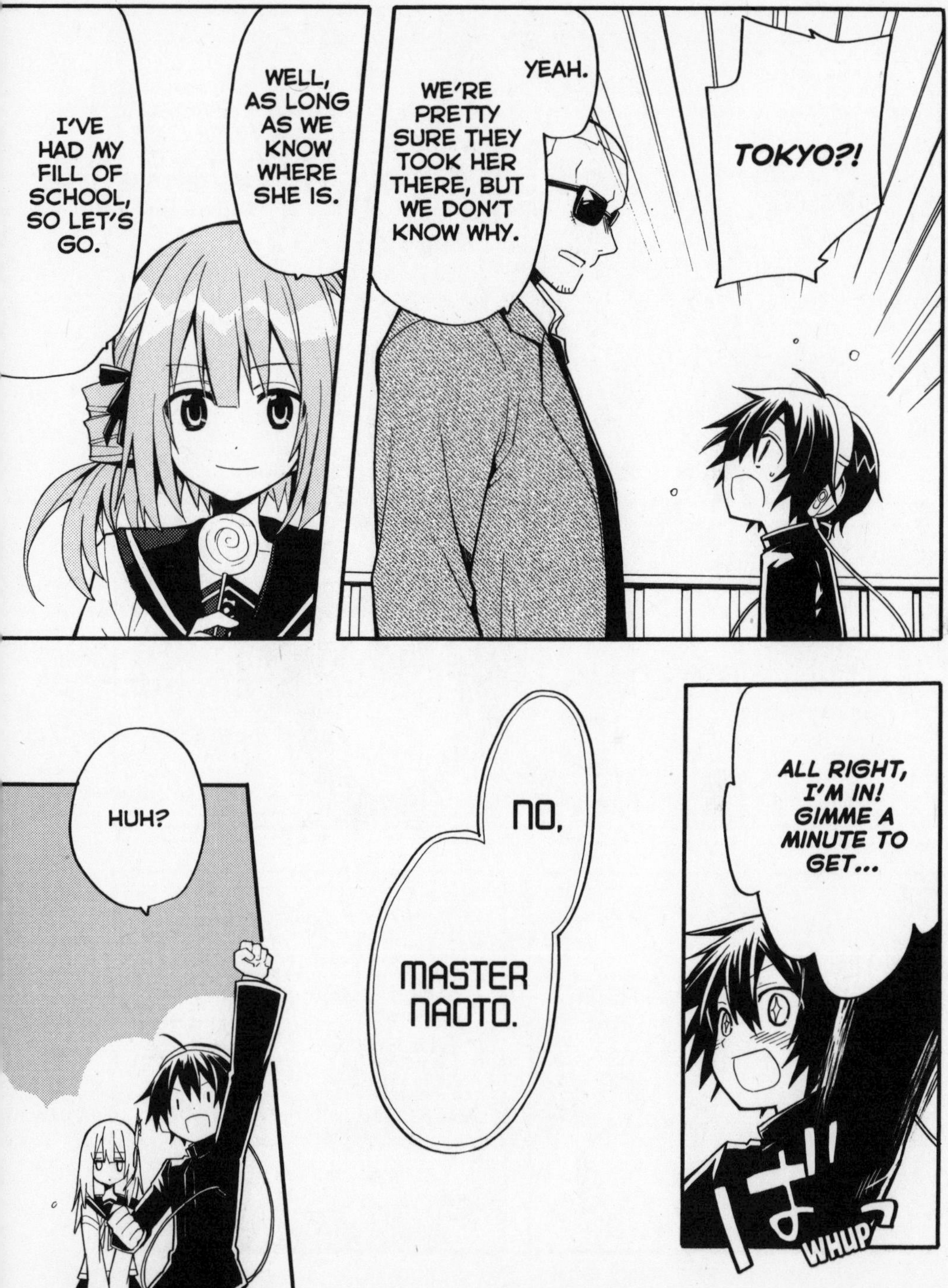
TOKYO?!
YEAH.
WE'RE PRETTY SURE THEY TOOK HER THERE, BUT WE DON'T KNOW WHY.
WELL, AS LONG AS WE KNOW WHERE SHE IS.
I'VE HAD MY FILL OF SCHOOL, SO LET'S GO.
ALL RIGHT, I'M IN! GIMME A MINUTE TO GET...
WHUP
NO,
MASTER NAOTO.
HUH?

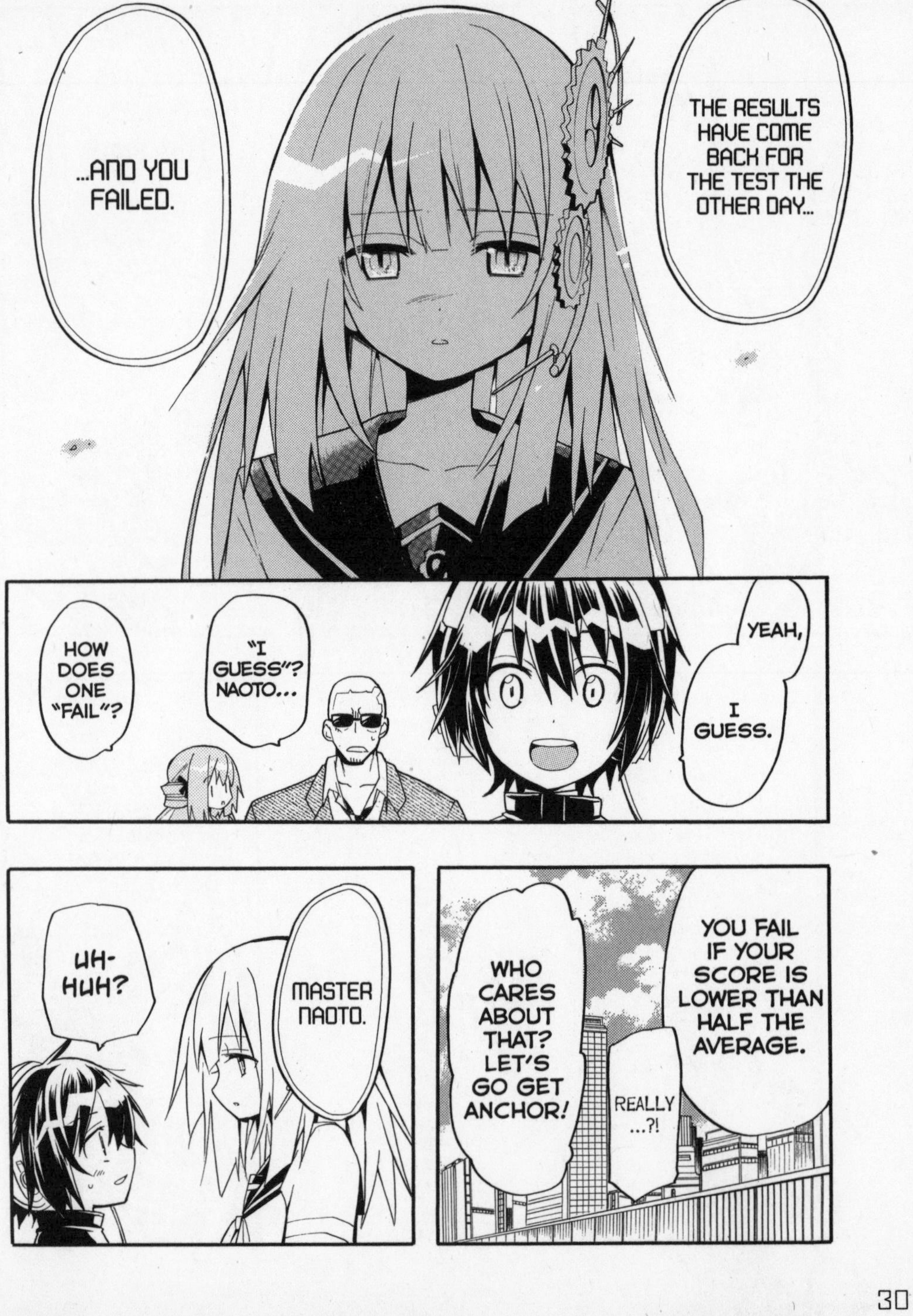
THE RESULTS HAVE COME BACK FOR THE TEST THE OTHER DAY...
...AND YOU FAILED.
YEAH,
I GUESS.
"I GUESS"? NAOTO...
HOW DOES ONE "FAIL"?
YOU FAIL IF YOUR SCORE IS LOWER THAN HALF THE AVERAGE.
REALLY ...?!
WHO CARES ABOUT THAT? LET'S GO GET ANCHOR!
MASTER NAOTO.
UH-HUH?

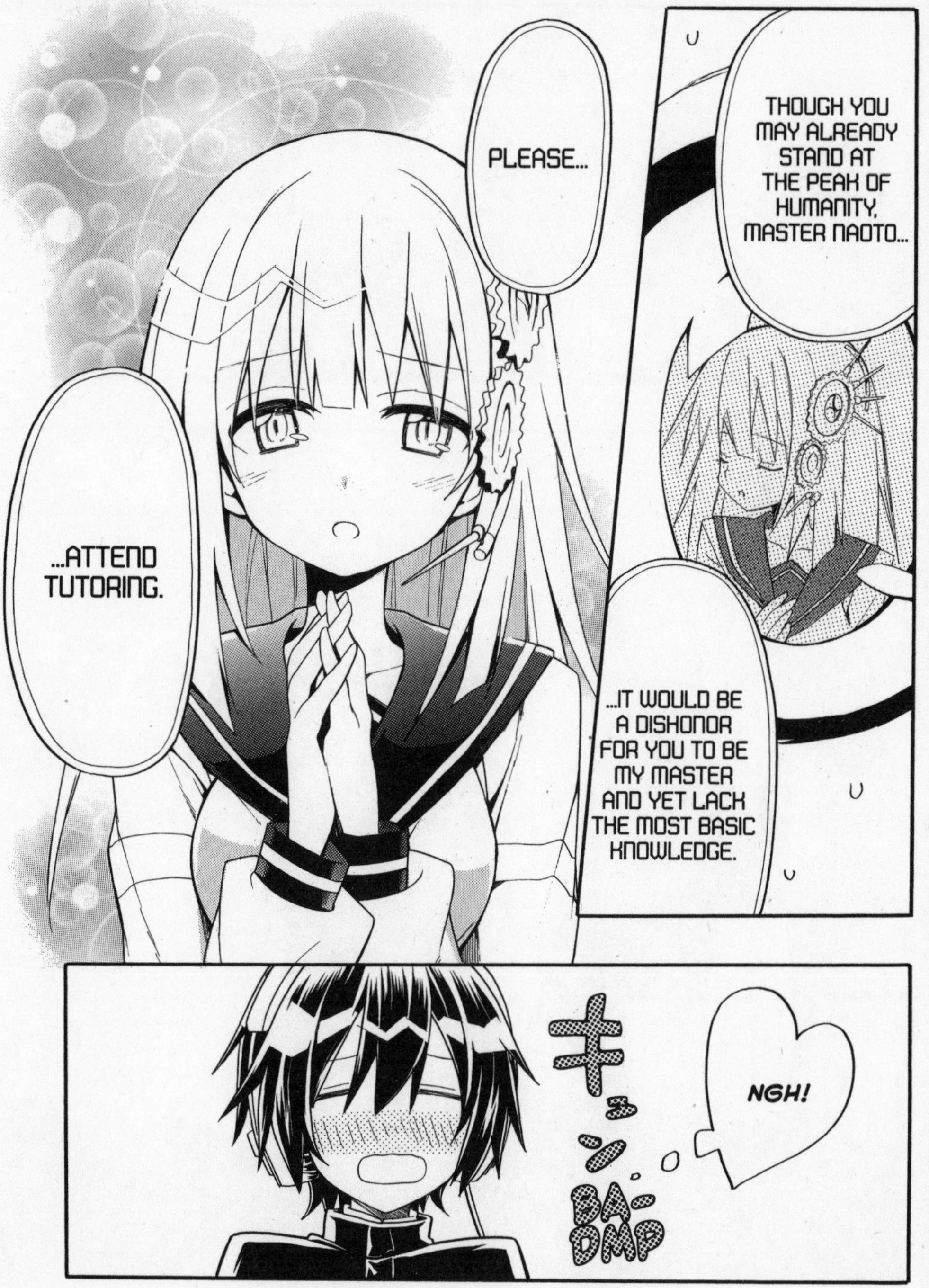
THOUGH YOU MAY ALREADY STAND AT THE PEAK OF HUMANITY, MASTER NAOTO...
...IT WOULD BE A DISHONOR FOR YOU TO BE MY MASTER AND YET LACK THE MOST BASIC KNOWLEDGE.
PLEASE...
...ATTEND TUTORING.
NGH!
BA-DMP

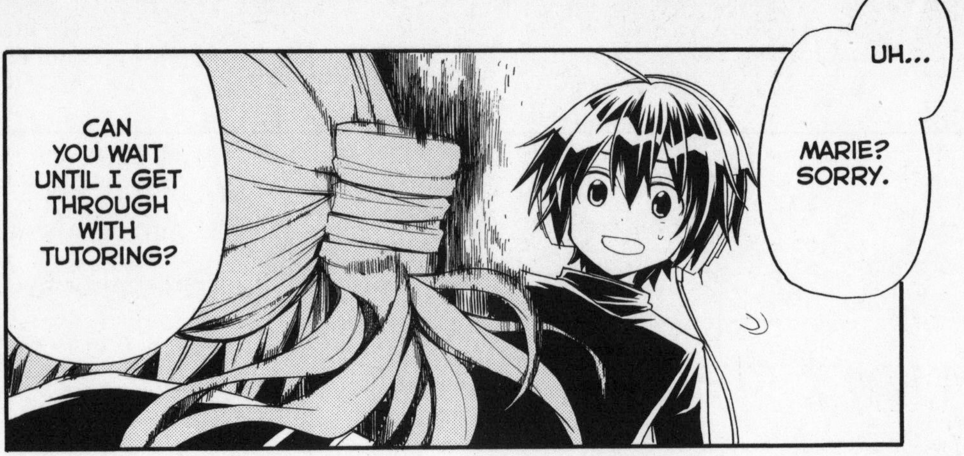
UH...
MARIE? SORRY.
CAN YOU WAIT UNTIL I GET THROUGH WITH TUTORING?

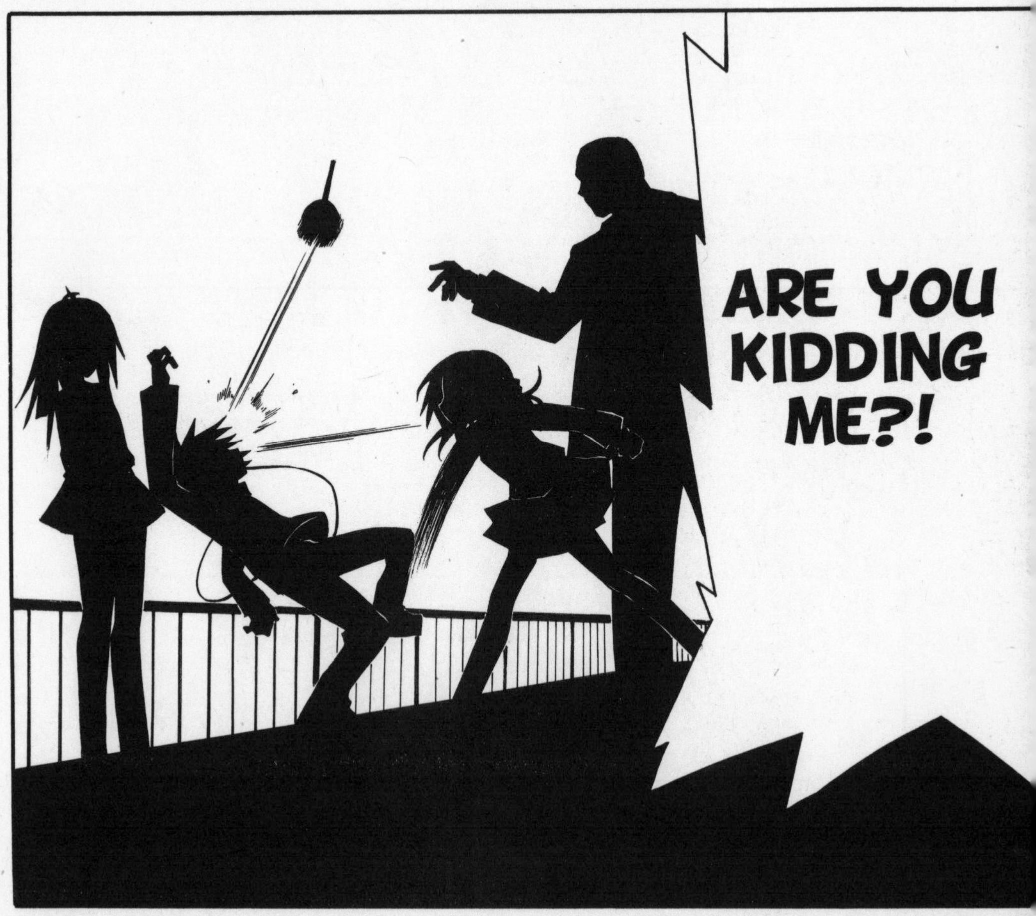
ARE YOU KIDDING ME?!

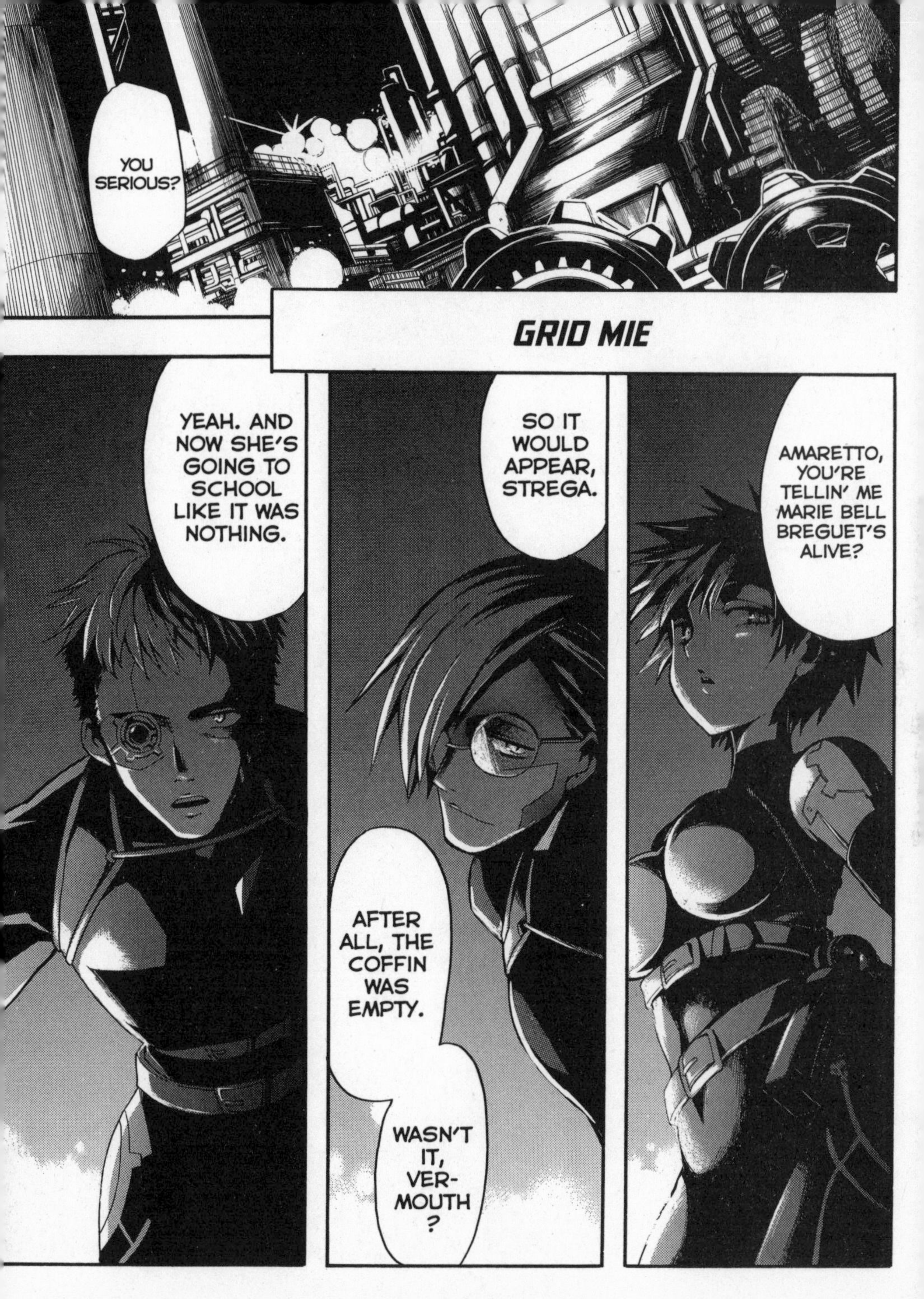
YOU SERIOUS?
GRID MIE
AMARETTO, YOU'RE TELLIN' ME MARIE BELL BREGUET'S ALIVE?
SO IT WOULD APPEAR, STREGA.
AFTER ALL, THE COFFIN WAS EMPTY.
WASN'T IT, VER-MOUTH?
YEAH. AND NOW SHE'S GOING TO SCHOOL LIKE IT WAS NOTHING.

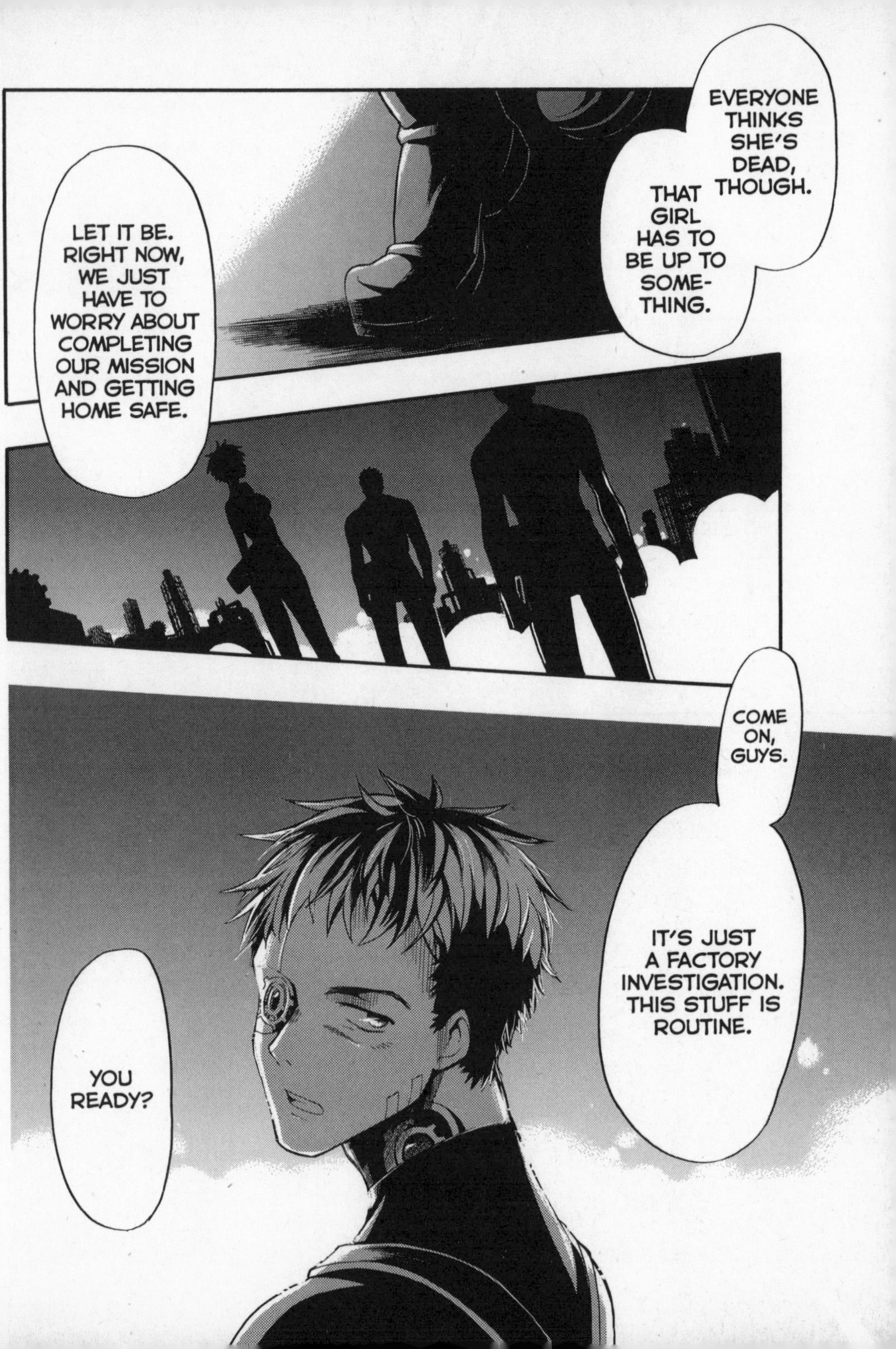
EVERYONE THINKS SHE'S DEAD, THOUGH.
THAT GIRL HAS TO BE UP TO SOME-THING.
LET IT BE. RIGHT NOW, WE JUST HAVE TO WORRY ABOUT COMPLETING OUR MISSION AND GETTING HOME SAFE.
COME ON, GUYS.
IT'S JUST A FACTORY INVESTIGATION. THIS STUFF IS ROUTINE.
YOU READY?

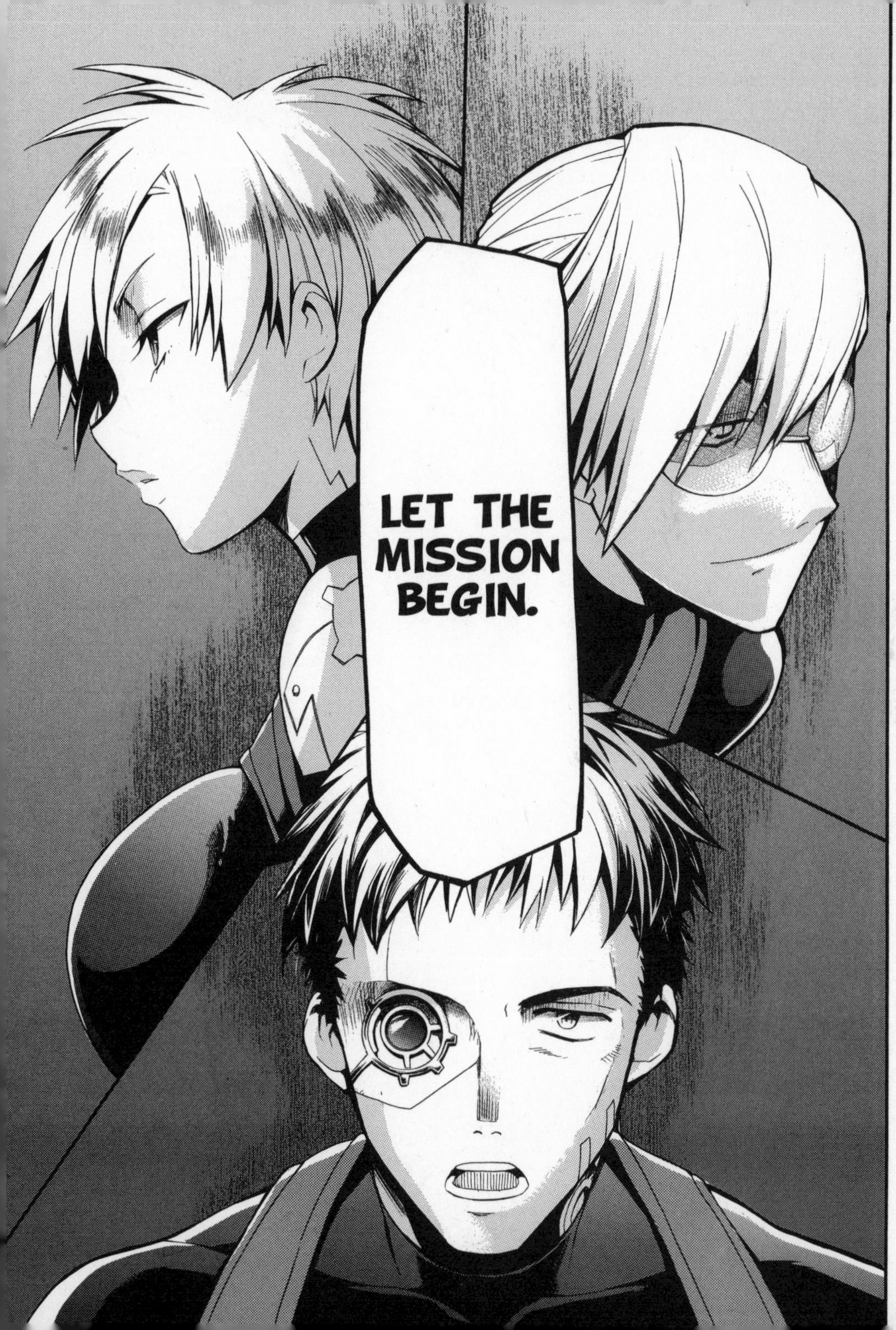
LET THE MISSION BEGIN.

CLOCKWORK
PLANET

Clock 12: Starter

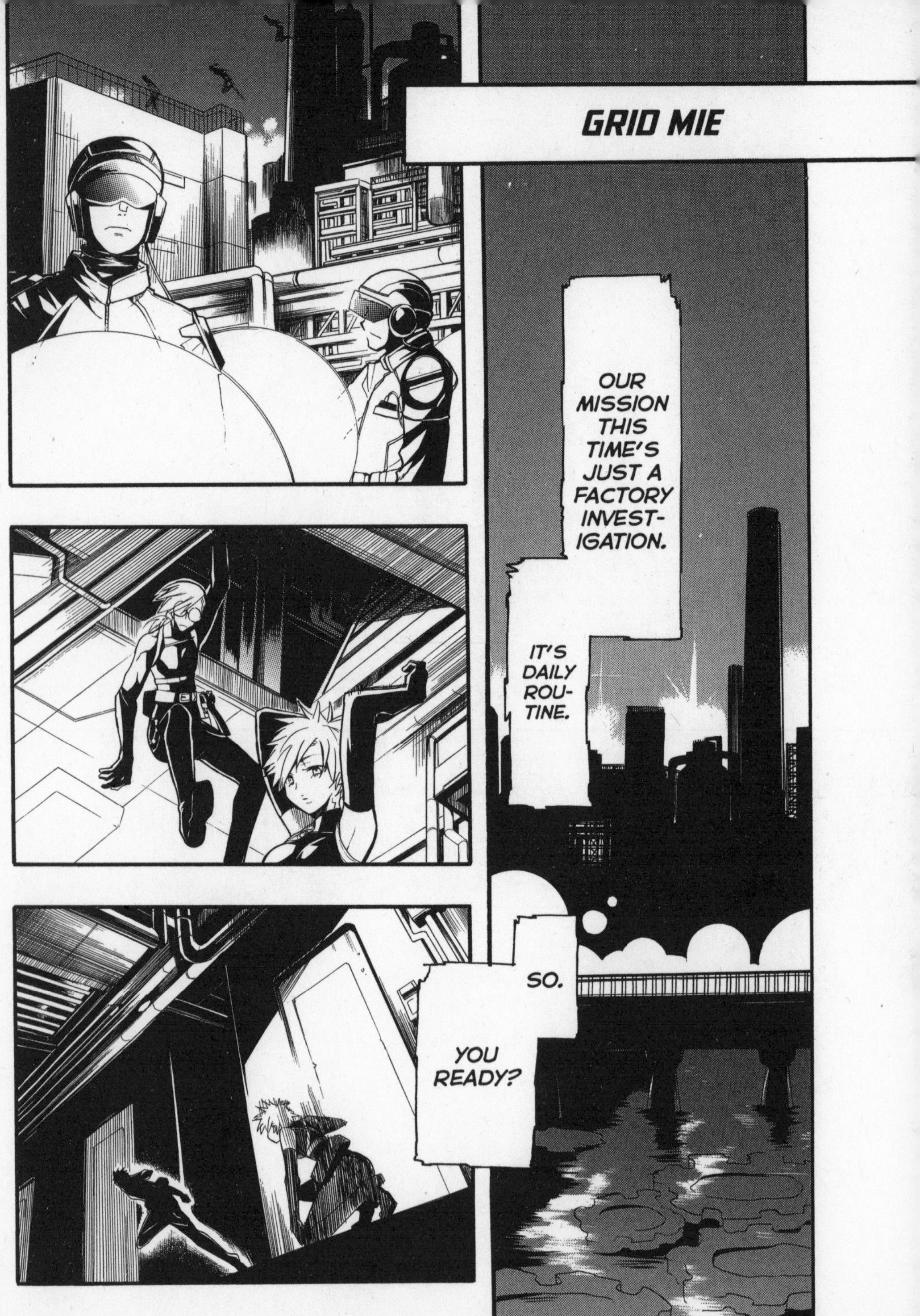
GRID MIE
OUR MISSION THIS TIME'S JUST A FACTORY INVESTIGATION.
IT'S DAILY ROUTINE.
SO.
YOU READY?

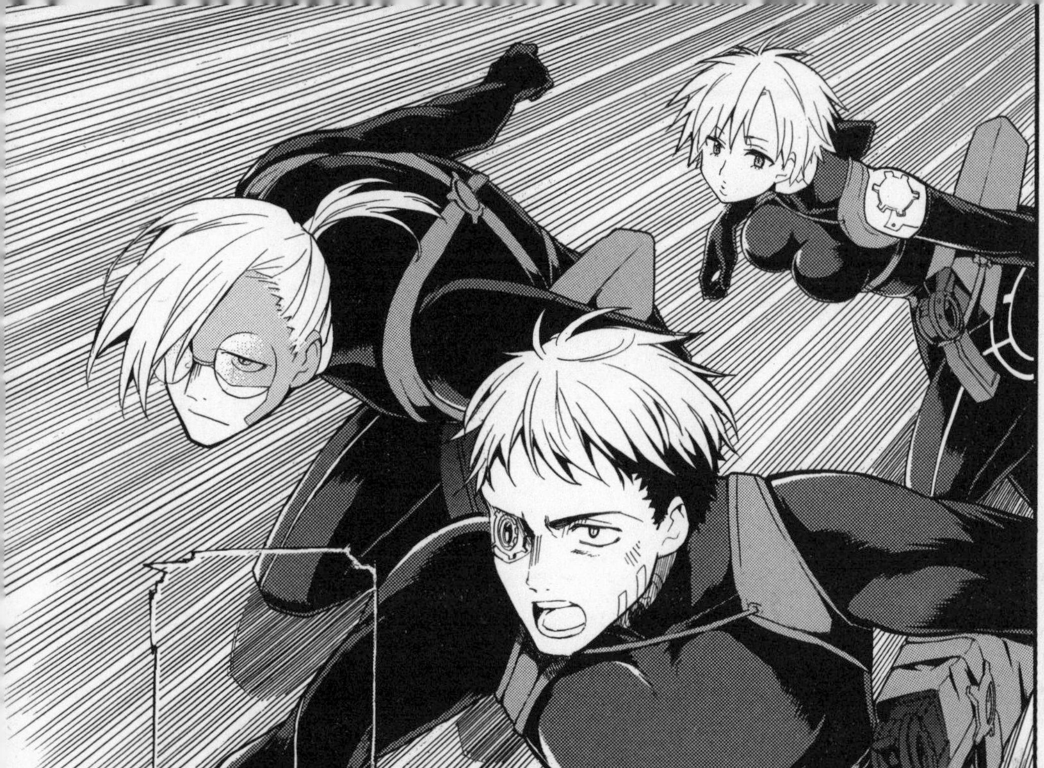
LET THE MISSION BEGIN.

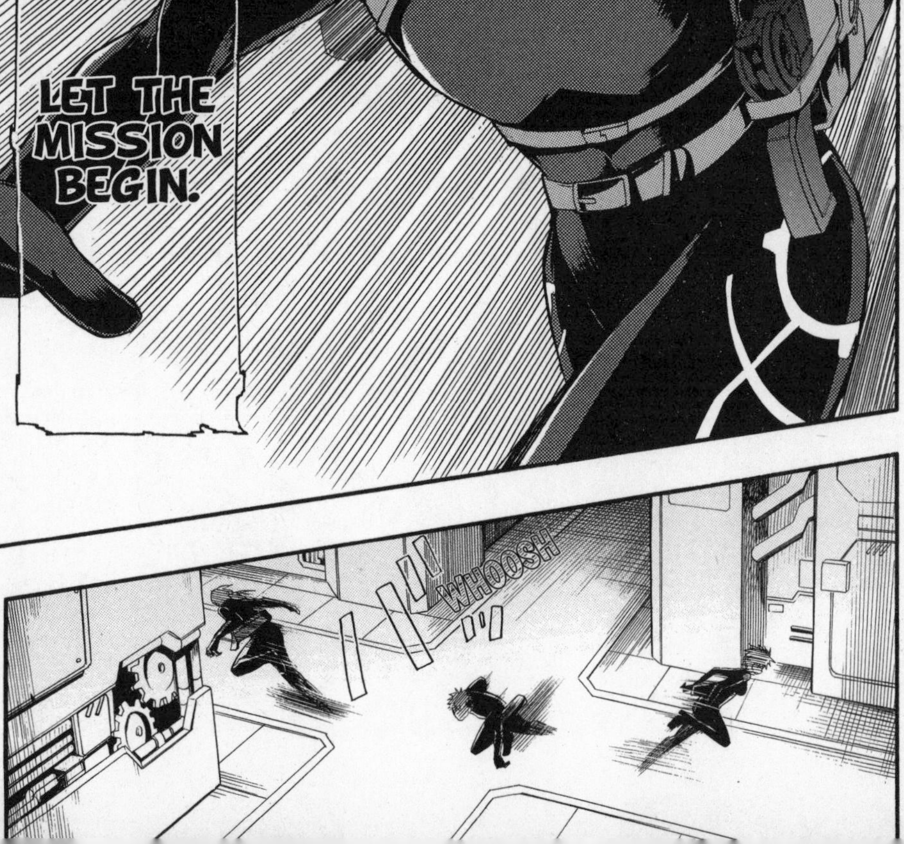
WHOOSH

MYSTERIOUS FACTORY UNDER A FRONT COMPANY, EH?

NOT THAT UNUSUAL, IS IT?

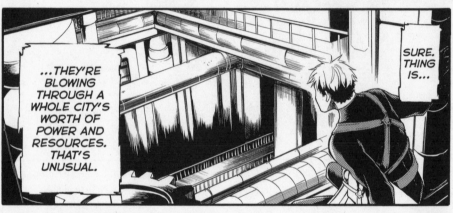

...THEY'RE BLOWING THROUGH A WHOLE CITY'S WORTH OF POWER AND RESOURCES. THAT'S UNUSUAL.

SURE. THING IS...

IN LIGHT OF THE LEVEL OF SECURITY ON THE WAY TO THE TARGET...

...I WOULD HAVE TO CONCLUDE THERE IS SOMETHING VERY UNUSUAL HERE.

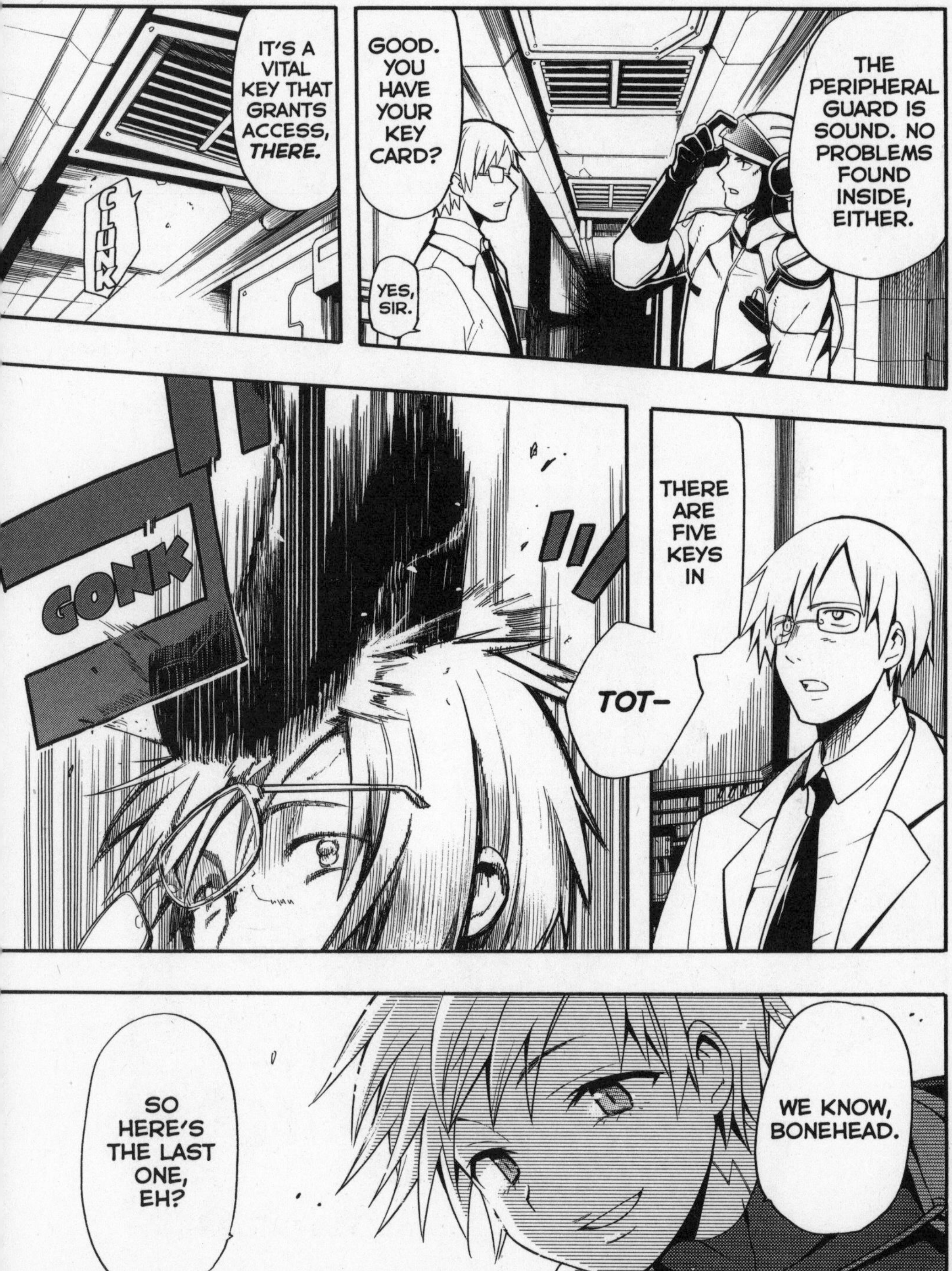
THE PERIPHERAL GUARD IS SOUND. NO PROBLEMS FOUND INSIDE, EITHER.
GOOD. YOU HAVE YOUR KEY CARD?
YES, SIR.
IT'S A VITAL KEY THAT GRANTS ACCESS, THERE.
CLUNK
THERE ARE FIVE KEYS IN
TOT–
GONK
WE KNOW, BONEHEAD.
SO HERE'S THE LAST ONE, EH?

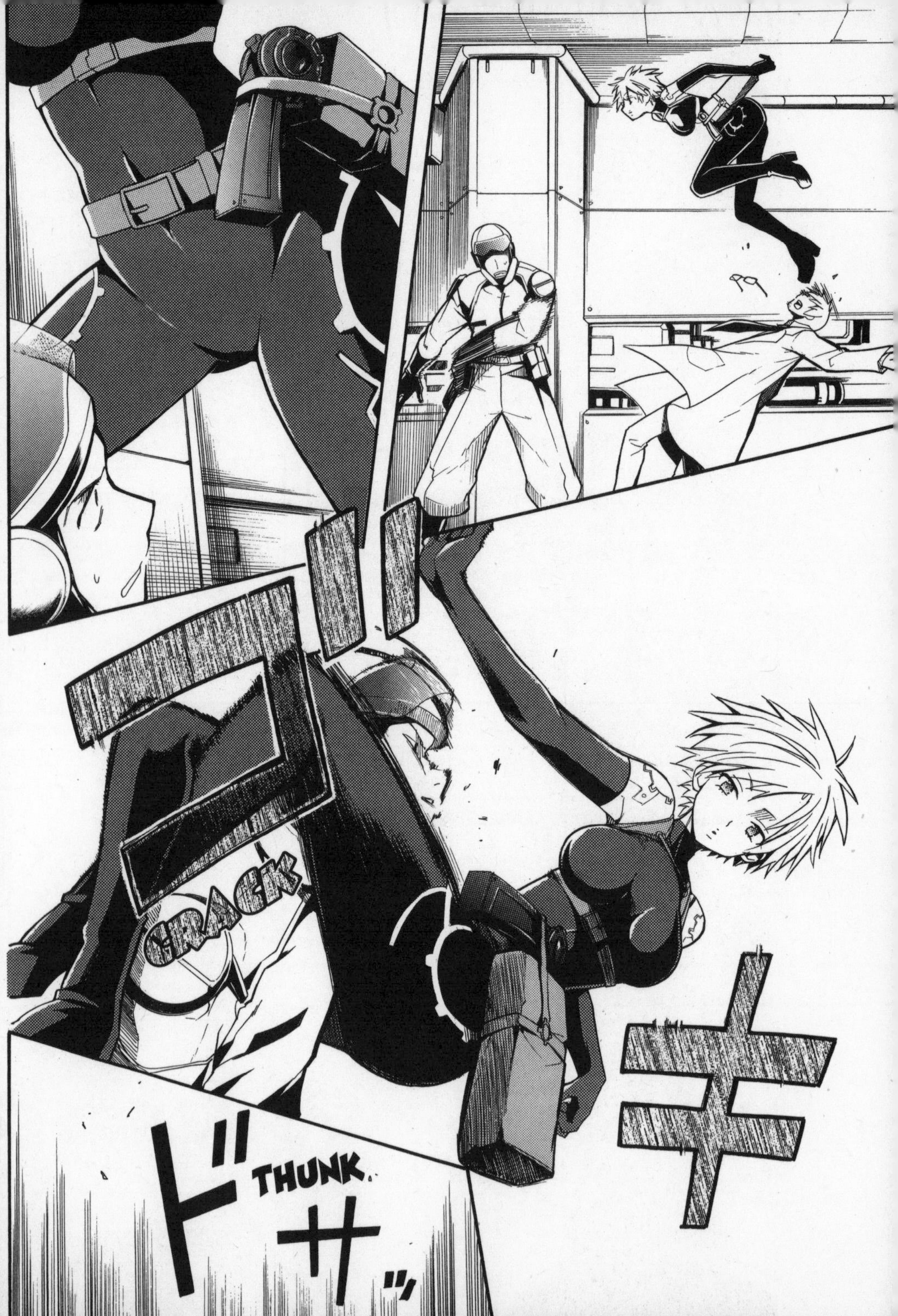
ゴキ
CRACK
ドサッ
THUNK

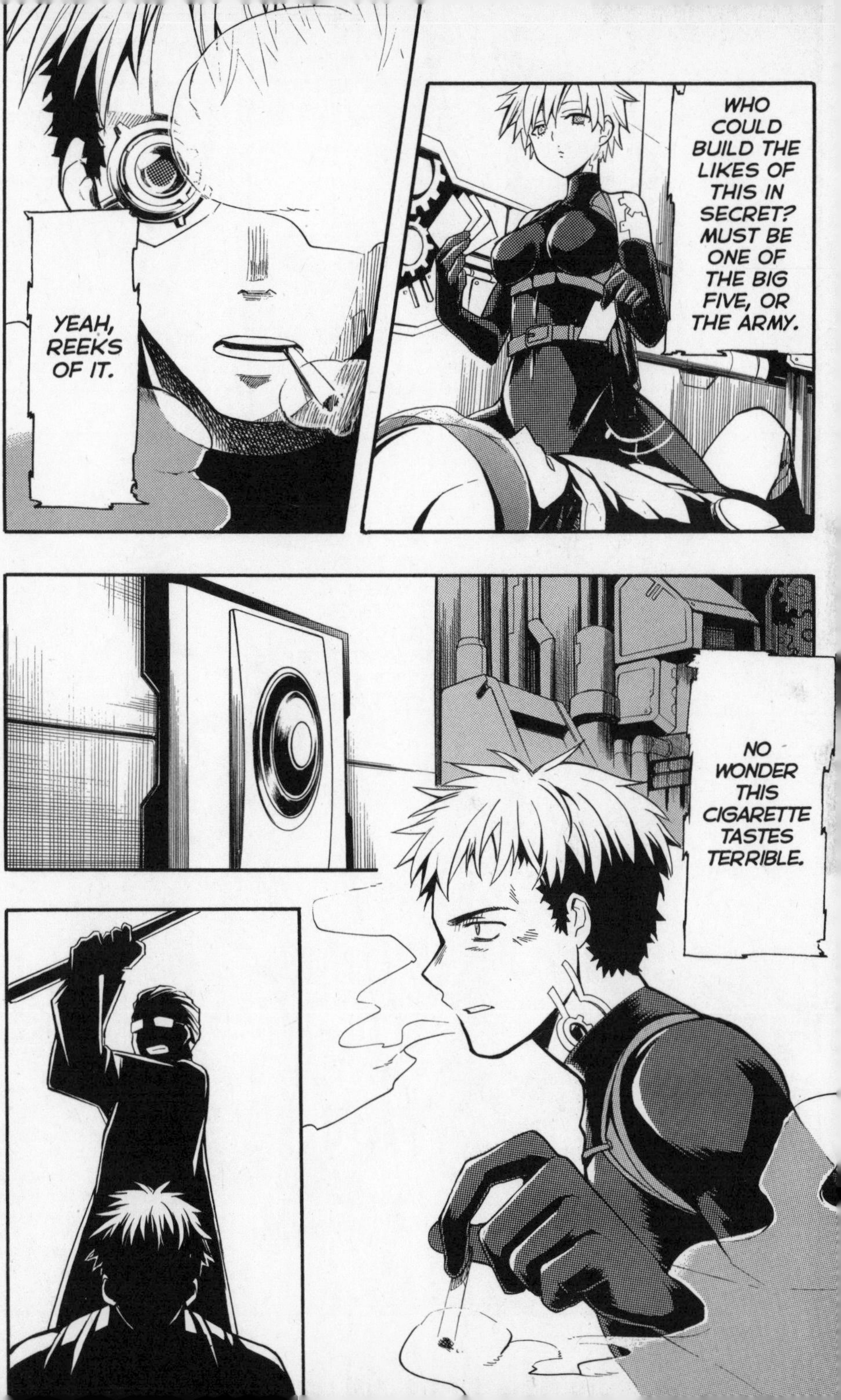
WHO COULD BUILD THE LIKES OF THIS IN SECRET? MUST BE ONE OF THE BIG FIVE, OR THE ARMY.
YEAH, REEKS OF IT.
NO WONDER THIS CIGARETTE TASTES TERRIBLE.

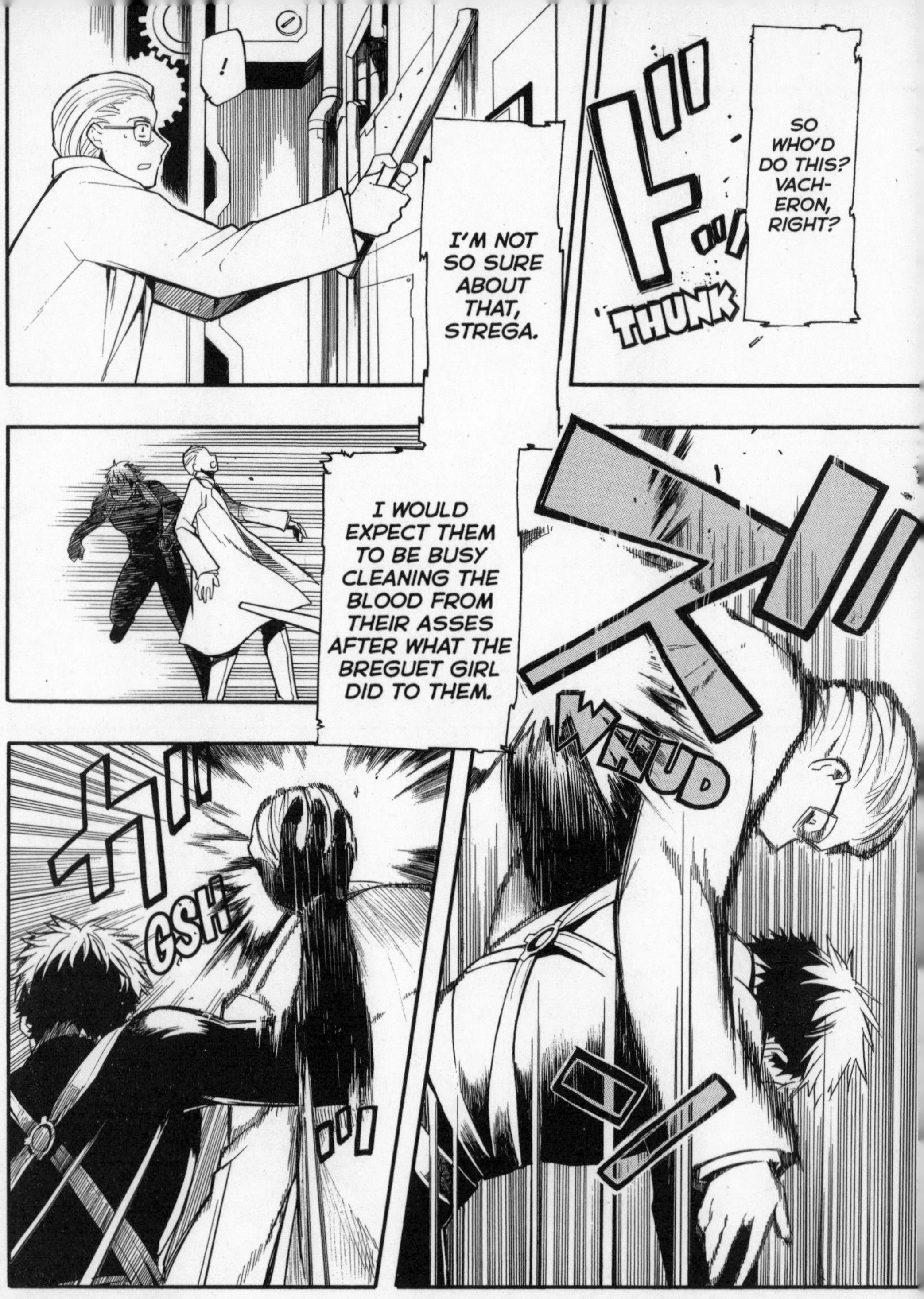
SO WHO'D DO THIS? VACHERON, RIGHT?
THUNK
I'M NOT SO SURE ABOUT THAT, STREGA.
WHUD
I WOULD EXPECT THEM TO BE BUSY CLEANING THE BLOOD FROM THEIR ASSES AFTER WHAT THE BREGUET GIRL DID TO THEM.
GSH

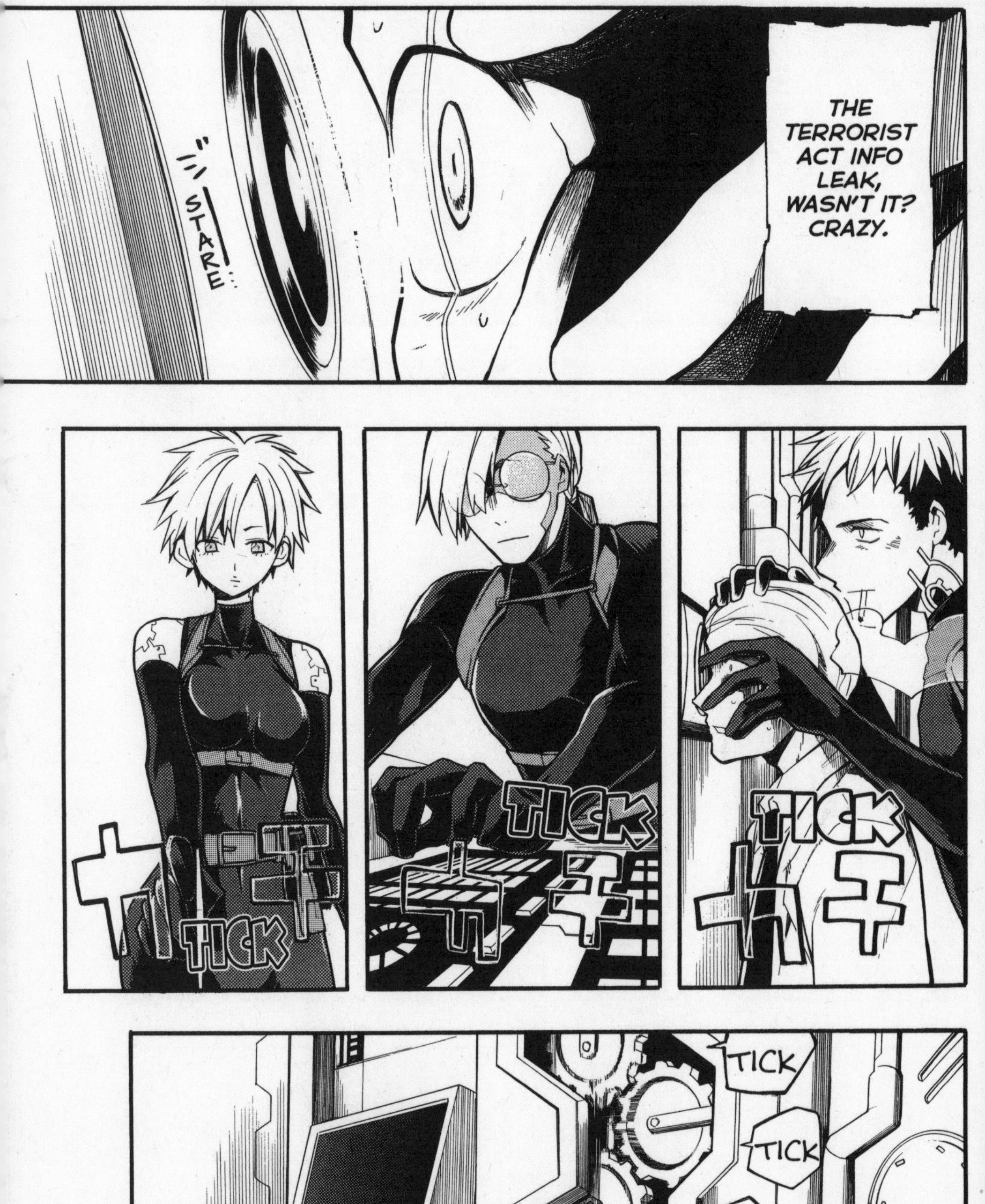
THE TERRORIST ACT INFO LEAK, WASN'T IT? CRAZY.
STARE
TICK
TICK
TICK
TICK
TICK
TICK

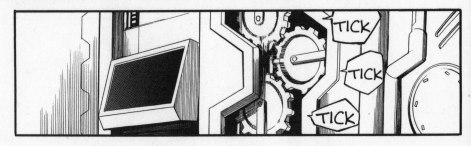

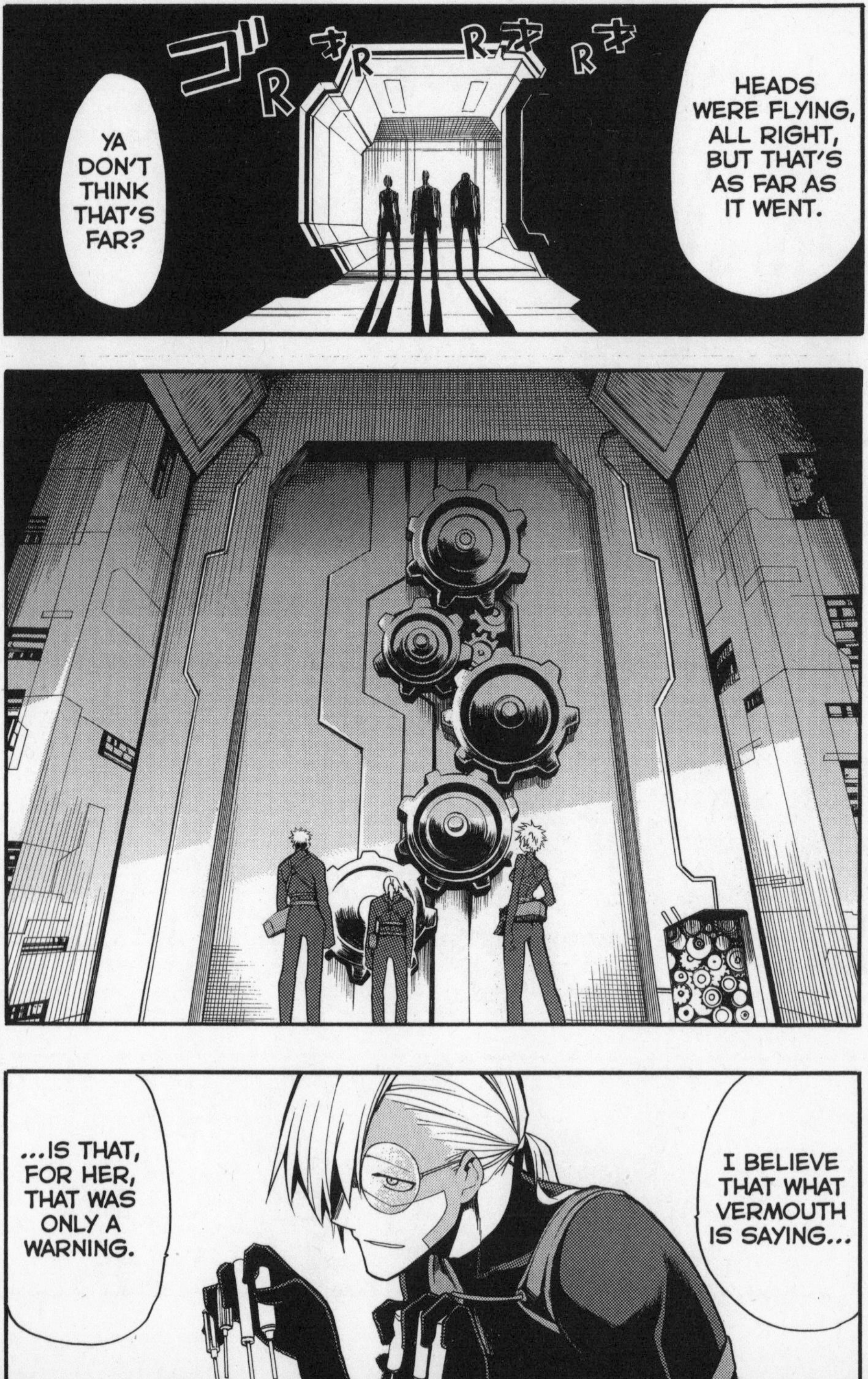
HEADS WERE FLYING, ALL RIGHT, BUT THAT'S AS FAR AS IT WENT.
YA DON'T THINK THAT'S FAR?
I BELIEVE THAT WHAT VERMOUTH IS SAYING...
...IS THAT, FOR HER, THAT WAS ONLY A WARNING.

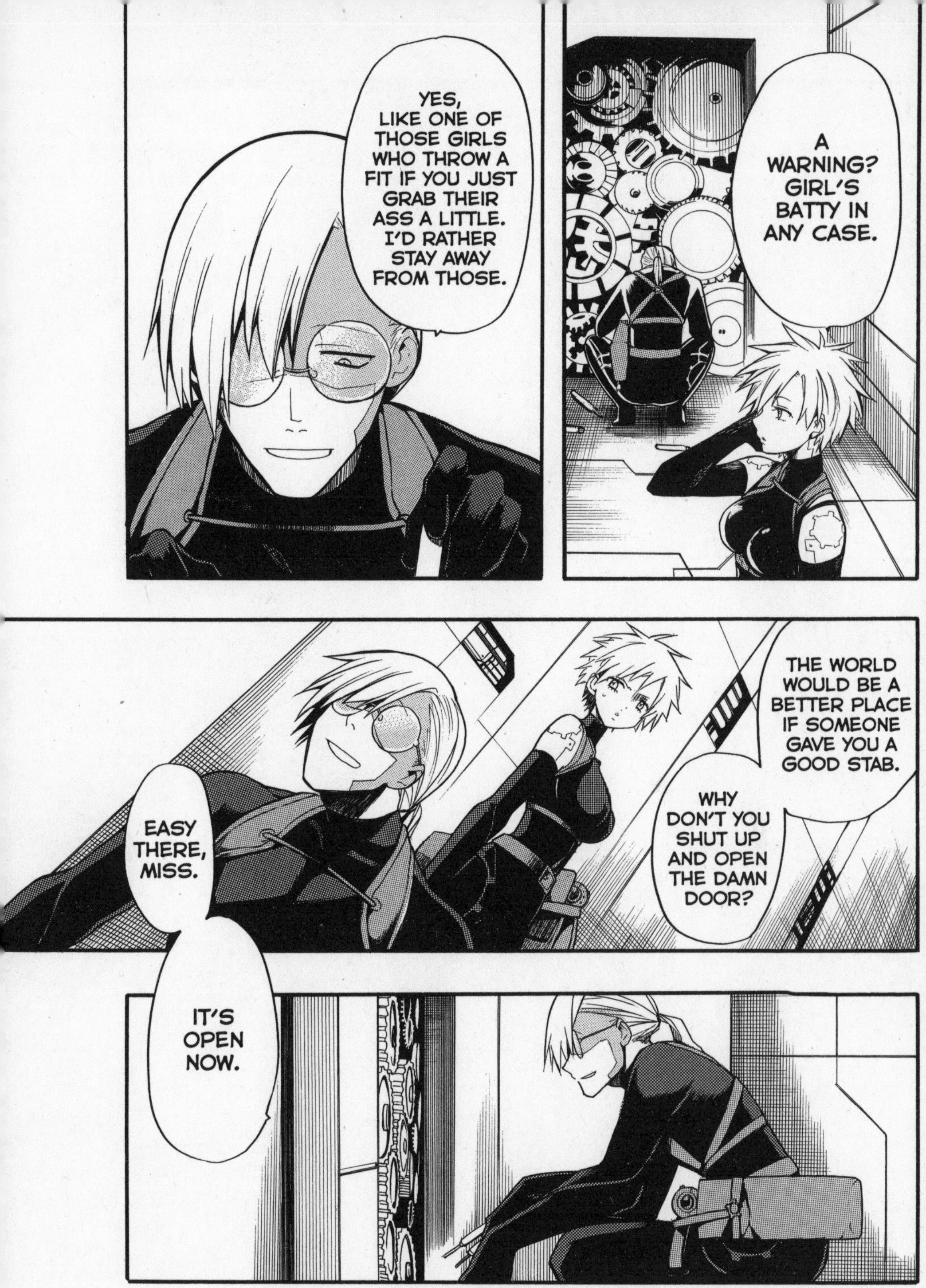
A WARNING? GIRL'S BATTY IN ANY CASE.
YES, LIKE ONE OF THOSE GIRLS WHO THROW A FIT IF YOU JUST GRAB THEIR ASS A LITTLE. I'D RATHER STAY AWAY FROM THOSE.
THE WORLD WOULD BE A BETTER PLACE IF SOMEONE GAVE YOU A GOOD STAB.
WHY DON'T YOU SHUT UP AND OPEN THE DAMN DOOR?
EASY THERE, MISS.
IT'S OPEN NOW.

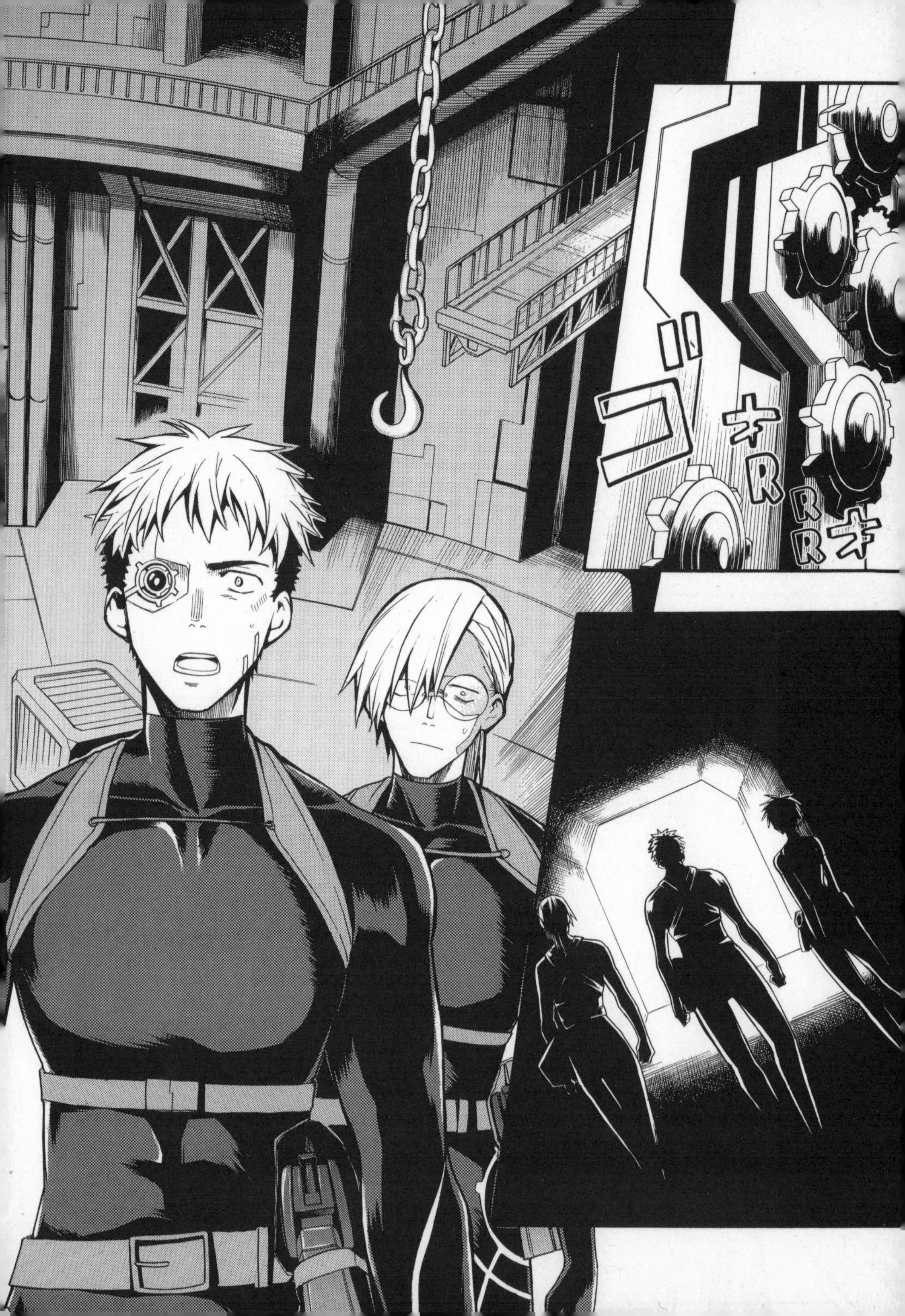
ゴオオ
RRR

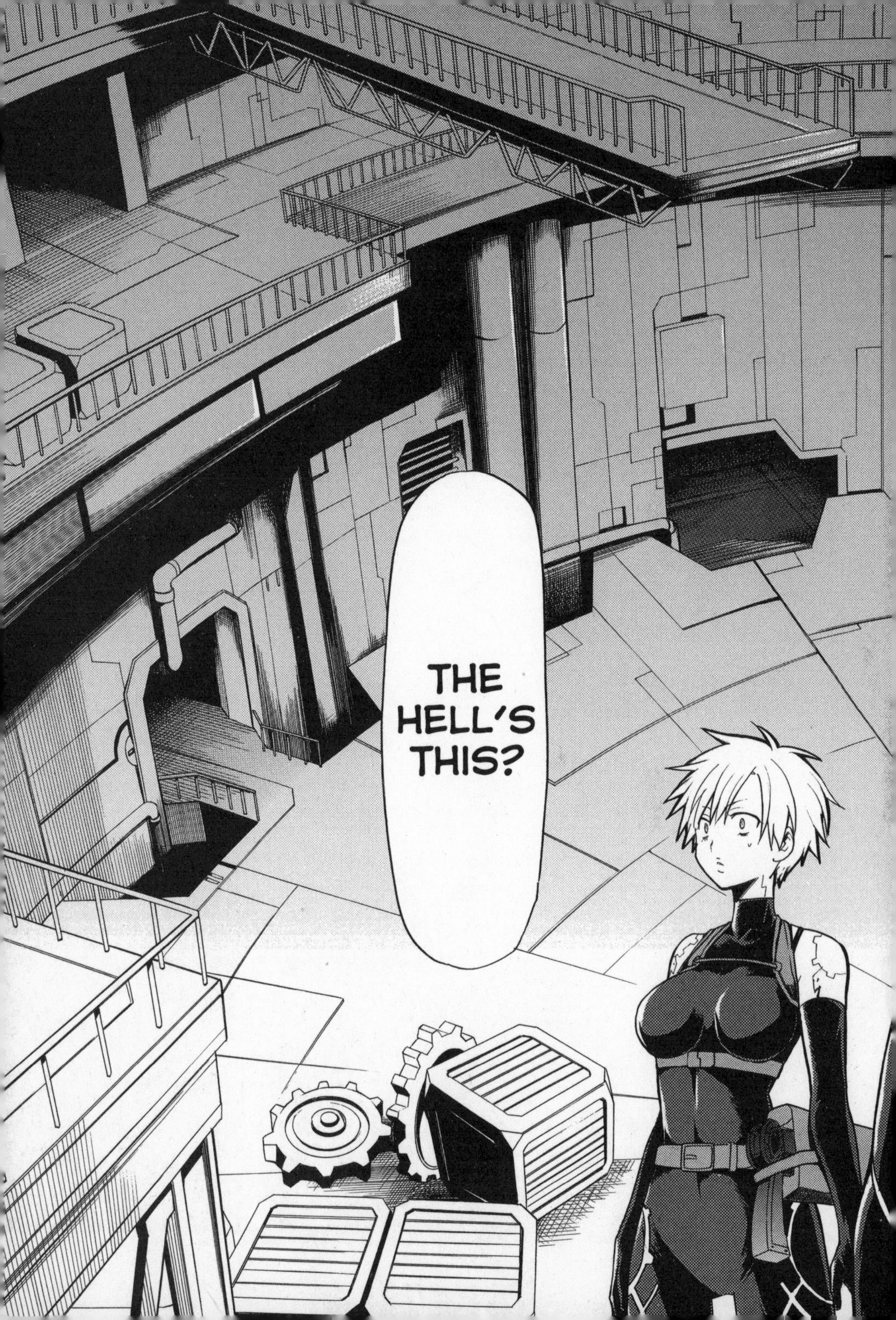
THE HELL'S THIS?

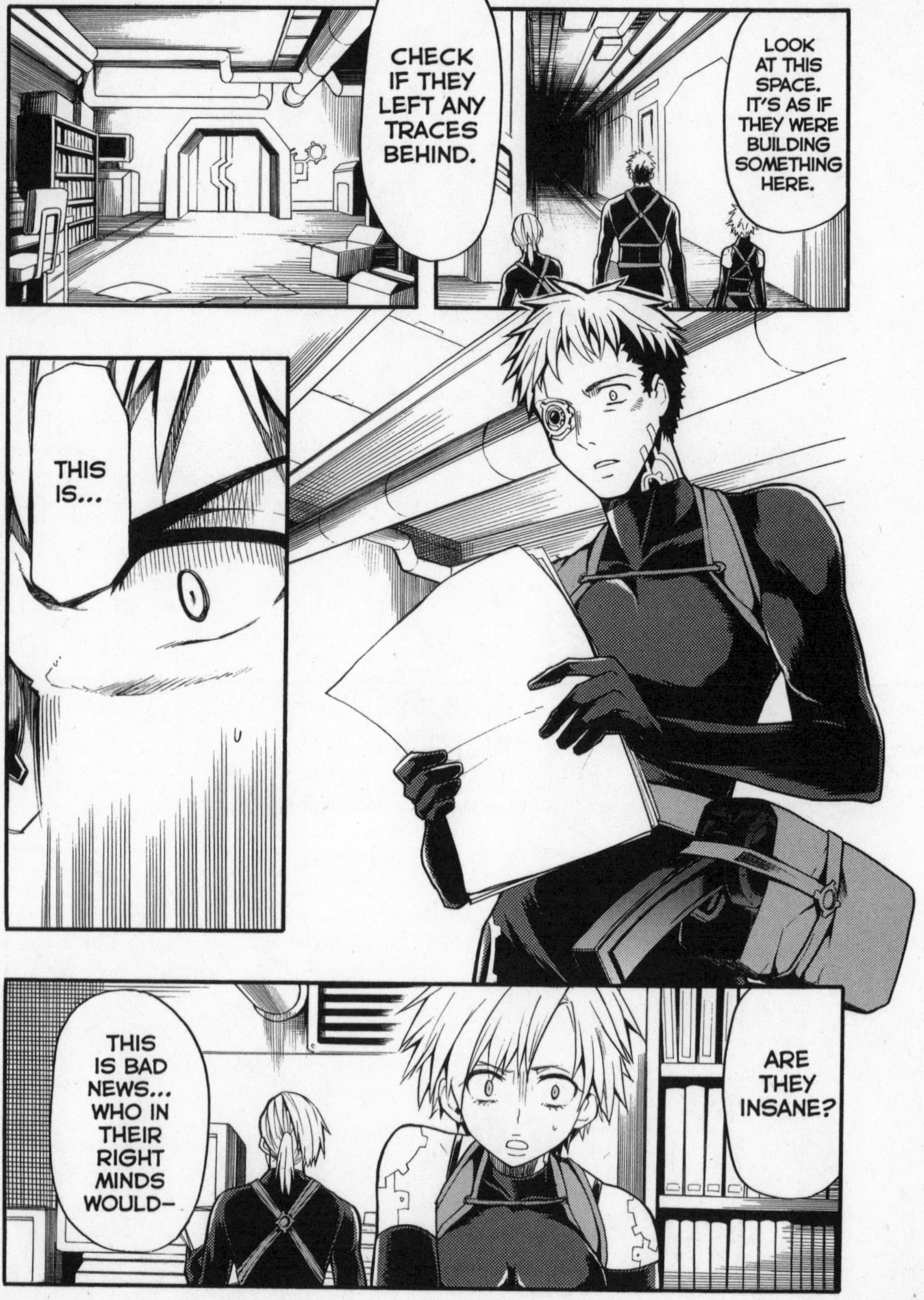
LOOK AT THIS SPACE. IT'S AS IF THEY WERE BUILDING SOMETHING HERE.
CHECK IF THEY LEFT ANY TRACES BEHIND.
THIS IS...
ARE THEY INSANE?
THIS IS BAD NEWS... WHO IN THEIR RIGHT MINDS WOULD-

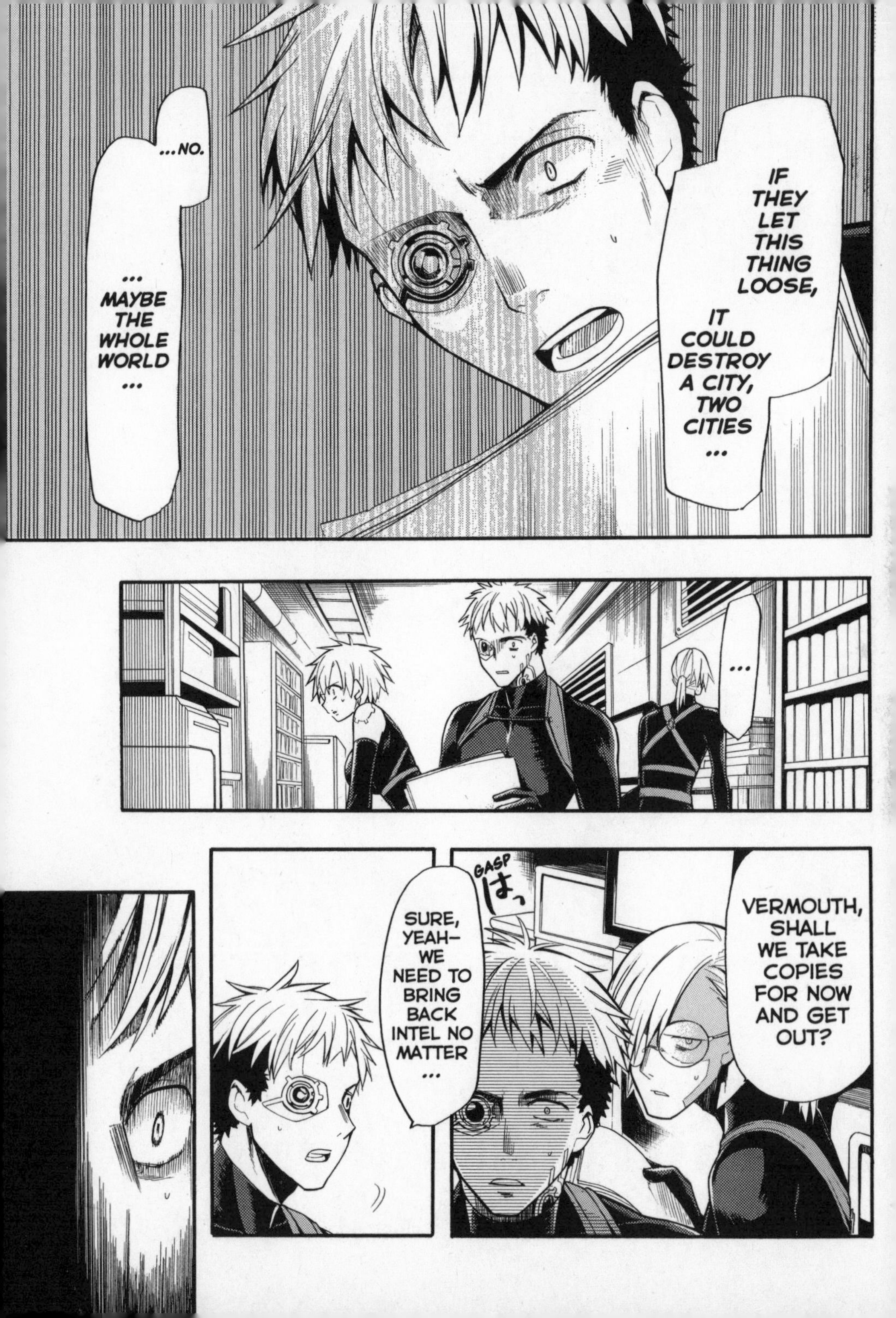
IF THEY LET THIS THING LOOSE,
IT COULD DESTROY A CITY, TWO CITIES ...
...NO.
... MAYBE THE WHOLE WORLD ...
...
VERMOUTH, SHALL WE TAKE COPIES FOR NOW AND GET OUT?
GASP
はっ
SURE, YEAH— WE NEED TO BRING BACK INTEL NO MATTER ...

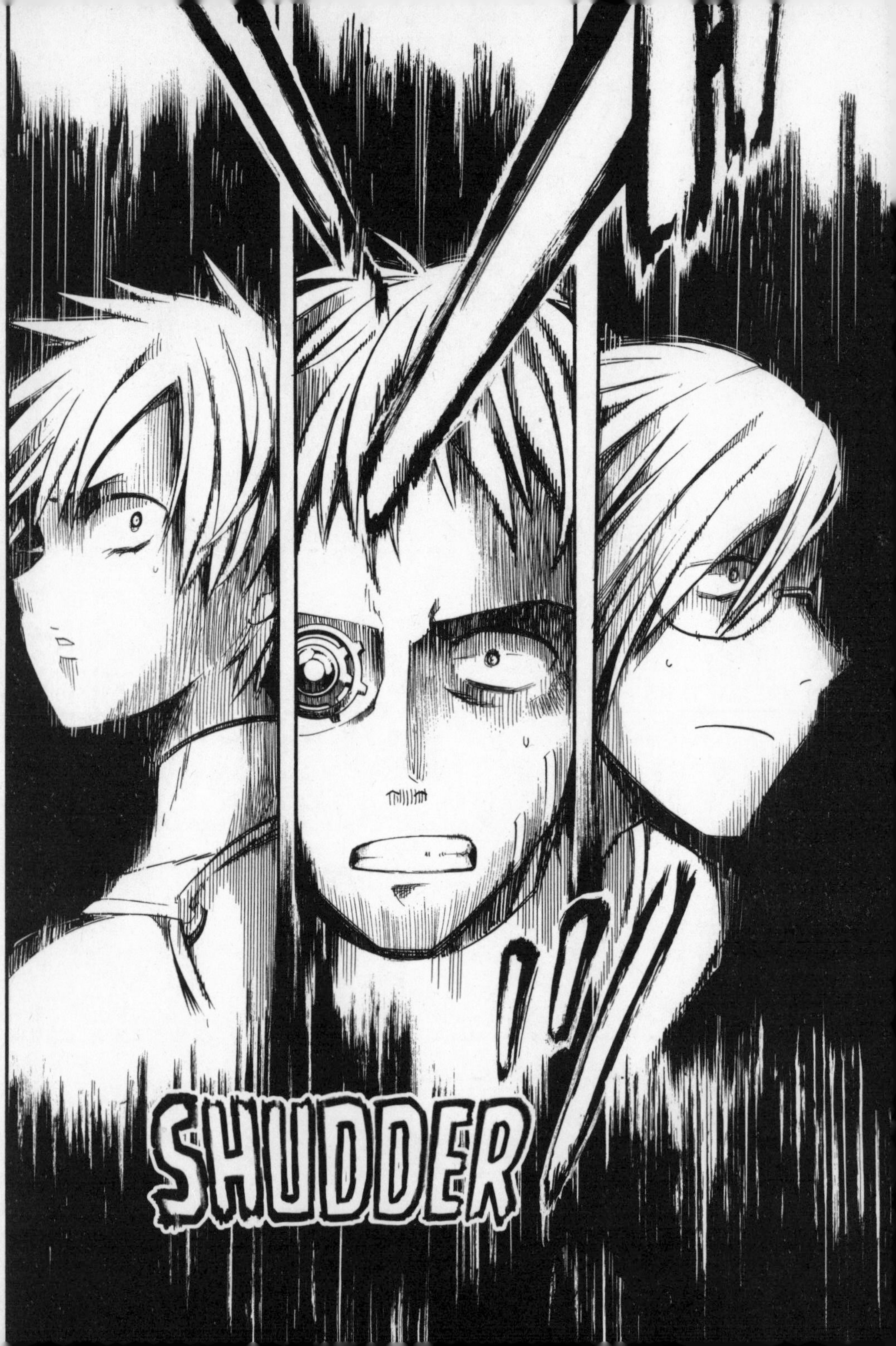
SHUDDER

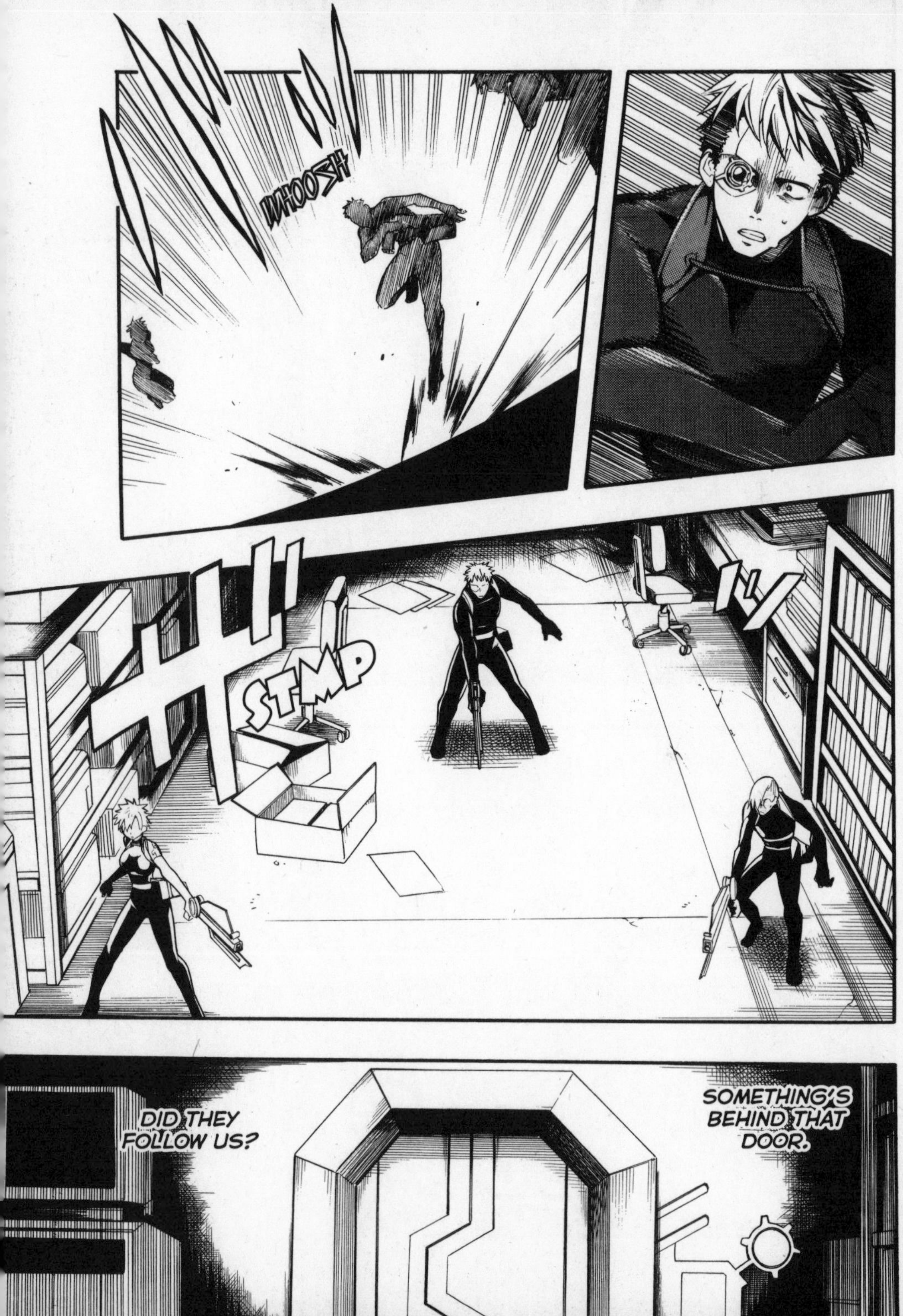
WHOOSH
STMP
SOMETHING'S BEHIND THAT DOOR.
DID THEY FOLLOW US?

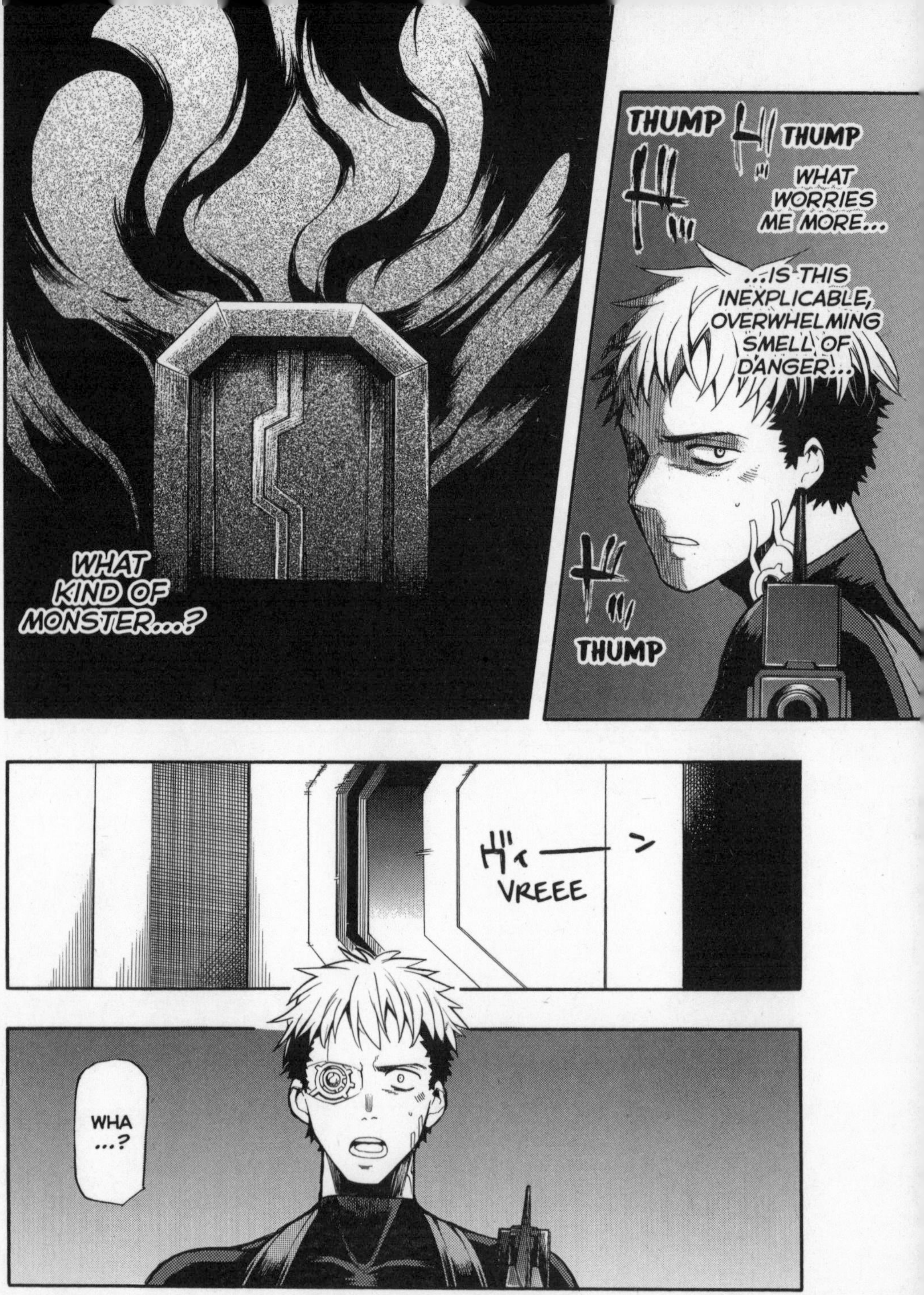
THUMP
THUMP
WHAT WORRIES ME MORE...
...IS THIS INEXPLICABLE, OVERWHELMING SMELL OF DANGER...
THUMP
WHAT KIND OF MONSTER...?
ヴィーーン
VREEE
WHA ...?

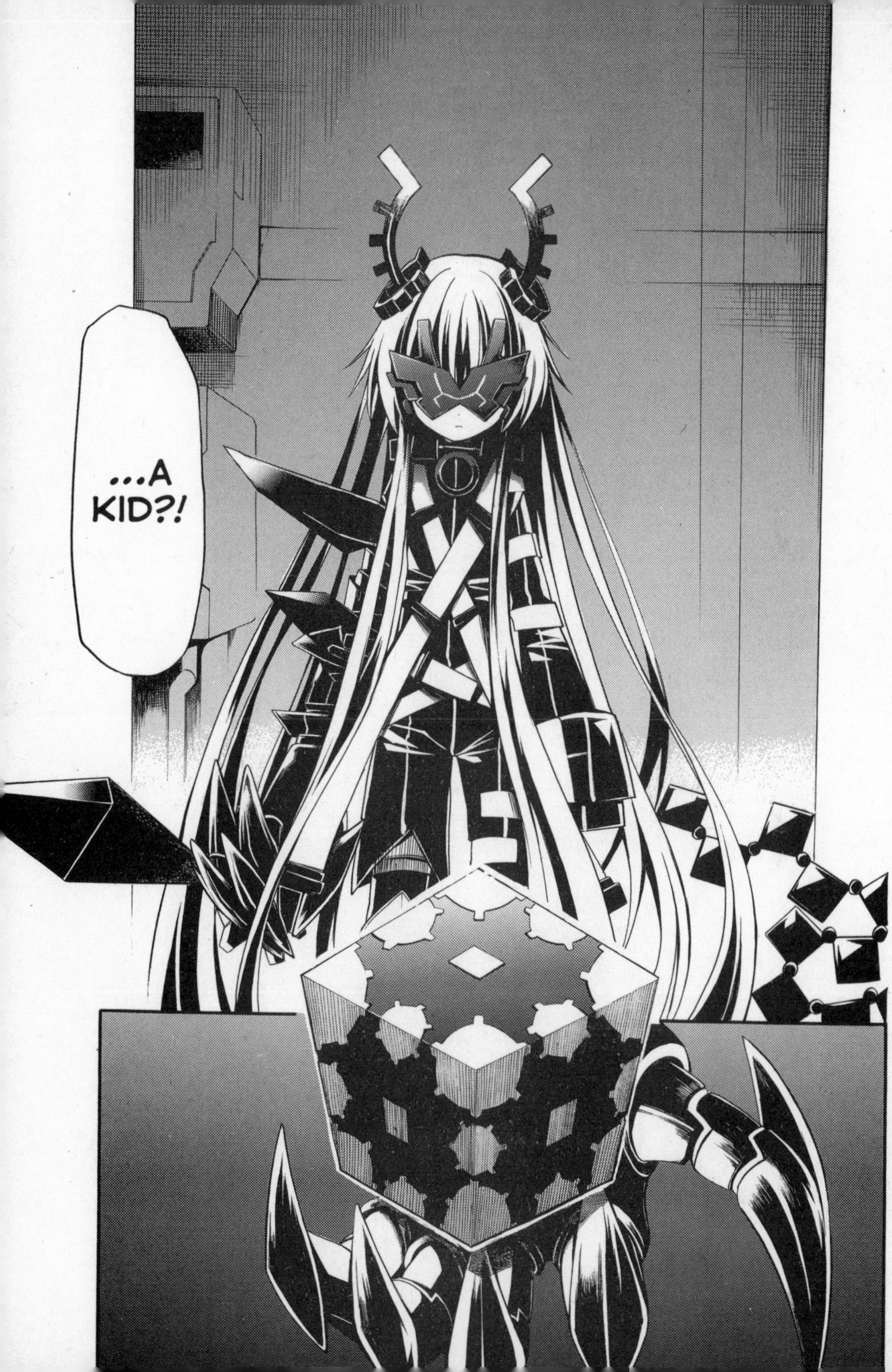
...A KID?!

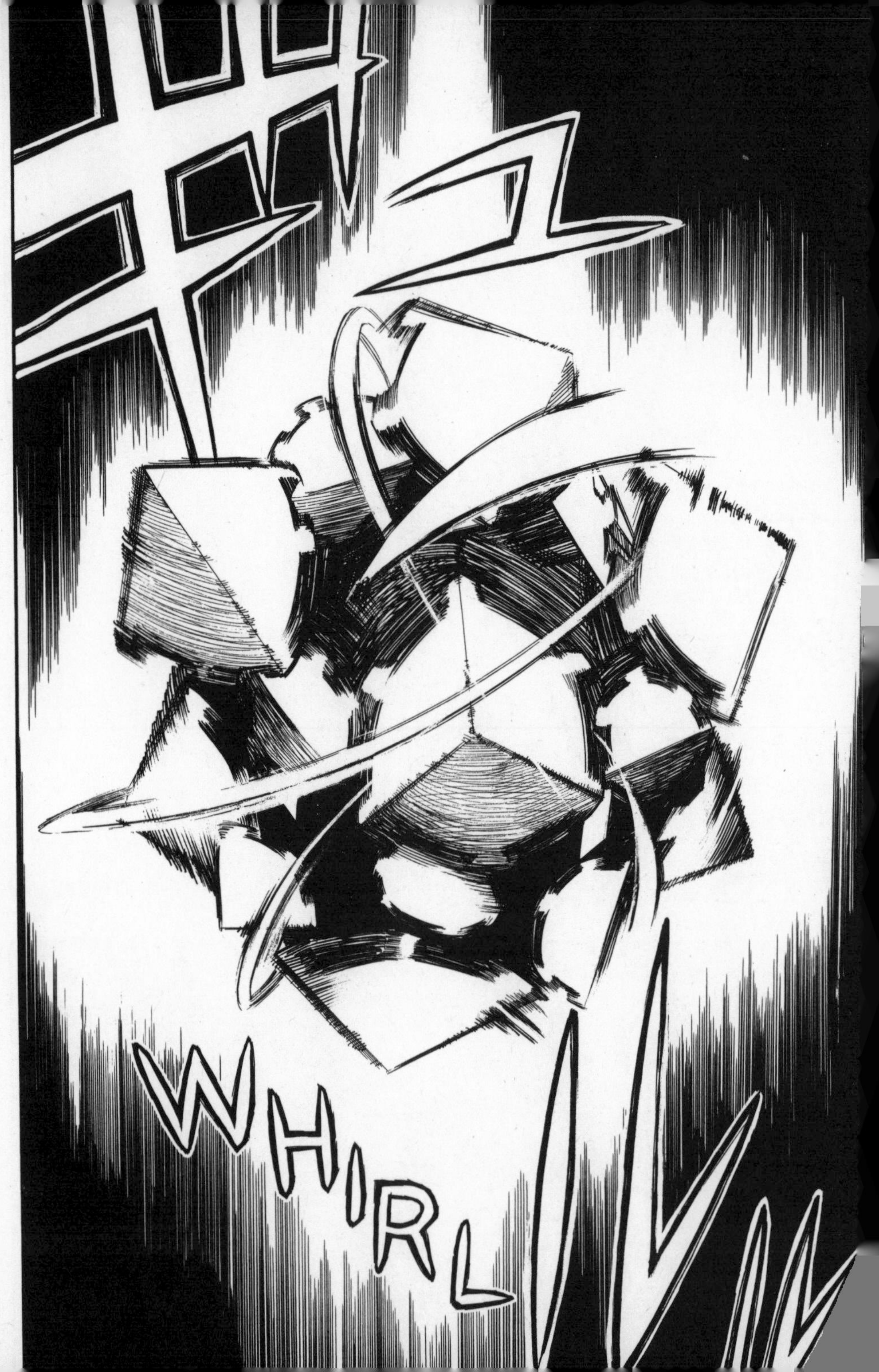
WHIRL

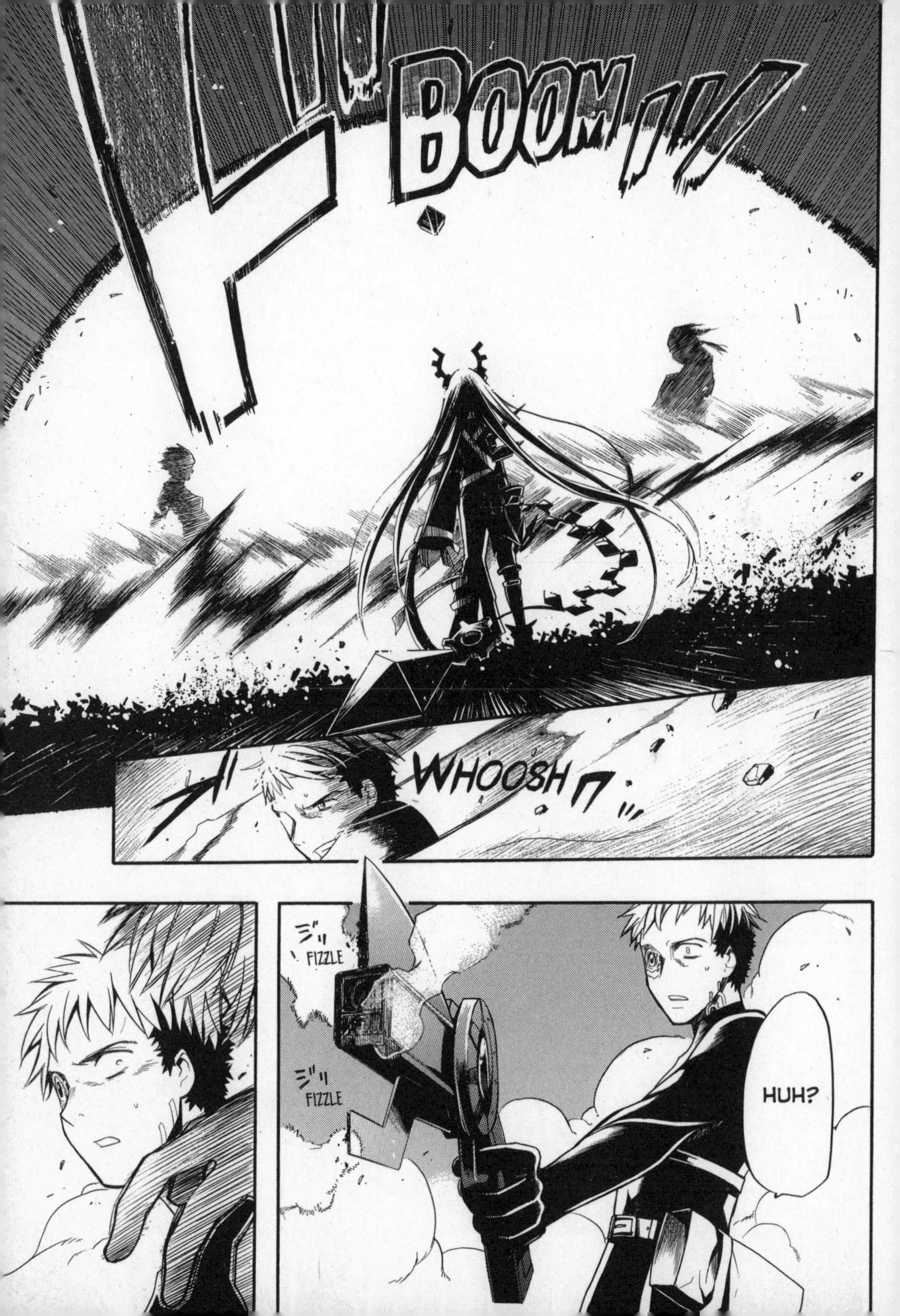
BOOM
WHOOSH
ジリ
FIZZLE
ジリ
FIZZLE
HUH?

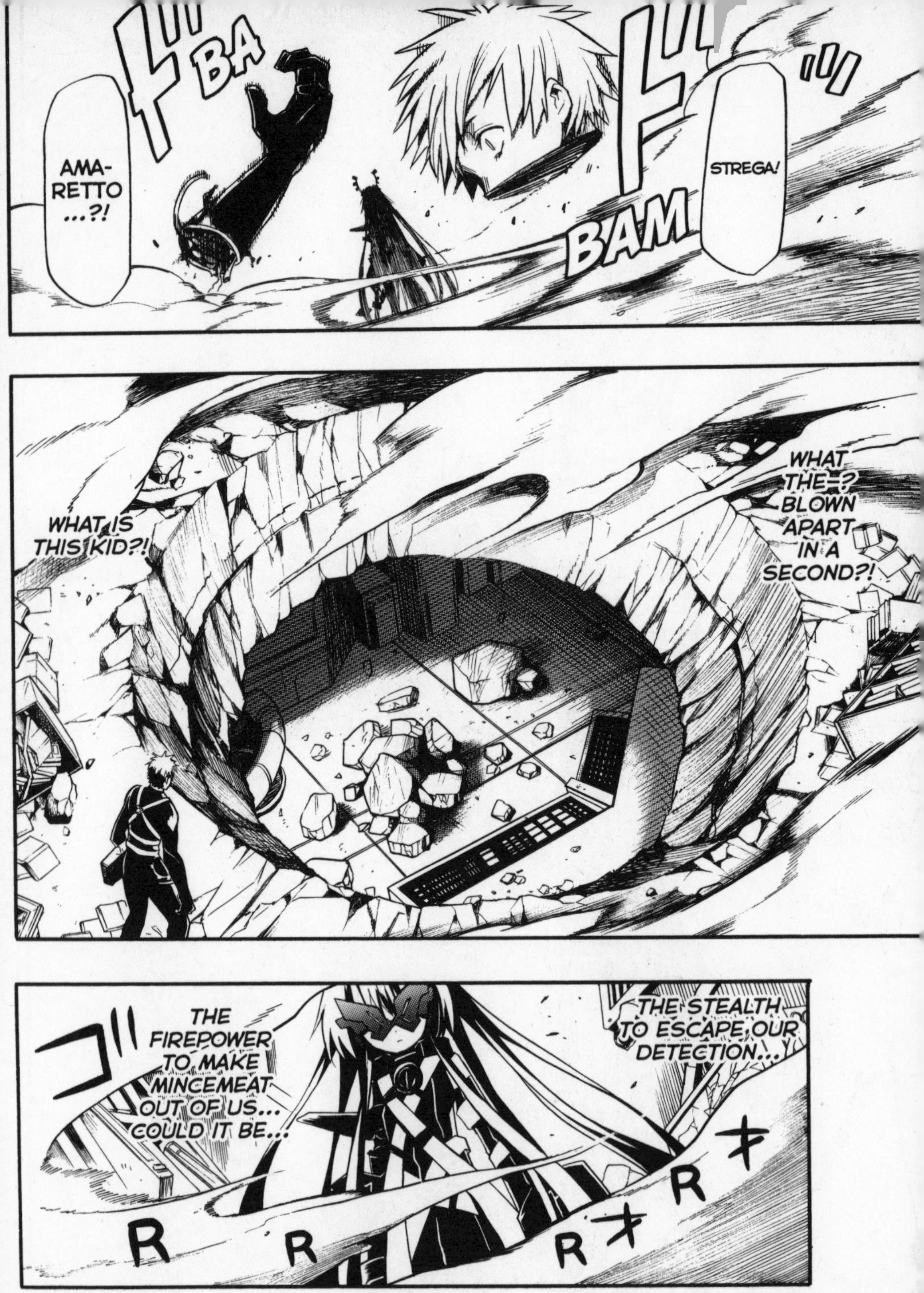
STREGA!
BAM
BA
AMA-RETTO ...?!
WHAT THE-? BLOWN APART IN A SECOND?!
WHAT IS THIS KID?!
THE STEALTH TO ESCAPE OUR DETECTION...
THE FIREPOWER TO MAKE MINCEMEAT OUT OF US... COULD IT BE...
R R R R

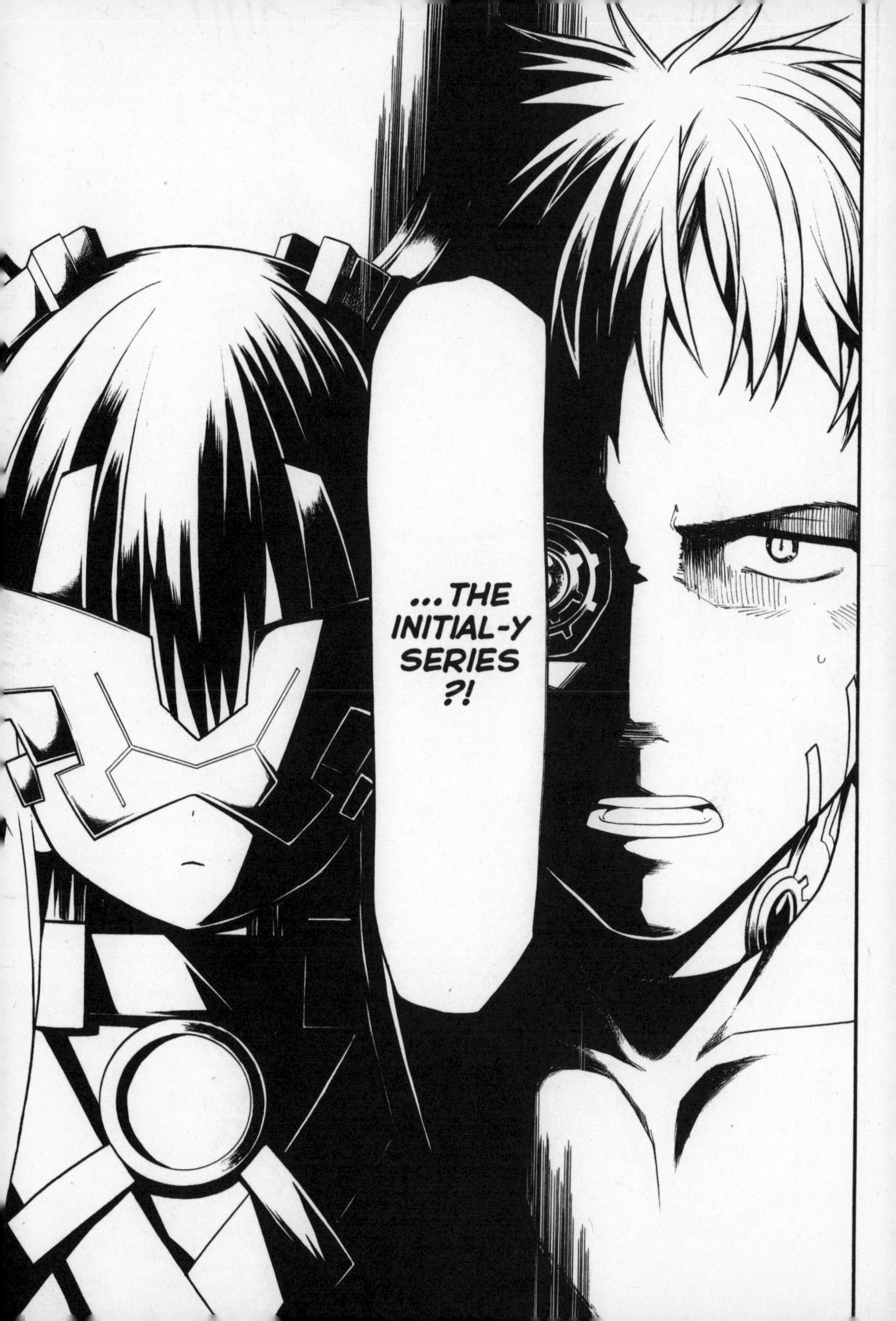
...THE INITIAL-Y SERIES ?!

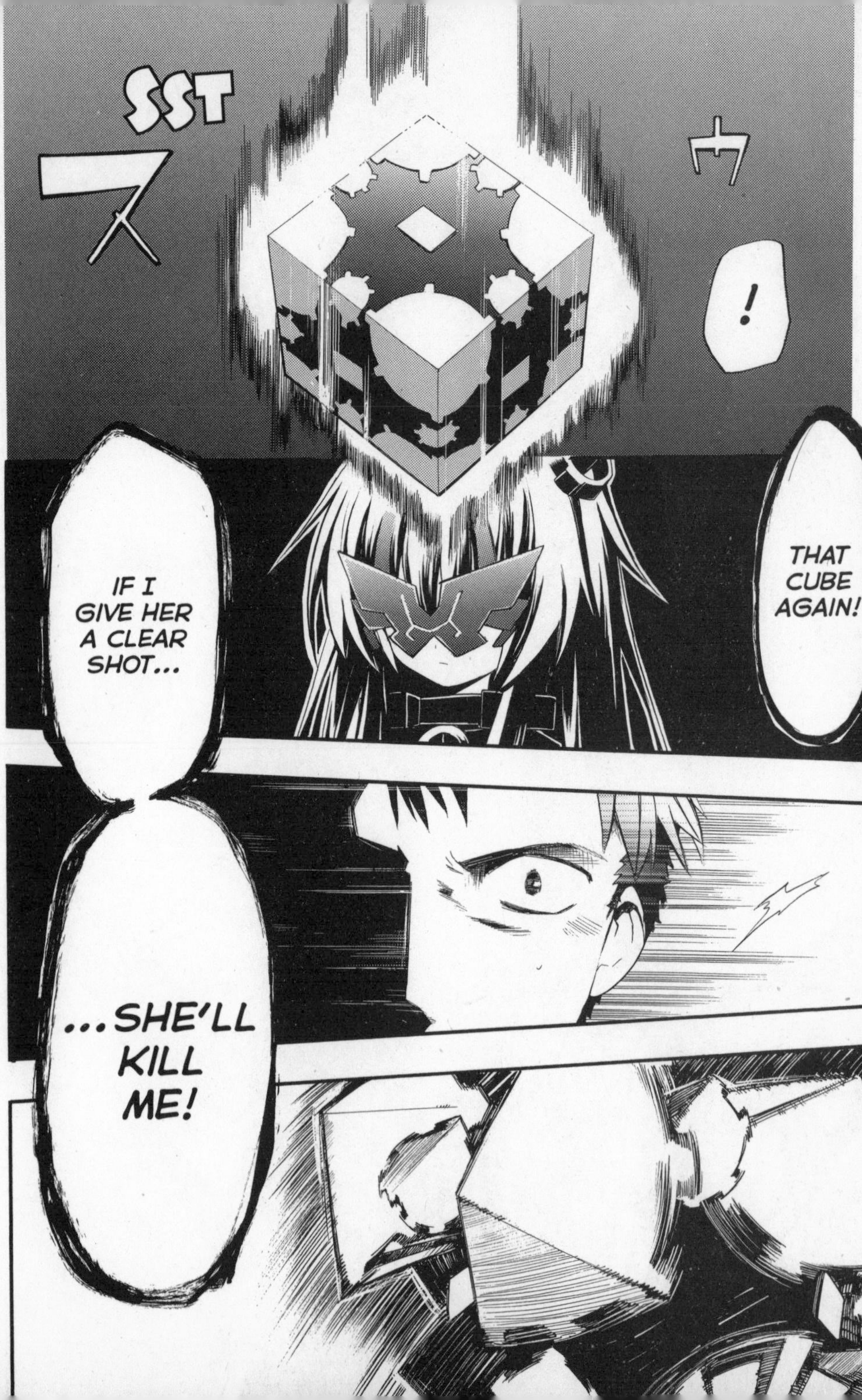

SST
!
THAT CUBE AGAIN!
IF I GIVE HER A CLEAR SHOT...
...SHE'LL KILL ME!

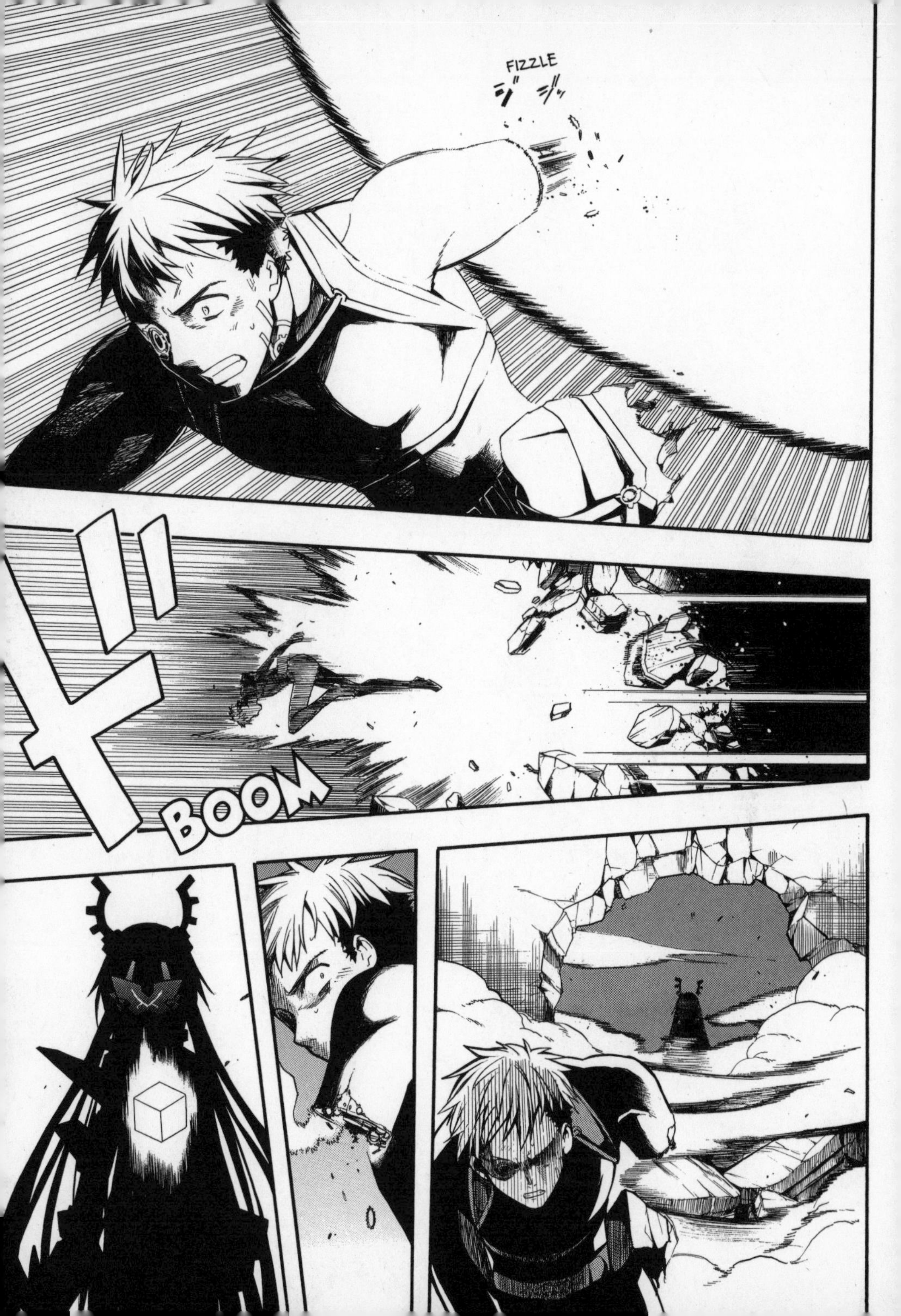
FIZZLE
ジ ジッ
ドン
BOOM

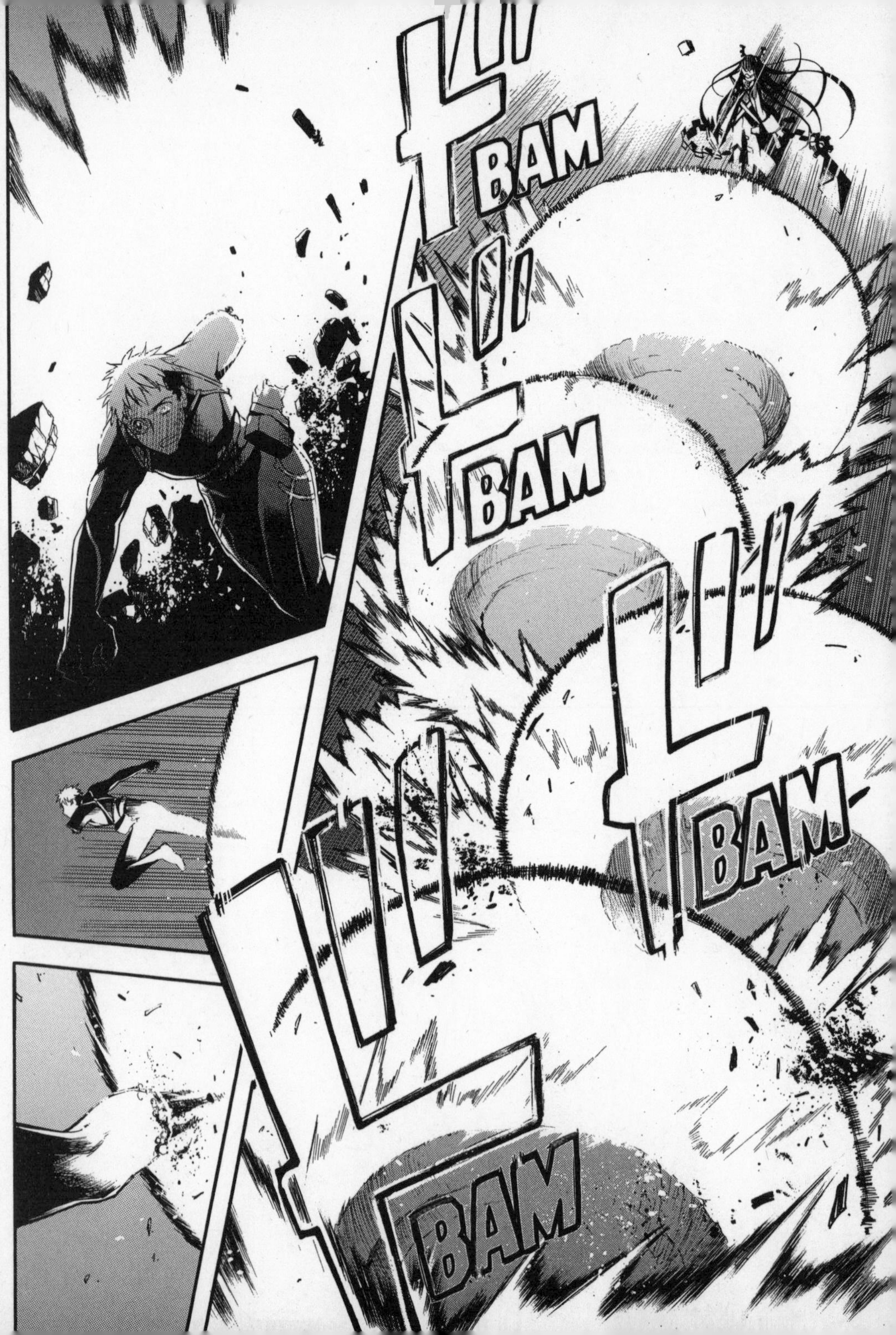
BAM
BAM
BAM
BAM

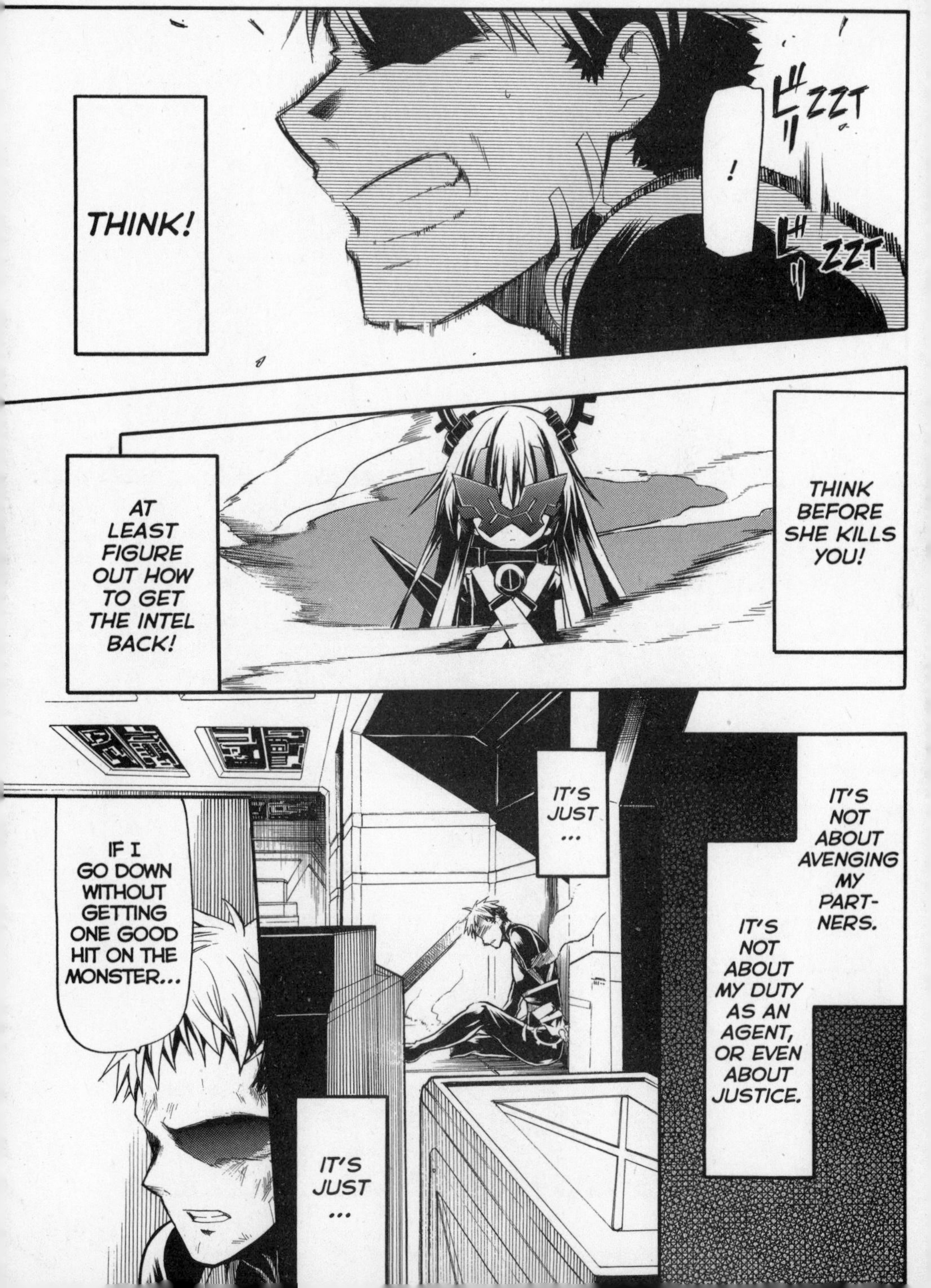
ZZZT
ZZZT
THINK!
THINK BEFORE SHE KILLS YOU!
AT LEAST FIGURE OUT HOW TO GET THE INTEL BACK!
IT'S NOT ABOUT AVENGING MY PARTNERS.
IT'S NOT ABOUT MY DUTY AS AN AGENT, OR EVEN ABOUT JUSTICE.
IT'S JUST ...
IF I GO DOWN WITHOUT GETTING ONE GOOD HIT ON THE MONSTER...
IT'S JUST ...

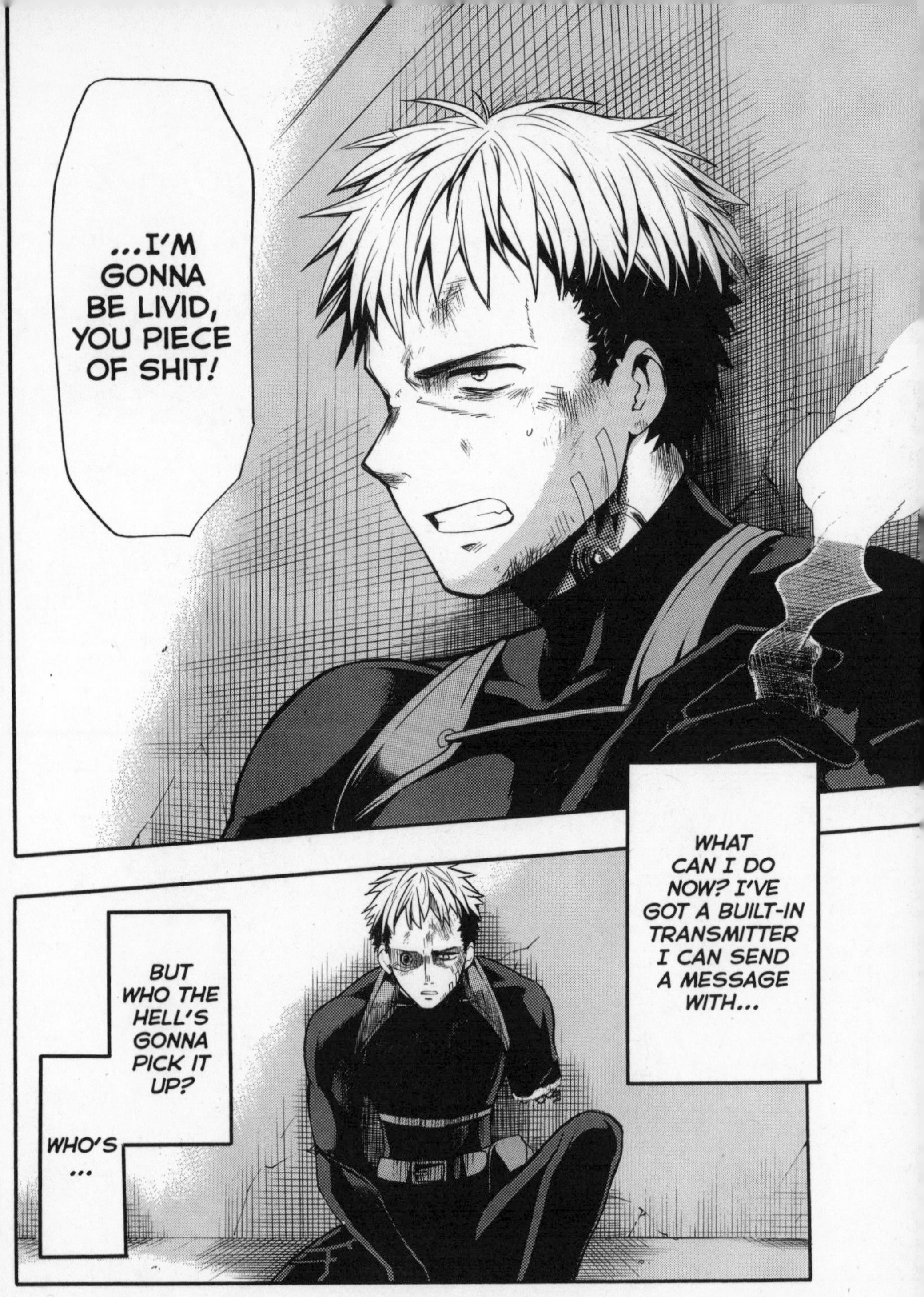
...I'M GONNA BE LIVID, YOU PIECE OF SHIT!
WHAT CAN I DO NOW? I'VE GOT A BUILT-IN TRANSMITTER I CAN SEND A MESSAGE WITH...
BUT WHO THE HELL'S GONNA PICK IT UP?
WHO'S ...

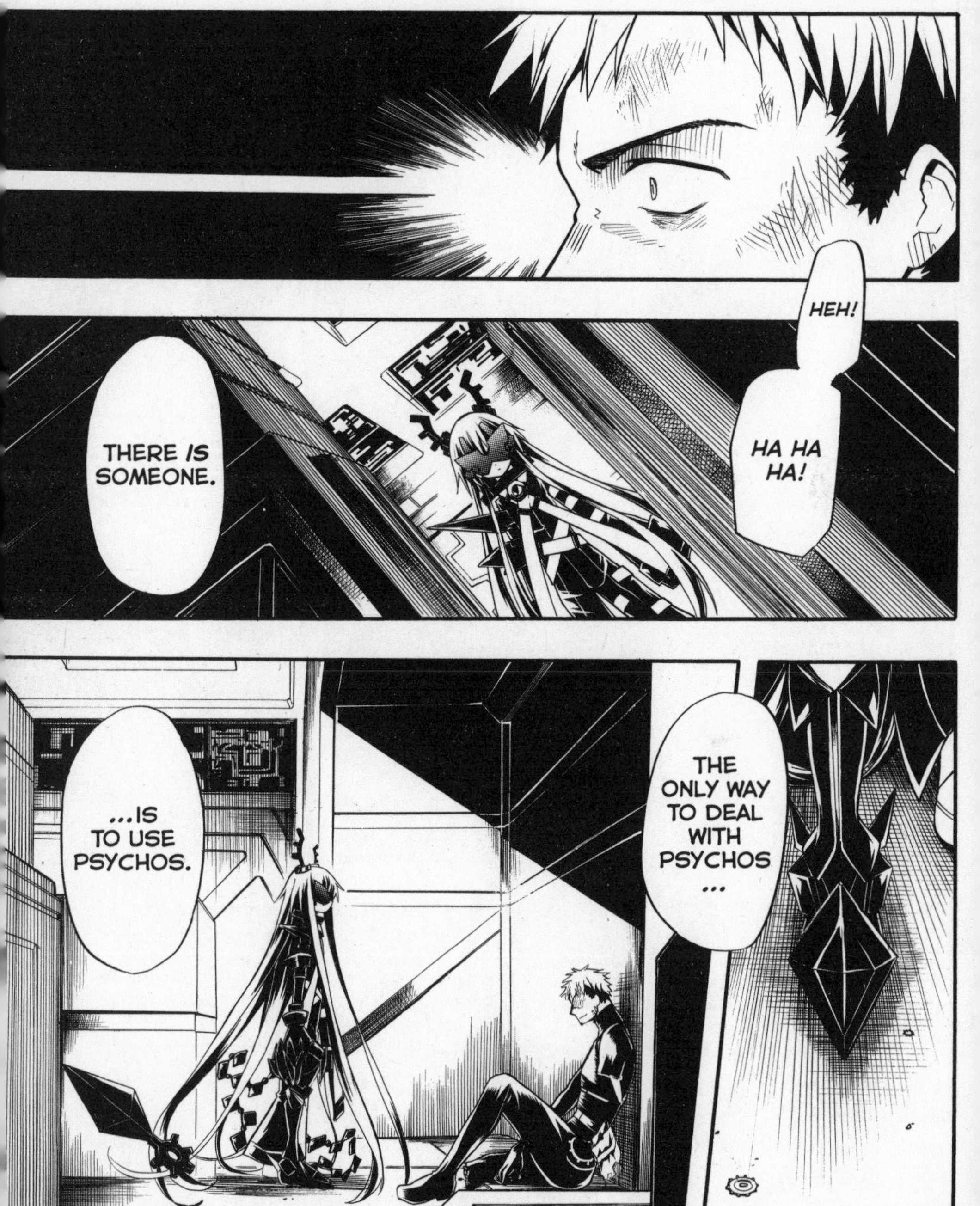
HEH!
HA HA HA!
THERE IS SOMEONE.
THE ONLY WAY TO DEAL WITH PSYCHOS ...
...IS TO USE PSYCHOS.

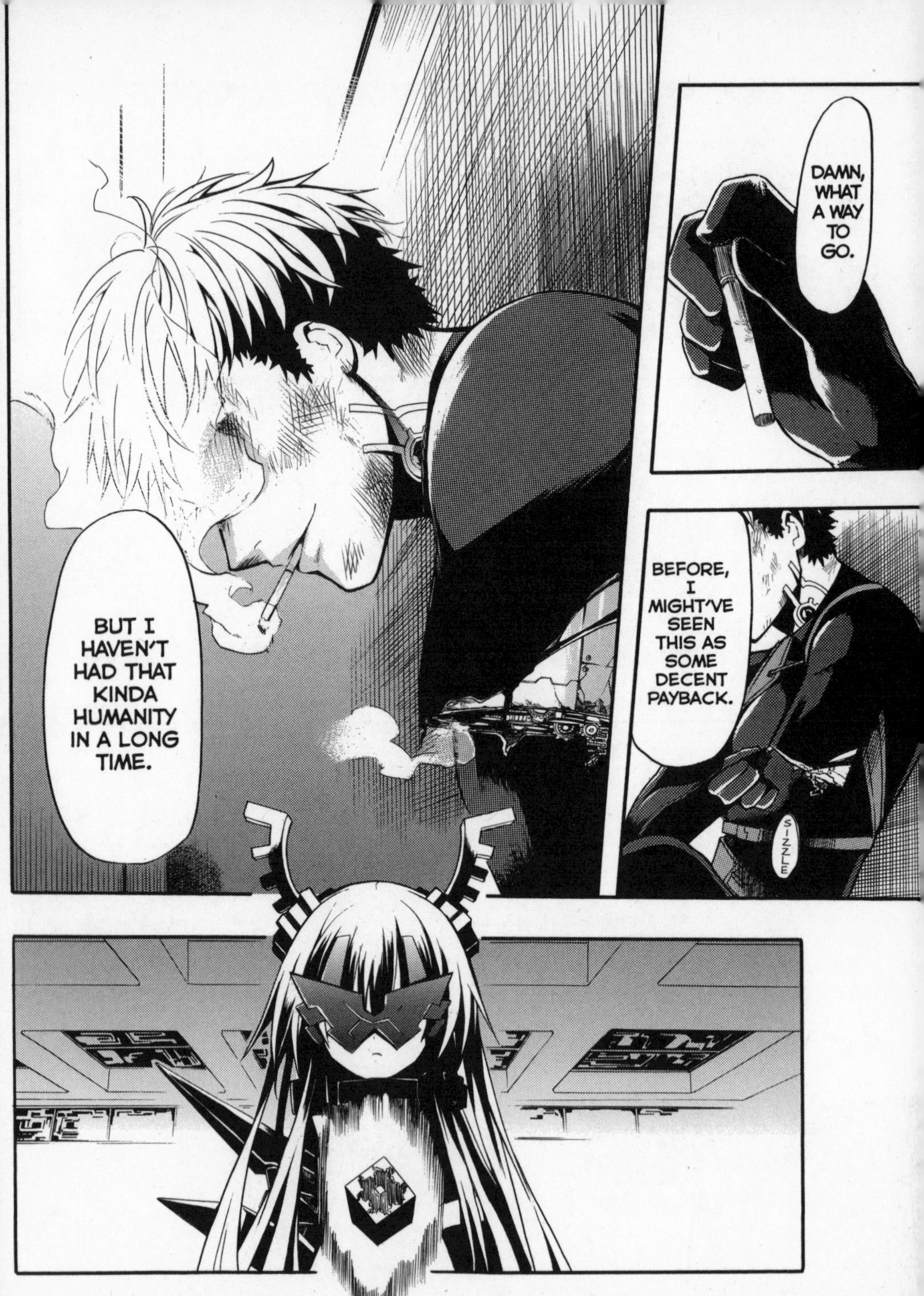
DAMN, WHAT A WAY TO GO.
BEFORE, I MIGHT'VE SEEN THIS AS SOME DECENT PAYBACK.
SIZZLE
BUT I HAVEN'T HAD THAT KINDA HUMANITY IN A LONG TIME.

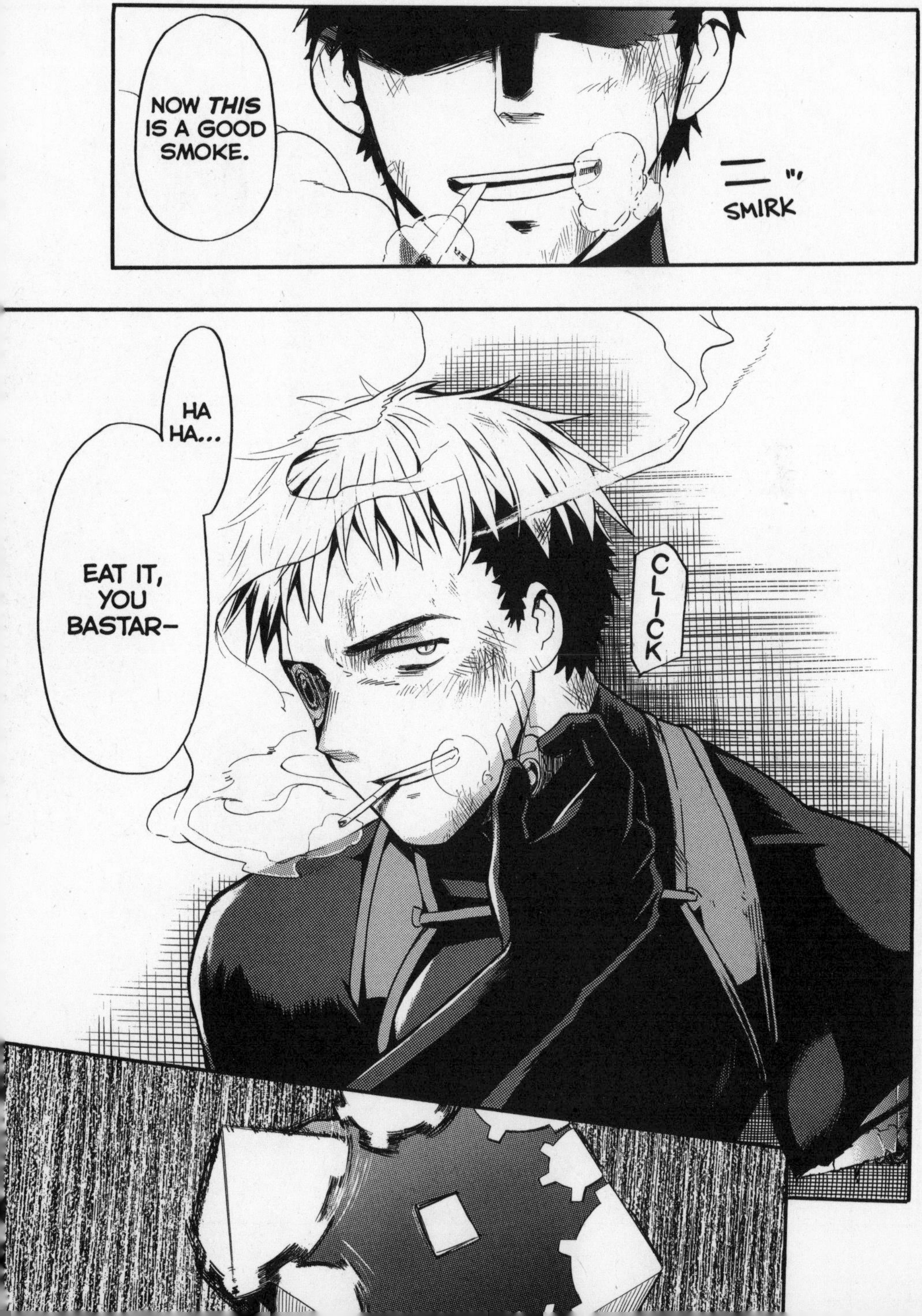
SMIRK
NOW THIS IS A GOOD SMOKE.
CLICK
HA HA...
EAT IT, YOU BASTAR-

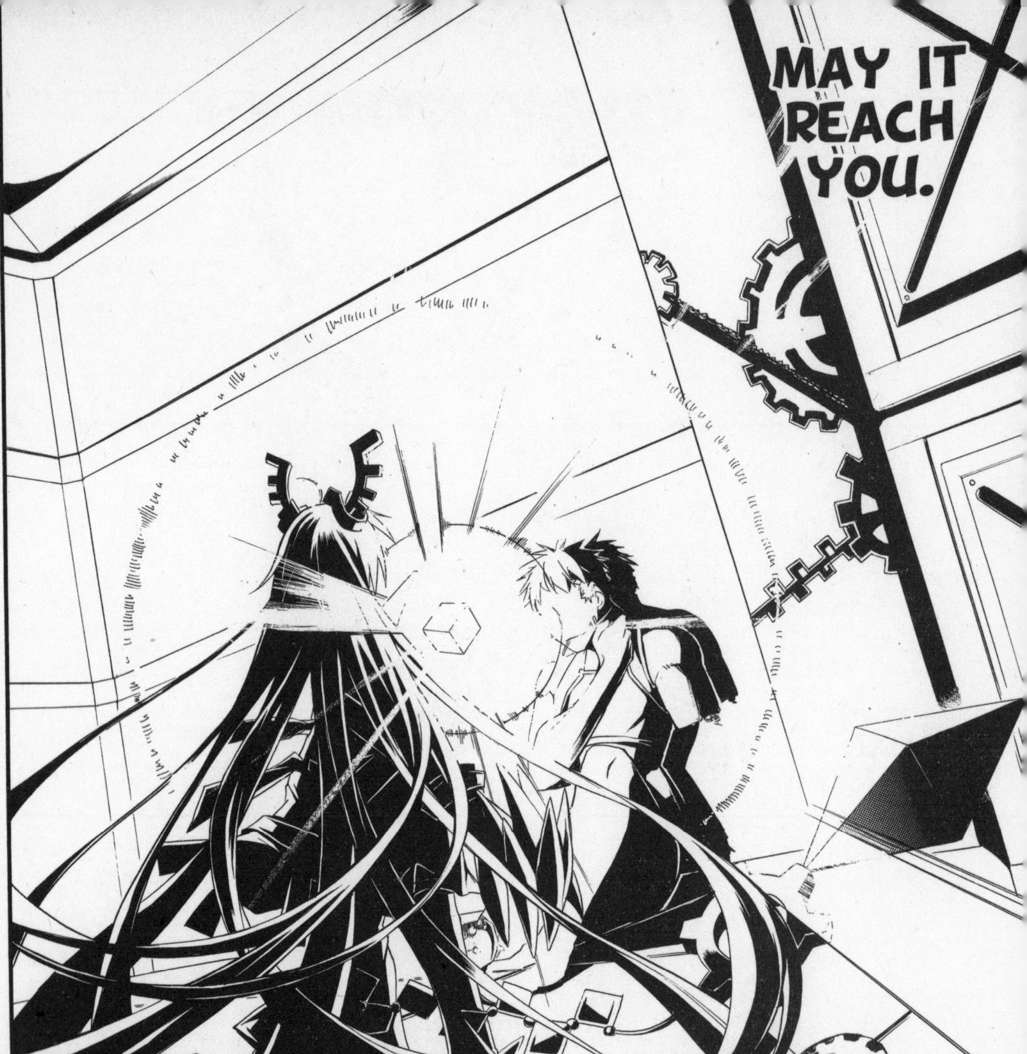
MAY IT REACH YOU.
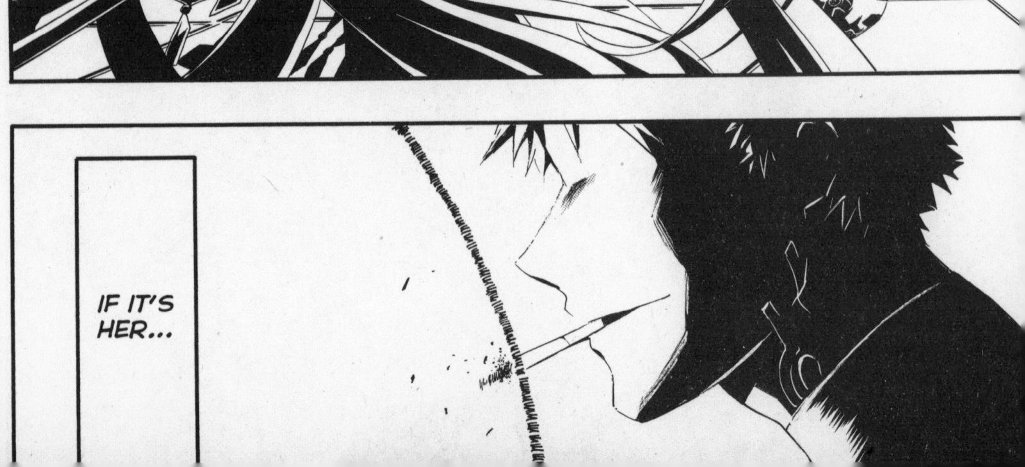
IF IT'S HER...

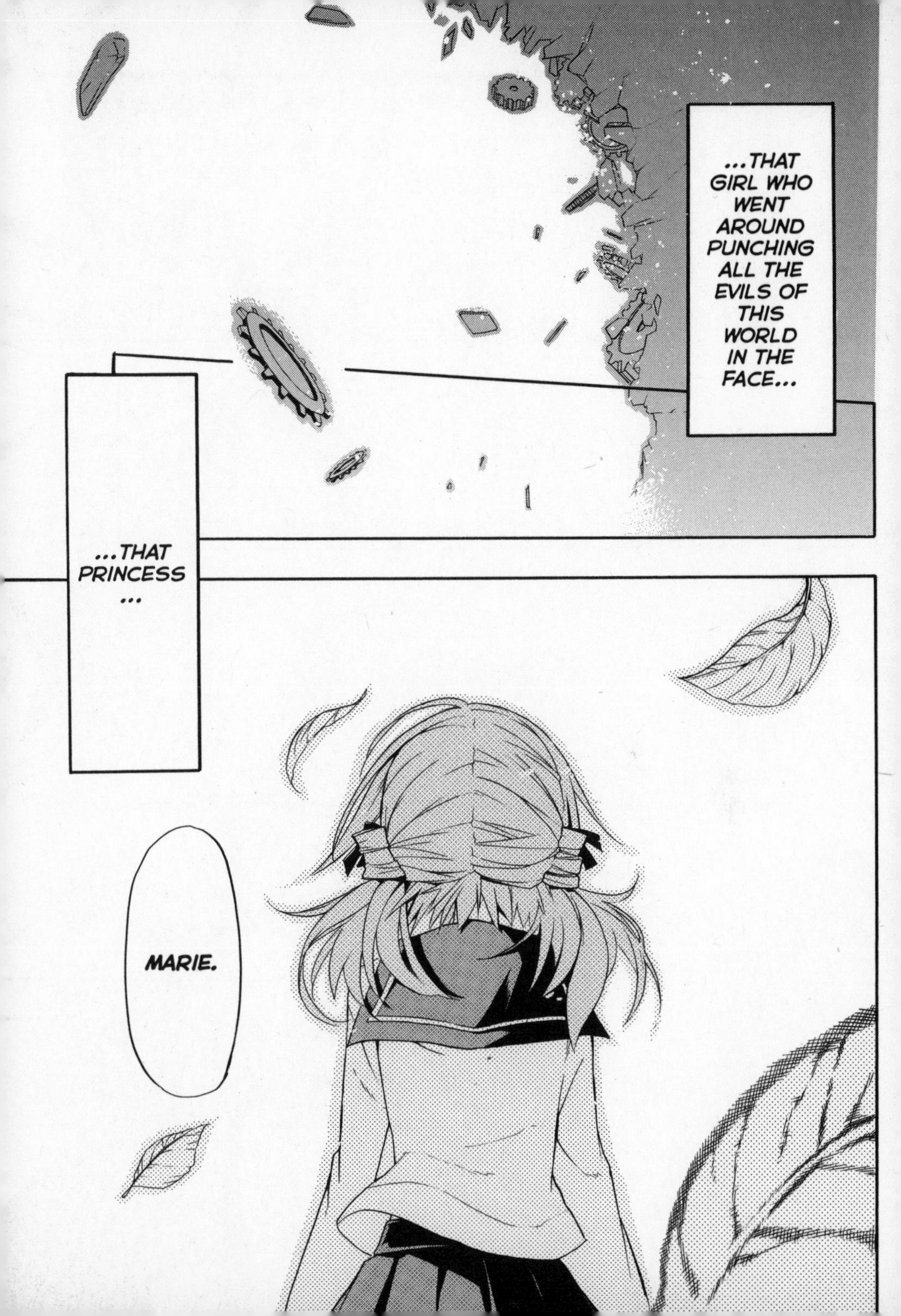
...THAT GIRL WHO WENT AROUND PUNCHING ALL THE EVILS OF THIS WORLD IN THE FACE...
...THAT PRINCESS ...
MARIE.

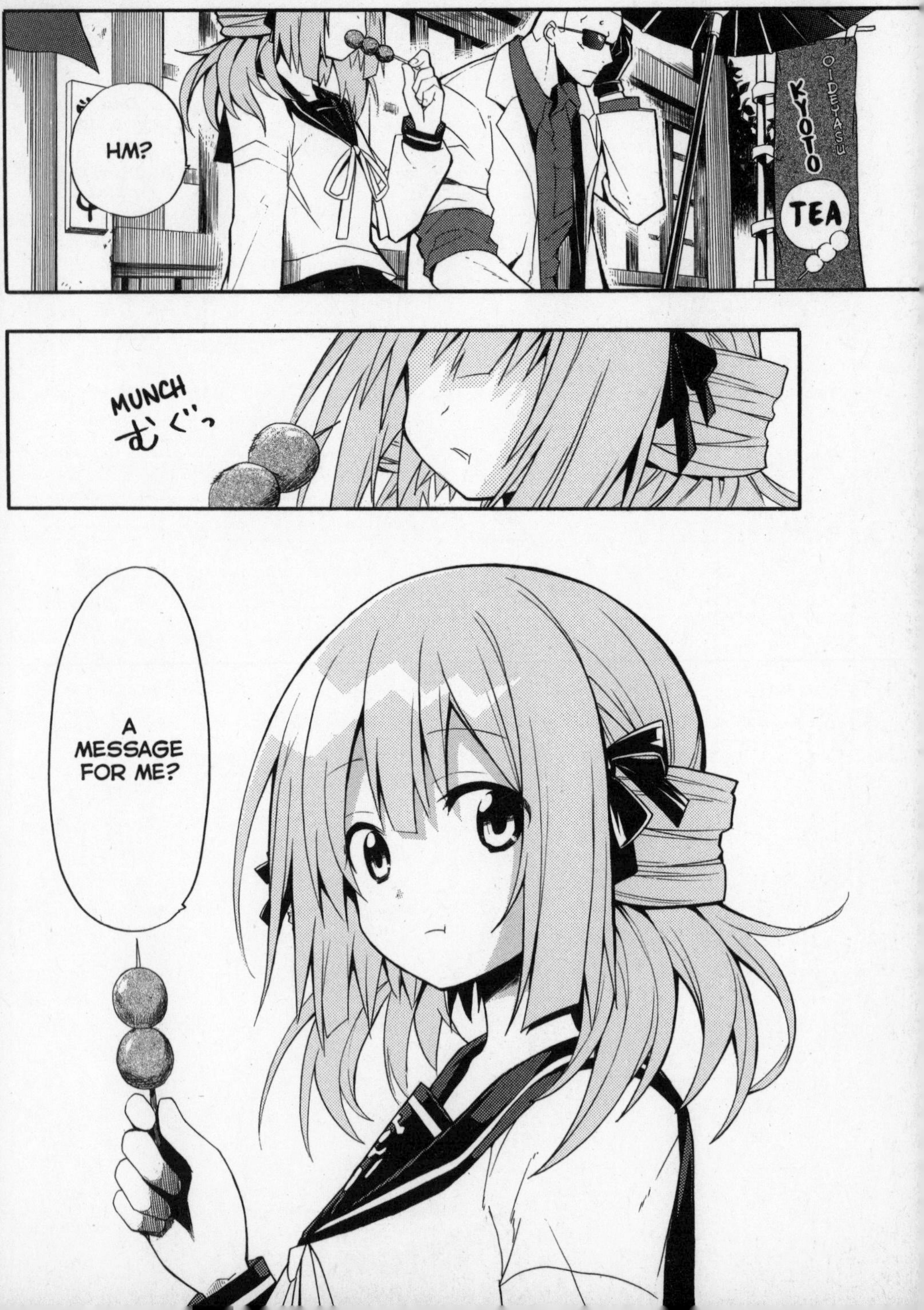
OIDEYASU
KYOTO
TEA
HM?
MUNCH
むぐっ
A MESSAGE FOR ME?

CLOCKWORK PLANET

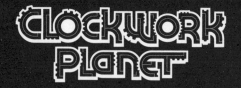

Clockwork Planet

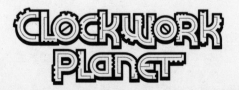

CLOCK 13: SEARCHER

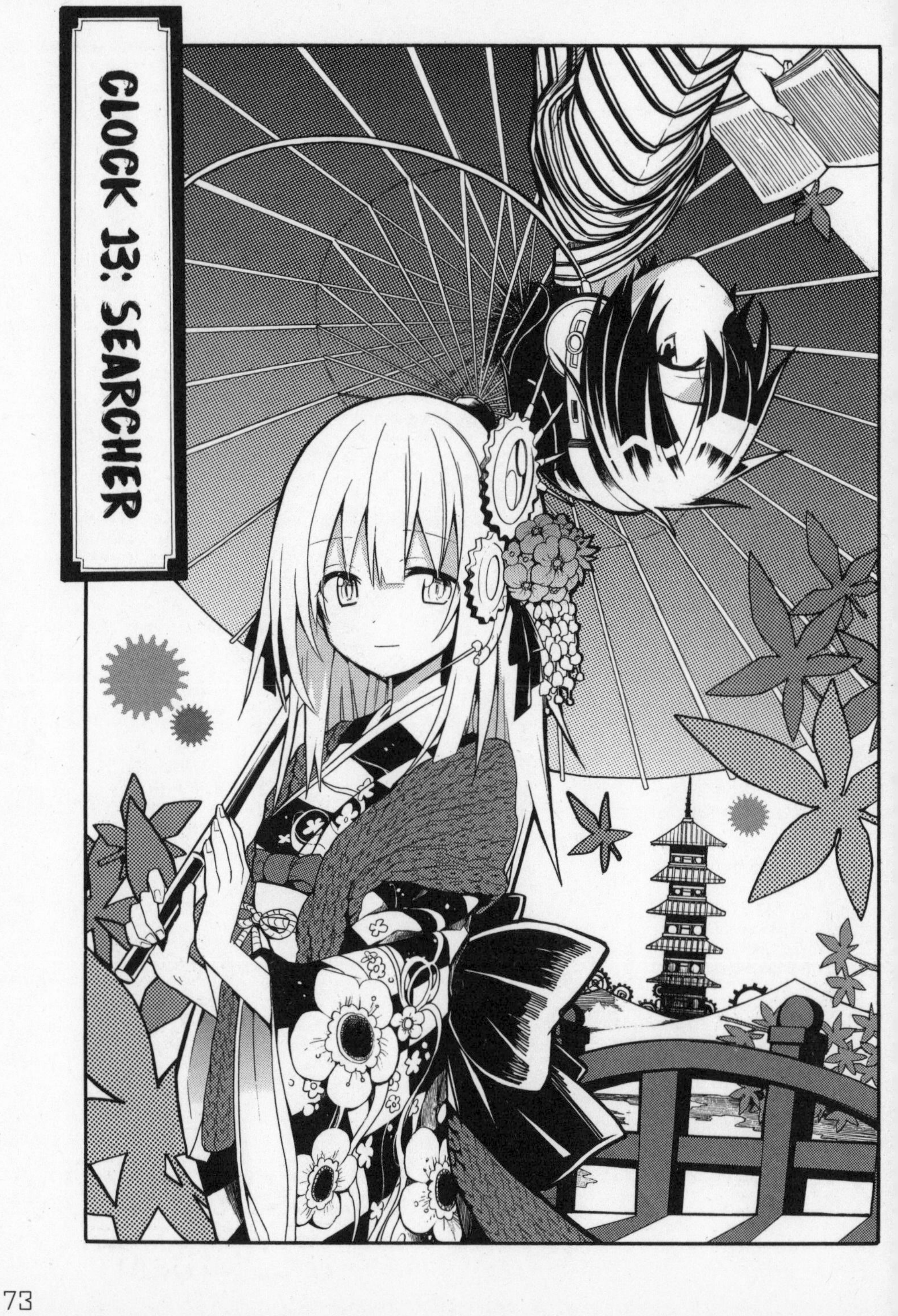

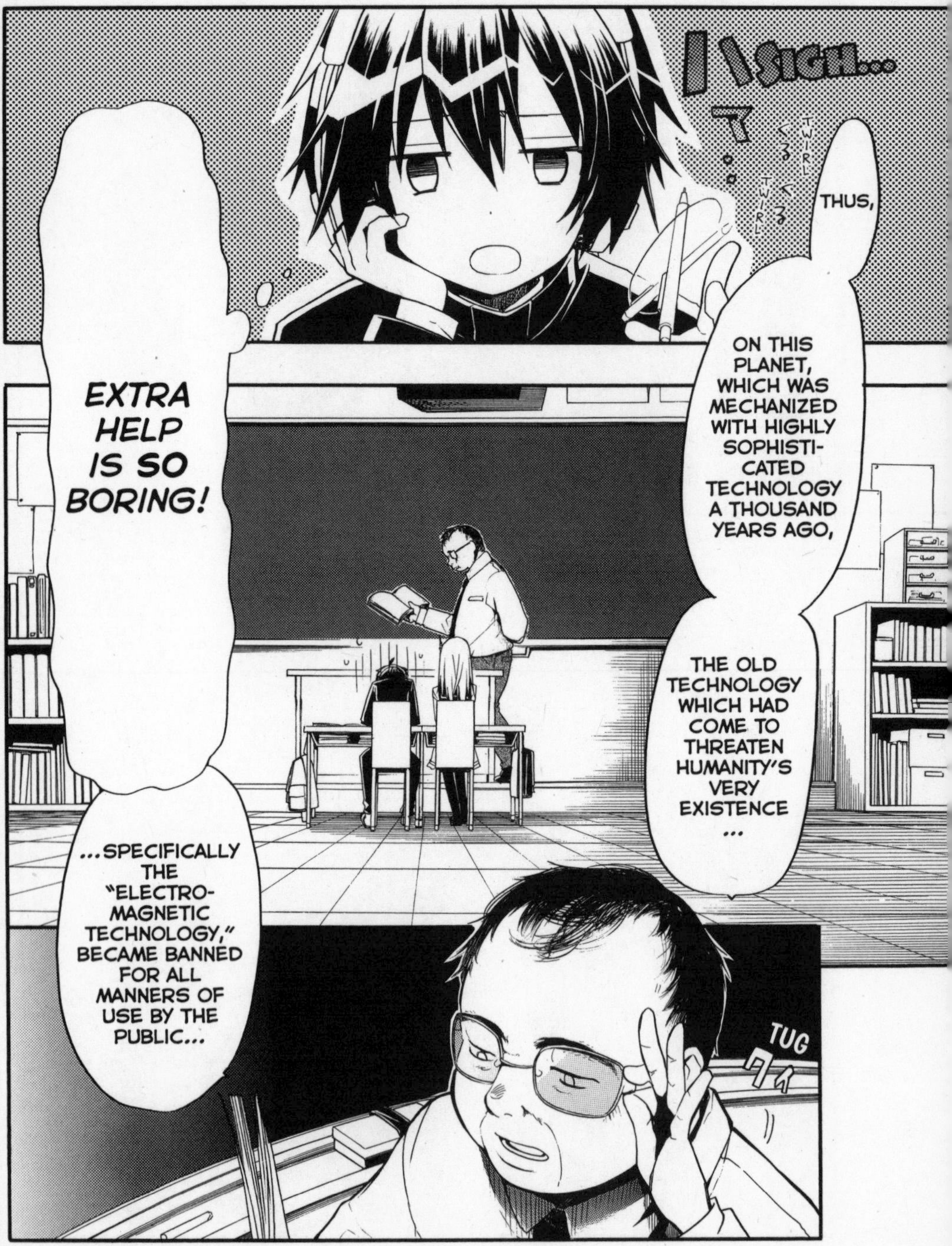
SIGH...
TWIRL
TWIRL
THUS,
EXTRA HELP IS SO BORING!
ON THIS PLANET, WHICH WAS MECHANIZED WITH HIGHLY SOPHISTICATED TECHNOLOGY A THOUSAND YEARS AGO,
THE OLD TECHNOLOGY WHICH HAD COME TO THREATEN HUMANITY'S VERY EXISTENCE ...
...SPECIFICALLY THE "ELECTRO-MAGNETIC TECHNOLOGY," BECAME BANNED FOR ALL MANNERS OF USE BY THE PUBLIC...
TUG

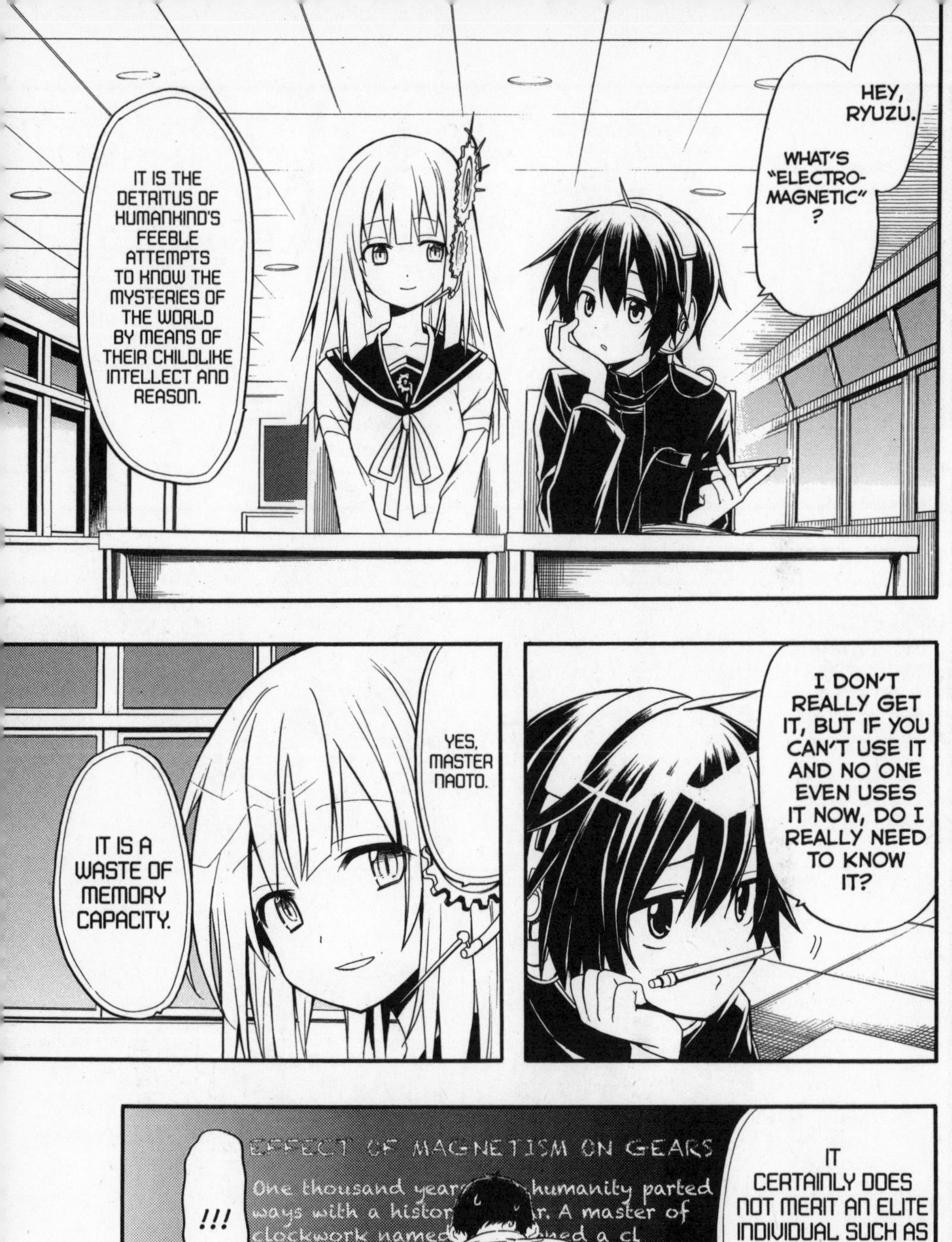

HEY, RYUZU.
WHAT'S "ELECTRO-MAGNETIC"?
IT IS THE DETRITUS OF HUMANKIND'S FEEBLE ATTEMPTS TO KNOW THE MYSTERIES OF THE WORLD BY MEANS OF THEIR CHILDLIKE INTELLECT AND REASON.
I DON'T REALLY GET IT, BUT IF YOU CAN'T USE IT AND NO ONE EVEN USES IT NOW, DO I REALLY NEED TO KNOW IT?
YES, MASTER NAOTO.
IT IS A WASTE OF MEMORY CAPACITY.
IT CERTAINLY DOES NOT MERIT AN ELITE INDIVIDUAL SUCH AS YOURSELF COMING IN ON HIS DAY OFF.
EFFECT OF MAGNETISM ON GEARS
!!!

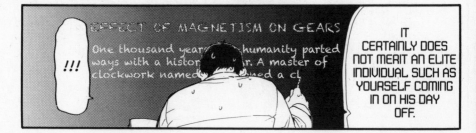

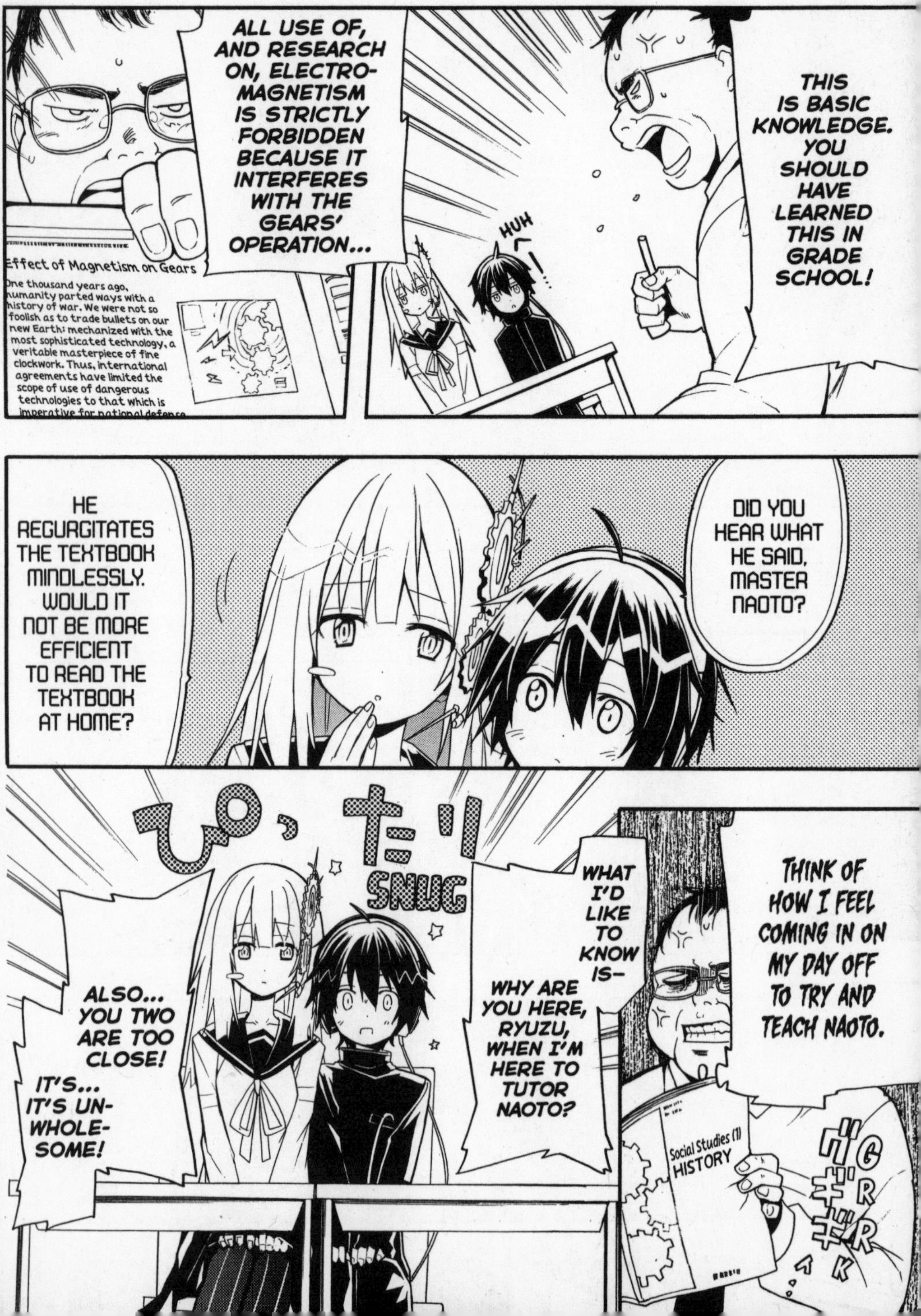
ALL USE OF, AND RESEARCH ON, ELECTRO-MAGNETISM IS STRICTLY FORBIDDEN BECAUSE IT INTERFERES WITH THE GEARS' OPERATION...
THIS IS BASIC KNOWLEDGE. YOU SHOULD HAVE LEARNED THIS IN GRADE SCHOOL!
HUH
Effect of Magnetism on Gears
One thousand years ago, humanity parted ways with a history of war. We were not so foolish as to trade bullets on our new Earth: mechanized with the most sophisticated technology, a veritable masterpiece of fine clockwork. Thus, international agreements have limited the scope of use of dangerous technologies to that which is imperative for national defense
DID YOU HEAR WHAT HE SAID, MASTER NAOTO?
HE REGURGITATES THE TEXTBOOK MINDLESSLY. WOULD IT NOT BE MORE EFFICIENT TO READ THE TEXTBOOK AT HOME?
THINK OF HOW I FEEL COMING IN ON MY DAY OFF TO TRY AND TEACH NAOTO.
GRRRK
WHAT I'D LIKE TO KNOW IS—
WHY ARE YOU HERE, RYUZU, WHEN I'M HERE TO TUTOR NAOTO?
Social Studies (1) HISTORY
ぴったり
SNUG
ALSO... YOU TWO ARE TOO CLOSE!
IT'S... IT'S UN-WHOLESOME!

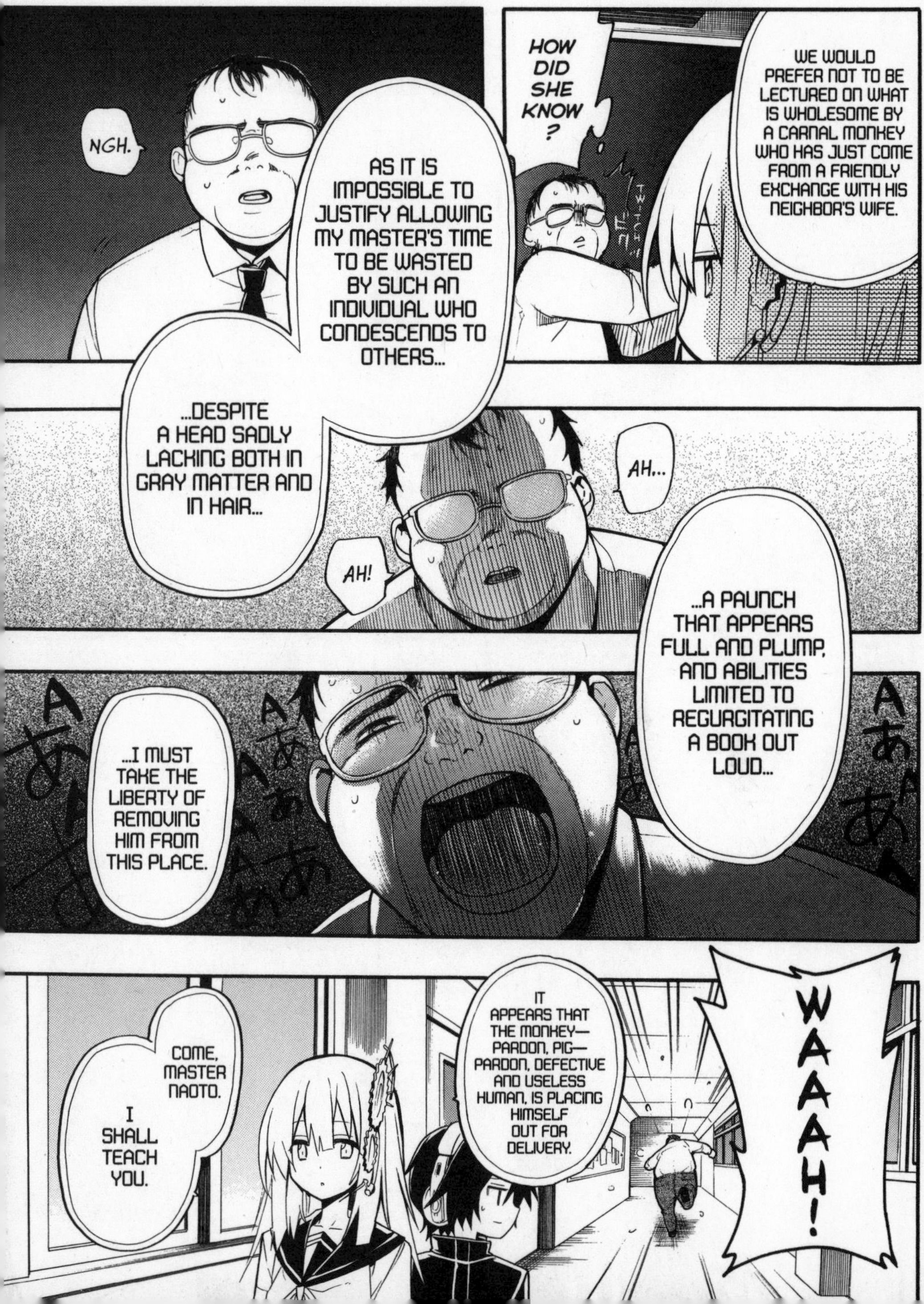
WE WOULD PREFER NOT TO BE LECTURED ON WHAT IS WHOLESOME BY A CARNAL MONKEY WHO HAS JUST COME FROM A FRIENDLY EXCHANGE WITH HIS NEIGHBOR'S WIFE.
HOW DID SHE KNOW?
TWITCH
AS IT IS IMPOSSIBLE TO JUSTIFY ALLOWING MY MASTER'S TIME TO BE WASTED BY SUCH AN INDIVIDUAL WHO CONDESCENDS TO OTHERS...
NGH.
...DESPITE A HEAD SADLY LACKING BOTH IN GRAY MATTER AND IN HAIR...
AH...
AH!
...A PAUNCH THAT APPEARS FULL AND PLUMP, AND ABILITIES LIMITED TO REGURGITATING A BOOK OUT LOUD...
...I MUST TAKE THE LIBERTY OF REMOVING HIM FROM THIS PLACE.
WAAAH!
IT APPEARS THAT THE MONKEY— PARDON, PIG— PARDON, DEFECTIVE AND USELESS HUMAN, IS PLACING HIMSELF OUT FOR DELIVERY.
COME, MASTER NAOTO.
I SHALL TEACH YOU.

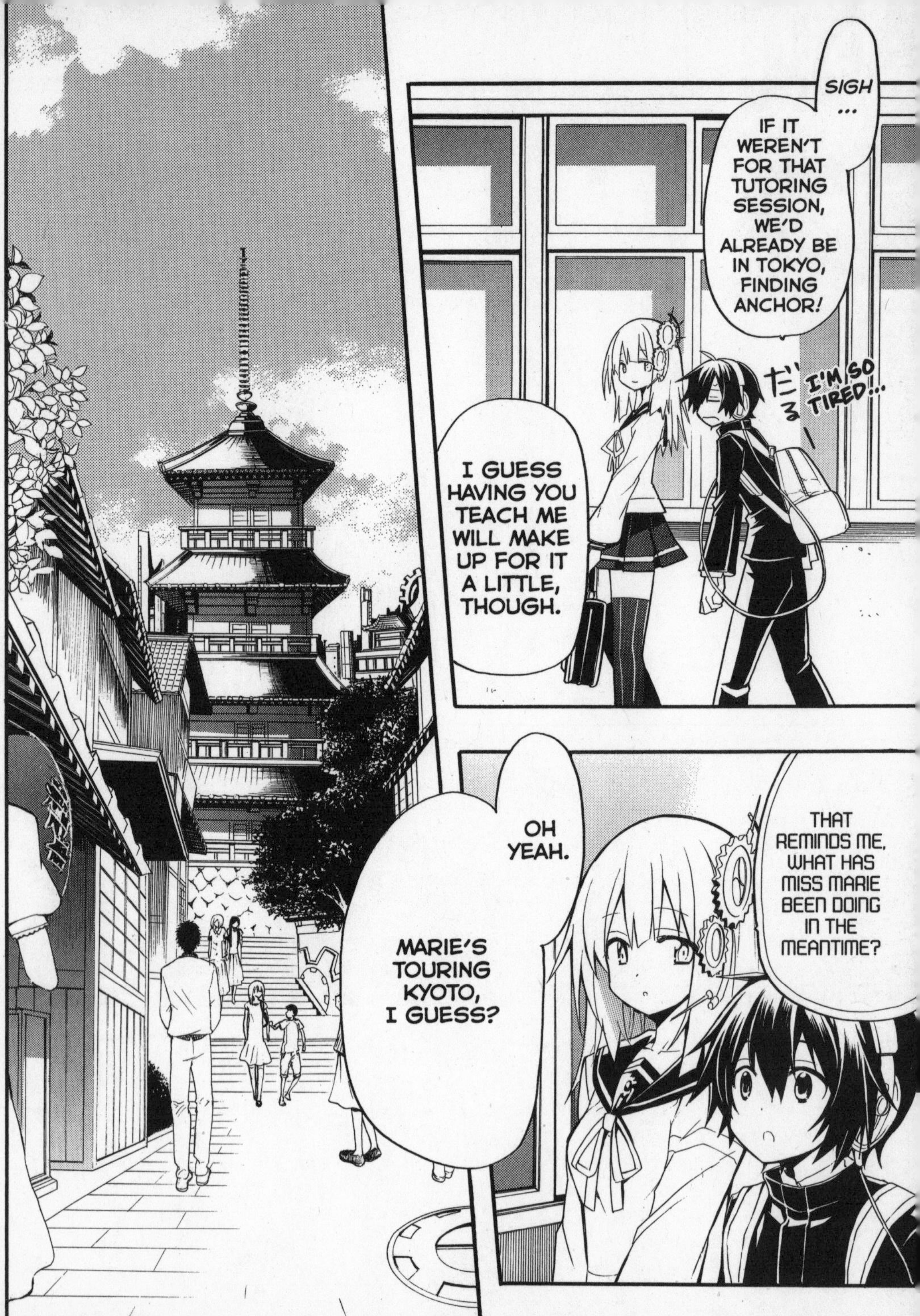
SIGH ...
IF IT WEREN'T FOR THAT TUTORING SESSION, WE'D ALREADY BE IN TOKYO, FINDING ANCHOR!
だる
I'M SO TIRED...
I GUESS HAVING YOU TEACH ME WILL MAKE UP FOR IT A LITTLE, THOUGH.
THAT REMINDS ME, WHAT HAS MISS MARIE BEEN DOING IN THE MEANTIME?
OH YEAH.
MARIE'S TOURING KYOTO, I GUESS?

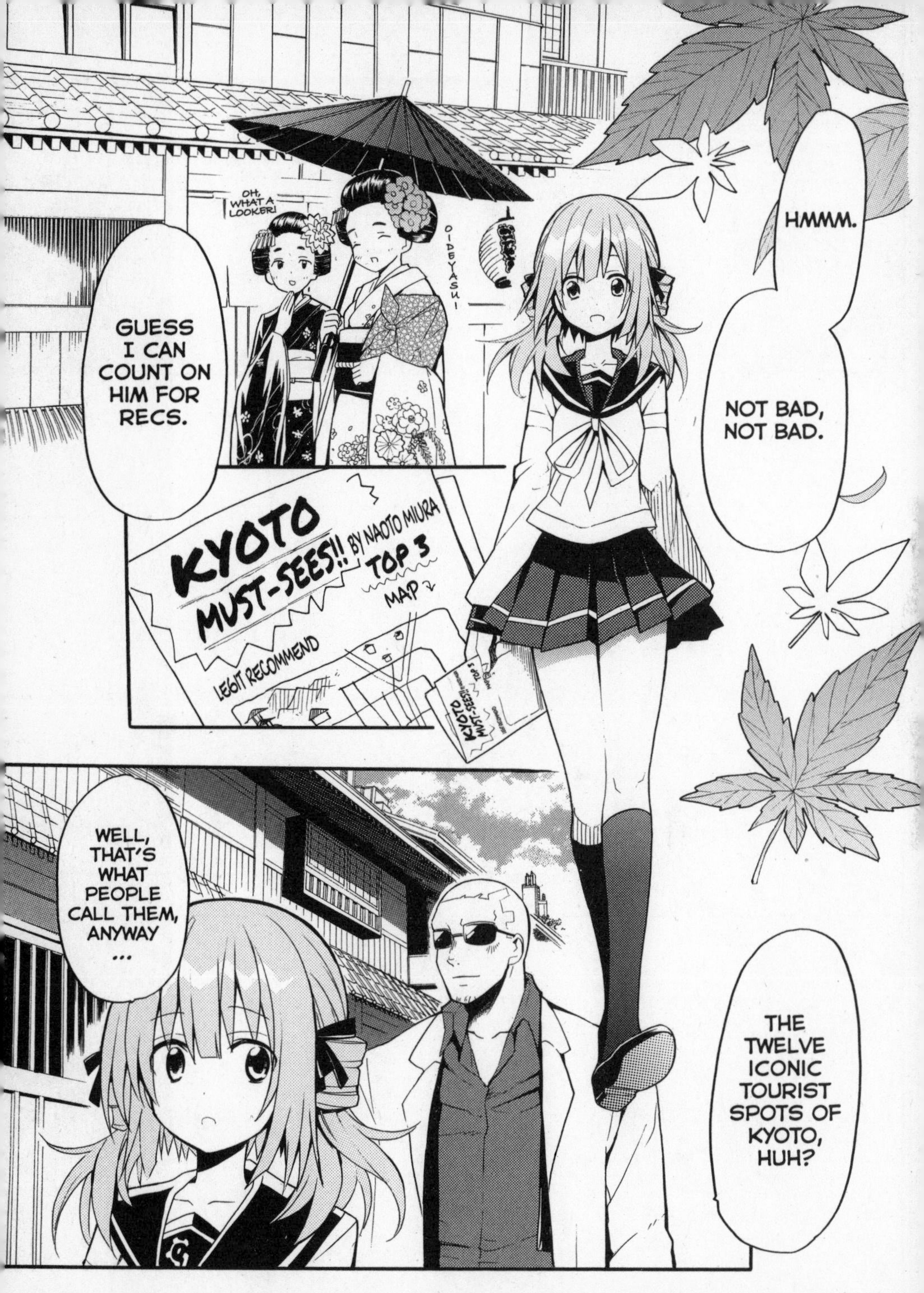
HMMM.
NOT BAD, NOT BAD.
OIDEYASU!
OH, WHAT A LOOKER!
GUESS I CAN COUNT ON HIM FOR RECS.
KYOTO MUST-SEES!!
BY NAOTO MIURA
TOP 3
MAP
LEGIT RECOMMEND
THE TWELVE ICONIC TOURIST SPOTS OF KYOTO, HUH?
WELL, THAT'S WHAT PEOPLE CALL THEM, ANYWAY...

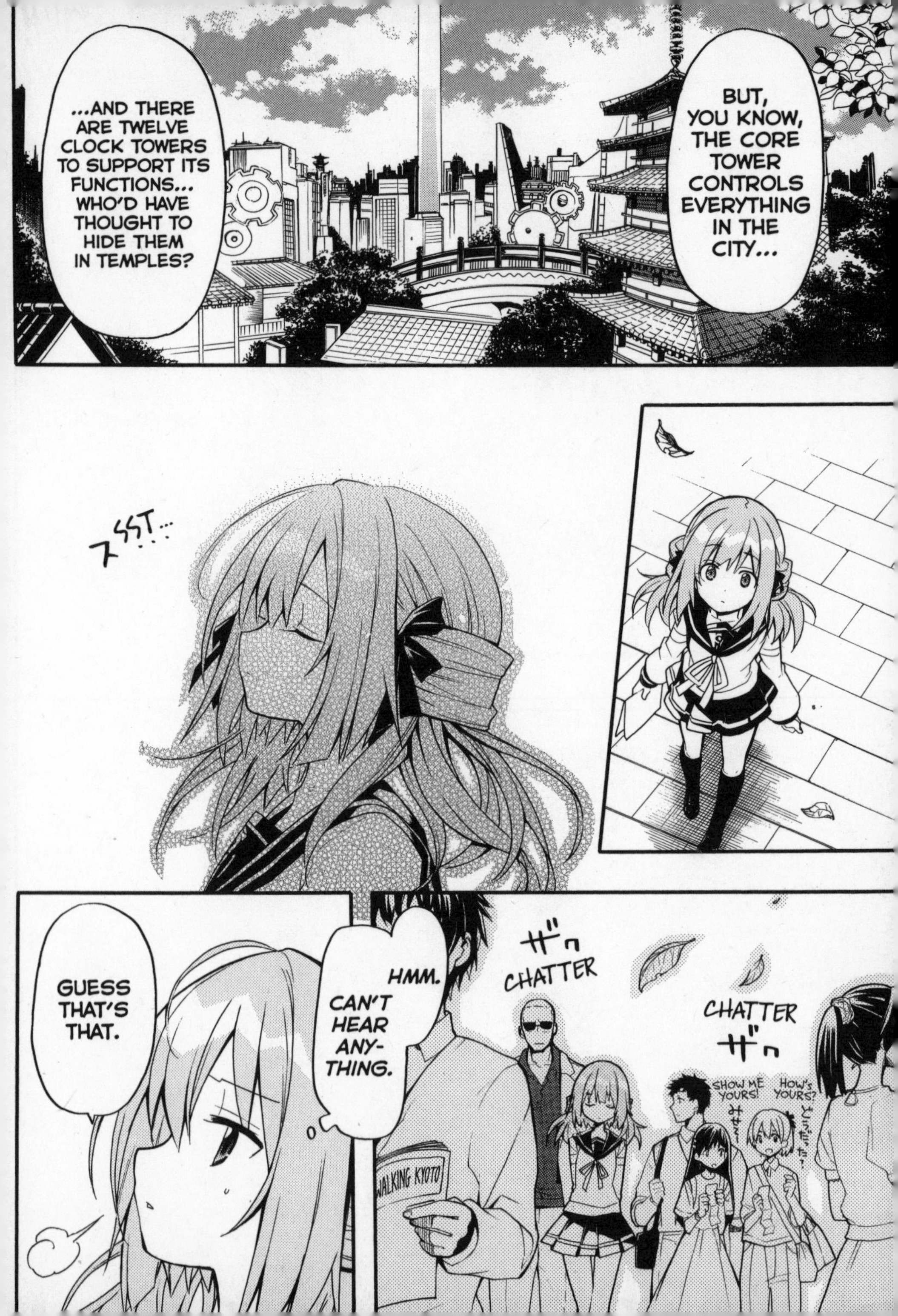

BUT, YOU KNOW, THE CORE TOWER CONTROLS EVERYTHING IN THE CITY...
...AND THERE ARE TWELVE CLOCK TOWERS TO SUPPORT ITS FUNCTIONS... WHO'D HAVE THOUGHT TO HIDE THEM IN TEMPLES?
スSST...
ザワ CHATTER
HOW'S YOURS?
SHOW ME YOURS!
CHATTER ザワ
HMM. CAN'T HEAR ANYTHING.
GUESS THAT'S THAT.
WALKING KYOTO

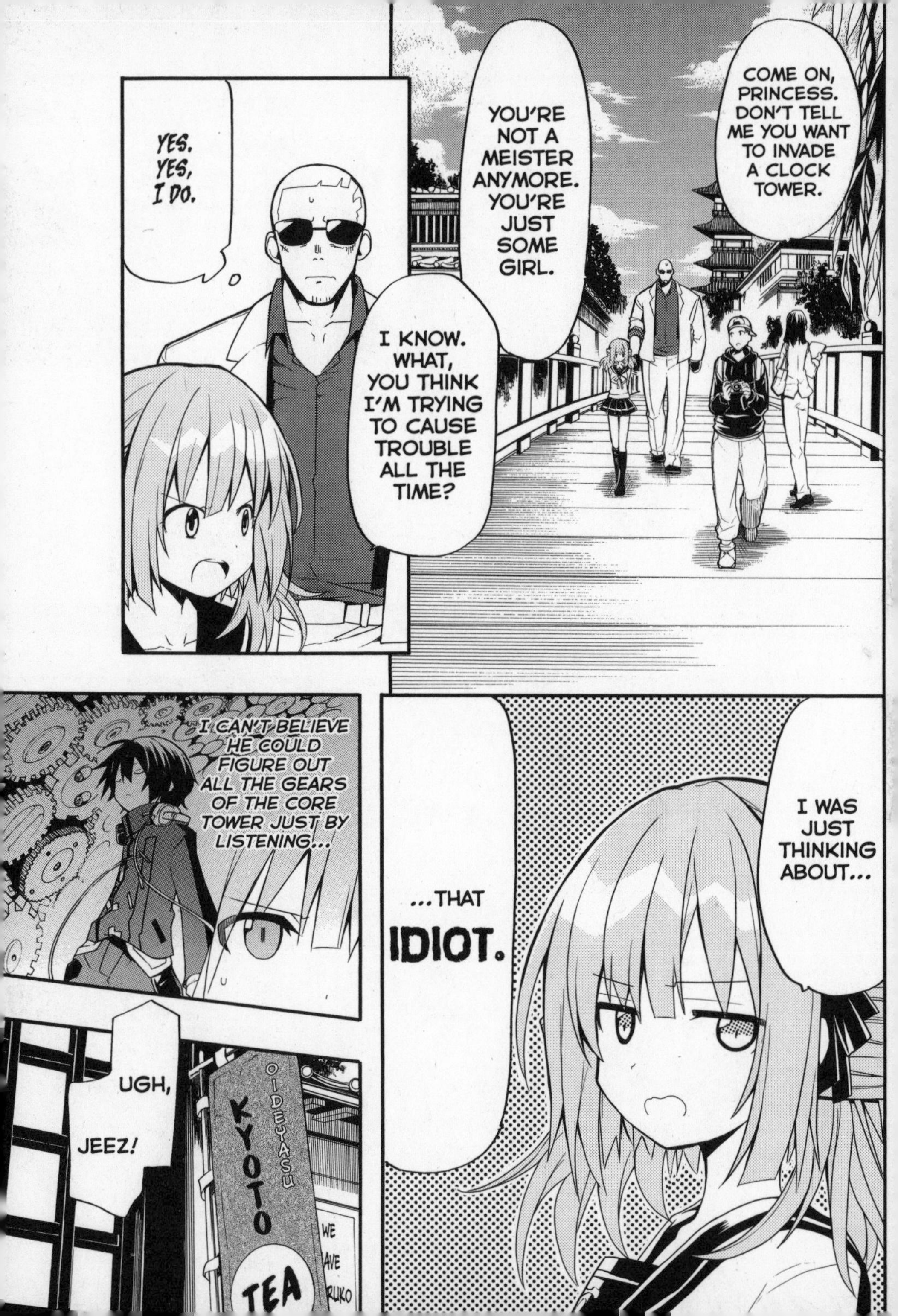
COME ON, PRINCESS. DON'T TELL ME YOU WANT TO INVADE A CLOCK TOWER.
YOU'RE NOT A MEISTER ANYMORE. YOU'RE JUST SOME GIRL.
I KNOW. WHAT, YOU THINK I'M TRYING TO CAUSE TROUBLE ALL THE TIME?
YES. YES, I DO.
I WAS JUST THINKING ABOUT...
...THAT IDIOT.
I CAN'T BELIEVE HE COULD FIGURE OUT ALL THE GEARS OF THE CORE TOWER JUST BY LISTENING...
UGH,
JEEZ!
OIDEYASU
KYOTO
TEA

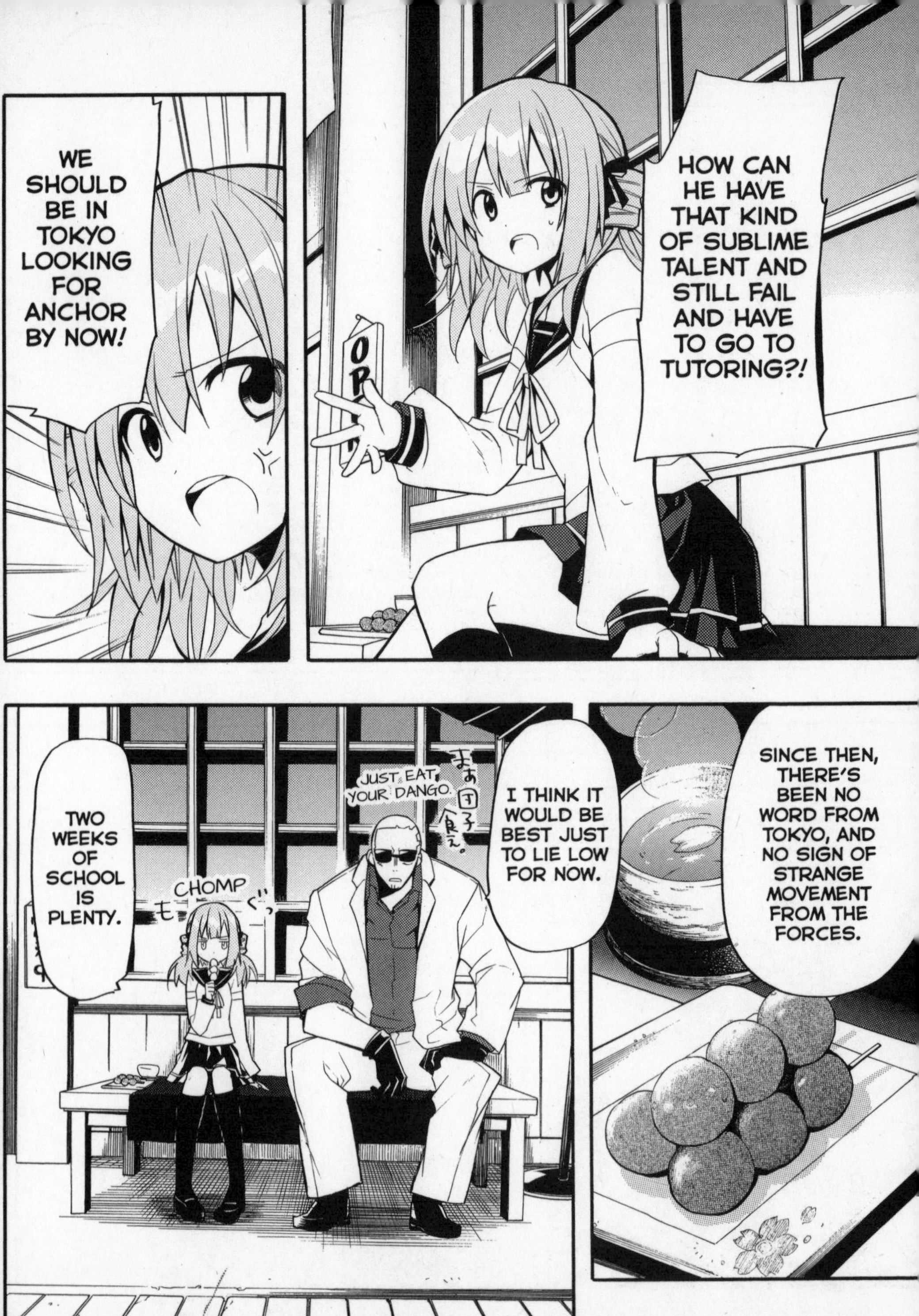
HOW CAN HE HAVE THAT KIND OF SUBLIME TALENT AND STILL FAIL AND HAVE TO GO TO TUTORING?!
WE SHOULD BE IN TOKYO LOOKING FOR ANCHOR BY NOW!
SINCE THEN, THERE'S BEEN NO WORD FROM TOKYO, AND NO SIGN OF STRANGE MOVEMENT FROM THE FORCES.
I THINK IT WOULD BE BEST JUST TO LIE LOW FOR NOW.
まあ団子食え。
JUST EAT YOUR DANGO.
CHOMP
TWO WEEKS OF SCHOOL IS PLENTY.

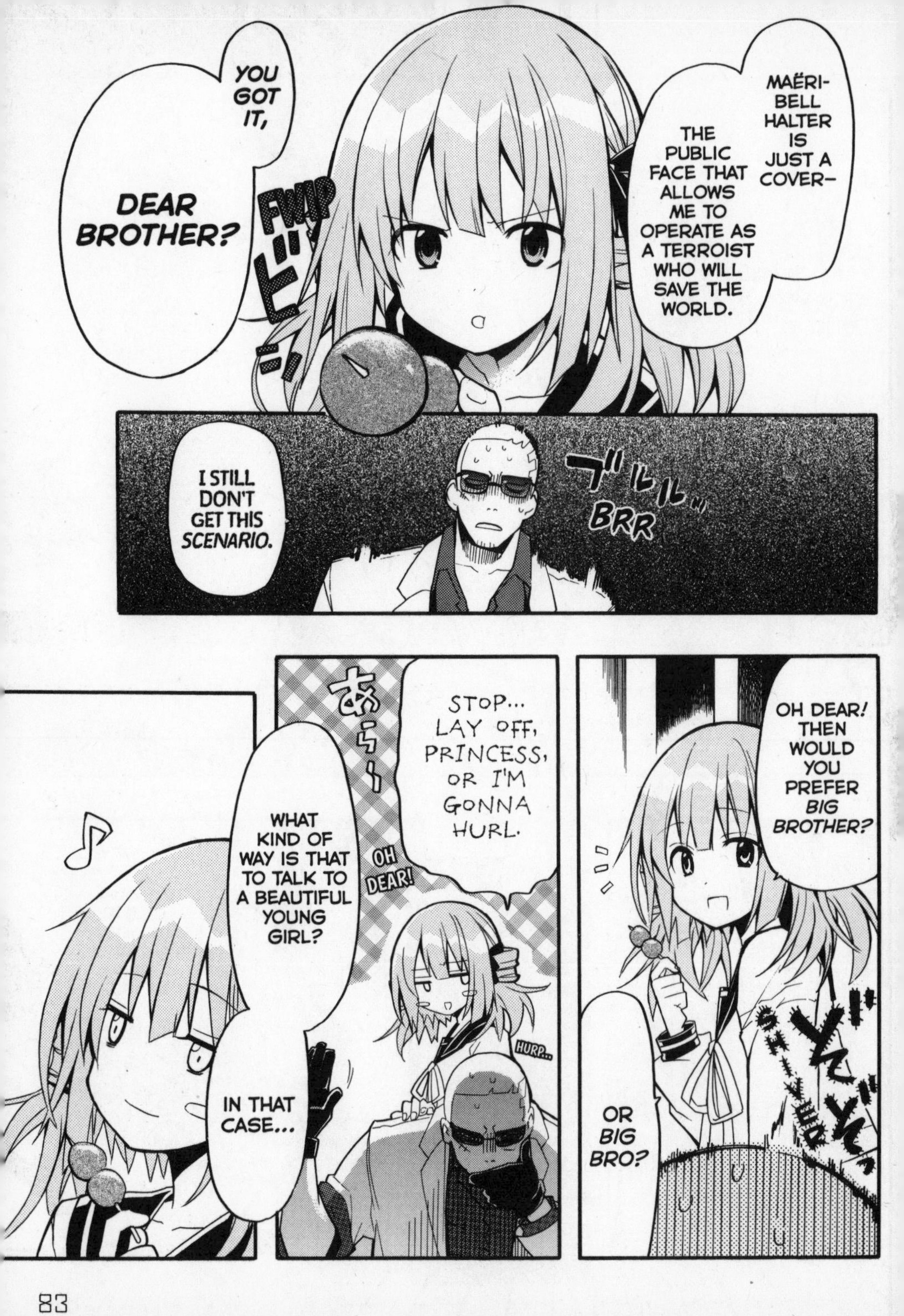
MAÉRI-BELL HALTER IS JUST A COVER— THE PUBLIC FACE THAT ALLOWS ME TO OPERATE AS A TERROIST WHO WILL SAVE THE WORLD.
FWIP
ビッ
YOU GOT IT, DEAR BROTHER?
ブルル
BRR
I STILL DON'T GET THIS SCENARIO.
OH DEAR! THEN WOULD YOU PREFER BIG BROTHER?
SHIVER
ゾゾゾ
OR BIG BRO?
STOP... LAY OFF, PRINCESS, OR I'M GONNA HURL.
あら～
OH DEAR!
HURP...
WHAT KIND OF WAY IS THAT TO TALK TO A BEAUTIFUL YOUNG GIRL?
IN THAT CASE...

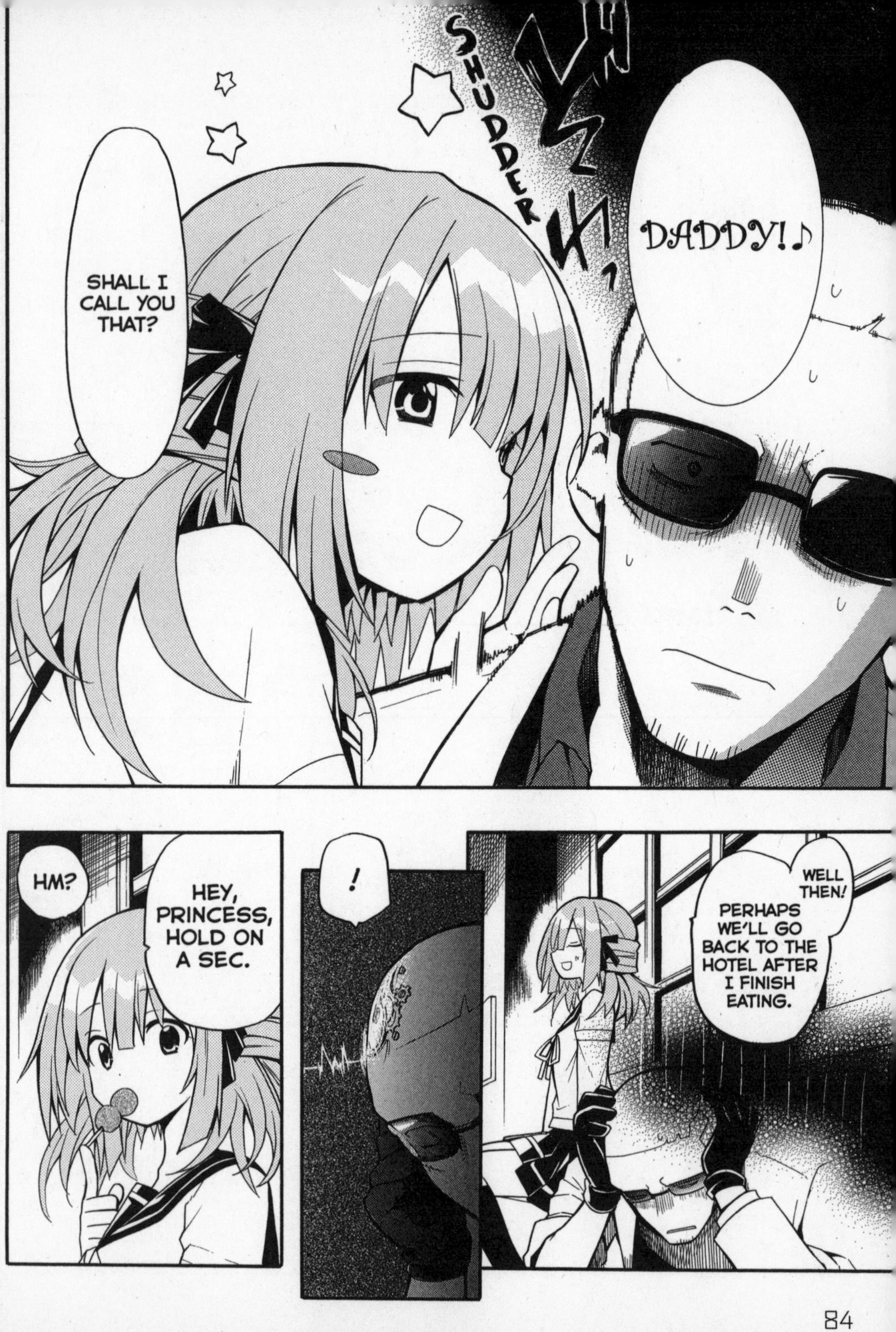
SHUDDER
DADDY!♪
SHALL I CALL YOU THAT?
WELL THEN!
PERHAPS WE'LL GO BACK TO THE HOTEL AFTER I FINISH EATING.
!
HEY, PRINCESS, HOLD ON A SEC.
HM?

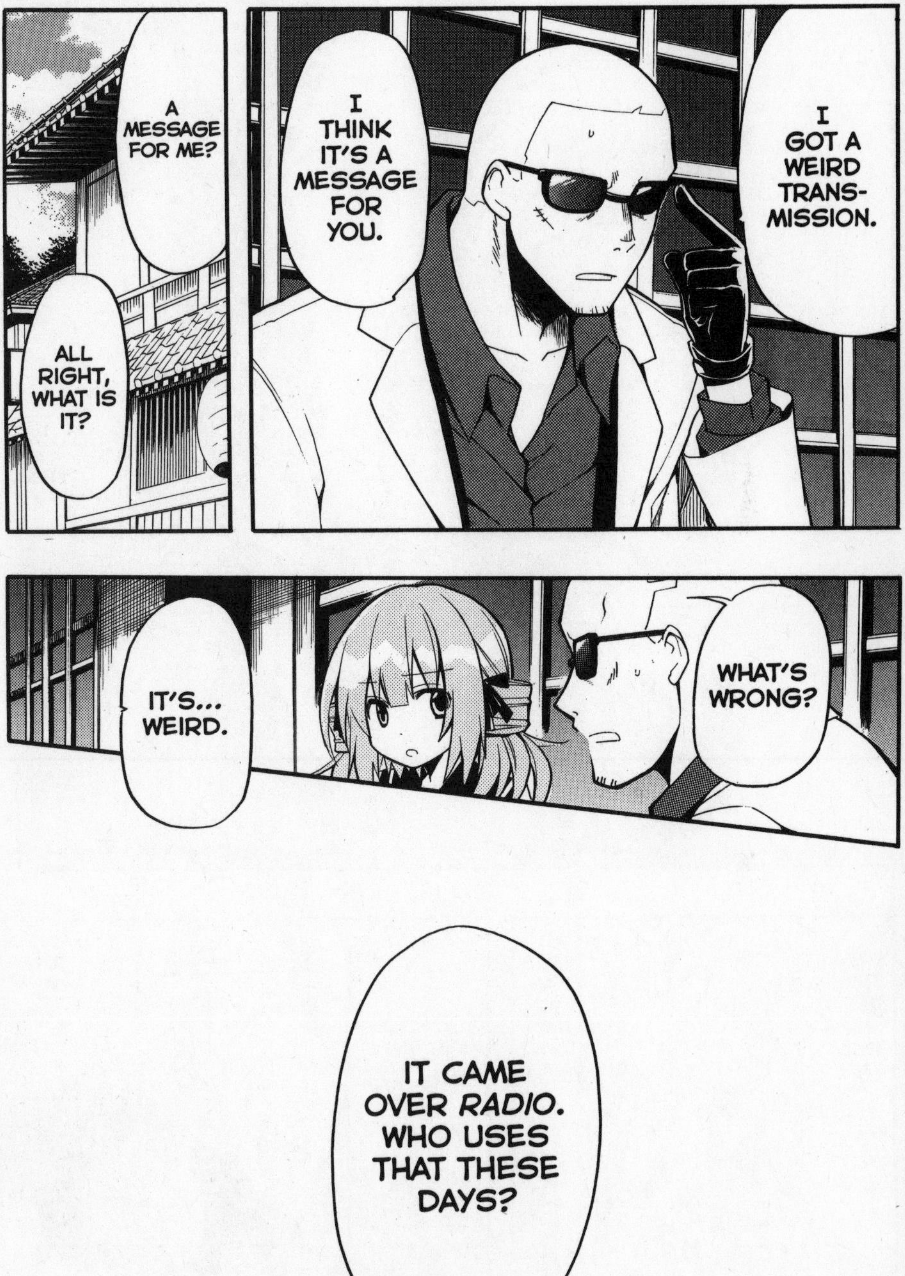
I GOT A WEIRD TRANS-MISSION.
I THINK IT'S A MESSAGE FOR YOU.
A MESSAGE FOR ME?
ALL RIGHT, WHAT IS IT?
WHAT'S WRONG?
IT'S... WEIRD.
IT CAME OVER *RADIO*. WHO USES THAT THESE DAYS?

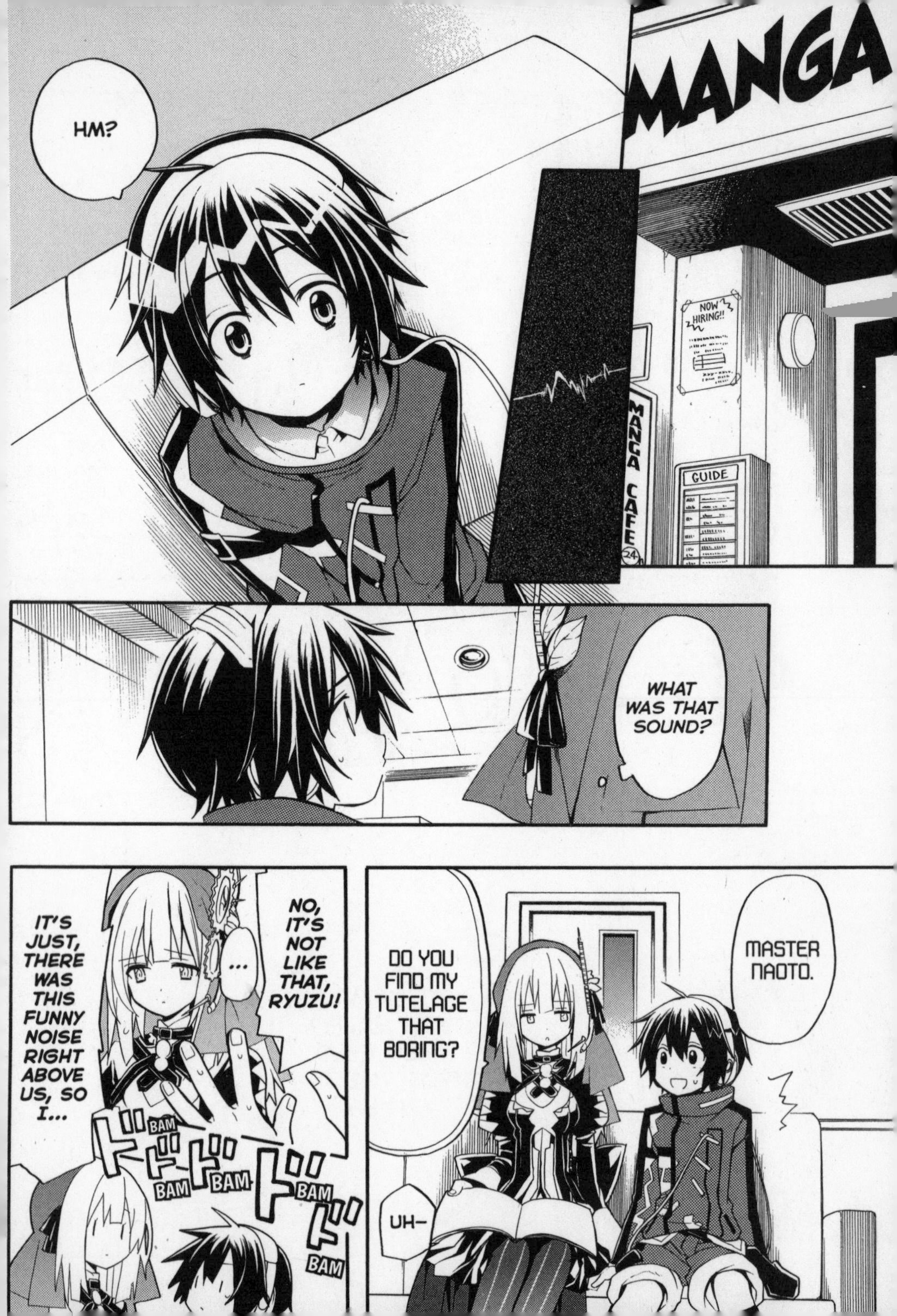
MANGA
NOW HIRING!!
MANGA CAFE 24
GUIDE
HM?
WHAT WAS THAT SOUND?
MASTER NAOTO.
DO YOU FIND MY TUTELAGE THAT BORING?
UH–
NO, IT'S NOT LIKE THAT, RYUZU!
...
IT'S JUST, THERE WAS THIS FUNNY NOISE RIGHT ABOVE US, SO I...
BAM
BAM
BAM
BAM
BAM

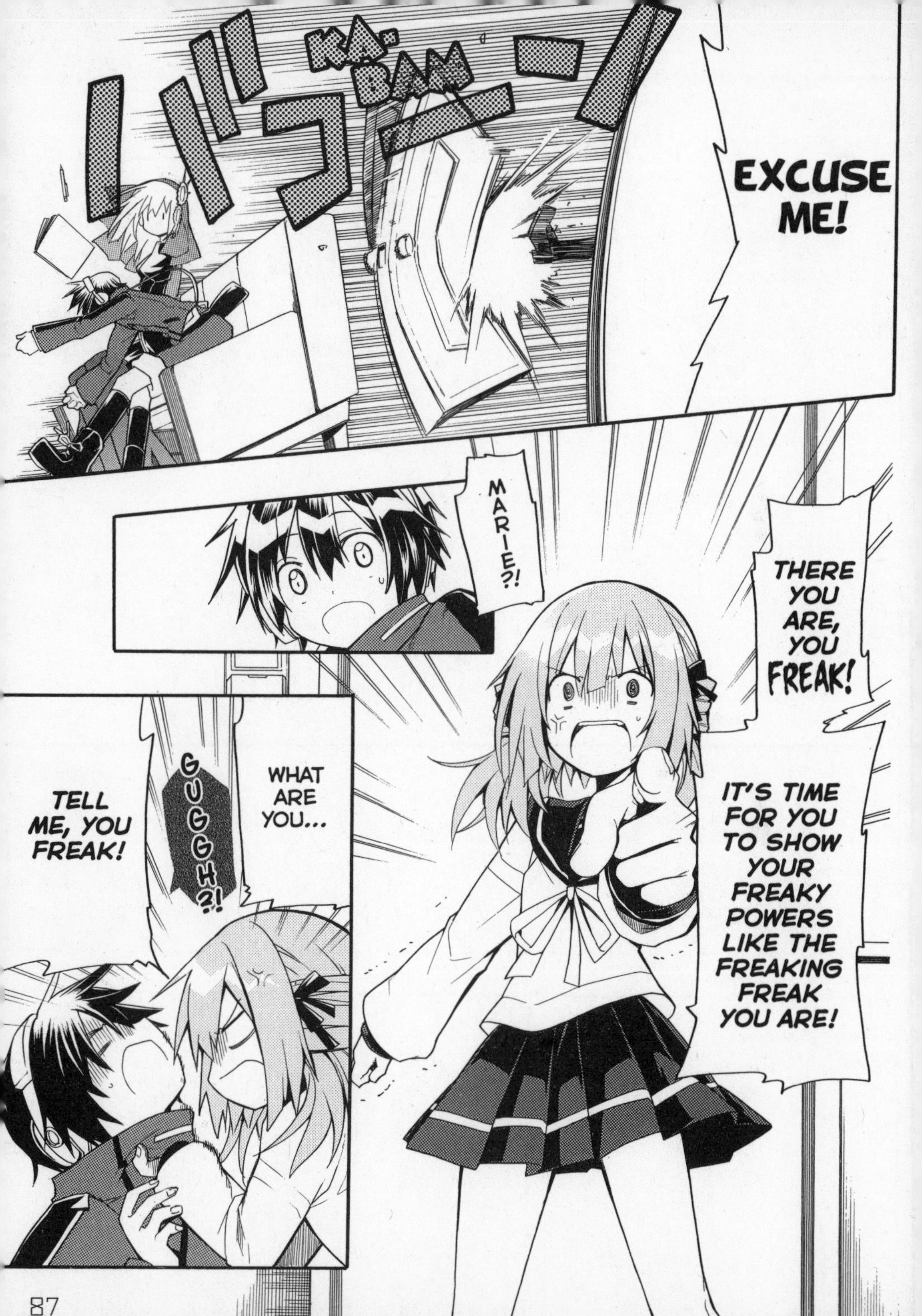
KA-BAM
EXCUSE ME!
THERE YOU ARE, YOU FREAK!
IT'S TIME FOR YOU TO SHOW YOUR FREAKY POWERS LIKE THE FREAKING FREAK YOU ARE!
MARIE?!
WHAT ARE YOU...
GUGGH?!
TELL ME, YOU FREAK!

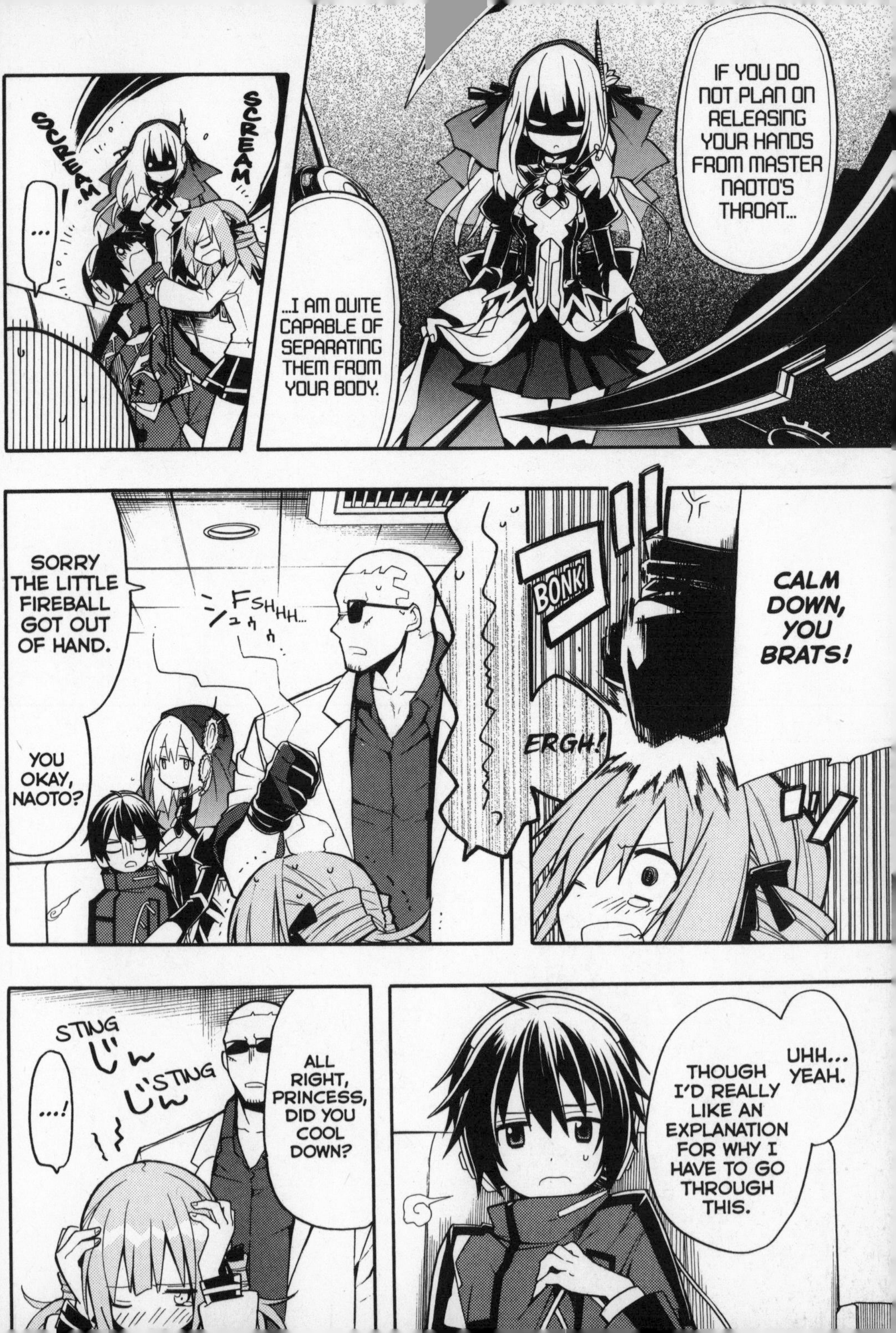
IF YOU DO NOT PLAN ON RELEASING YOUR HANDS FROM MASTER NAOTO'S THROAT...
...I AM QUITE CAPABLE OF SEPARATING THEM FROM YOUR BODY.
SCREAM
SCREAM
...
CALM DOWN, YOU BRATS!
BONK
ERGH!
SORRY THE LITTLE FIREBALL GOT OUT OF HAND.
FSHHH...
YOU OKAY, NAOTO?
UHH... YEAH.
THOUGH I'D REALLY LIKE AN EXPLANATION FOR WHY I HAVE TO GO THROUGH THIS.
ALL RIGHT, PRINCESS, DID YOU COOL DOWN?
STING
STING
...!

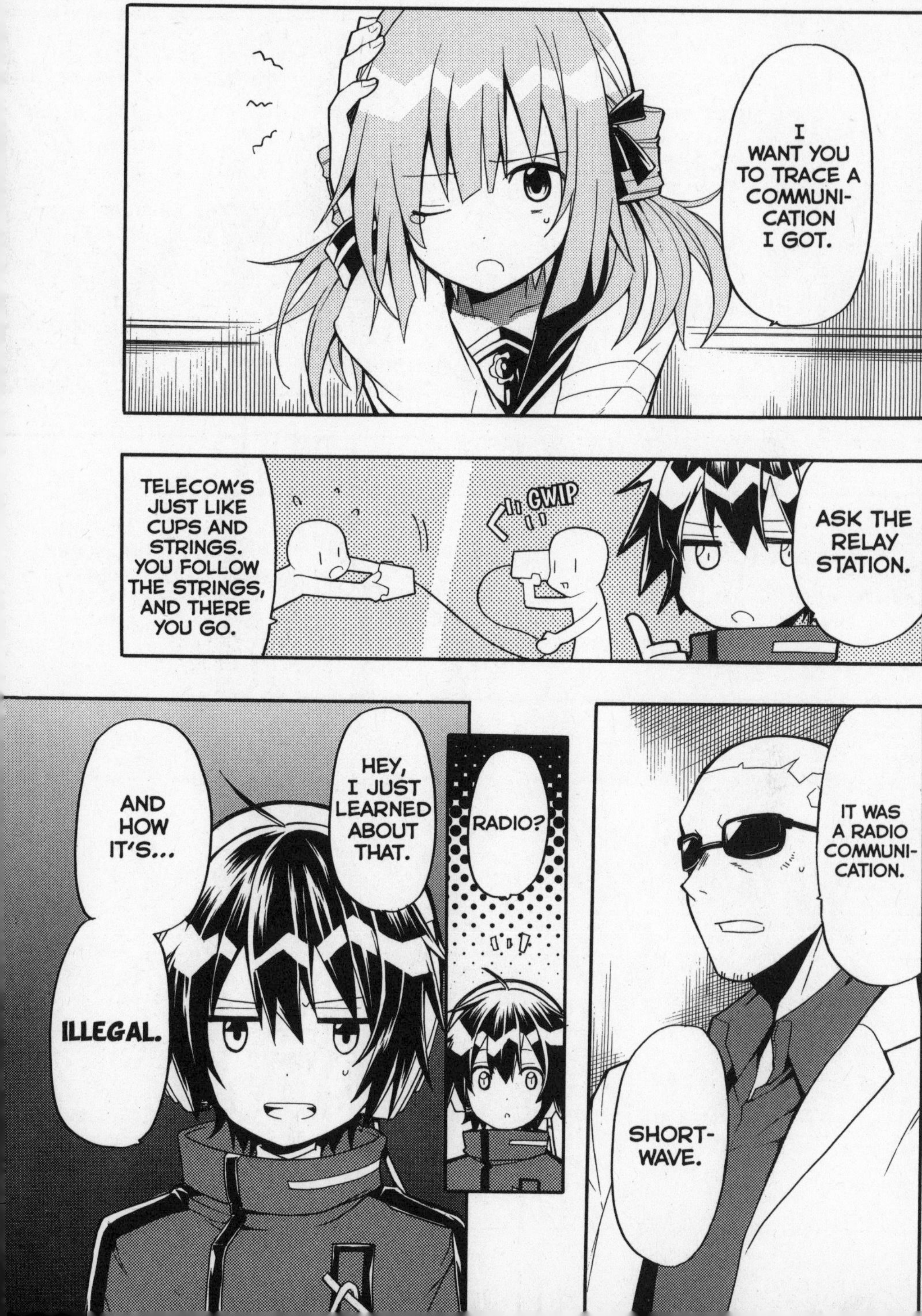
I WANT YOU TO TRACE A COMMUNI-CATION I GOT.
ASK THE RELAY STATION.
GWIP
TELECOM'S JUST LIKE CUPS AND STRINGS. YOU FOLLOW THE STRINGS, AND THERE YOU GO.
IT WAS A RADIO COMMUNI-CATION.
SHORT-WAVE.
RADIO?
HEY, I JUST LEARNED ABOUT THAT.
AND HOW IT'S...
ILLEGAL.

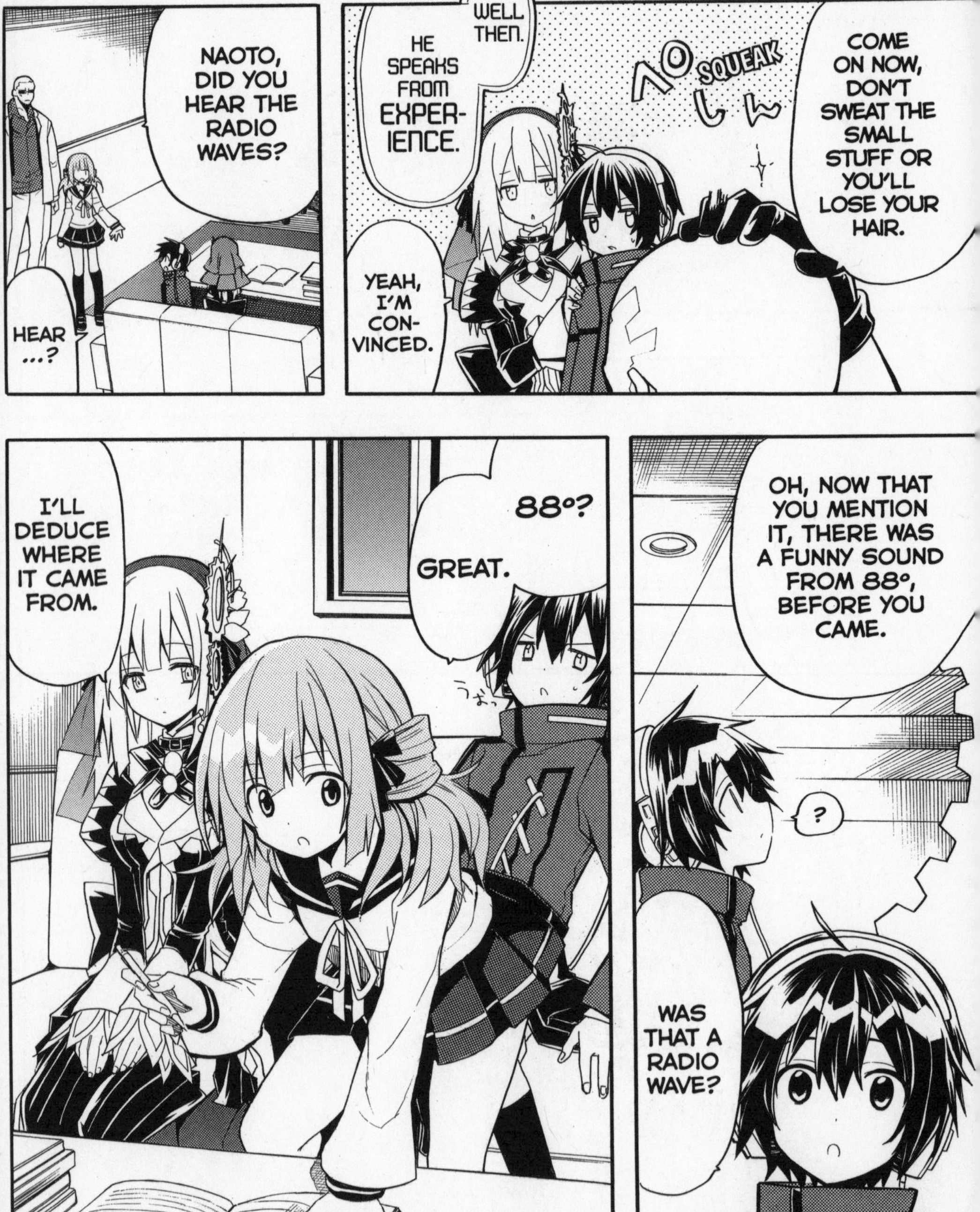
COME ON NOW, DON'T SWEAT THE SMALL STUFF OR YOU'LL LOSE YOUR HAIR.
SQUEAK
WELL THEN.
HE SPEAKS FROM EXPER-IENCE.
YEAH, I'M CON-VINCED.
NAOTO, DID YOU HEAR THE RADIO WAVES?
HEAR ...?
OH, NOW THAT YOU MENTION IT, THERE WAS A FUNNY SOUND FROM 88°, BEFORE YOU CAME.
?
WAS THAT A RADIO WAVE?
88°?
GREAT.
I'LL DEDUCE WHERE IT CAME FROM.

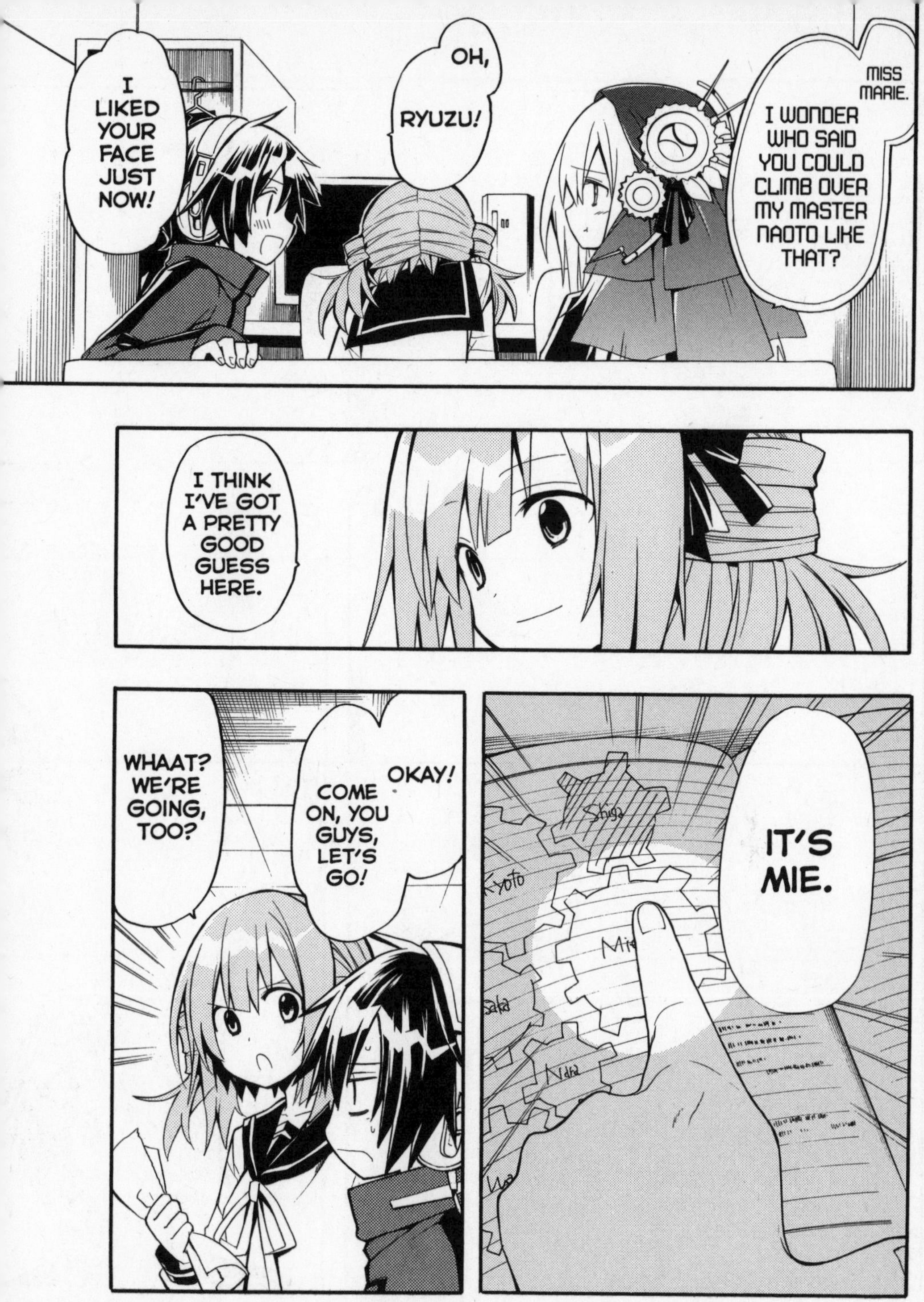
MISS MARIE.
I WONDER WHO SAID YOU COULD CLIMB OVER MY MASTER NAOTO LIKE THAT?
OH, RYUZU!
I LIKED YOUR FACE JUST NOW!
I THINK I'VE GOT A PRETTY GOOD GUESS HERE.
IT'S MIE.
Shiga
Kyoto
Mie
Nara
OKAY!
COME ON, YOU GUYS, LET'S GO!
WHAAT? WE'RE GOING, TOO?

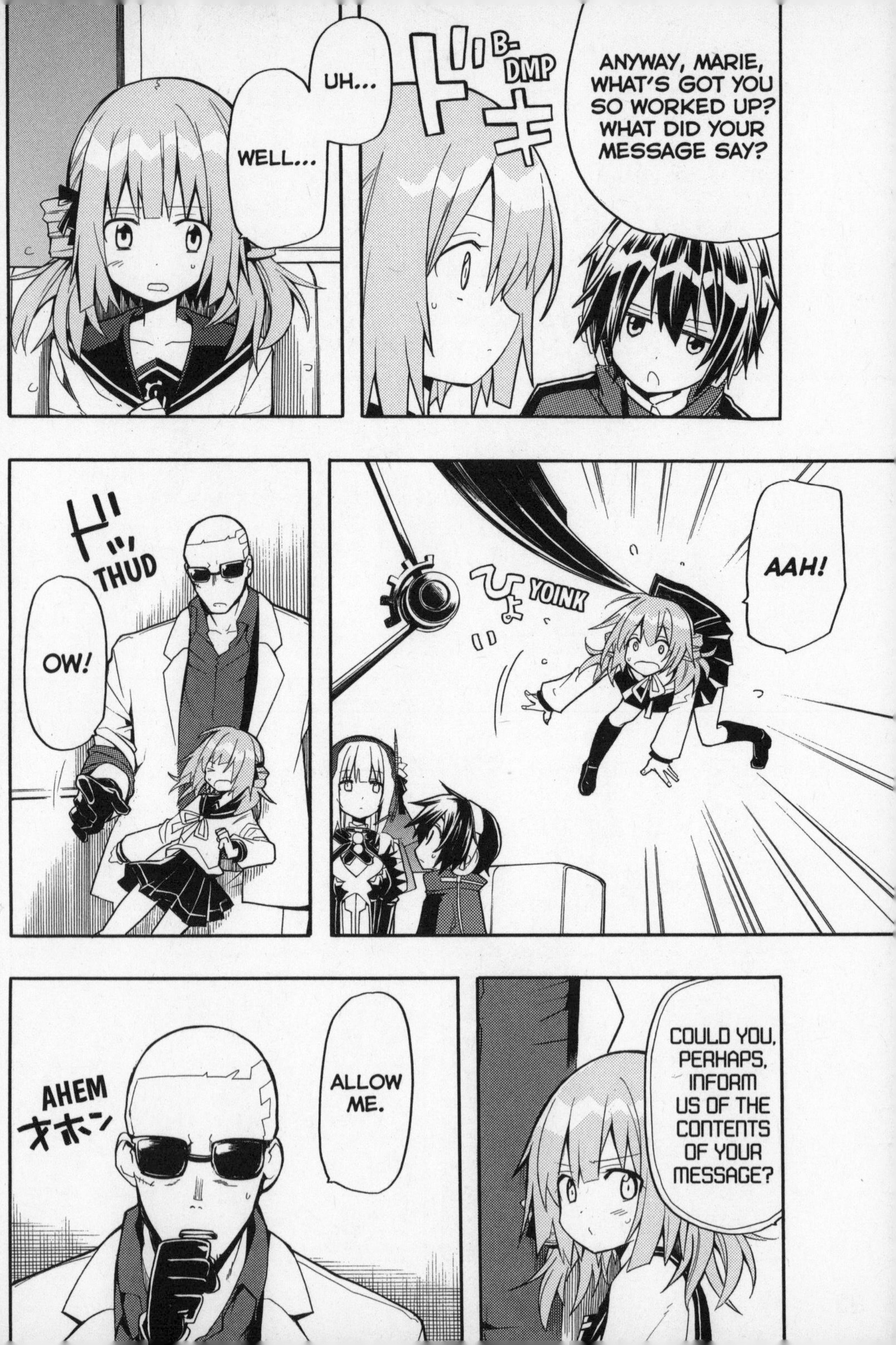
ANYWAY, MARIE, WHAT'S GOT YOU SO WORKED UP? WHAT DID YOUR MESSAGE SAY?
ドキ B-DMP
UH...
WELL...
AAH!
ひょ YOINK
ドッ THUD
OW!
COULD YOU, PERHAPS, INFORM US OF THE CONTENTS OF YOUR MESSAGE?
ALLOW ME.
AHEM オホン

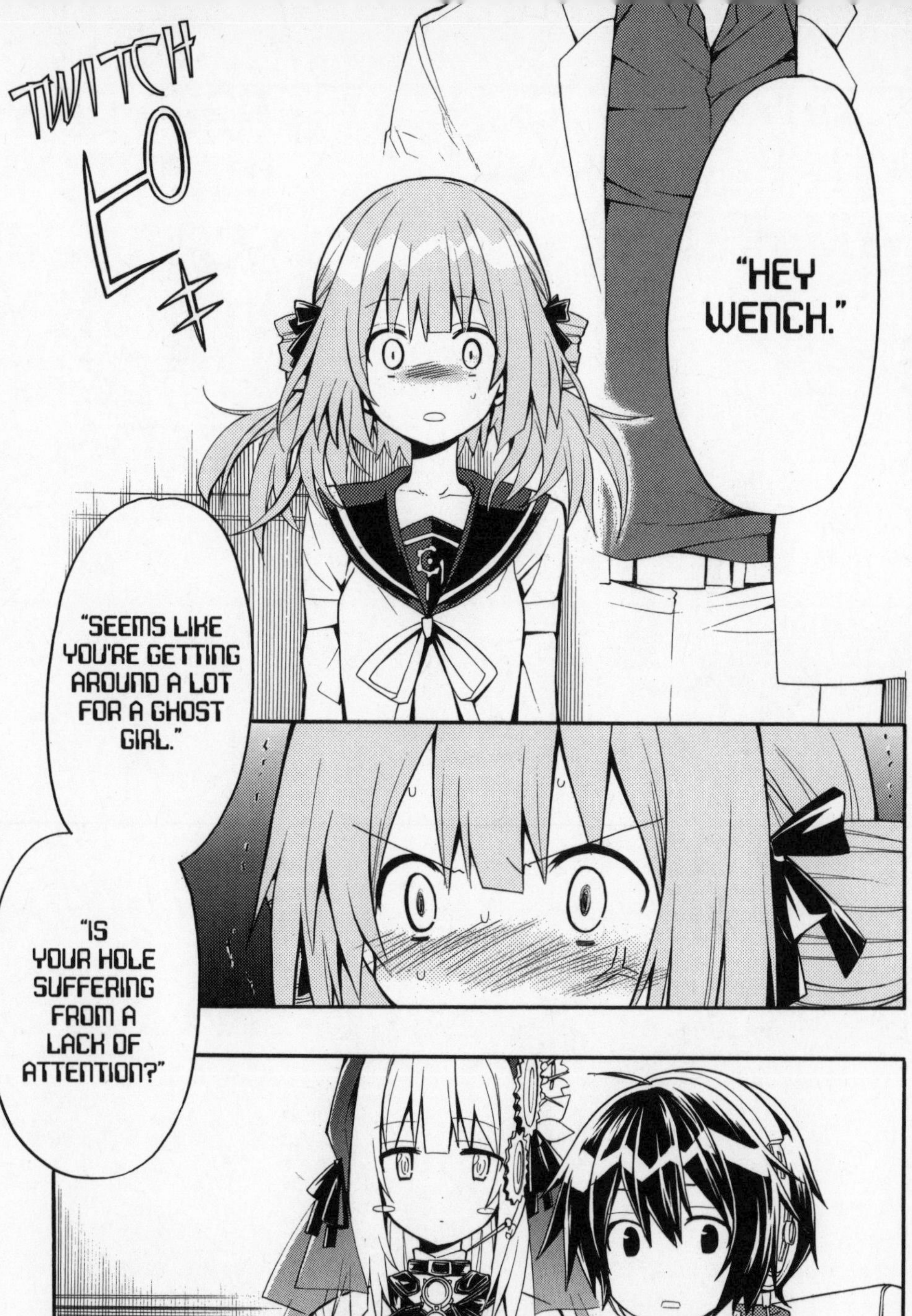
"HEY WENCH."
TWITCH
"SEEMS LIKE YOU'RE GETTING AROUND A LOT FOR A GHOST GIRL."
"IS YOUR HOLE SUFFERING FROM A LACK OF ATTENTION?"

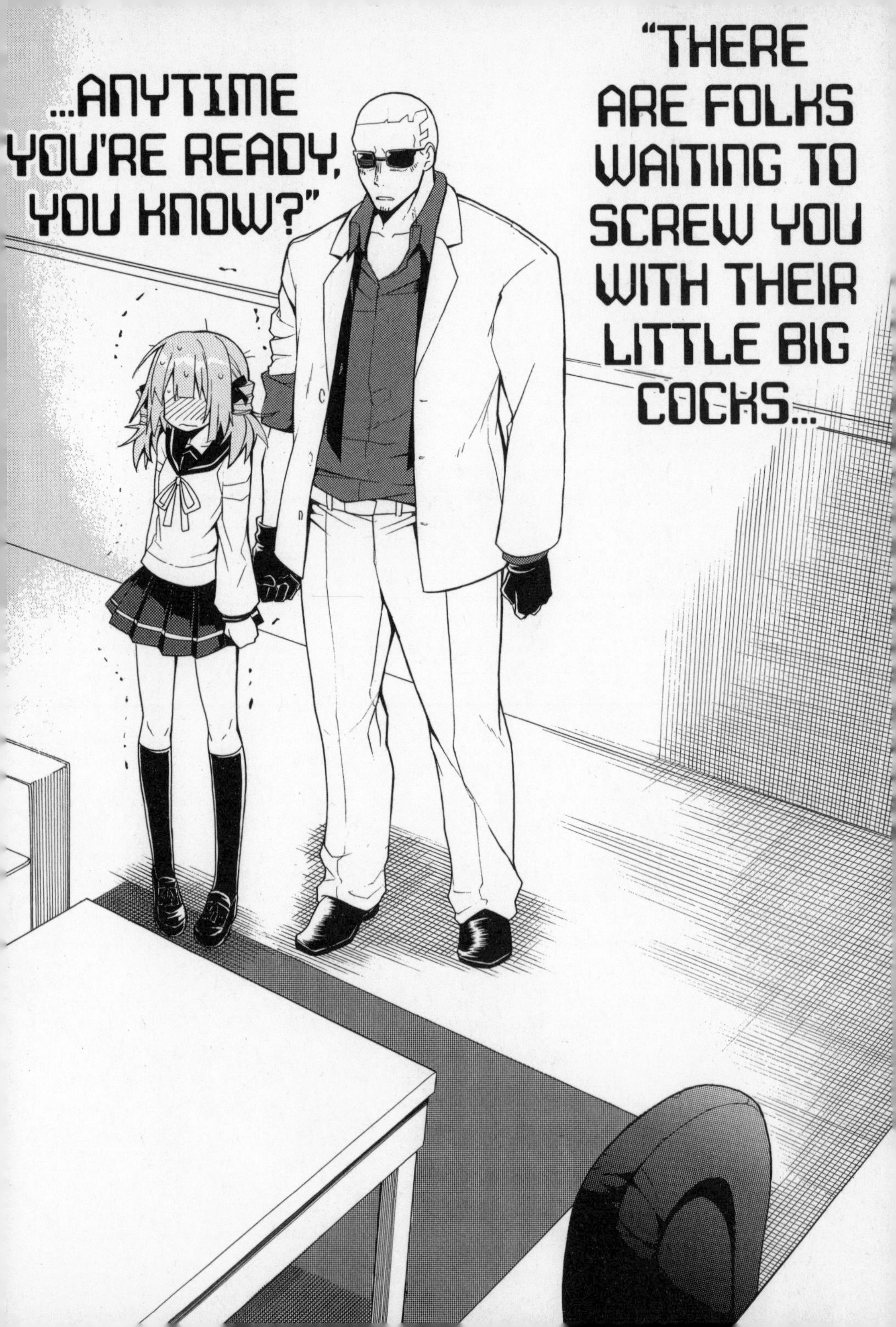
"THERE ARE FOLKS WAITING TO SCREW YOU WITH THEIR LITTLE BIG COCKS...
...ANYTIME YOU'RE READY, YOU KNOW?"

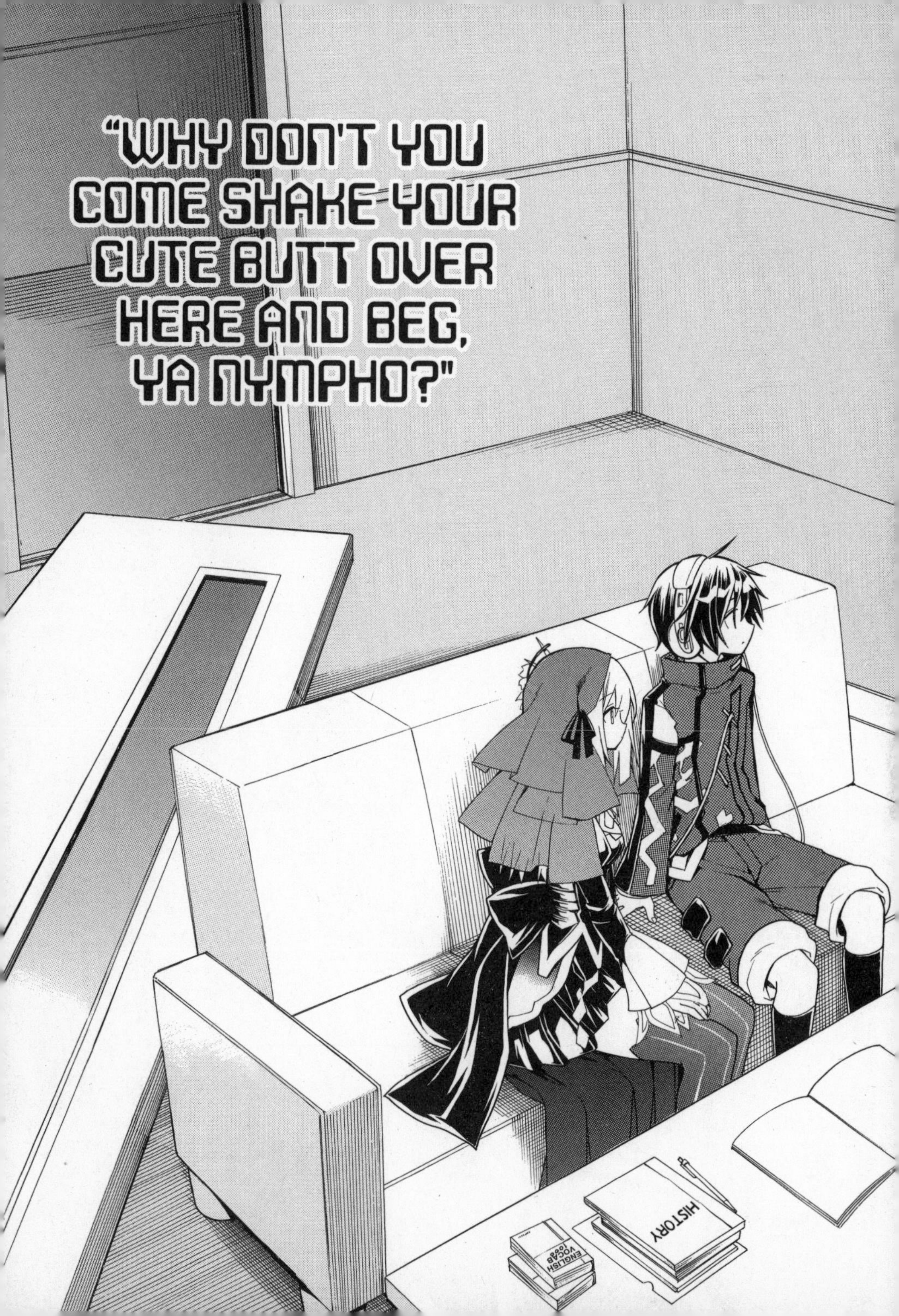
"WHY DON'T YOU COME SHAKE YOUR CUTE BUTT OVER HERE AND BEG, YA NYMPHO?"
HISTORY
ENGLISH VOCAB

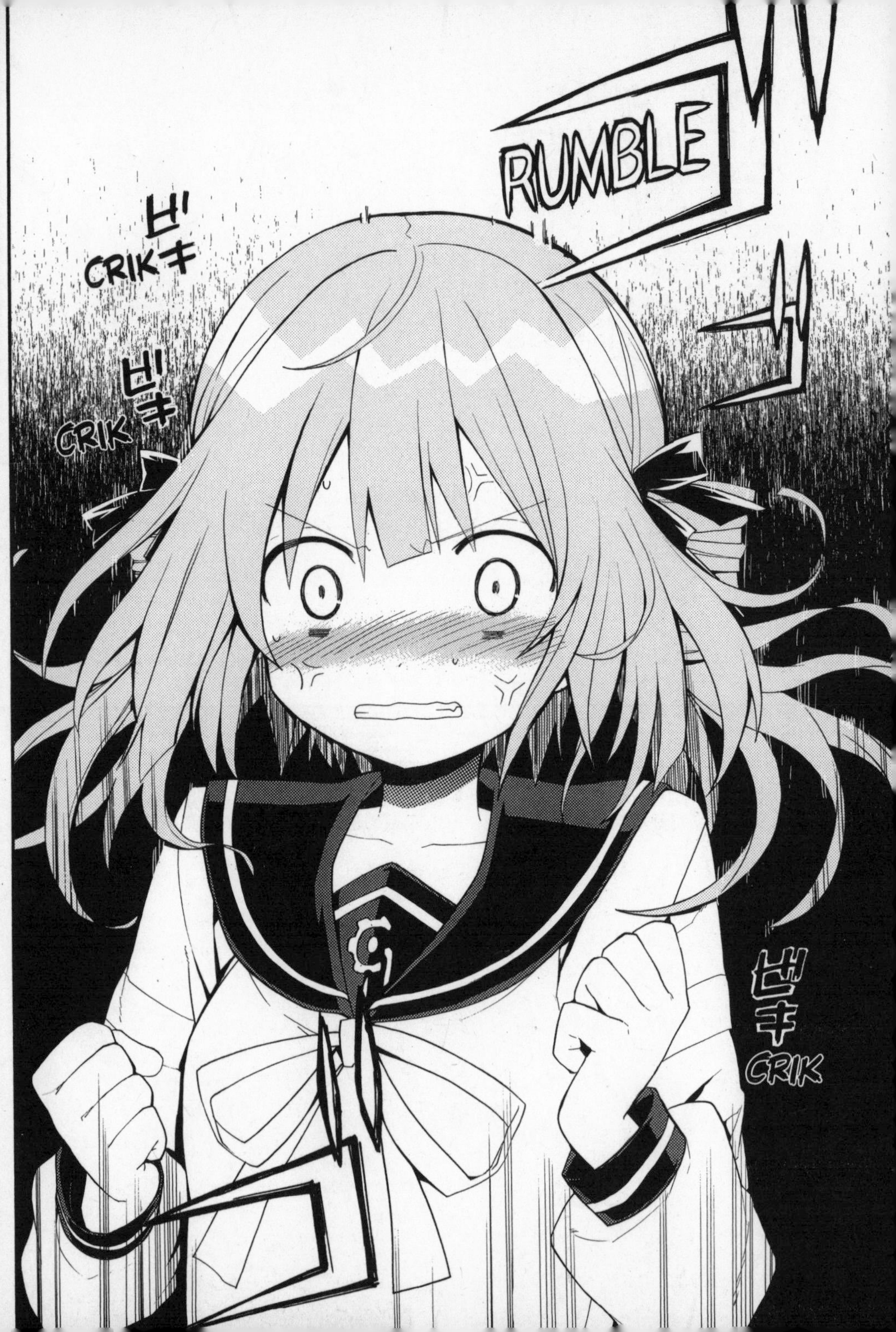
RUMBLE
ビキ
CRIK
ビキ
CRIK
ビキ
CRIK

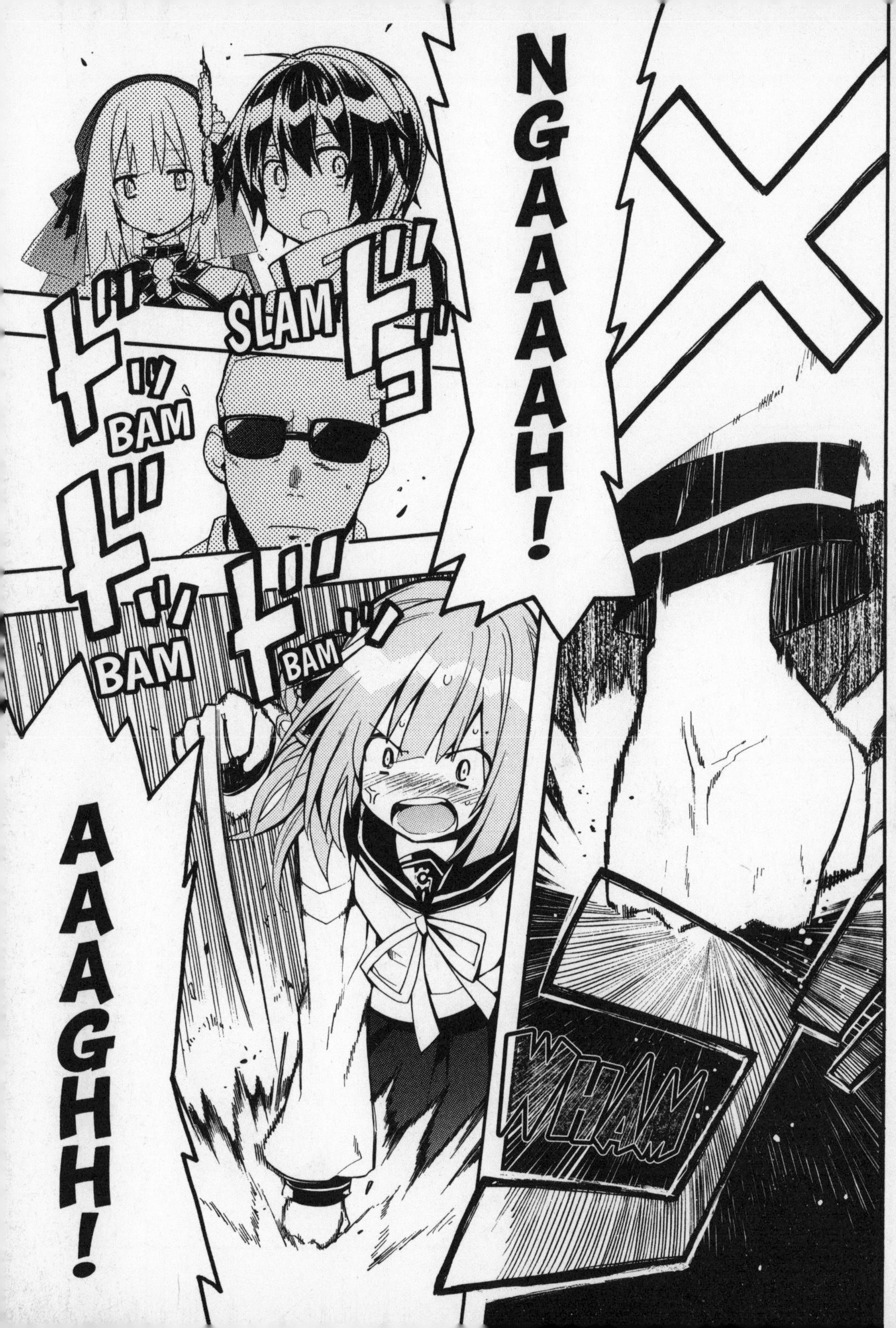
NGAAAAAH!
SLAM
BAM
BAM
BAM
AAAGHH!
WHAM

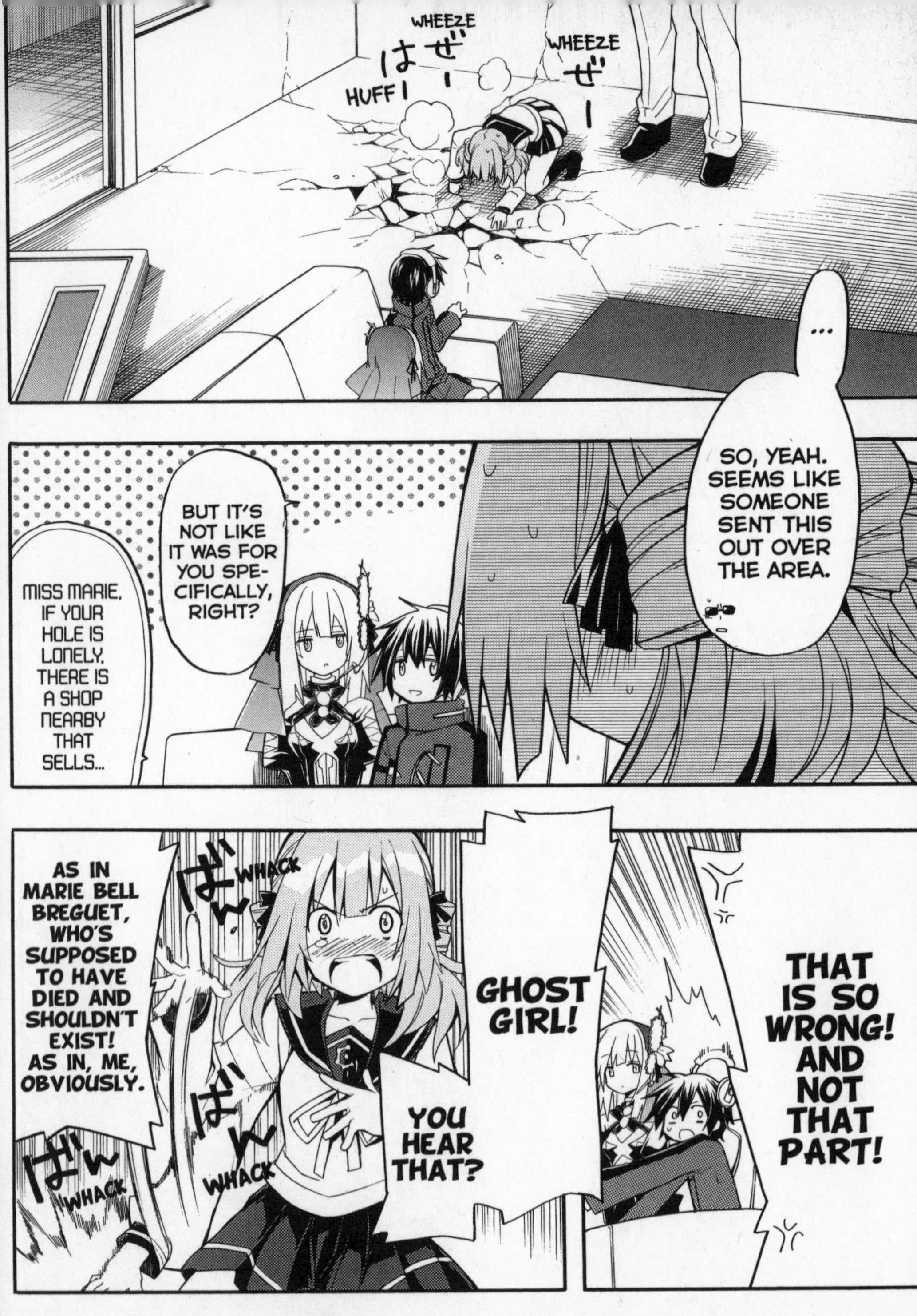
WHEEZE
ぜー
はぜー
WHEEZE
HUFF
...
SO, YEAH. SEEMS LIKE SOMEONE SENT THIS OUT OVER THE AREA.
BUT IT'S NOT LIKE IT WAS FOR YOU SPE-CIFICALLY, RIGHT?
MISS MARIE, IF YOUR HOLE IS LONELY, THERE IS A SHOP NEARBY THAT SELLS...
THAT IS SO WRONG! AND NOT THAT PART!
GHOST GIRL!
YOU HEAR THAT?
AS IN MARIE BELL BREGUET, WHO'S SUPPOSED TO HAVE DIED AND SHOULDN'T EXIST! AS IN, ME, OBVIOUSLY.
ばん WHACK
ばん WHACK
ばん WHACK

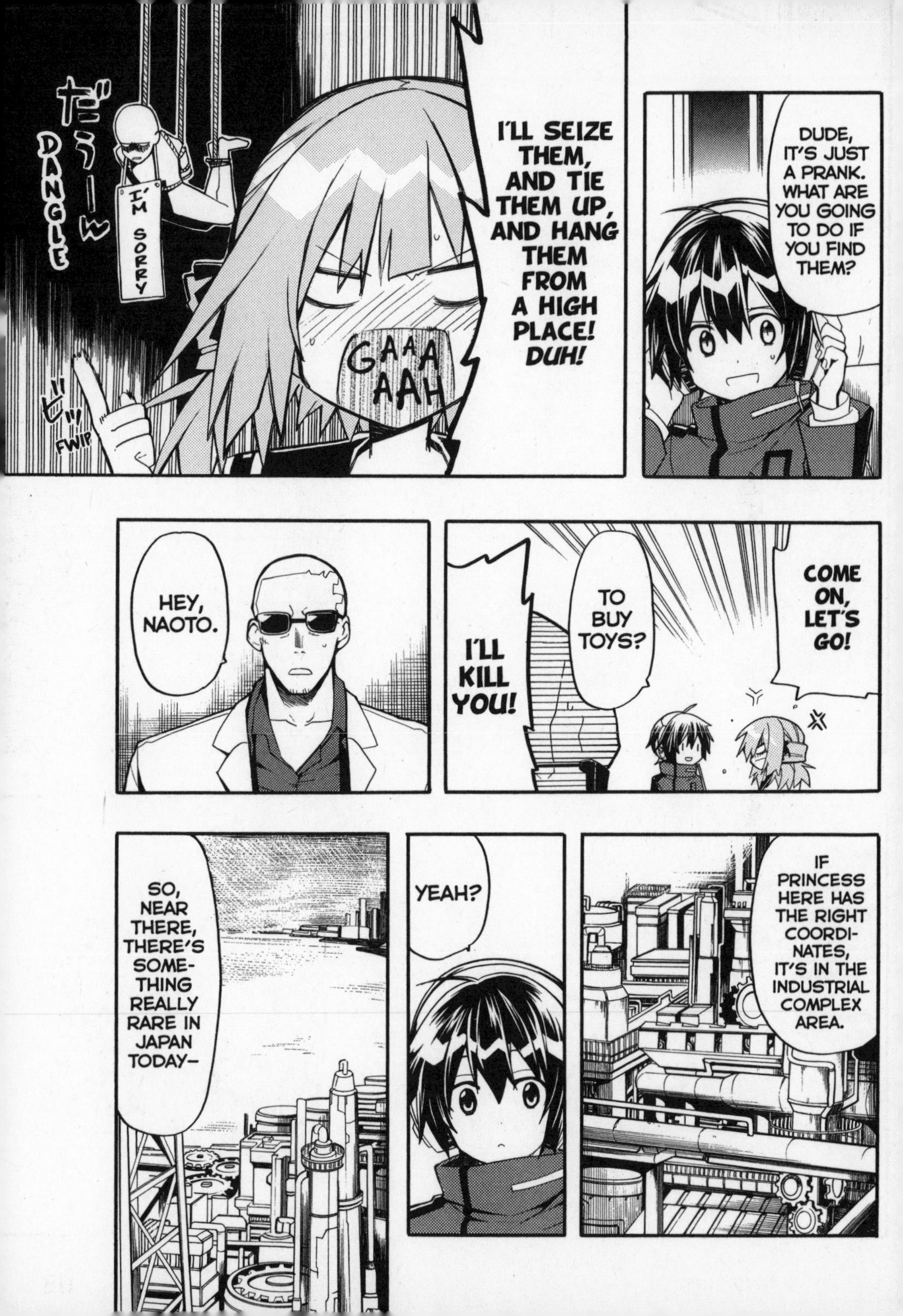
DUDE, IT'S JUST A PRANK. WHAT ARE YOU GOING TO DO IF YOU FIND THEM?
I'LL SEIZE THEM, AND TIE THEM UP, AND HANG THEM FROM A HIGH PLACE! DUH!
GAAAAAH
だらーん
DANGLE
I'M SORRY
ビッ
FWIP
COME ON, LET'S GO!
TO BUY TOYS?
I'LL KILL YOU!
HEY, NAOTO.
IF PRINCESS HERE HAS THE RIGHT COORDINATES, IT'S IN THE INDUSTRIAL COMPLEX AREA.
YEAH?
SO, NEAR THERE, THERE'S SOMETHING REALLY RARE IN JAPAN TODAY–

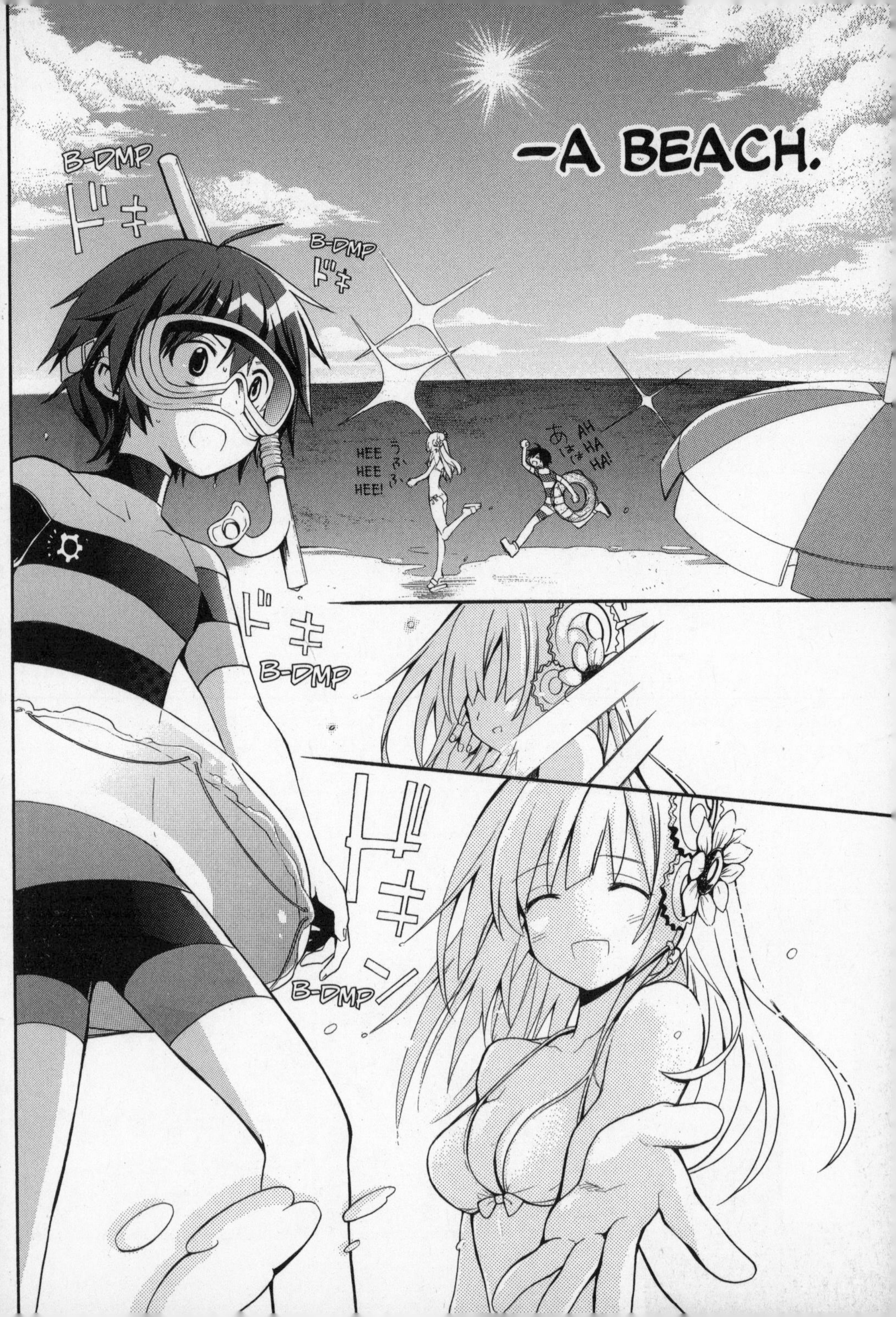
—A BEACH.
AH HA HA!
あはは
HEE HEE HEE!
うふふ
B-DMP
ドキ
B-DMP
ドキ
ドキ
B-DMP
ドキーン
B-DMP

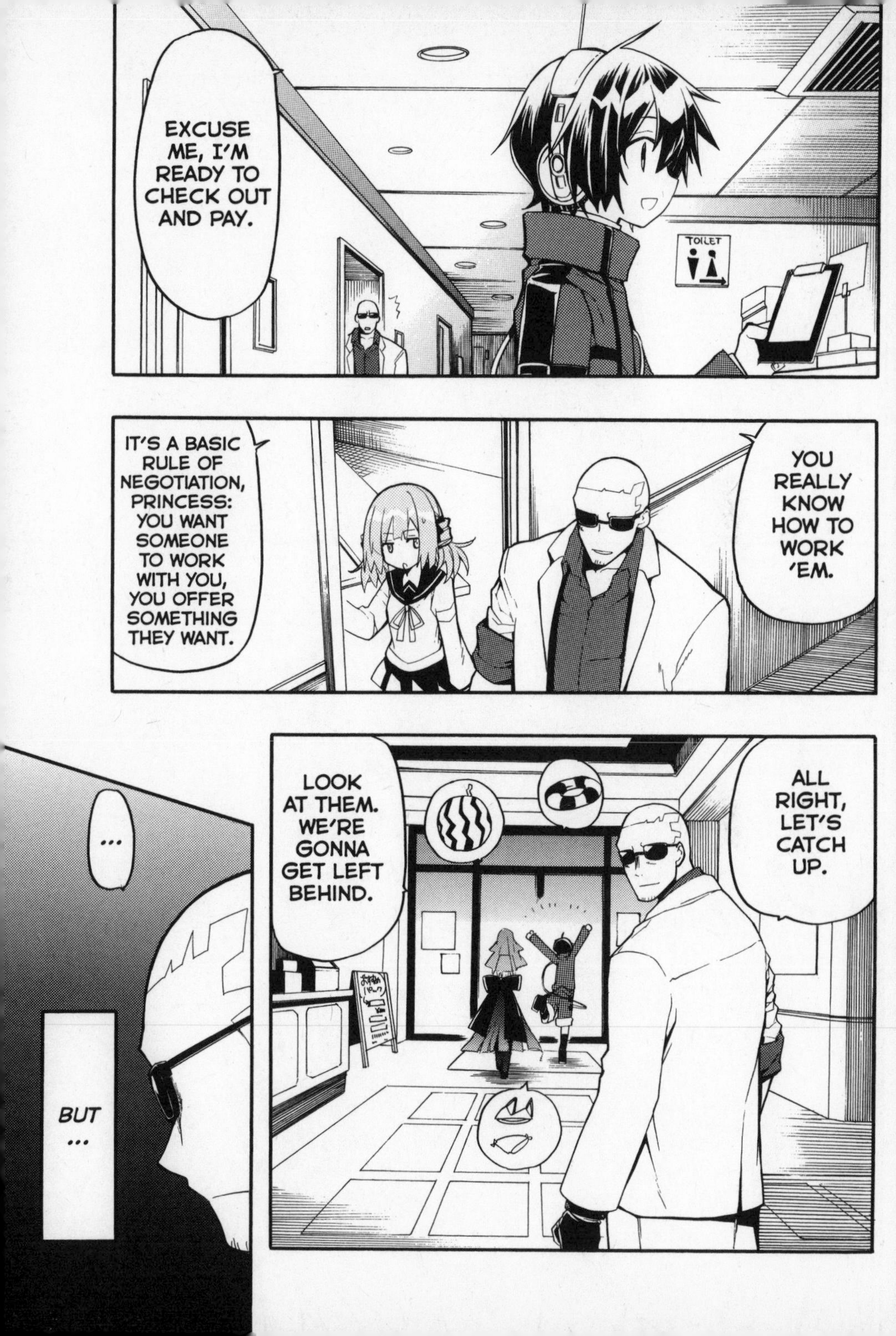
EXCUSE ME, I'M READY TO CHECK OUT AND PAY.
TOILET
YOU REALLY KNOW HOW TO WORK 'EM.
IT'S A BASIC RULE OF NEGOTIATION, PRINCESS: YOU WANT SOMEONE TO WORK WITH YOU, YOU OFFER SOMETHING THEY WANT.
ALL RIGHT, LET'S CATCH UP.
LOOK AT THEM. WE'RE GONNA GET LEFT BEHIND.
...
BUT ...

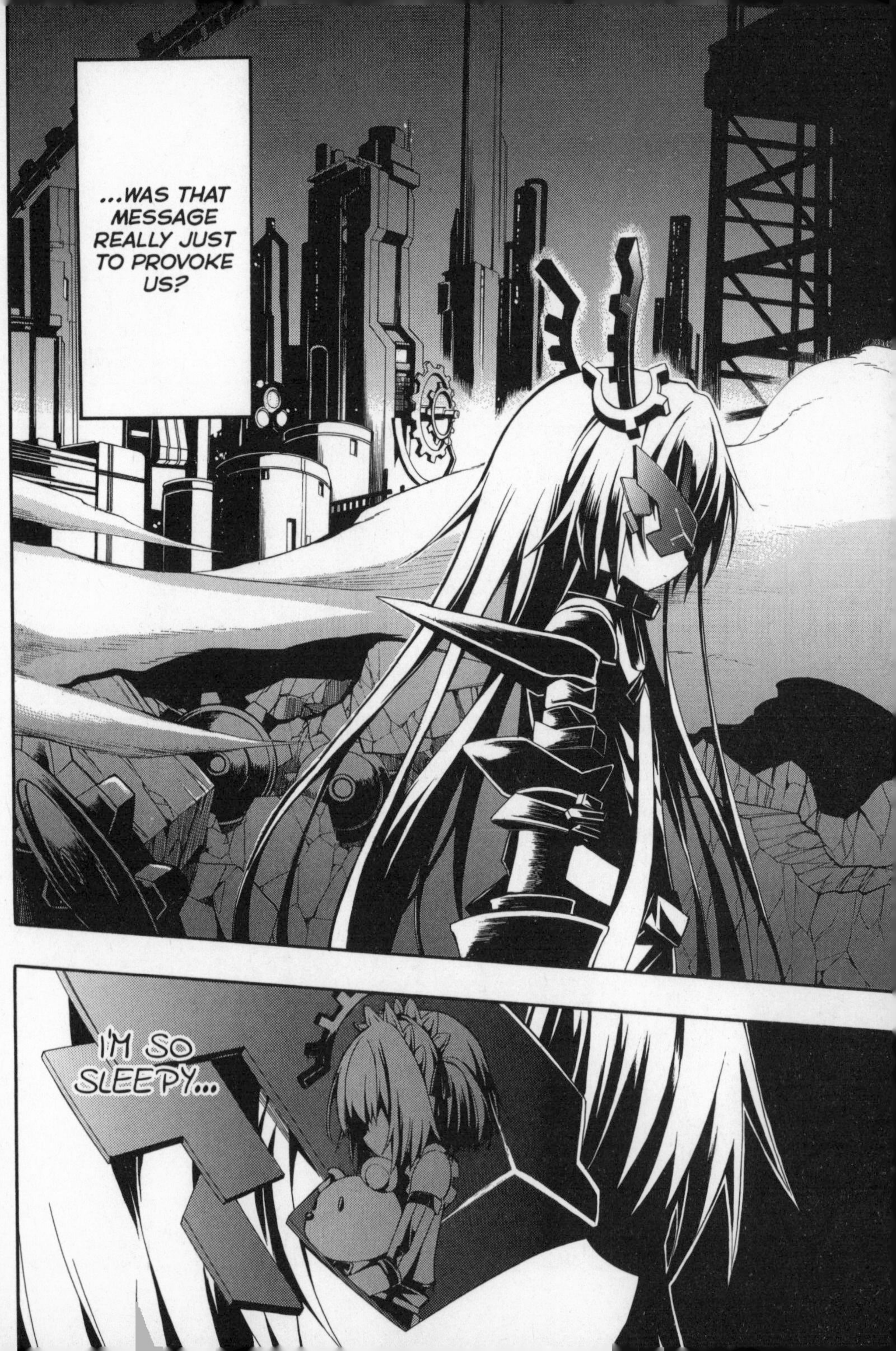
...WAS THAT MESSAGE REALLY JUST TO PROVOKE US?
I'M SO SLEEPY...

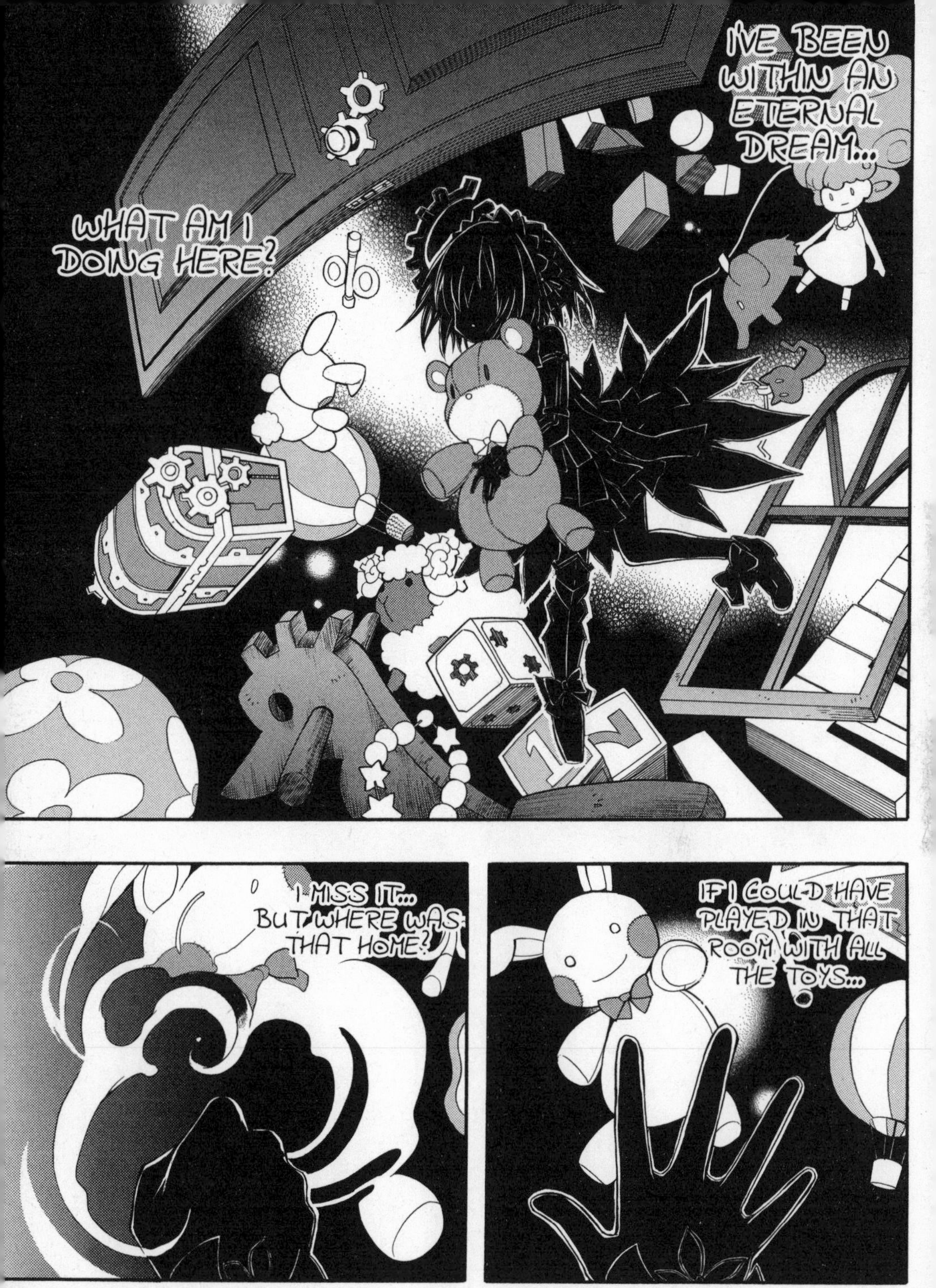
I'VE BEEN WITHIN AN ETERNAL DREAM...
WHAT AM I DOING HERE?
IF I COULD HAVE PLAYED IN THAT ROOM WITH ALL THE TOYS...
I MISS IT... BUT WHERE WAS THAT HOME?

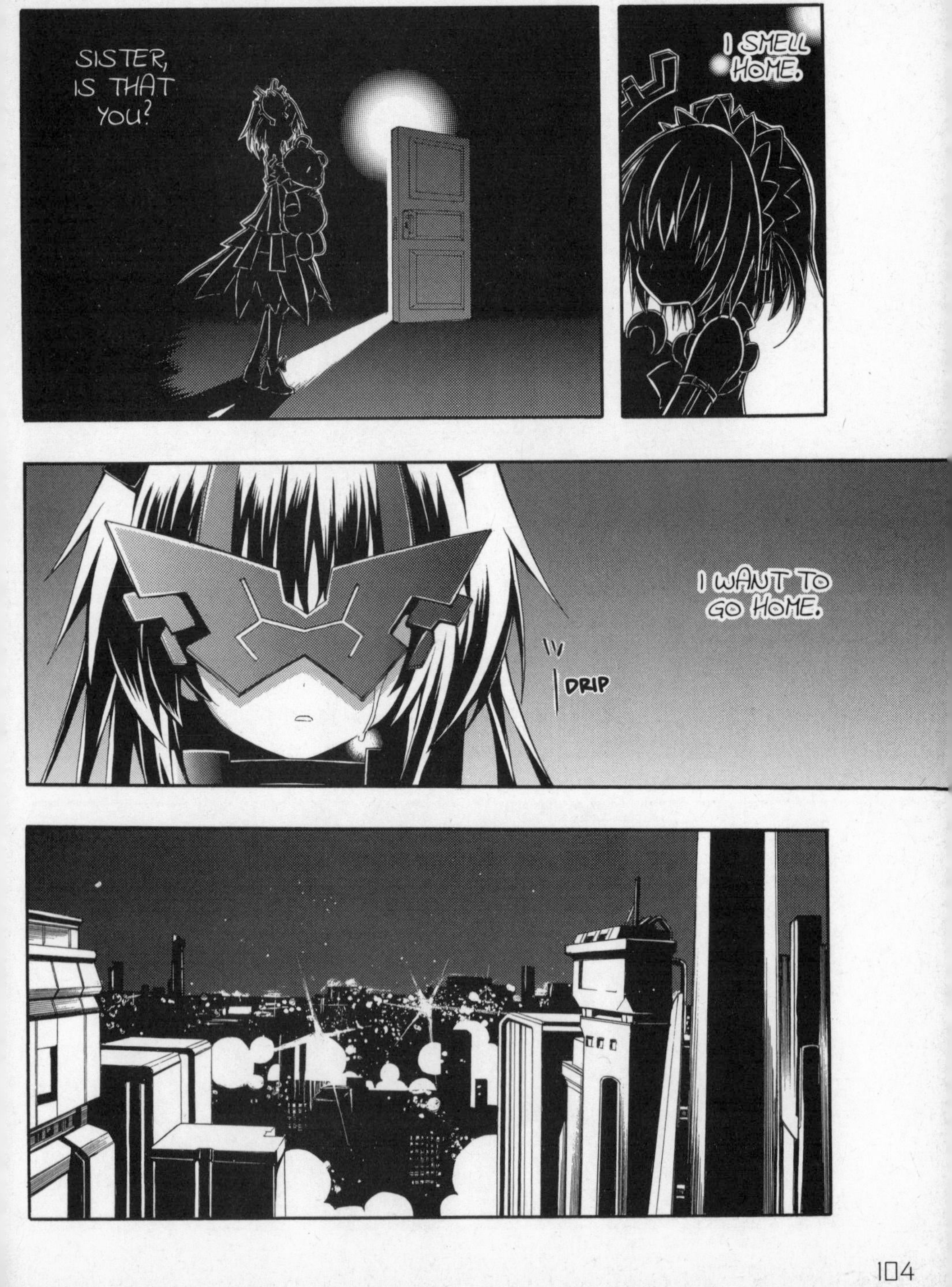
I SMELL HOME.
SISTER, IS THAT YOU?
I WANT TO GO HOME.
DRIP

CLOCKWORK PLANET

CLOCKWORK PLANET

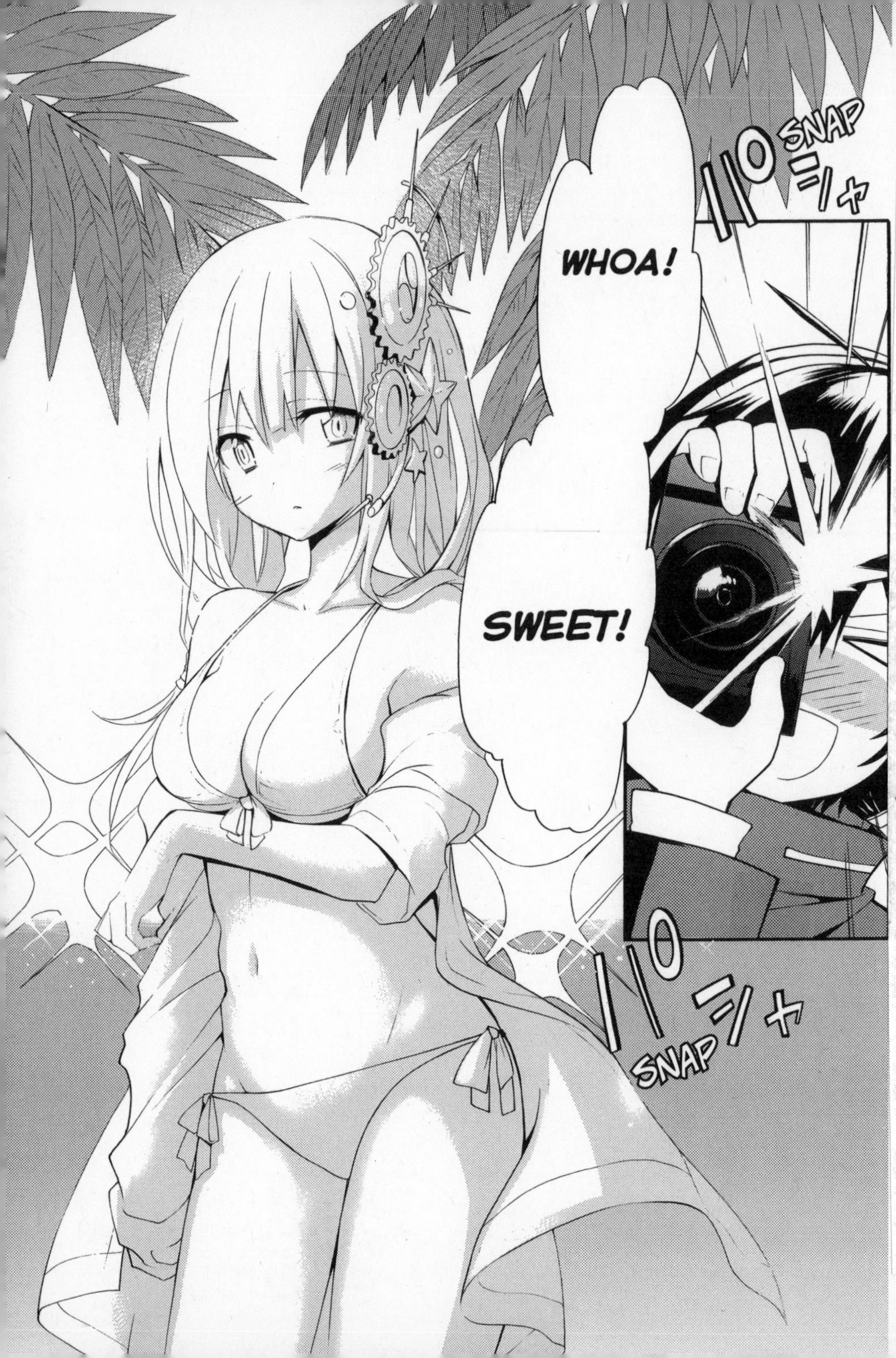
SNAP
WHOA!
SWEET!
SNAP

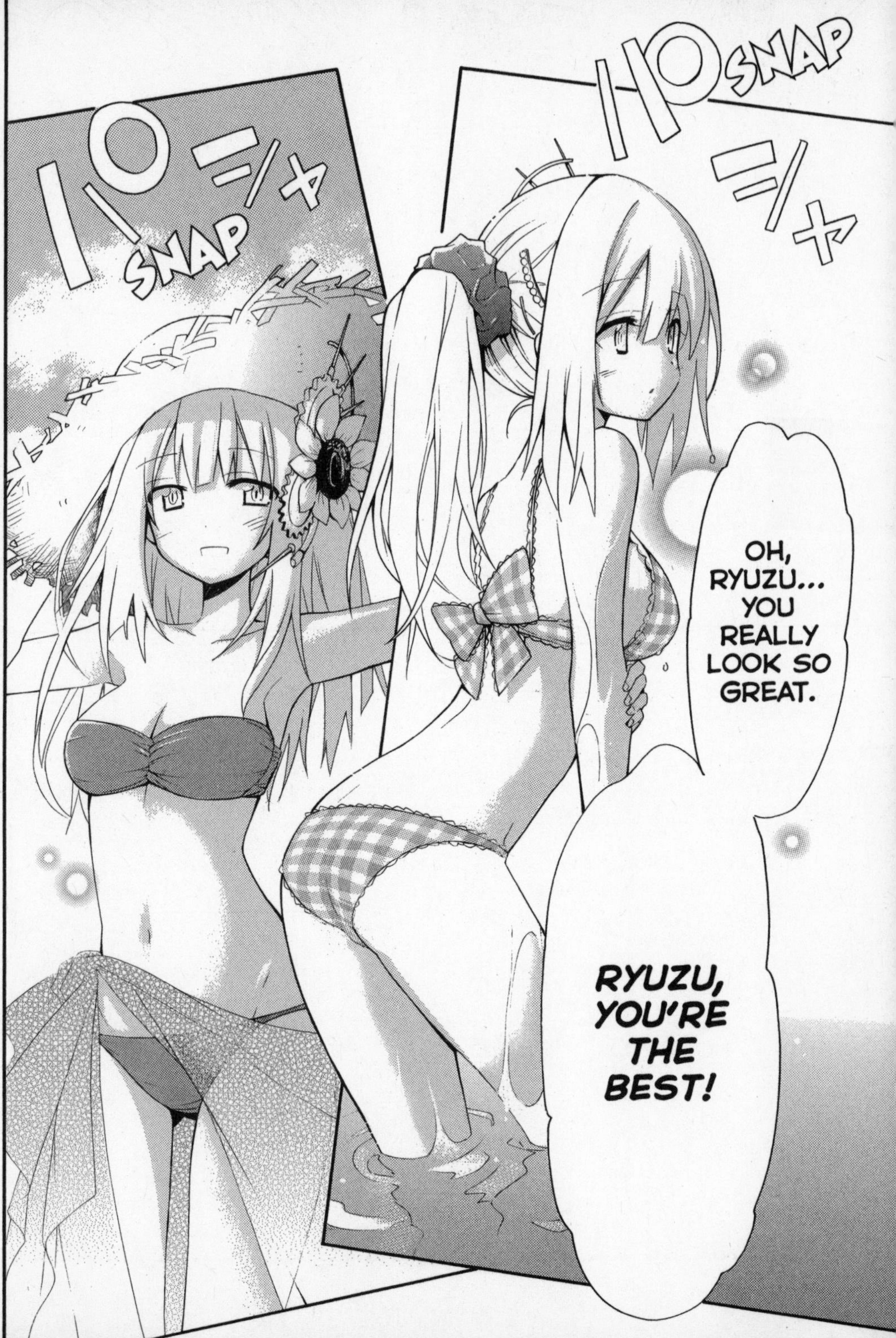
パシャ
SNAP
OH, RYUZU... YOU REALLY LOOK SO GREAT.
RYUZU, YOU'RE THE BEST!
パシャ
SNAP

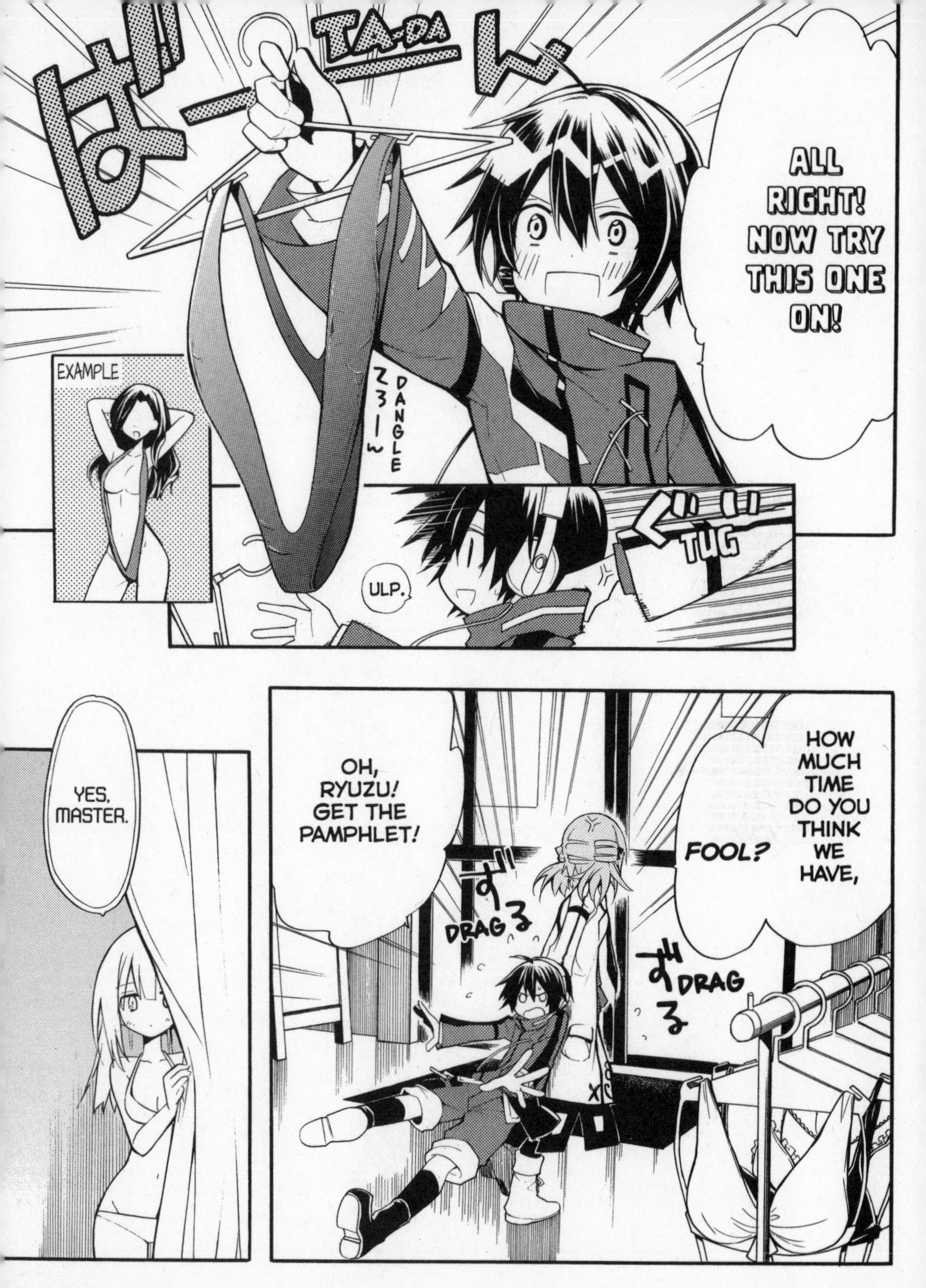
TA-DA
ALL RIGHT! NOW TRY THIS ONE ON!
DANGLE
EXAMPLE
TUG
ULP.
HOW MUCH TIME DO YOU THINK WE HAVE, FOOL?
OH, RYUZU! GET THE PAMPHLET!
DRAG
DRAG
YES, MASTER.

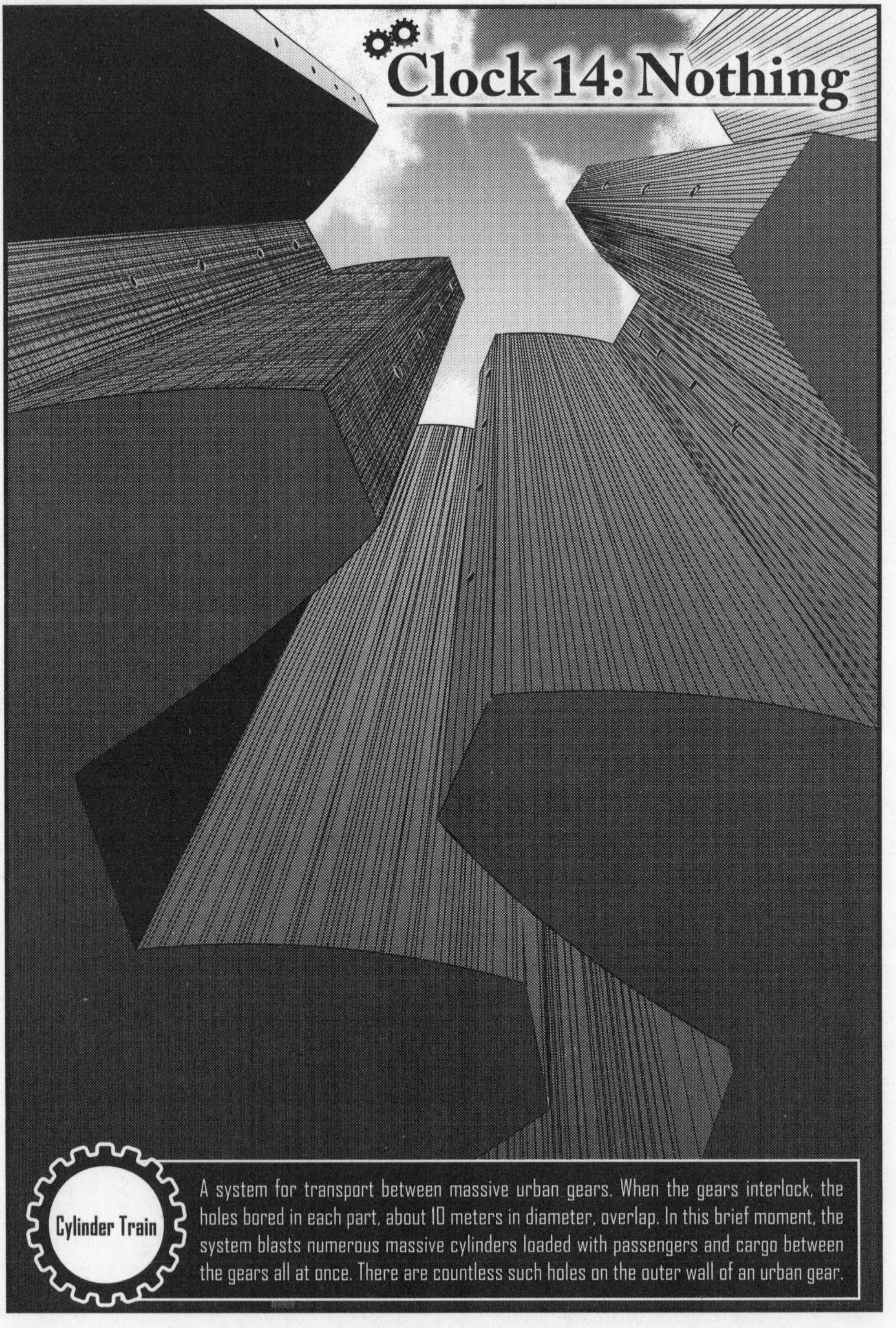
Clock 14: Nothing
Cylinder Train
A system for transport between massive urban gears. When the gears interlock, the holes bored in each part, about 10 meters in diameter, overlap. In this brief moment, the system blasts numerous massive cylinders loaded with passengers and cargo between the gears all at once. There are countless such holes on the outer wall of an urban gear.

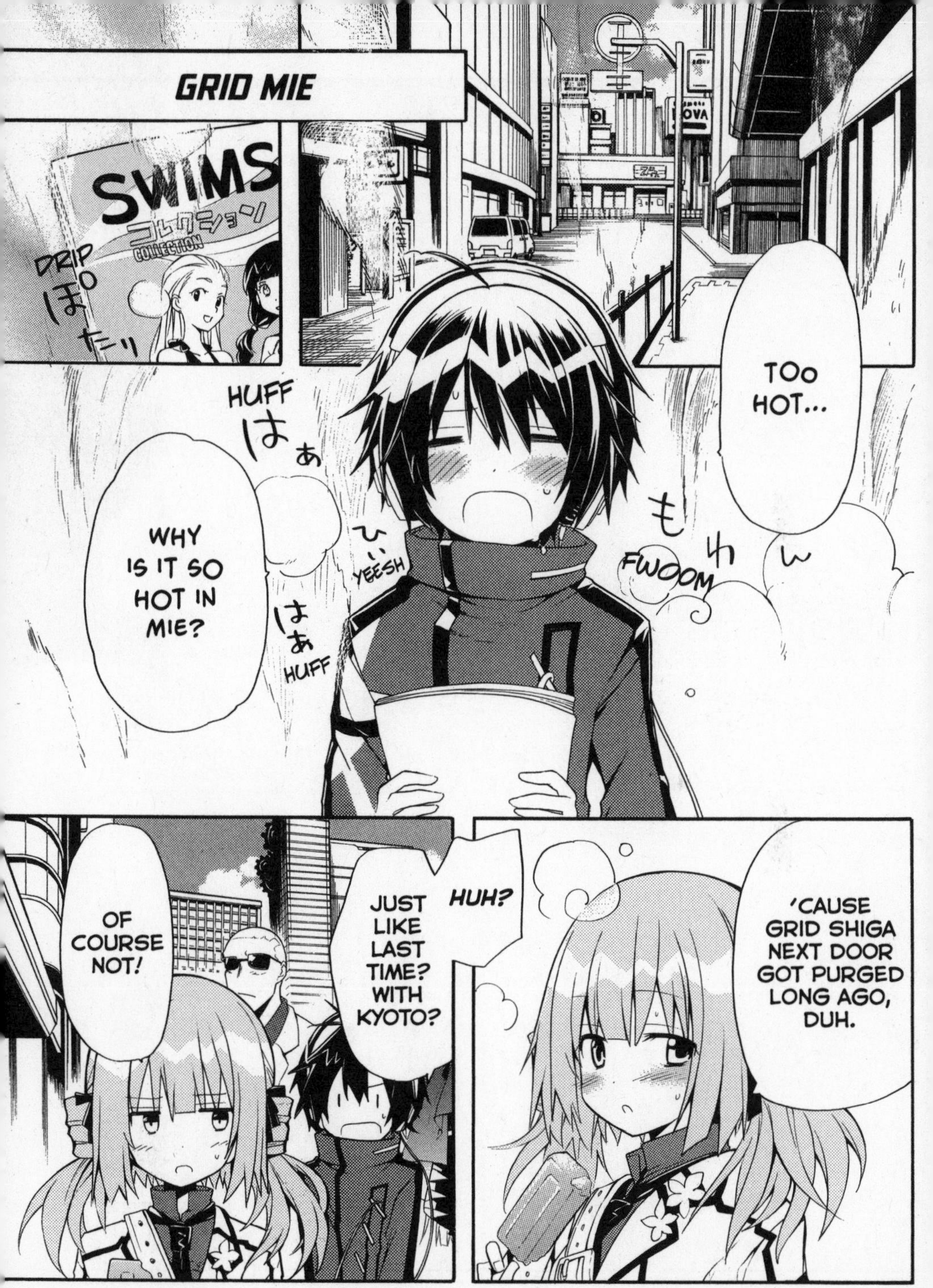
GRID MIE
SWIMS
コレクション
COLLECTION
ぽたり
DRIP
TOO HOT...
もわん
FWOOM
ひぃ
YEESH
はぁ
HUFF
WHY IS IT SO HOT IN MIE?
はぁ
HUFF
'CAUSE GRID SHIGA NEXT DOOR GOT PURGED LONG AGO, DUH.
HUH?
JUST LIKE LAST TIME? WITH KYOTO?
OF COURSE NOT!

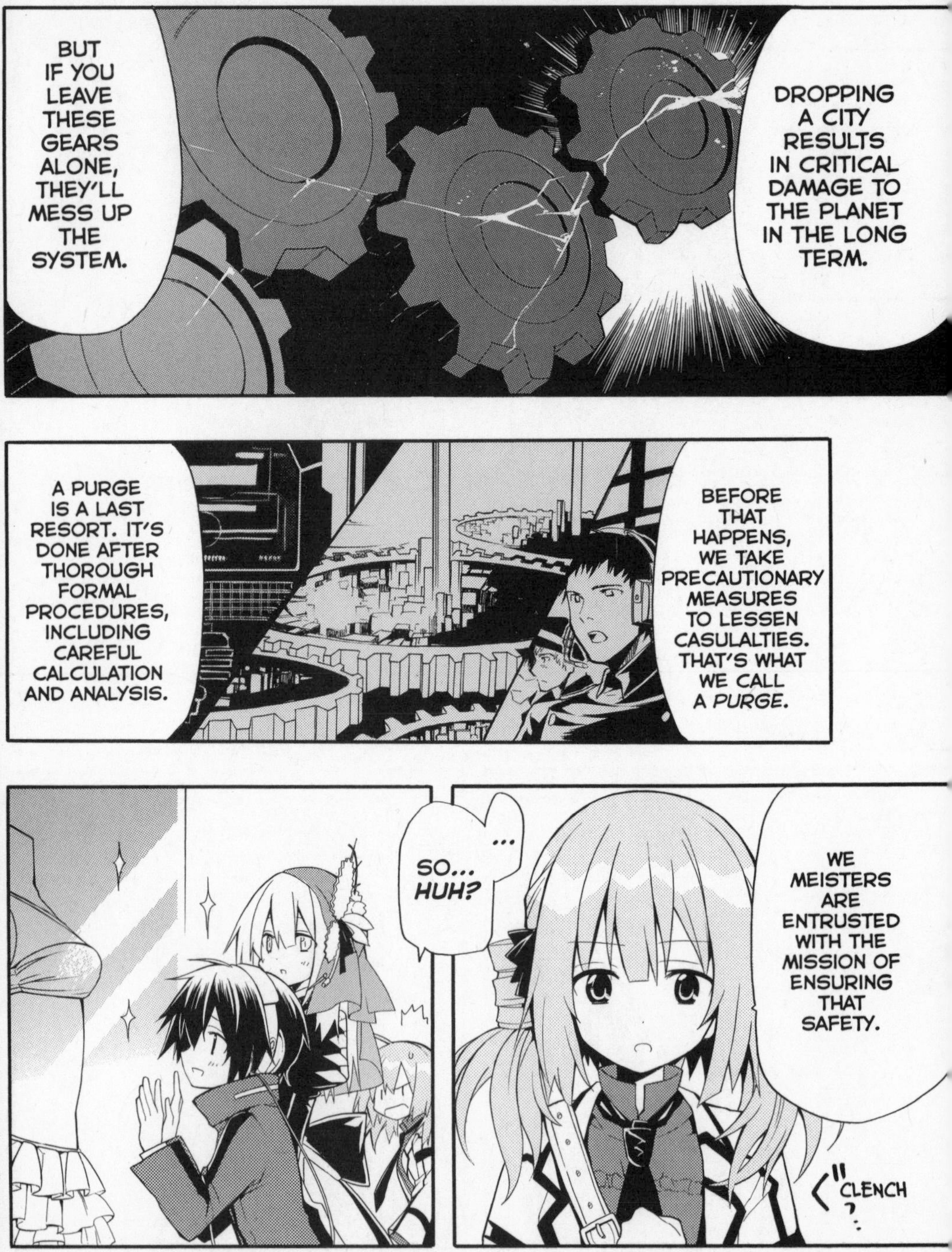
DROPPING A CITY RESULTS IN CRITICAL DAMAGE TO THE PLANET IN THE LONG TERM.
BUT IF YOU LEAVE THESE GEARS ALONE, THEY'LL MESS UP THE SYSTEM.
BEFORE THAT HAPPENS, WE TAKE PRECAUTIONARY MEASURES TO LESSEN CASULALTIES. THAT'S WHAT WE CALL A *PURGE*.
A PURGE IS A LAST RESORT. IT'S DONE AFTER THOROUGH FORMAL PROCEDURES, INCLUDING CAREFUL CALCULATION AND ANALYSIS.
WE MEISTERS ARE ENTRUSTED WITH THE MISSION OF ENSURING THAT SAFETY.
CLENCH
...
SO... *HUH?*

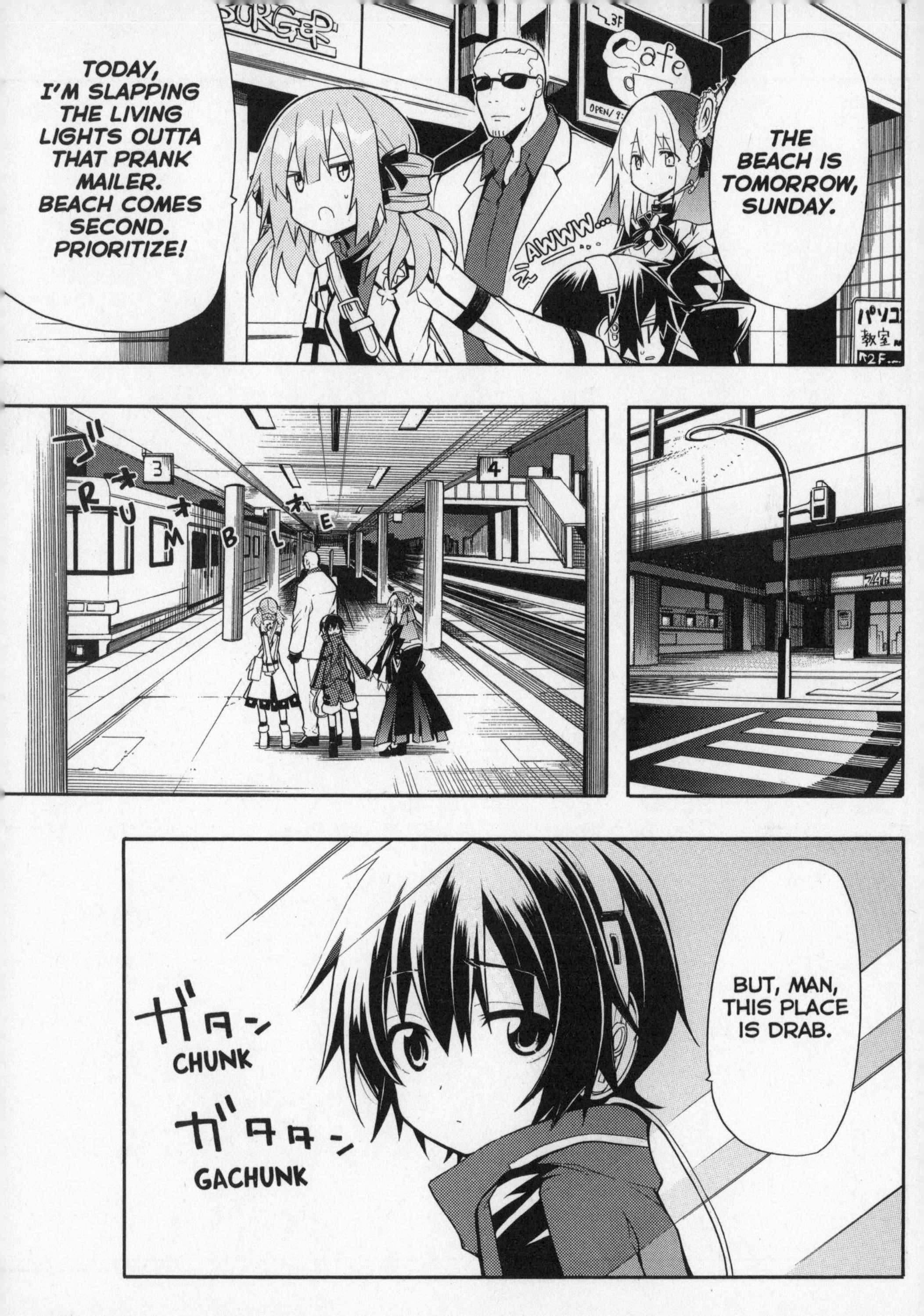
THE BEACH IS TOMORROW, SUNDAY.
AWWW...
TODAY, I'M SLAPPING THE LIVING LIGHTS OUTTA THAT PRANK MAILER. BEACH COMES SECOND. PRIORITIZE!
ゴオオ
RUMBLE
BUT, MAN, THIS PLACE IS DRAB.
ガタン
CHUNK
ガタタン
GACHUNK

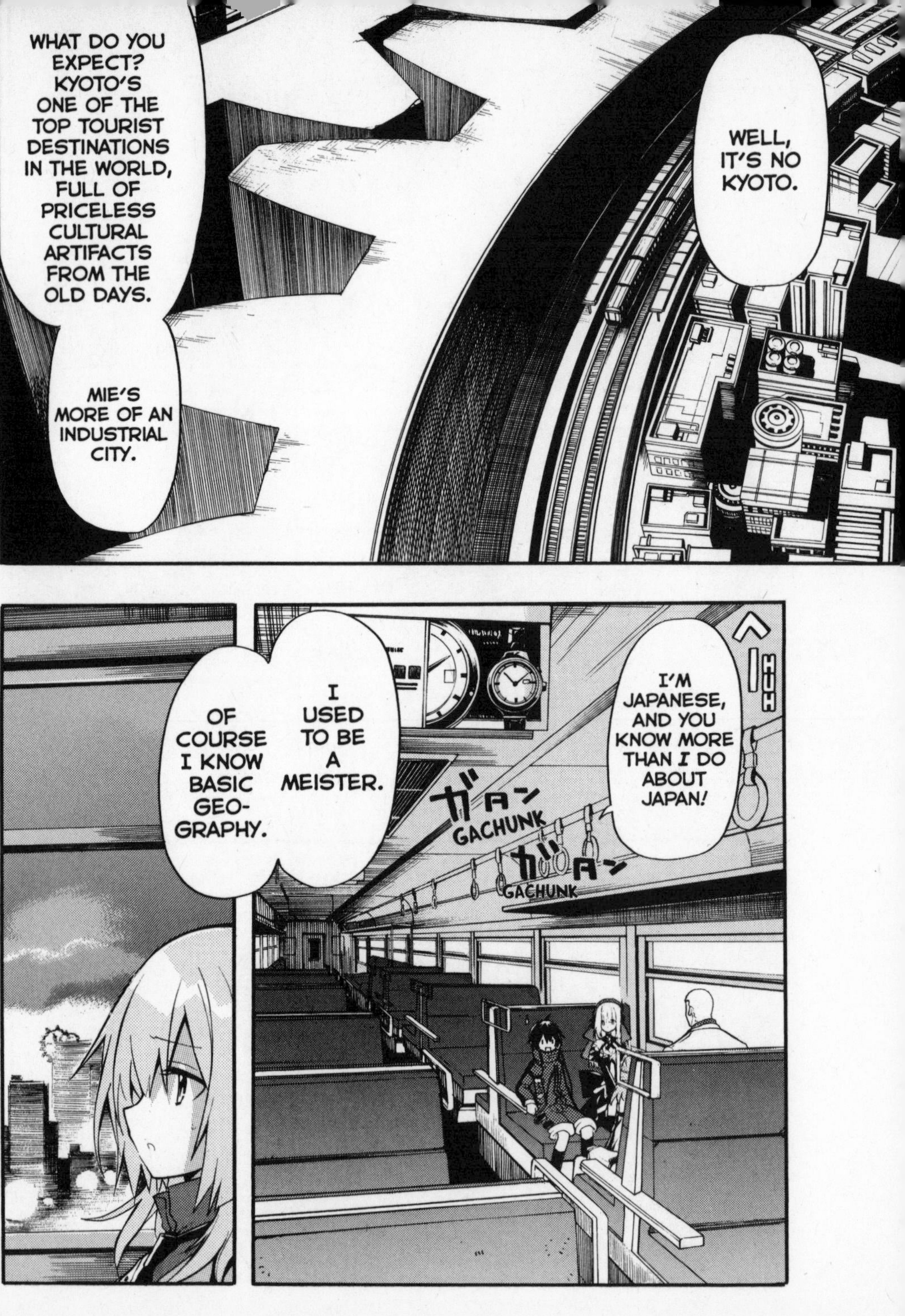
WELL, IT'S NO KYOTO.
WHAT DO YOU EXPECT? KYOTO'S ONE OF THE TOP TOURIST DESTINATIONS IN THE WORLD, FULL OF PRICELESS CULTURAL ARTIFACTS FROM THE OLD DAYS.
MIE'S MORE OF AN INDUSTRIAL CITY.
HUH
I'M JAPANESE, AND YOU KNOW MORE THAN *I* DO ABOUT JAPAN!
ガタン GACHUNK
ガタン GACHUNK
I USED TO BE A MEISTER.
OF COURSE I KNOW BASIC GEO-GRAPHY.

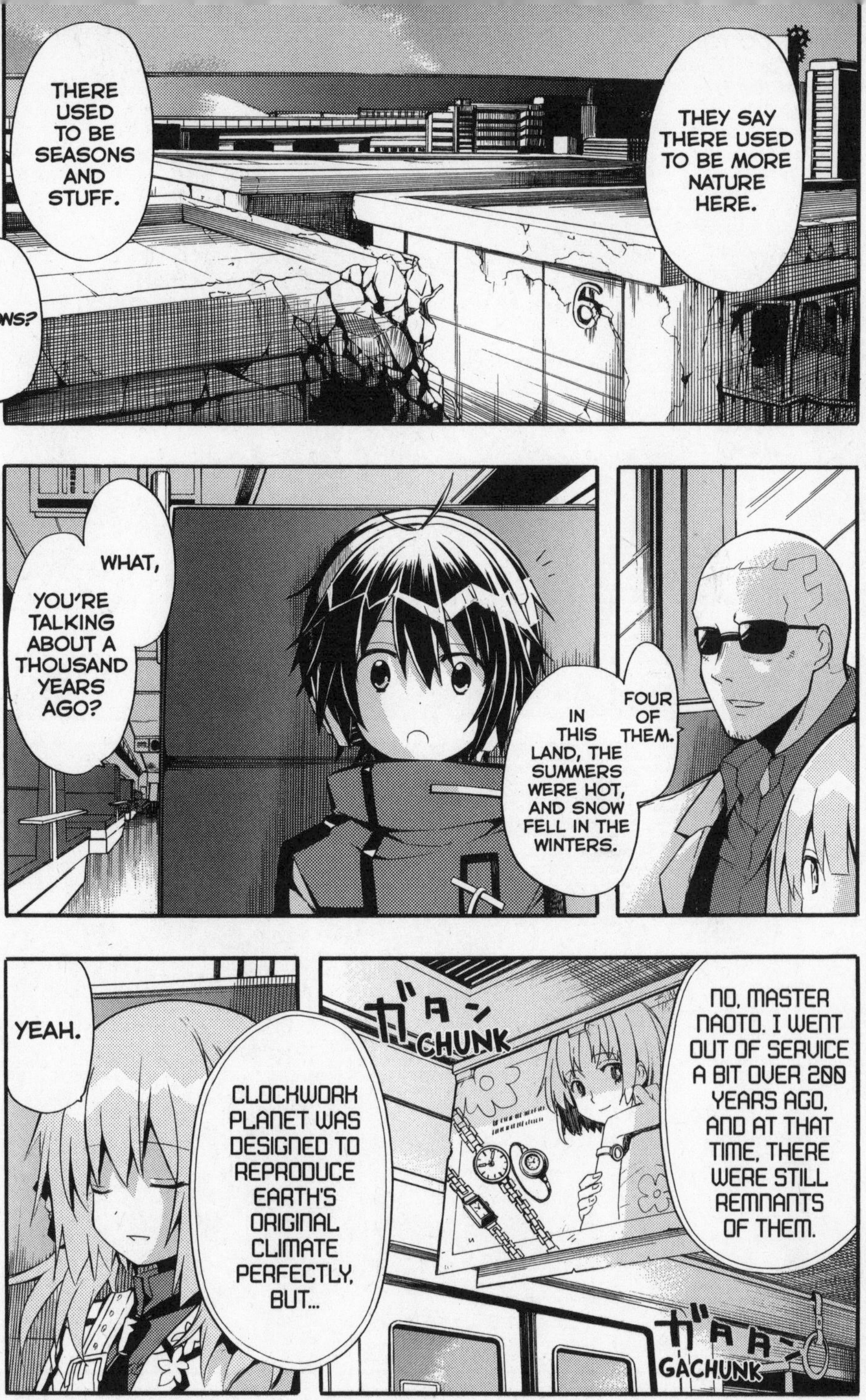
THEY SAY THERE USED TO BE MORE NATURE HERE.
THERE USED TO BE SEASONS AND STUFF.
SEASONS?
FOUR OF THEM.
IN THIS LAND, THE SUMMERS WERE HOT, AND SNOW FELL IN THE WINTERS.
WHAT,
YOU'RE TALKING ABOUT A THOUSAND YEARS AGO?
NO, MASTER NAOTO. I WENT OUT OF SERVICE A BIT OVER 200 YEARS AGO, AND AT THAT TIME, THERE WERE STILL REMNANTS OF THEM.
ガタン
CHUNK
ガタタン
GACHUNK
YEAH.
CLOCKWORK PLANET WAS DESIGNED TO REPRODUCE EARTH'S ORIGINAL CLIMATE PERFECTLY, BUT...

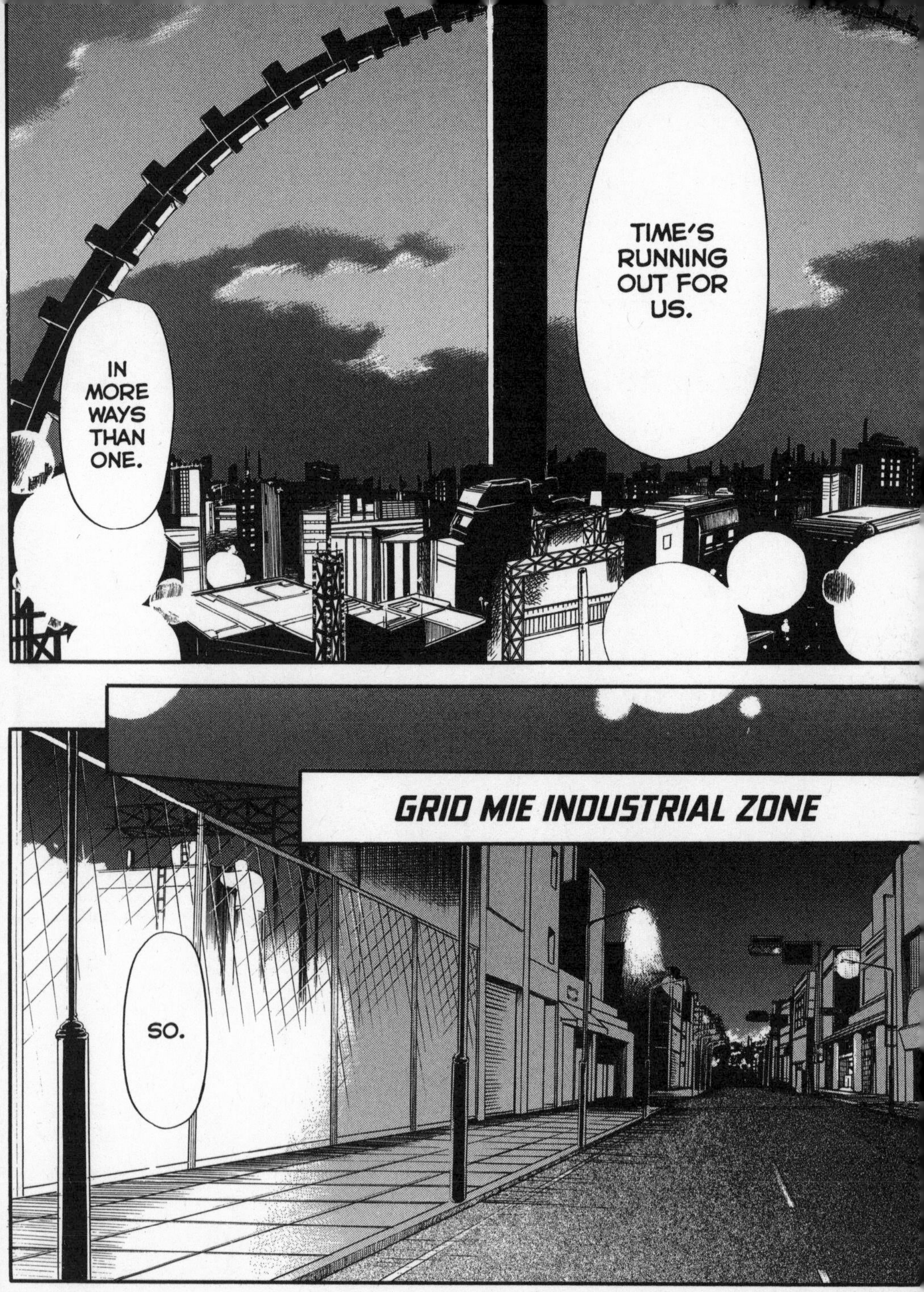
TIME'S RUNNING OUT FOR US.
IN MORE WAYS THAN ONE.
GRID MIE INDUSTRIAL ZONE
SO.

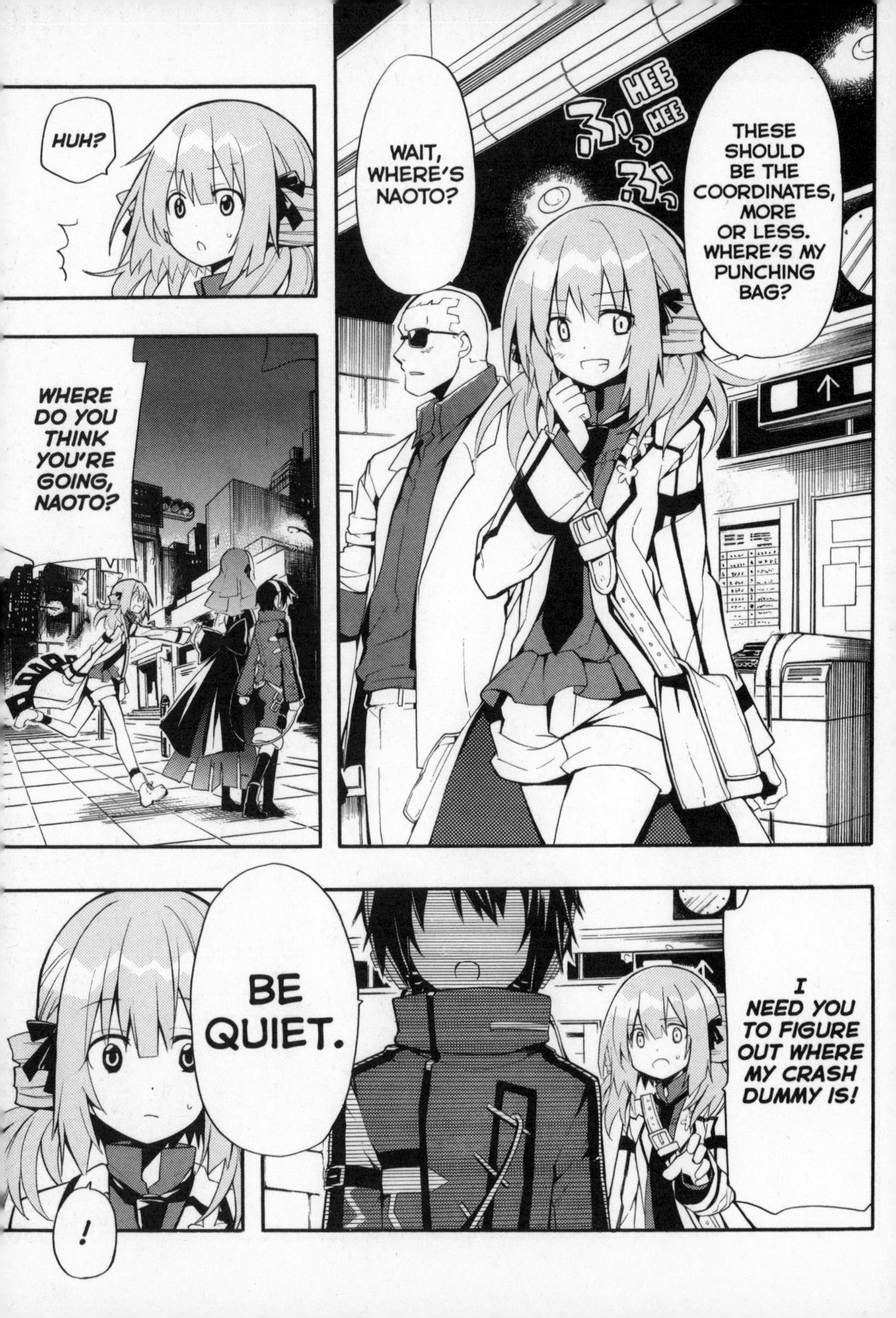
THESE SHOULD BE THE COORDINATES, MORE OR LESS. WHERE'S MY PUNCHING BAG?
HEE HEE
WAIT, WHERE'S NAOTO?
HUH?
WHERE DO YOU THINK YOU'RE GOING, NAOTO?
I NEED YOU TO FIGURE OUT WHERE MY CRASH DUMMY IS!
BE QUIET.
!

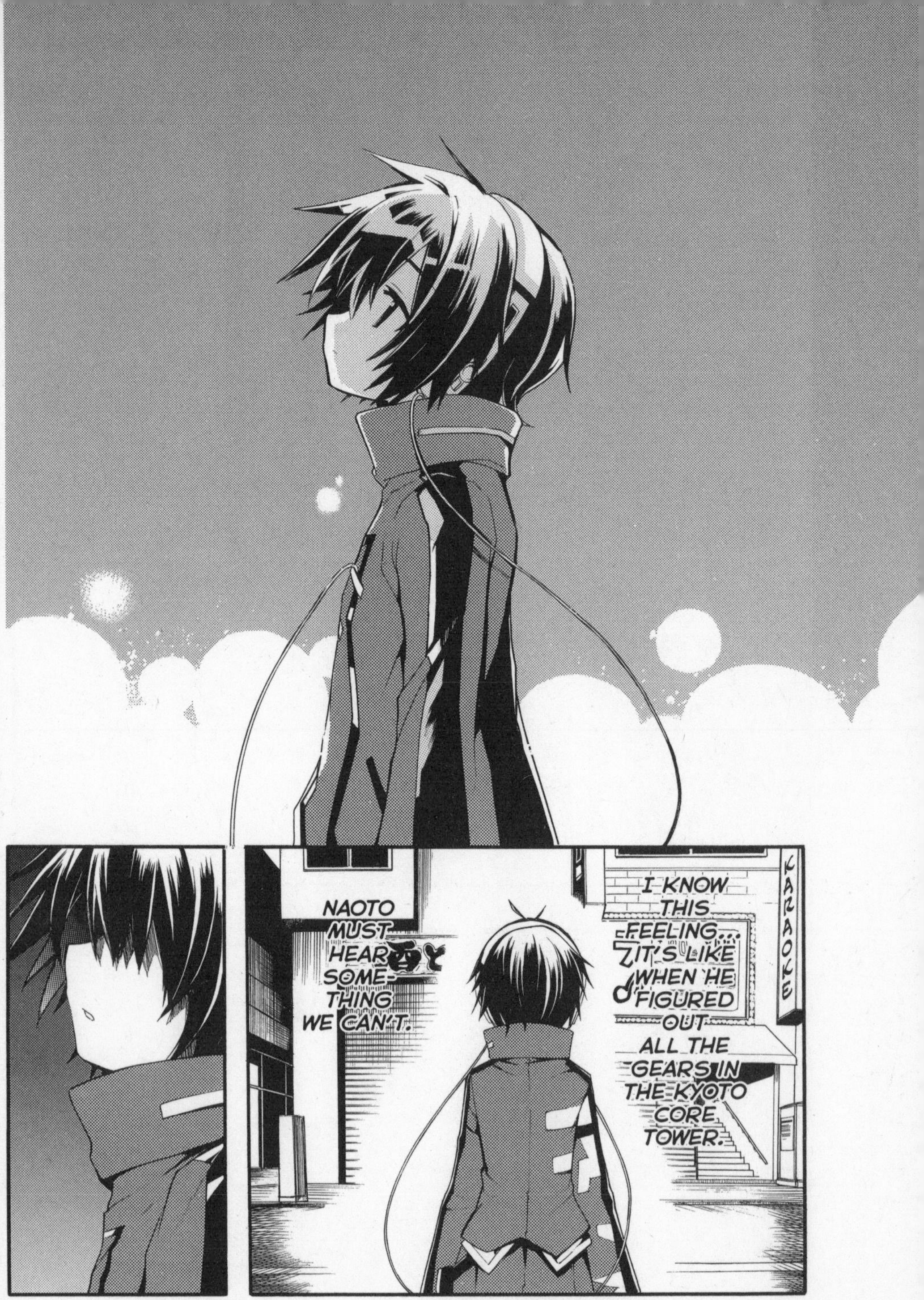
KARAOKE
I KNOW THIS FEELING... IT'S LIKE WHEN HE FIGURED OUT ALL THE GEARS IN THE KYOTO CORE TOWER.
NAOTO MUST HEAR SOMETHING WE CAN'T.

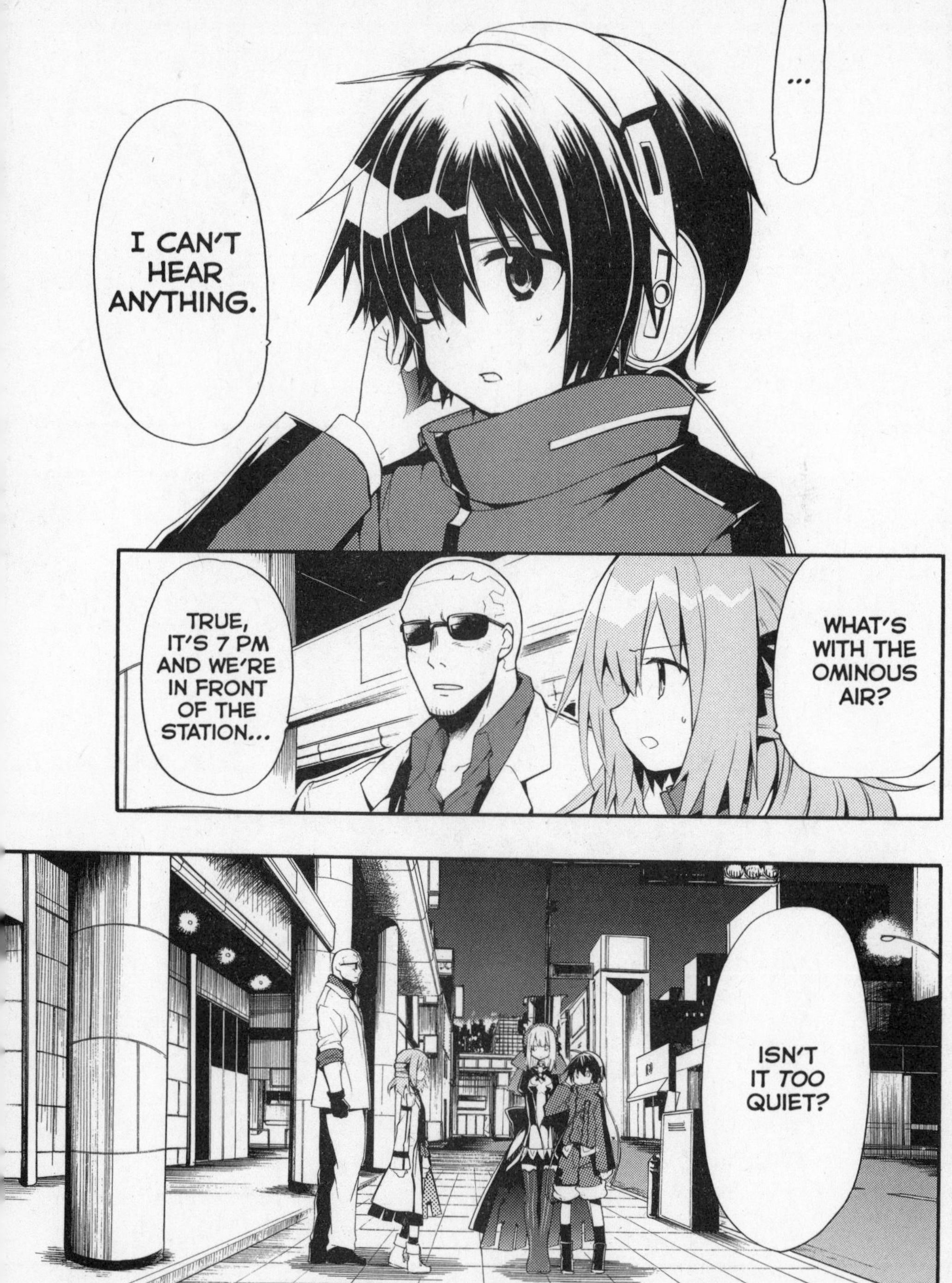
...
I CAN'T HEAR ANYTHING.
WHAT'S WITH THE OMINOUS AIR?
TRUE, IT'S 7 PM AND WE'RE IN FRONT OF THE STATION...
ISN'T IT *TOO* QUIET?

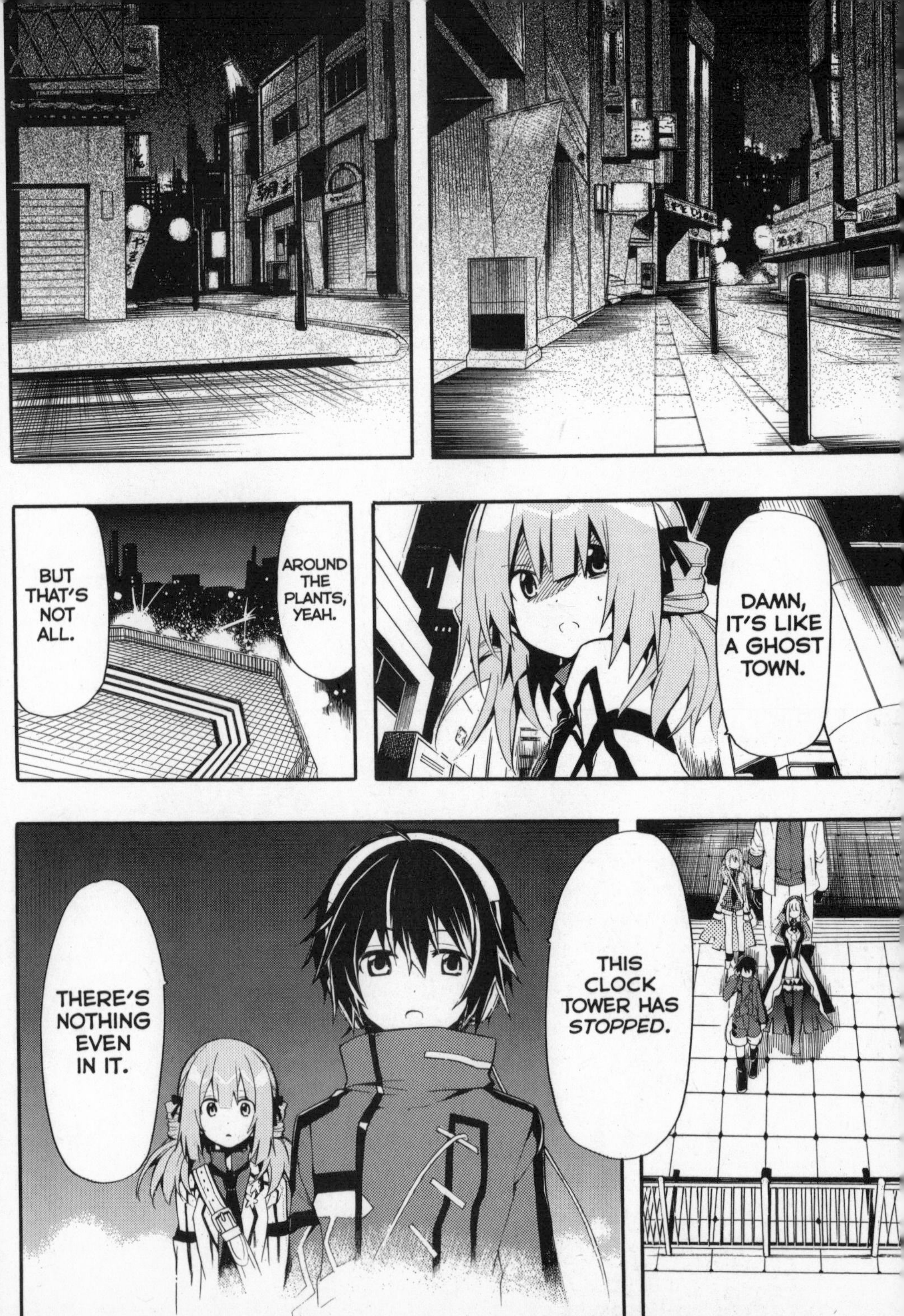
DAMN, IT'S LIKE A GHOST TOWN.
AROUND THE PLANTS, YEAH.
BUT THAT'S NOT ALL.
THIS CLOCK TOWER HAS STOPPED.
THERE'S NOTHING EVEN IN IT.

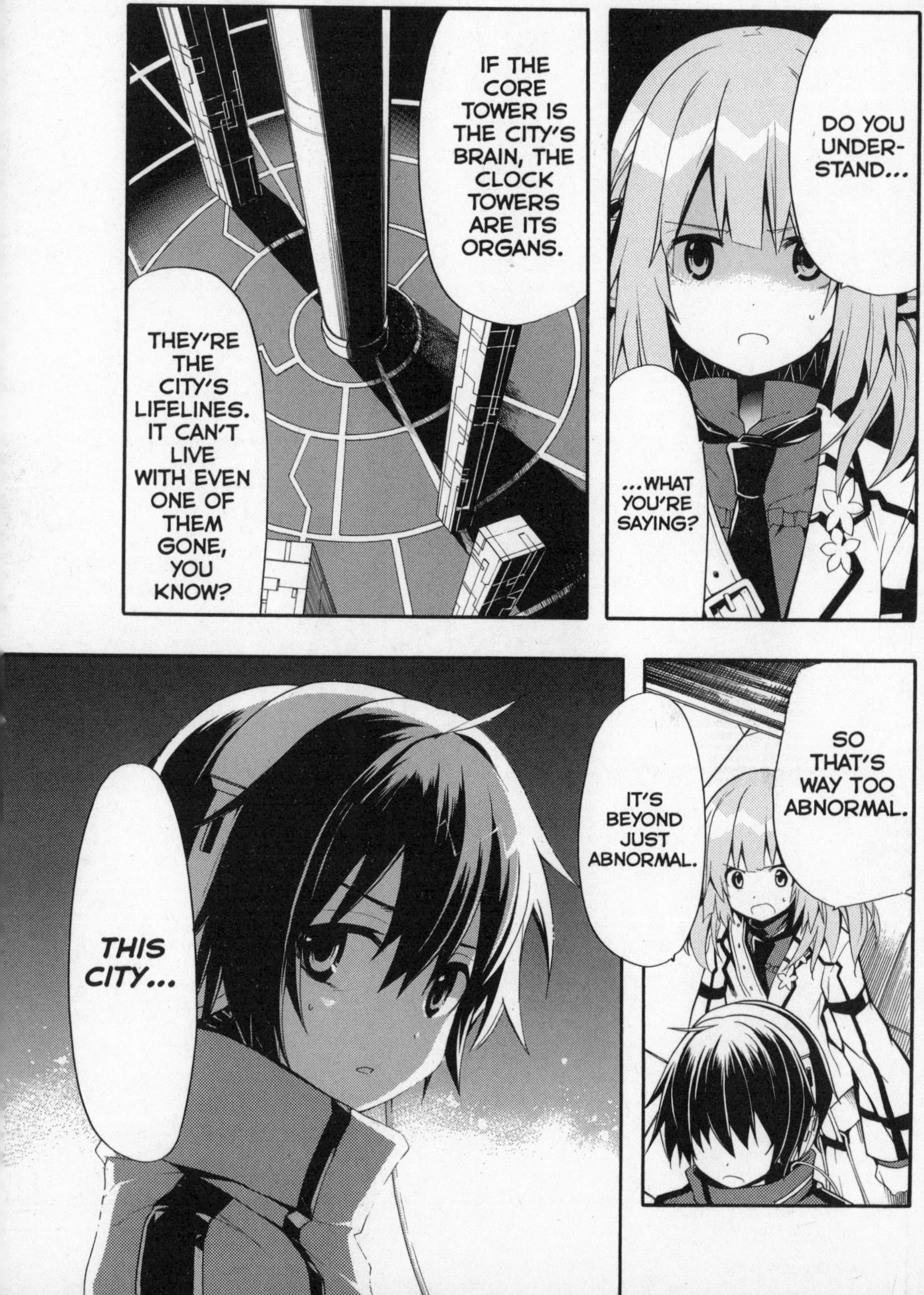
DO YOU UNDERSTAND...
...WHAT YOU'RE SAYING?
IF THE CORE TOWER IS THE CITY'S BRAIN, THE CLOCK TOWERS ARE ITS ORGANS.
THEY'RE THE CITY'S LIFELINES. IT CAN'T LIVE WITH EVEN ONE OF THEM GONE, YOU KNOW?
SO THAT'S WAY TOO ABNORMAL.
IT'S BEYOND JUST ABNORMAL.
THIS CITY...

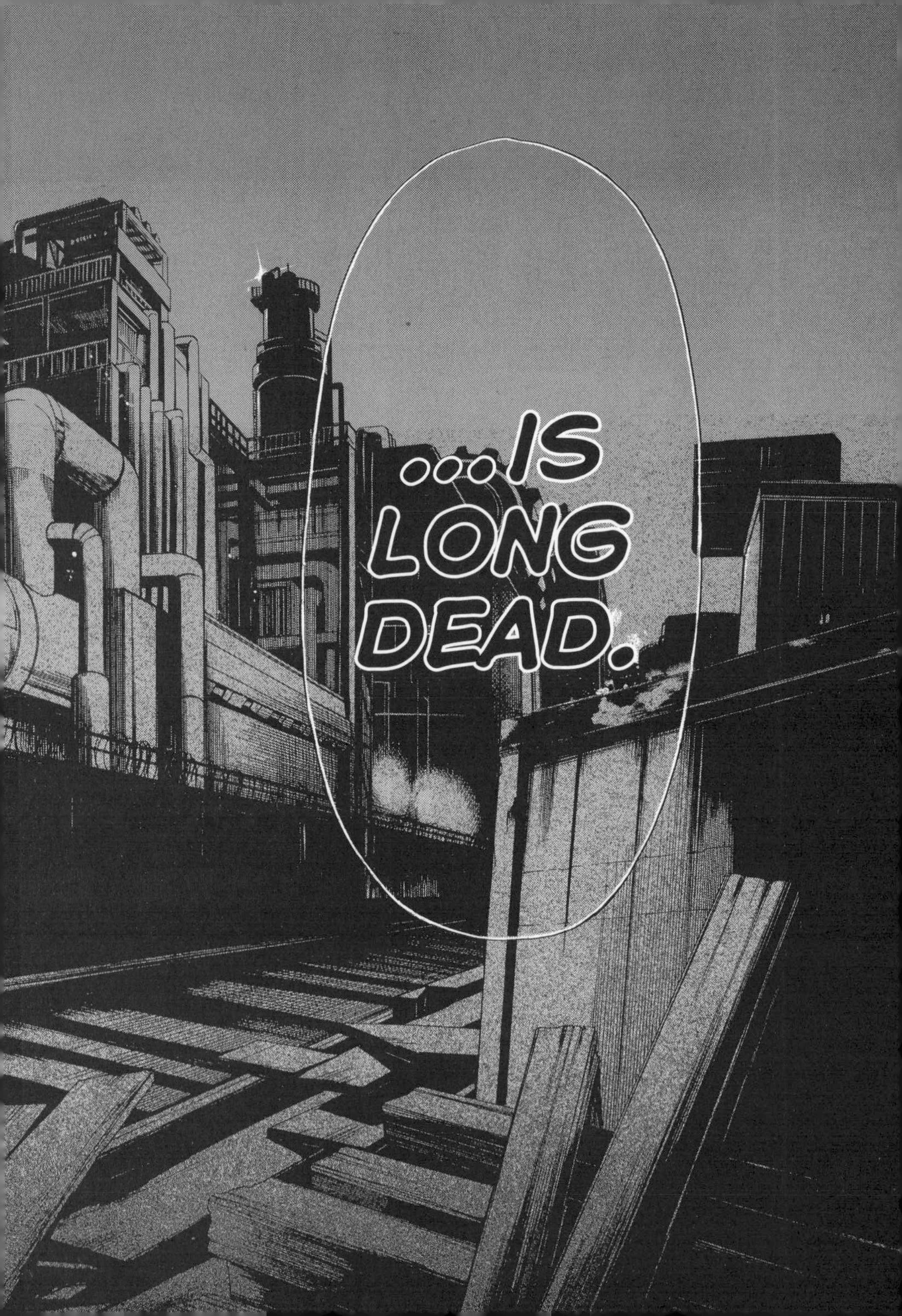
...IS LONG DEAD.

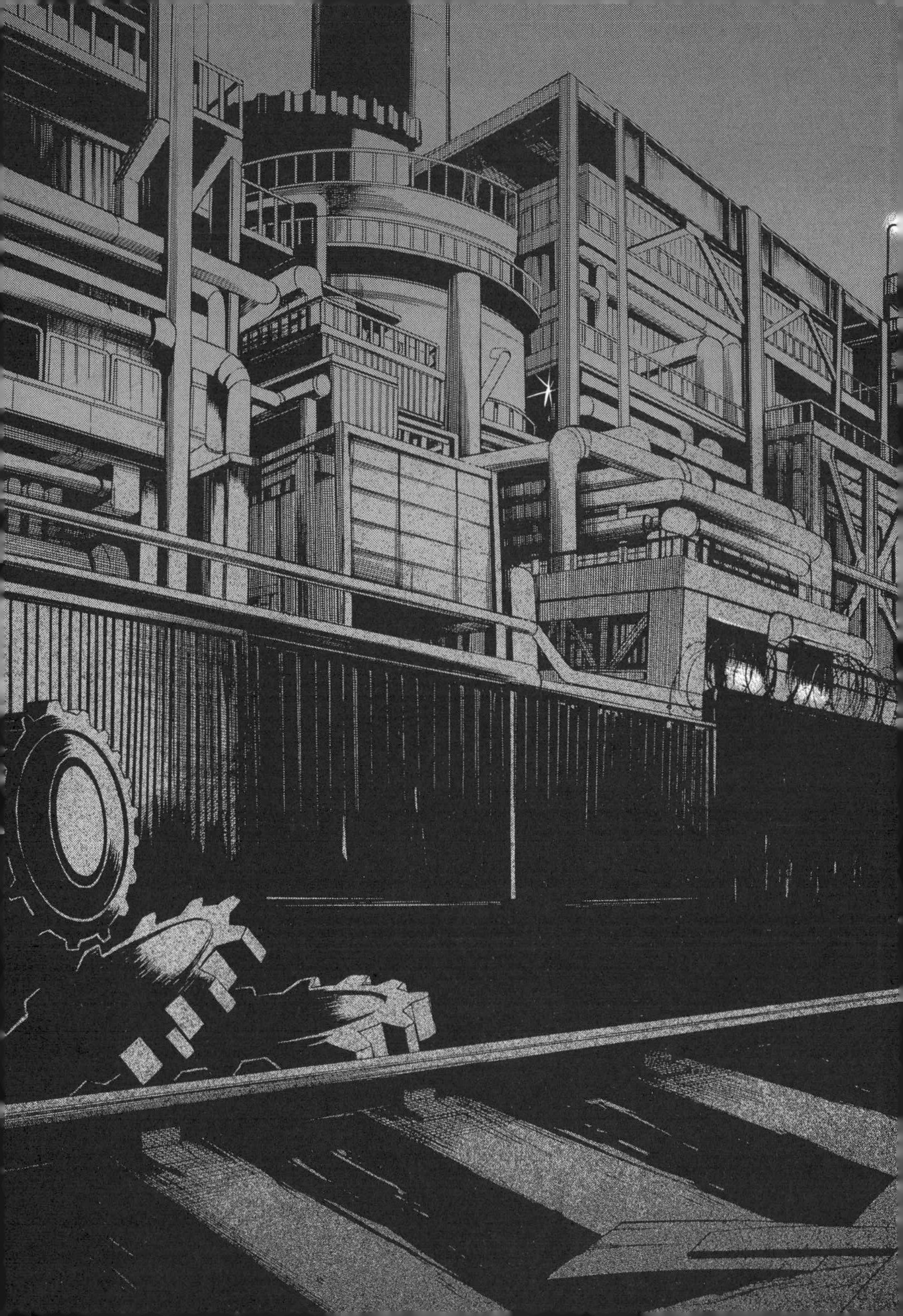

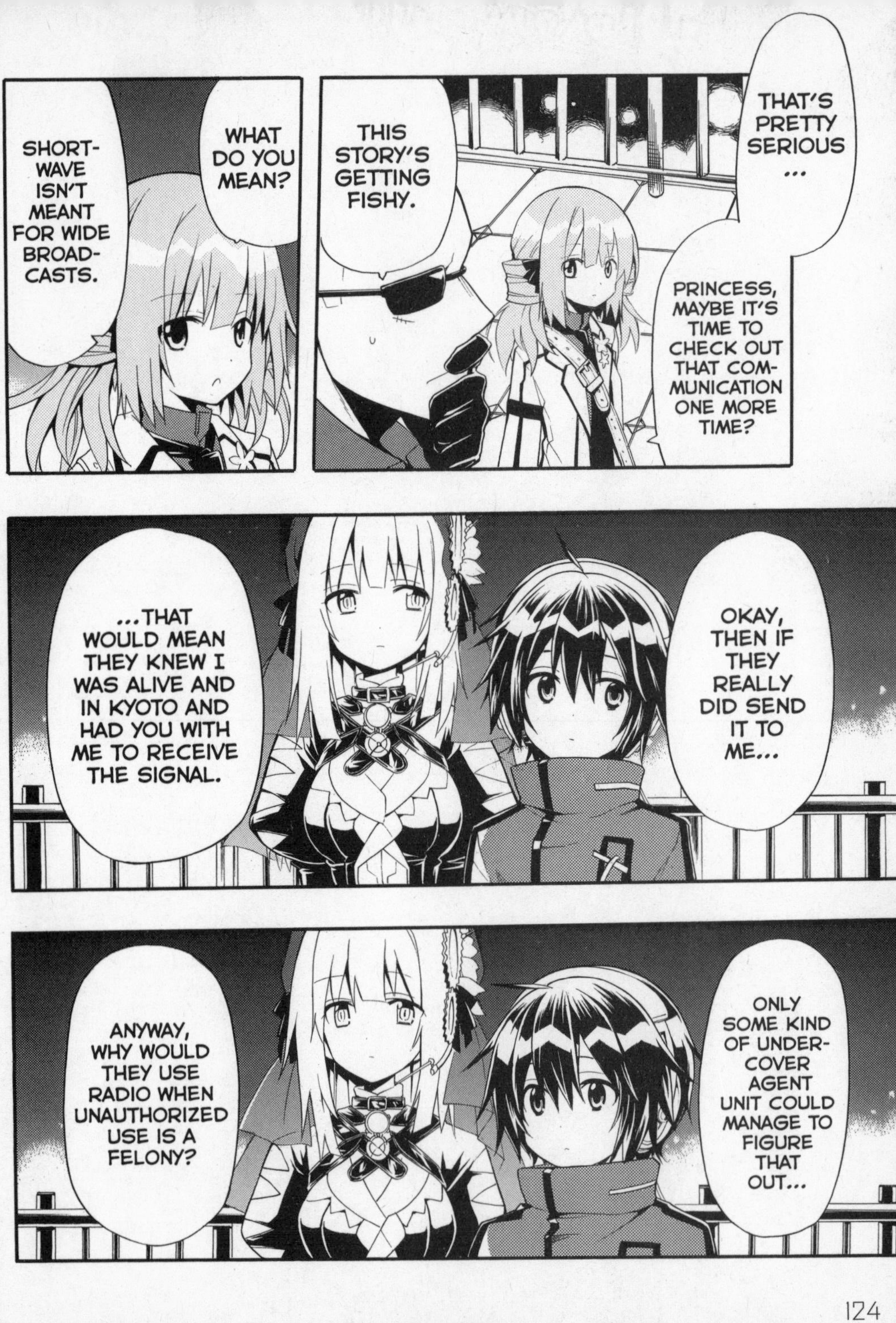
THAT'S PRETTY SERIOUS...
THIS STORY'S GETTING FISHY.
PRINCESS, MAYBE IT'S TIME TO CHECK OUT THAT COMMUNICATION ONE MORE TIME?
WHAT DO YOU MEAN?
SHORT-WAVE ISN'T MEANT FOR WIDE BROAD-CASTS.
OKAY, THEN IF THEY REALLY DID SEND IT TO ME...
...THAT WOULD MEAN THEY KNEW I WAS ALIVE AND IN KYOTO AND HAD YOU WITH ME TO RECEIVE THE SIGNAL.
ONLY SOME KIND OF UNDER-COVER AGENT UNIT COULD MANAGE TO FIGURE THAT OUT...
ANYWAY, WHY WOULD THEY USE RADIO WHEN UNAUTHORIZED USE IS A FELONY?

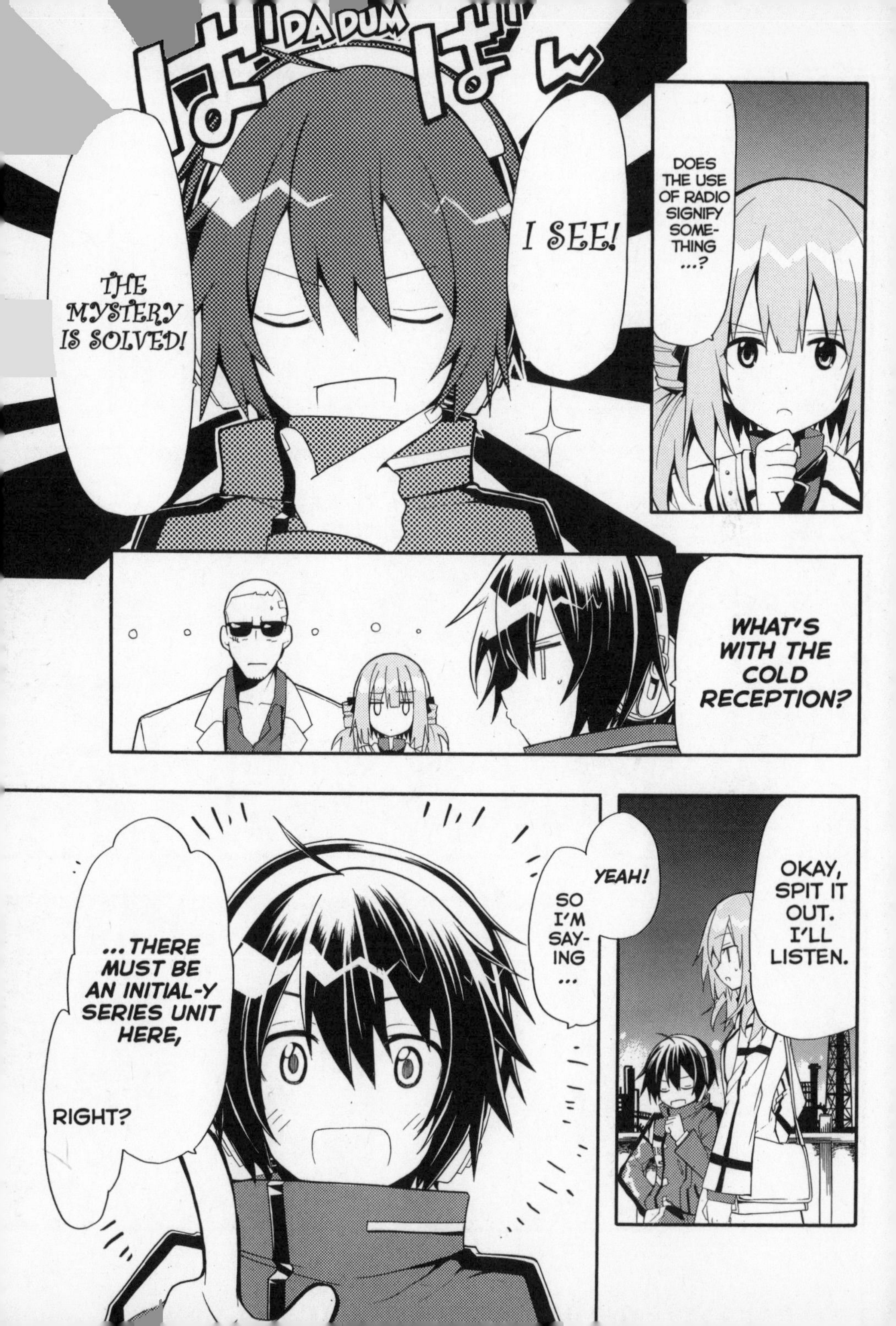
DOES THE USE OF RADIO SIGNIFY SOMETHING...?
DA DUM
I SEE!
THE MYSTERY IS SOLVED!
WHAT'S WITH THE COLD RECEPTION?
OKAY, SPIT IT OUT. I'LL LISTEN.
YEAH!
SO I'M SAYING...
...THERE MUST BE AN INITIAL-Y SERIES UNIT HERE,
RIGHT?

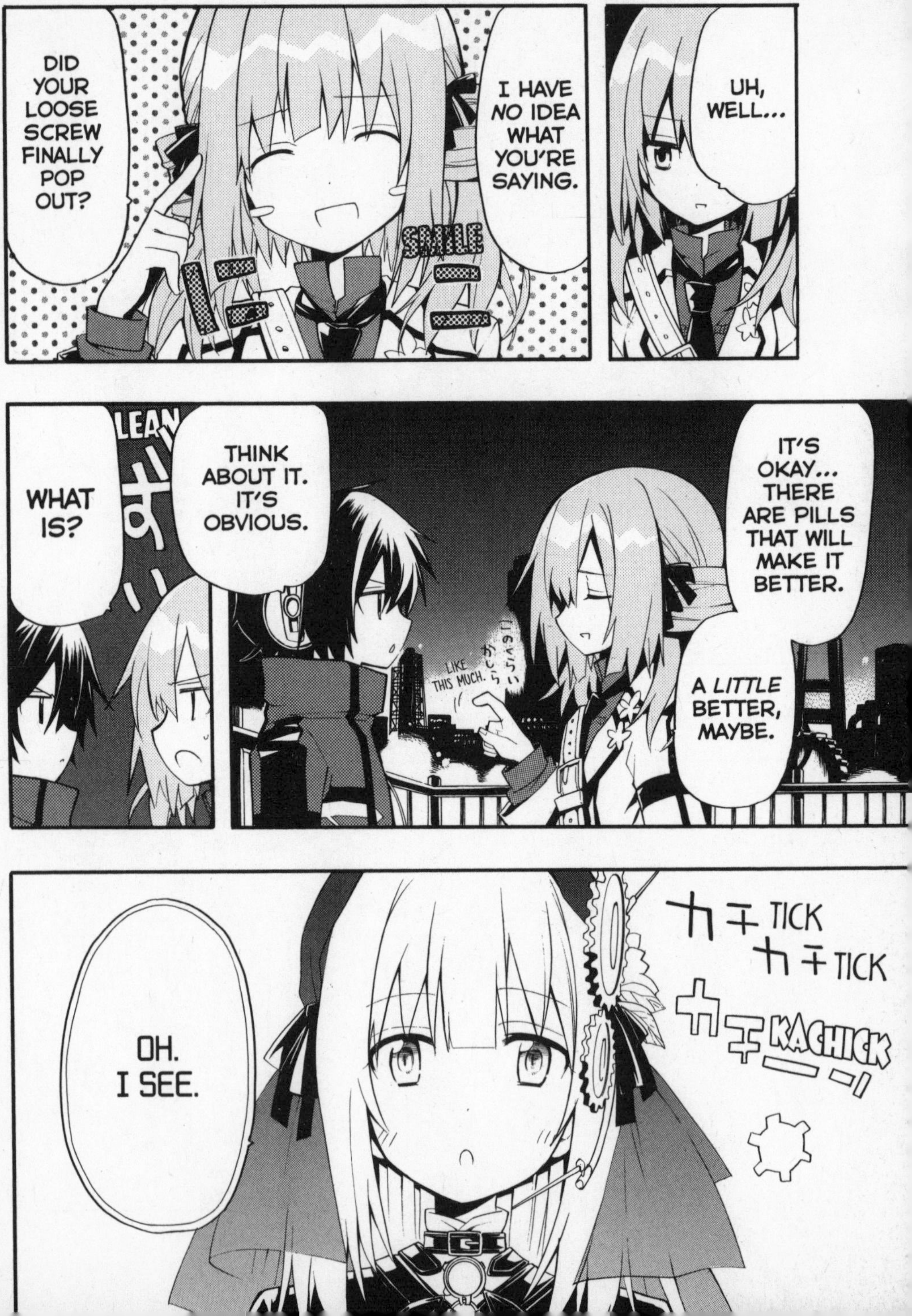
UH, WELL...
I HAVE *NO* IDEA WHAT YOU'RE SAYING.
SMILE
DID YOUR LOOSE SCREW FINALLY POP OUT?
IT'S OKAY... THERE ARE PILLS THAT WILL MAKE IT BETTER.
A *LITTLE* BETTER, MAYBE.
LIKE THIS MUCH.
THINK ABOUT IT. IT'S OBVIOUS.
LEAN
WHAT IS?
カチ TICK
カチ TICK
カチーーッ KACHICK
OH. I SEE.

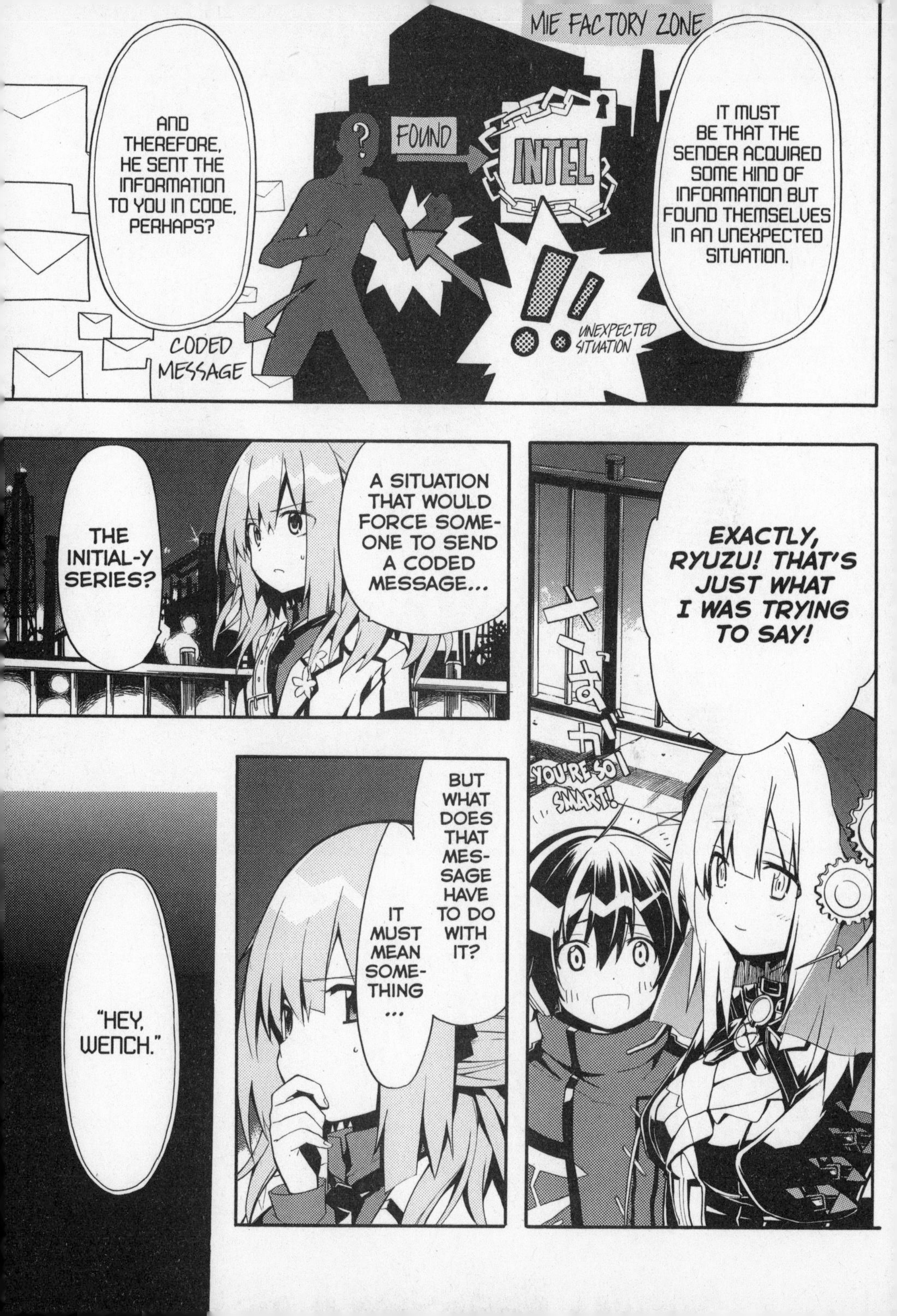
MIE FACTORY ZONE
IT MUST BE THAT THE SENDER ACQUIRED SOME KIND OF INFORMATION BUT FOUND THEMSELVES IN AN UNEXPECTED SITUATION.
INTEL
FOUND
UNEXPECTED SITUATION
AND THEREFORE, HE SENT THE INFORMATION TO YOU IN CODE, PERHAPS?
CODED MESSAGE
EXACTLY, RYUZU! THAT'S JUST WHAT I WAS TRYING TO SAY!
YOU'RE SO! SMART!
A SITUATION THAT WOULD FORCE SOME-ONE TO SEND A CODED MESSAGE...
THE INITIAL-Y SERIES?
BUT WHAT DOES THAT MES-SAGE HAVE TO DO WITH IT?
IT MUST MEAN SOME-THING...
"HEY, WENCH."

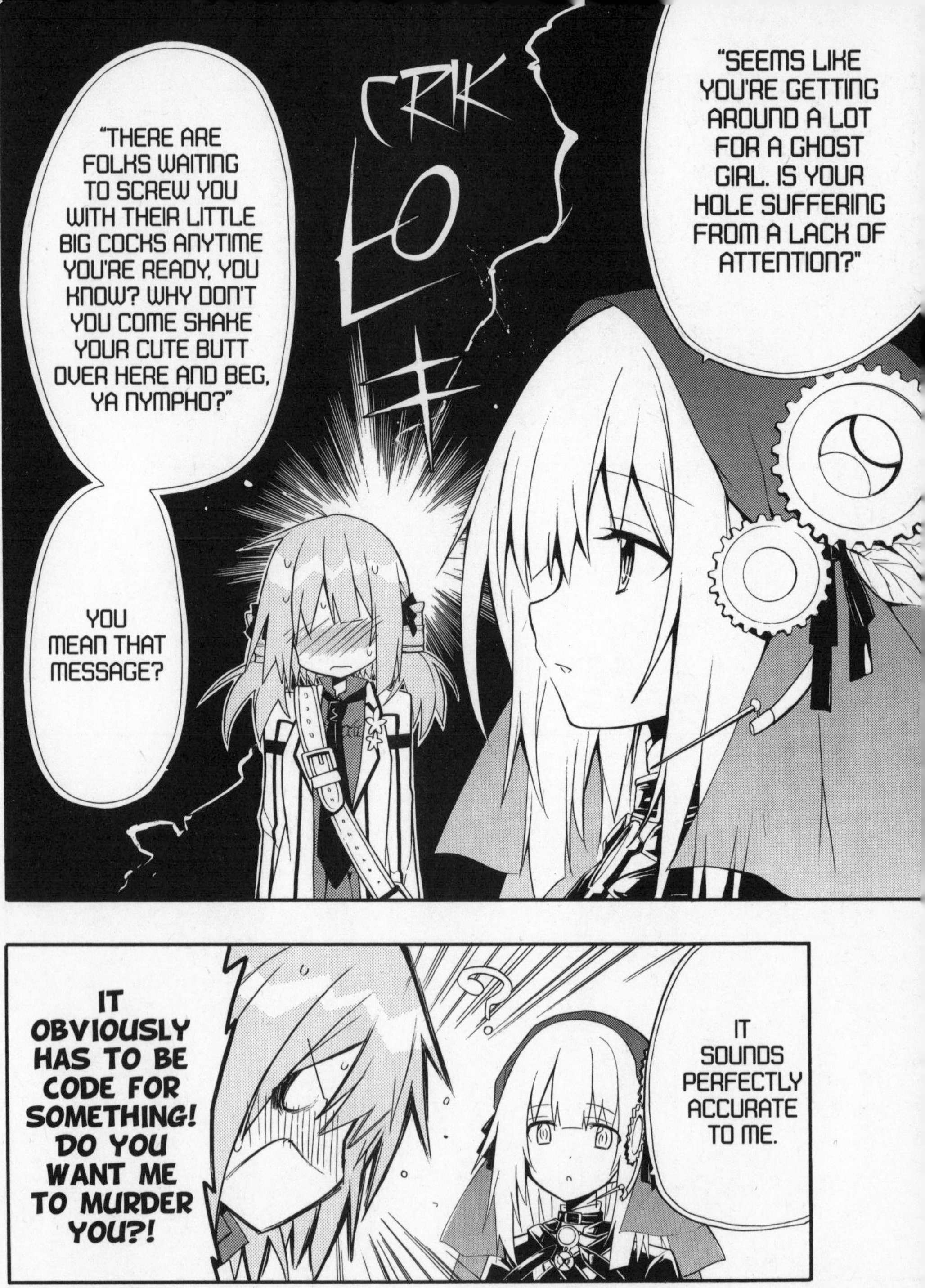
"SEEMS LIKE YOU'RE GETTING AROUND A LOT FOR A GHOST GIRL. IS YOUR HOLE SUFFERING FROM A LACK OF ATTENTION?"
"THERE ARE FOLKS WAITING TO SCREW YOU WITH THEIR LITTLE BIG COCKS ANYTIME YOU'RE READY, YOU KNOW? WHY DON'T YOU COME SHAKE YOUR CUTE BUTT OVER HERE AND BEG, YA NYMPHO?"
CRIK
YOU MEAN THAT MESSAGE?
IT SOUNDS PERFECTLY ACCURATE TO ME.
IT OBVIOUSLY HAS TO BE CODE FOR SOMETHING! DO YOU WANT ME TO MURDER YOU?!

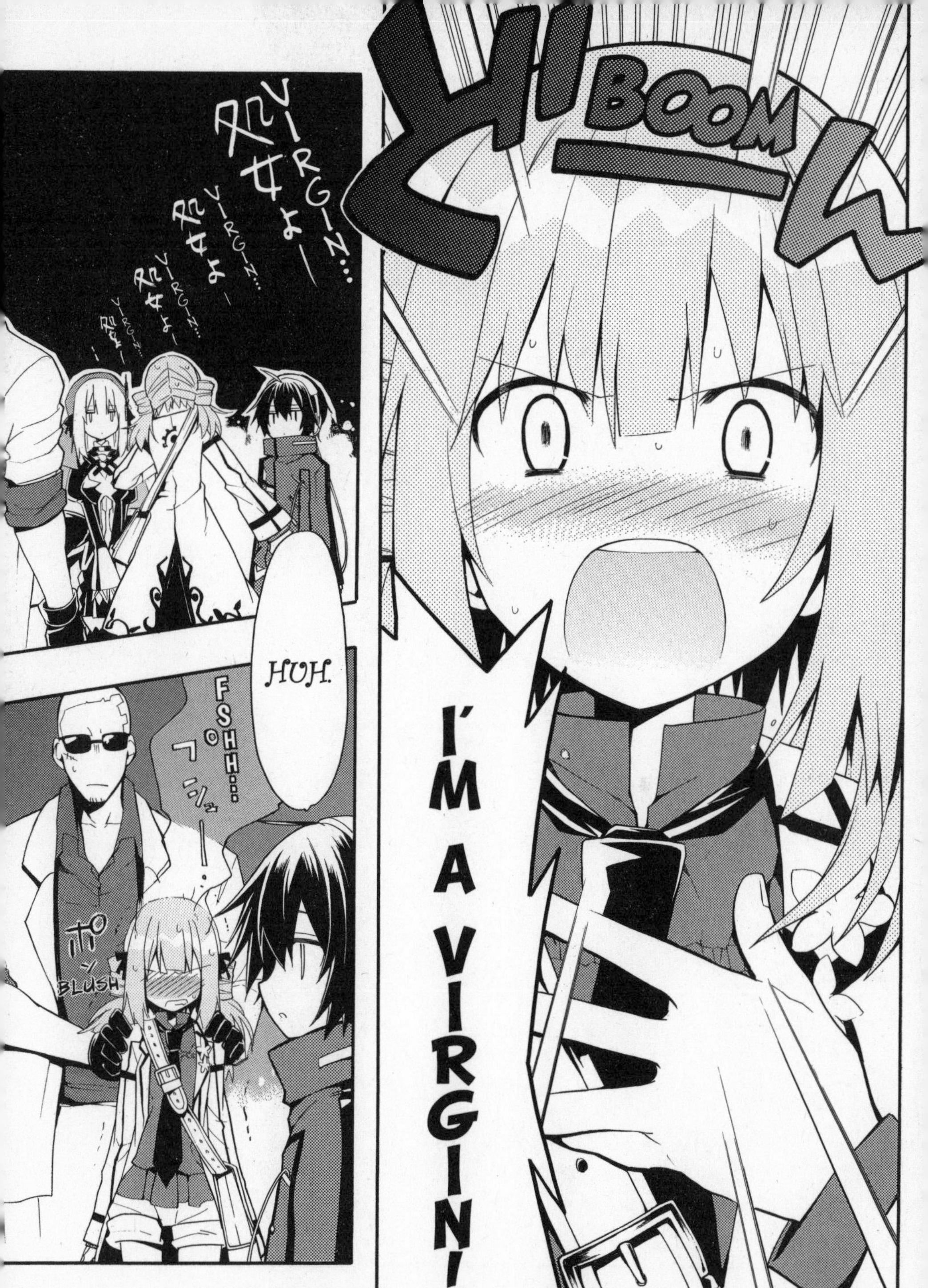
BOOM
I'M A VIRGIN!
VIRGIN...
VIRGIN...
VIRGIN...
VIRGIN...
HUH.
FSHH...
BLUSH

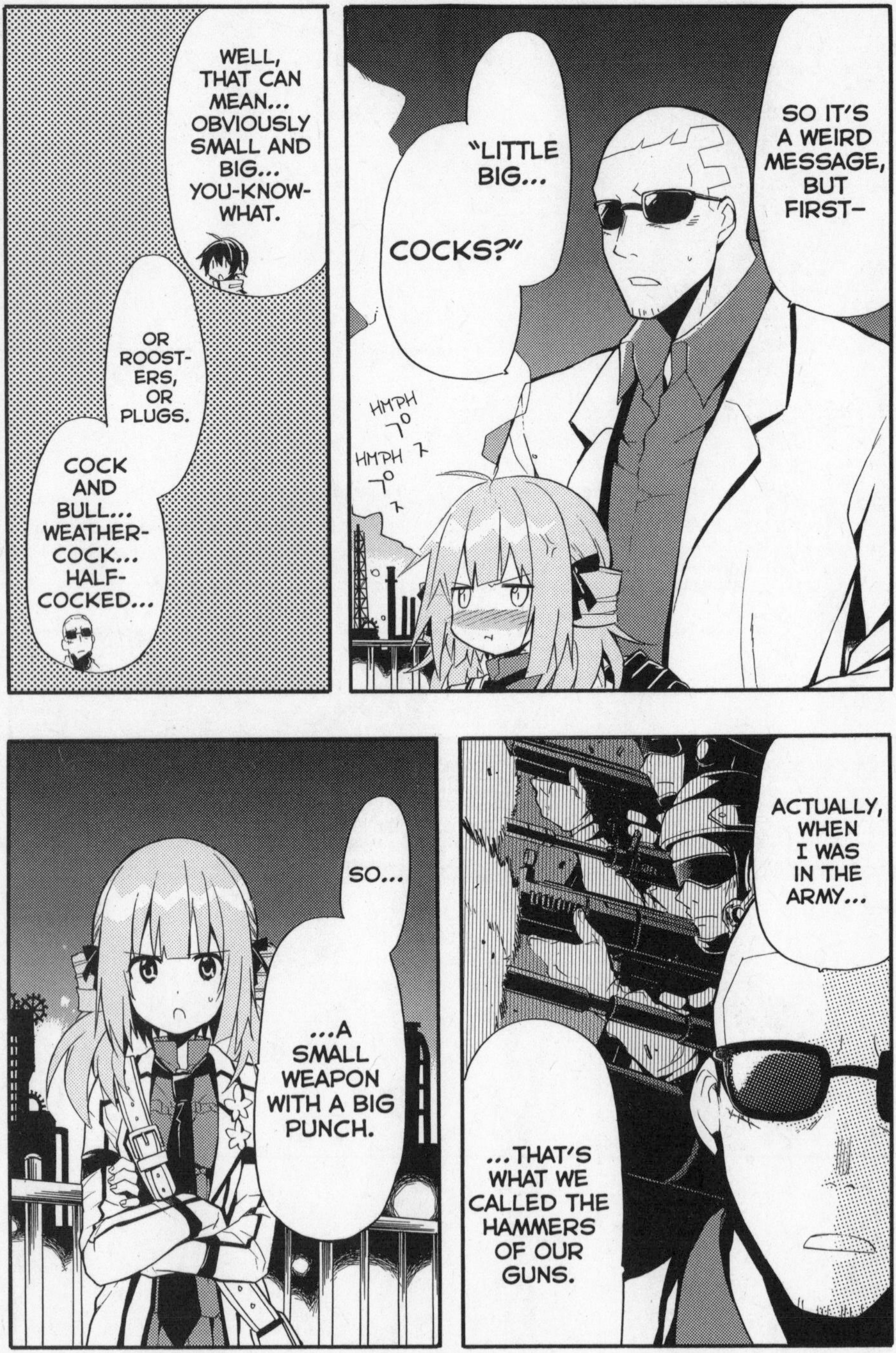
SO IT'S A WEIRD MESSAGE, BUT FIRST–
"LITTLE BIG... COCKS?"
HMPH HMPH
WELL, THAT CAN MEAN... OBVIOUSLY SMALL AND BIG... YOU-KNOW-WHAT.
OR ROOSTERS, OR PLUGS.
COCK AND BULL... WEATHERCOCK... HALF-COCKED...
ACTUALLY, WHEN I WAS IN THE ARMY...
...THAT'S WHAT WE CALLED THE HAMMERS OF OUR GUNS.
SO...
...A SMALL WEAPON WITH A BIG PUNCH.

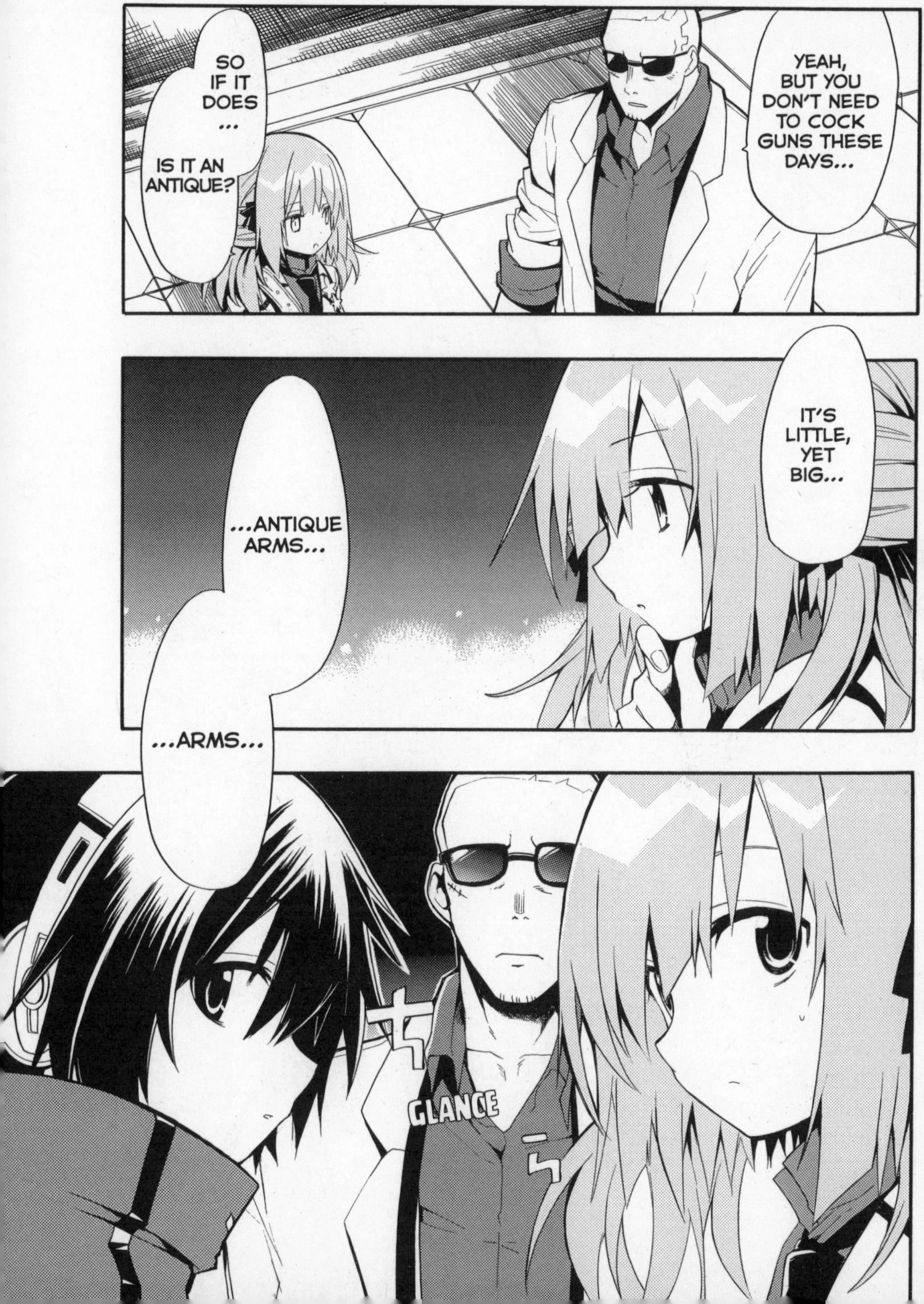
YEAH, BUT YOU DON'T NEED TO COCK GUNS THESE DAYS...
SO IF IT DOES ... IS IT AN ANTIQUE?
IT'S LITTLE, YET BIG...
...ANTIQUE ARMS...
...ARMS...
GLANCE

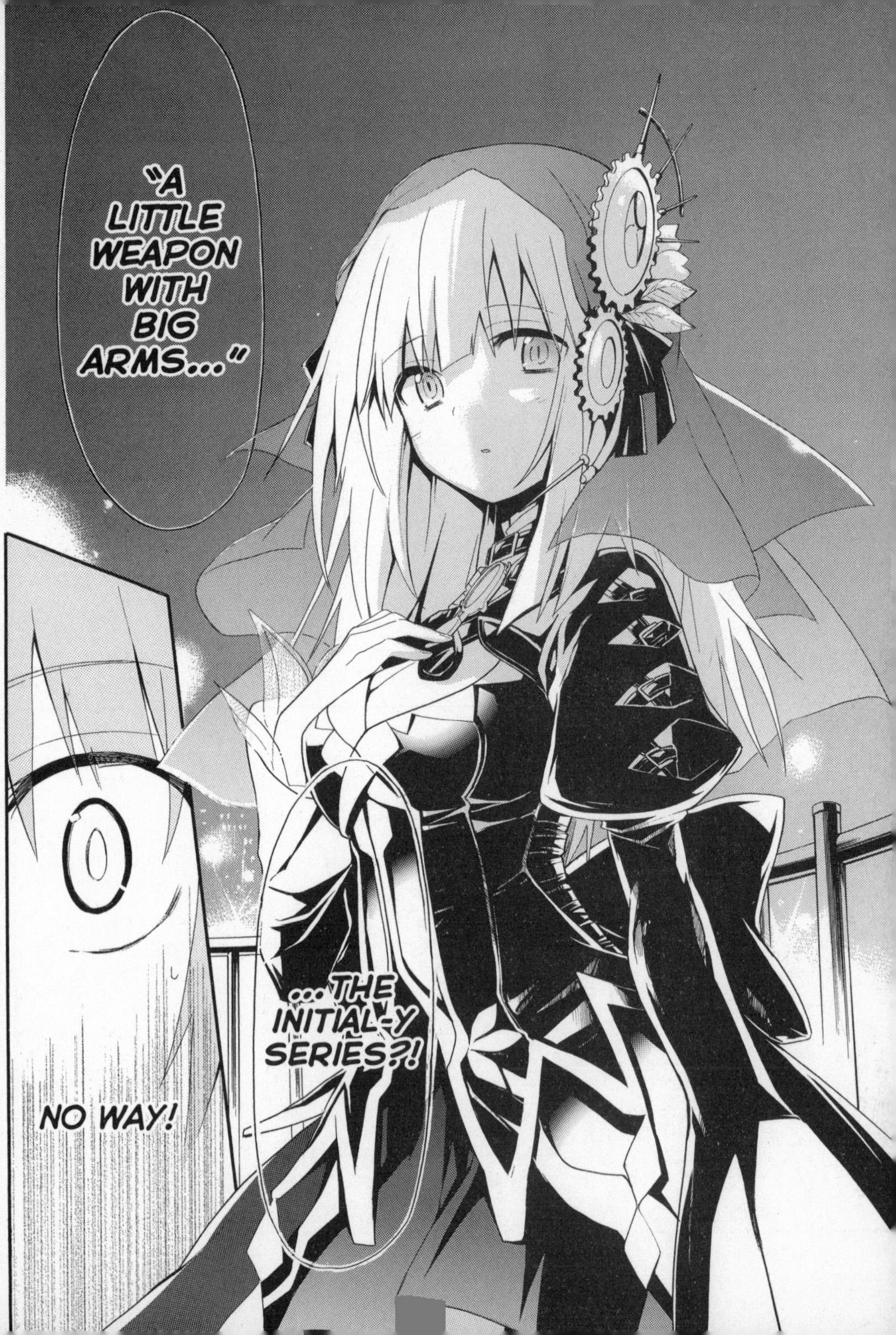
"A LITTLE WEAPON WITH BIG ARMS..."
...THE INITIAL-Y SERIES?!
NO WAY!

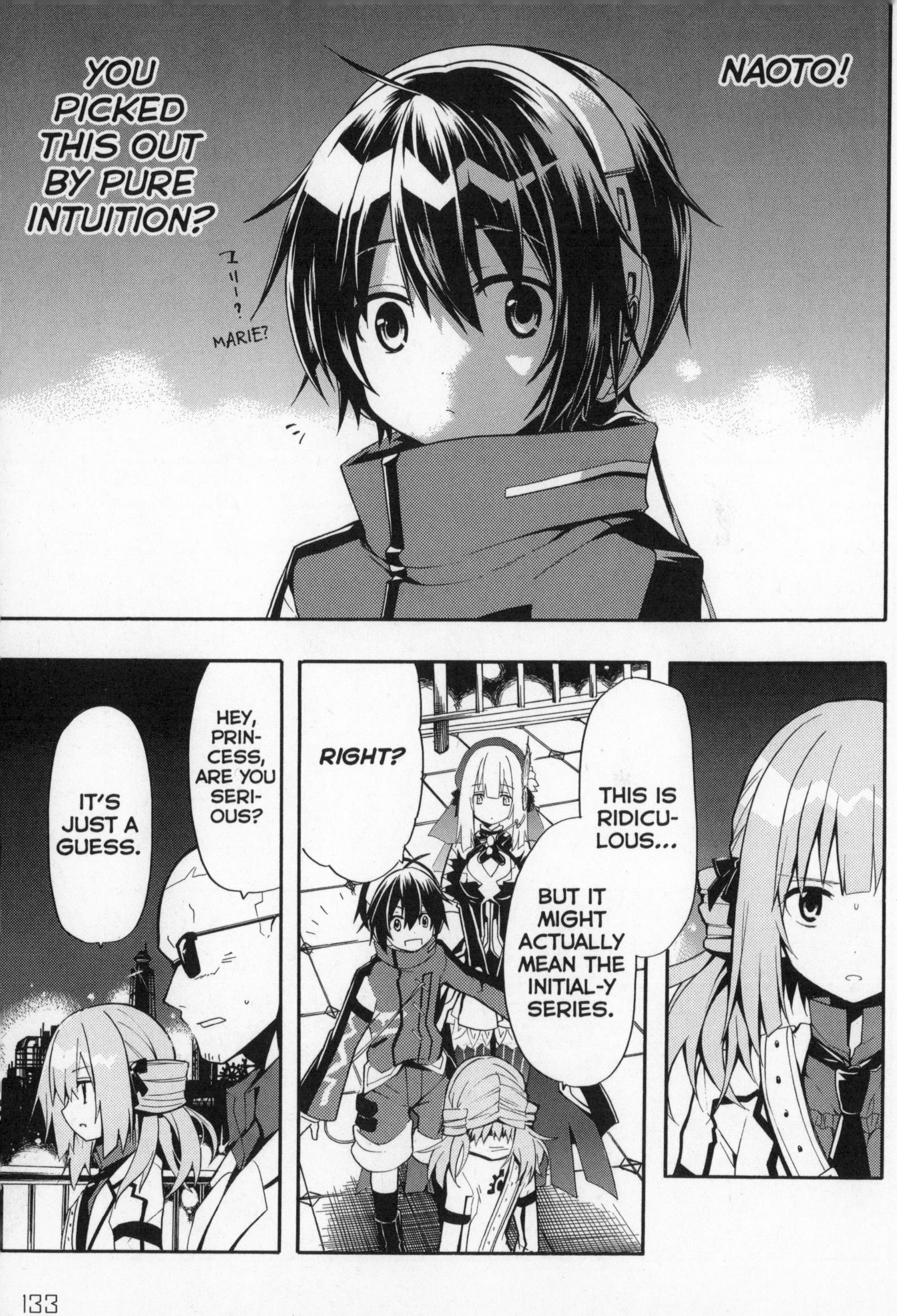
NAOTO!
YOU PICKED THIS OUT BY PURE INTUITION?
MARIE?
THIS IS RIDICULOUS...
BUT IT MIGHT ACTUALLY MEAN THE INITIAL-Y SERIES.
RIGHT?
HEY, PRINCESS, ARE YOU SERIOUS?
IT'S JUST A GUESS.

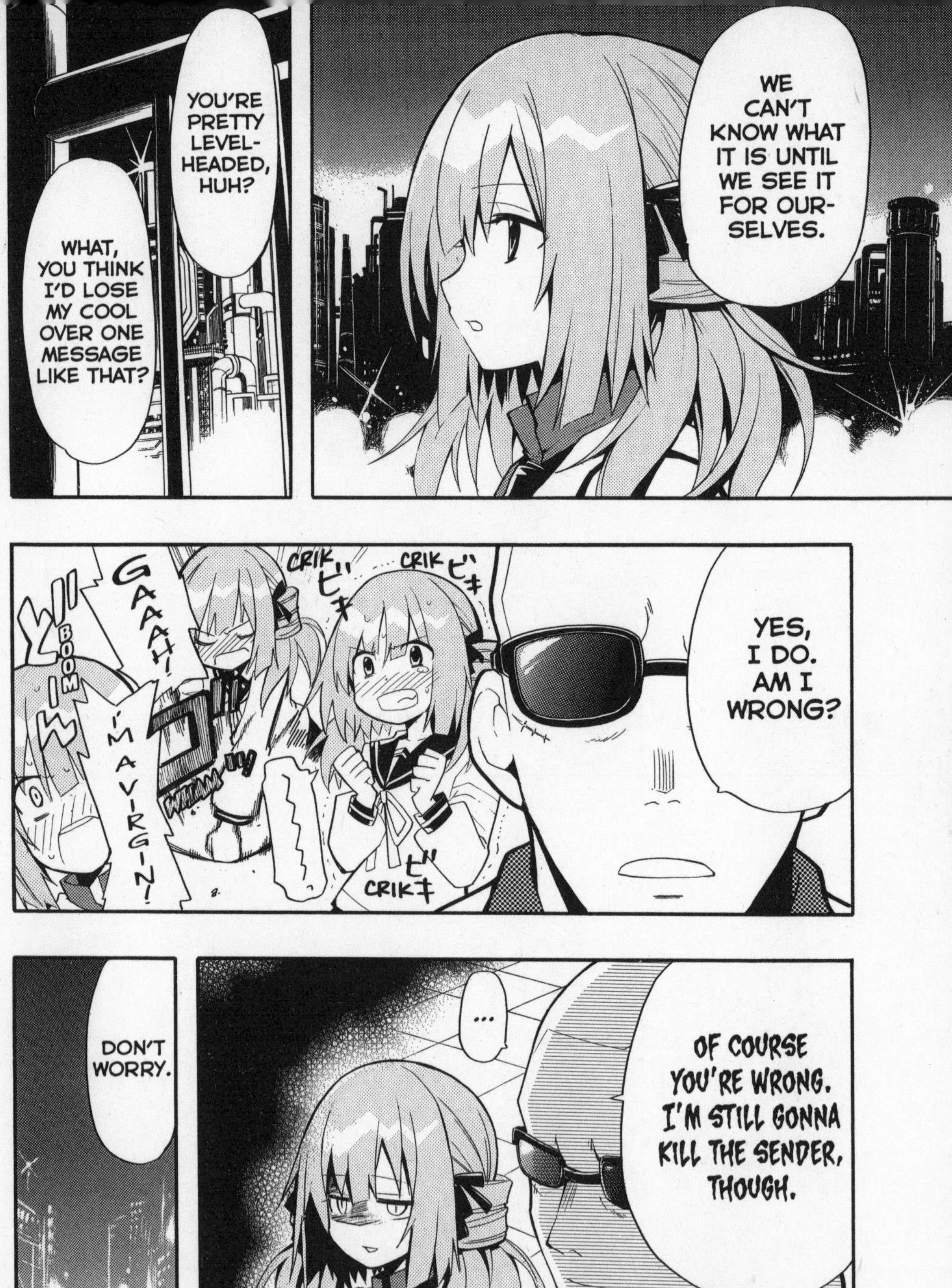
WE CAN'T KNOW WHAT IT IS UNTIL WE SEE IT FOR OURSELVES.
YOU'RE PRETTY LEVEL-HEADED, HUH?
WHAT, YOU THINK I'D LOSE MY COOL OVER ONE MESSAGE LIKE THAT?
YES, I DO. AM I WRONG?
CRIK
CRIK
GAAAH!
I'M A VIRGIN!
BOOM
CRIK
...
OF COURSE YOU'RE WRONG. I'M STILL GONNA KILL THE SENDER, THOUGH.
DON'T WORRY.

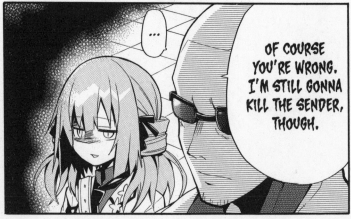

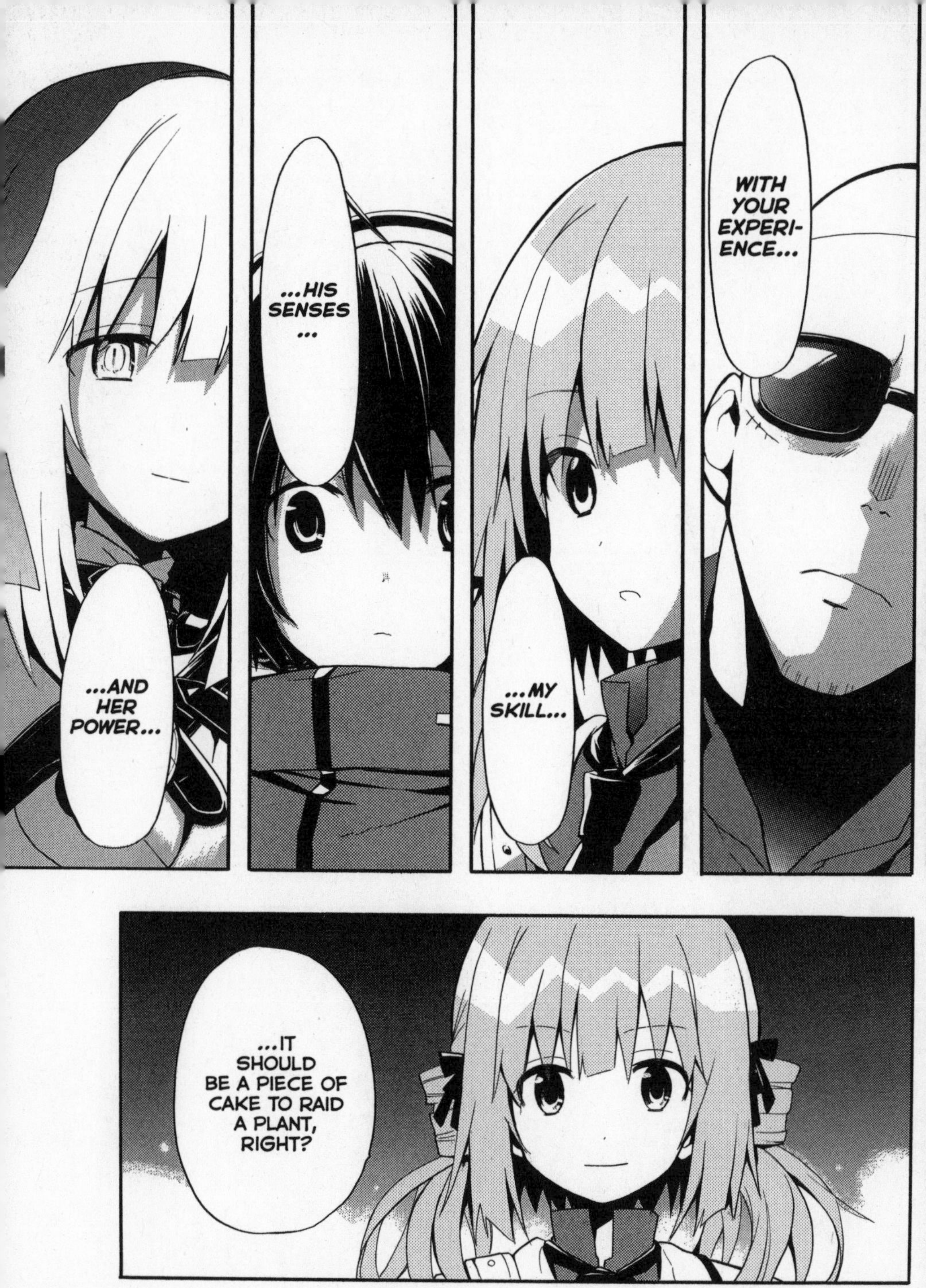
WITH YOUR EXPERI- ENCE...
...MY SKILL...
...HIS SENSES ...
...AND HER POWER...
...IT SHOULD BE A PIECE OF CAKE TO RAID A PLANT, RIGHT?

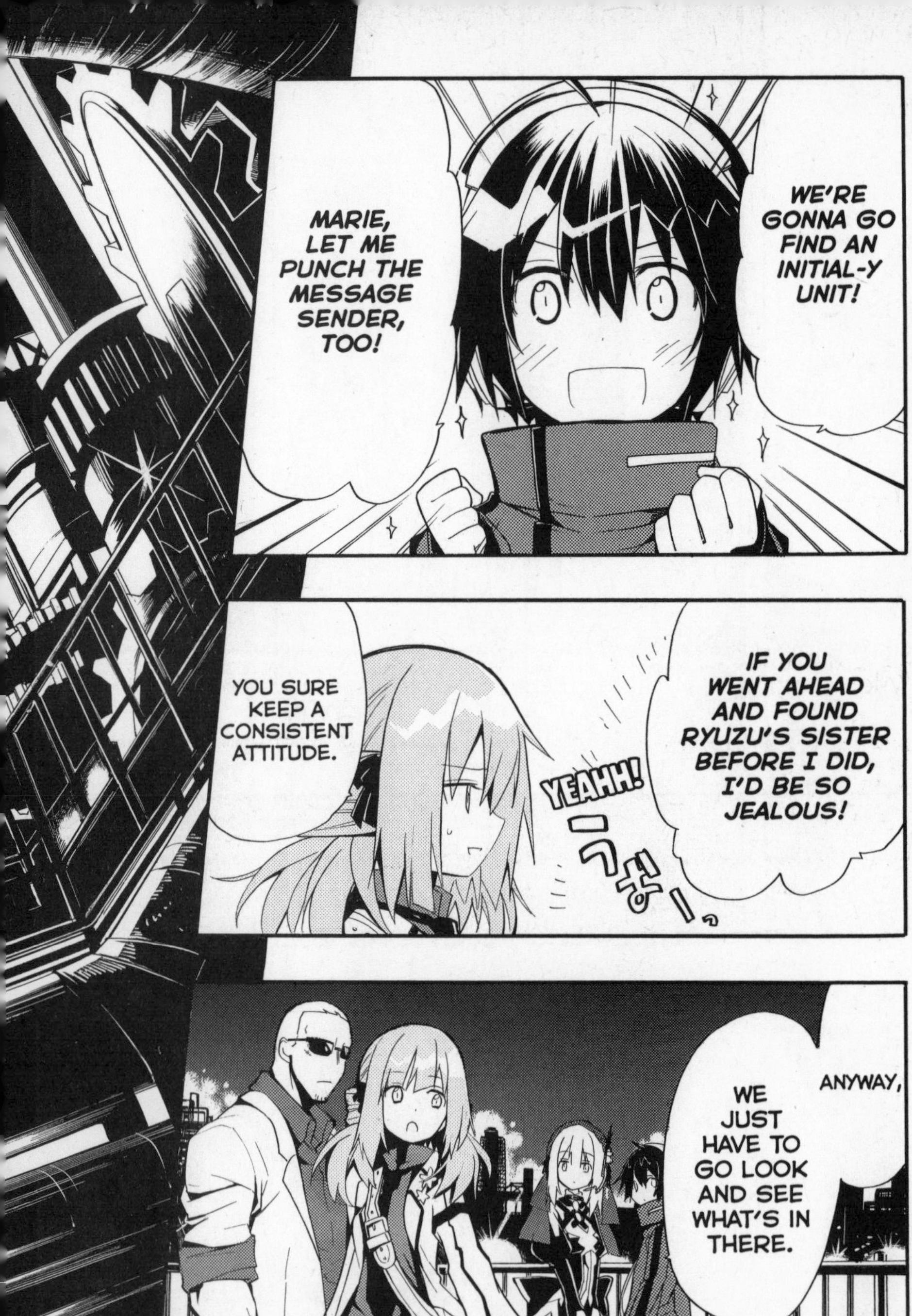
WE'RE GONNA GO FIND AN INITIAL-Y UNIT!
MARIE, LET ME PUNCH THE MESSAGE SENDER, TOO!
IF YOU WENT AHEAD AND FOUND RYUZU'S SISTER BEFORE I DID, I'D BE SO JEALOUS!
YEAHH!
YOU SURE KEEP A CONSISTENT ATTITUDE.
ANYWAY,
WE JUST HAVE TO GO LOOK AND SEE WHAT'S IN THERE.

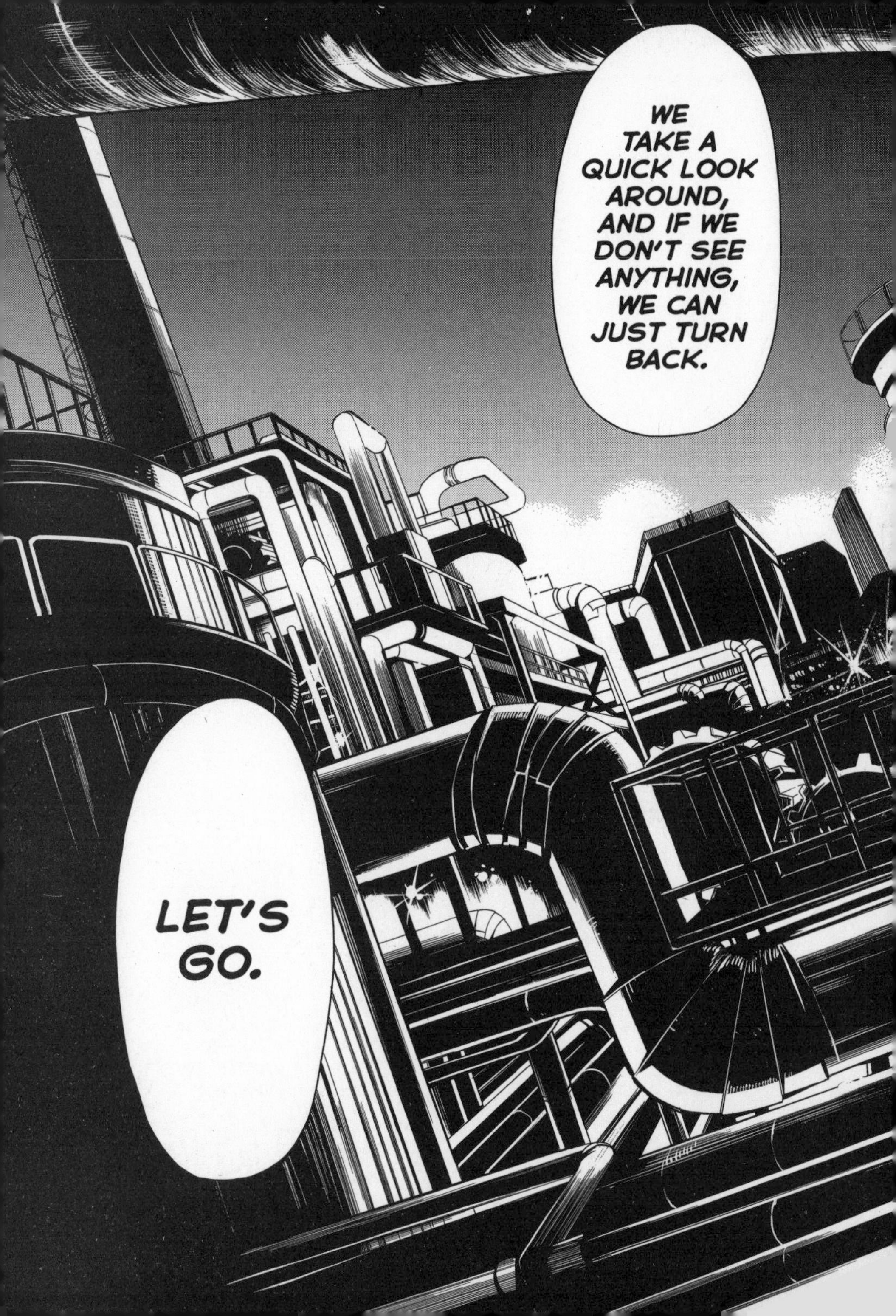
WE TAKE A QUICK LOOK AROUND, AND IF WE DON'T SEE ANYTHING, WE CAN JUST TURN BACK.
LET'S GO.

Clockwork Planet

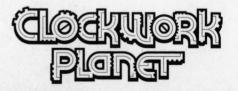

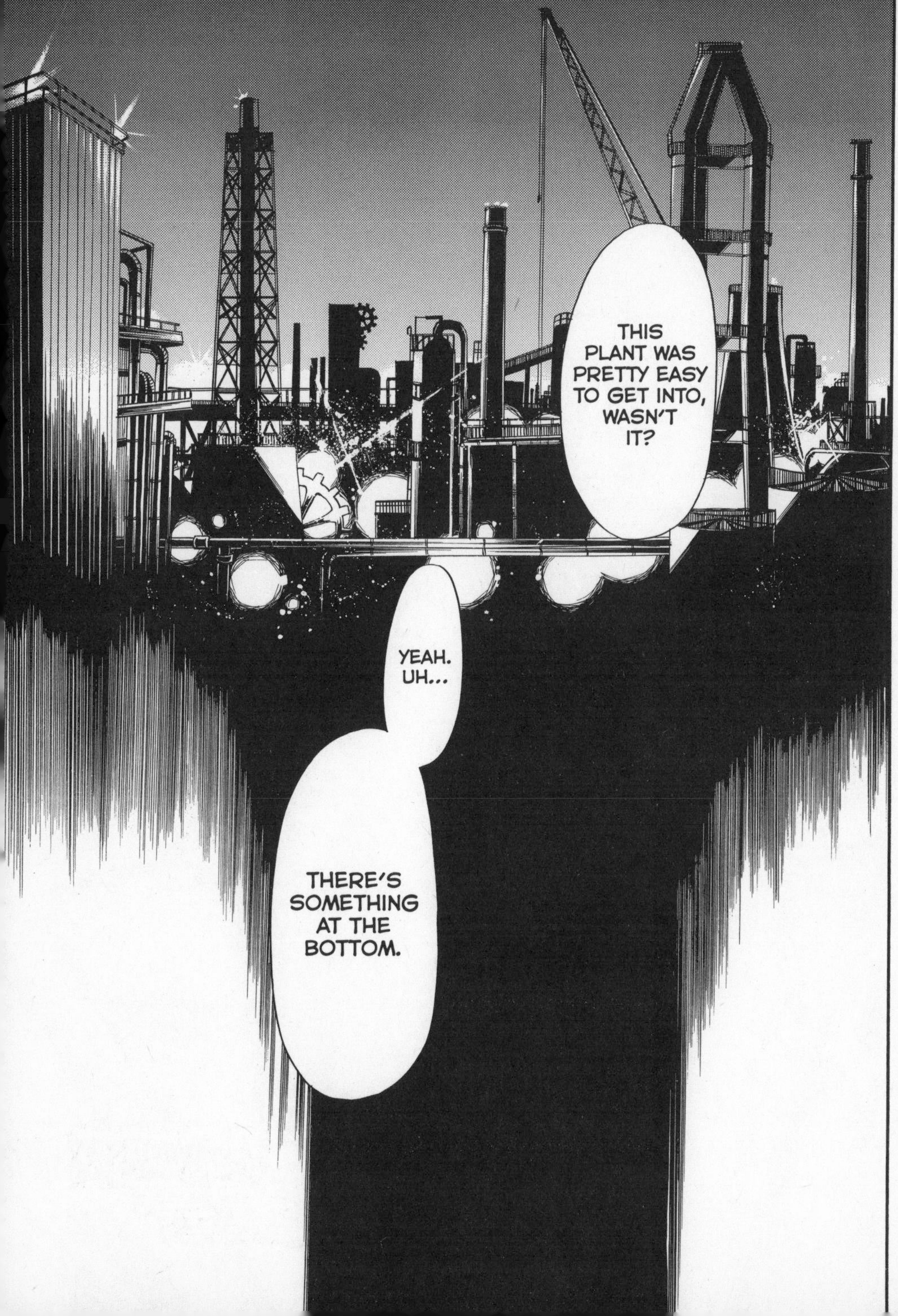
THIS PLANT WAS PRETTY EASY TO GET INTO, WASN'T IT?
YEAH. UH...
THERE'S SOMETHING AT THE BOTTOM.

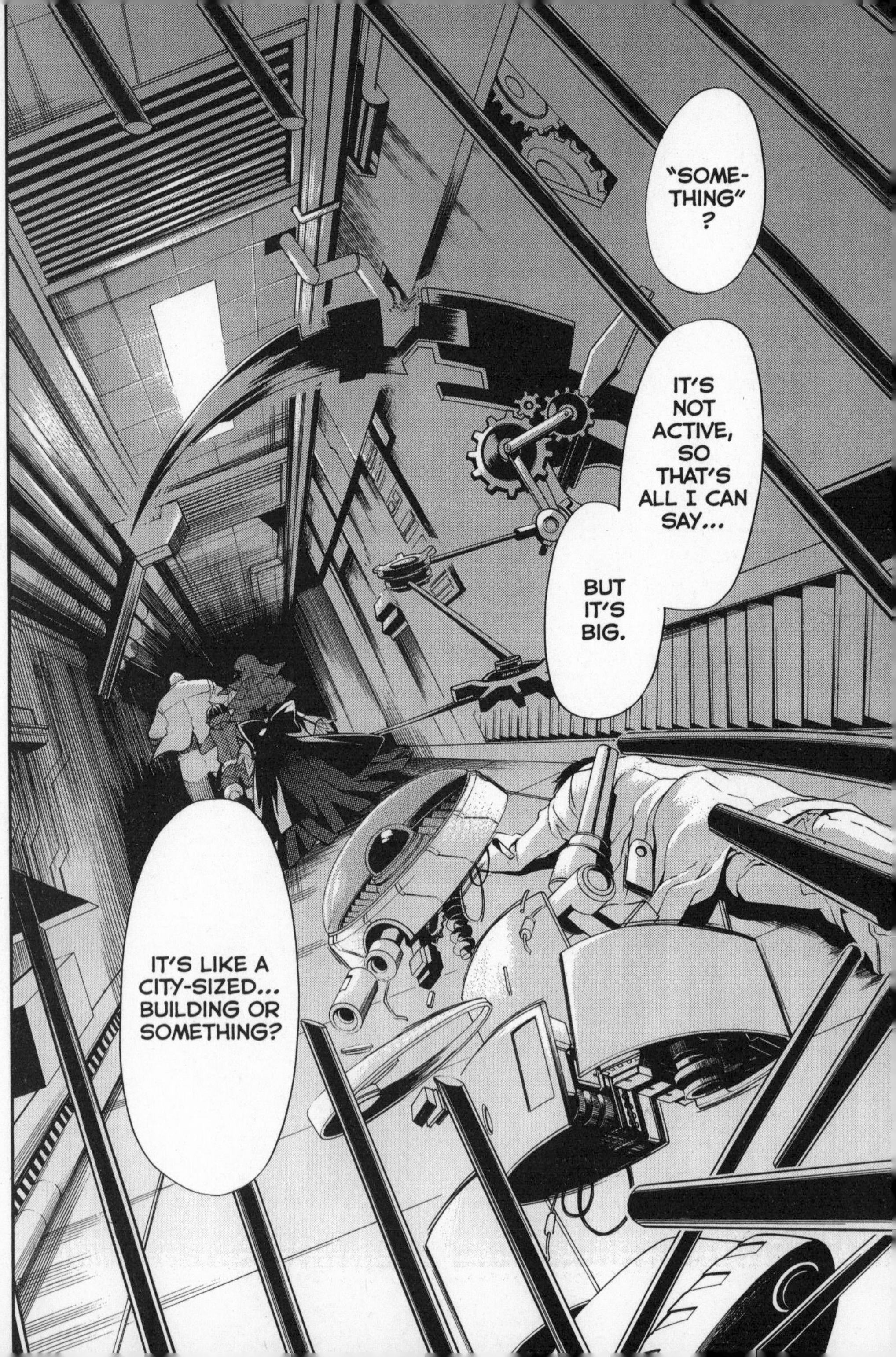
"SOME-THING"?
IT'S NOT ACTIVE, SO THAT'S ALL I CAN SAY...
BUT IT'S BIG.
IT'S LIKE A CITY-SIZED... BUILDING OR SOMETHING?

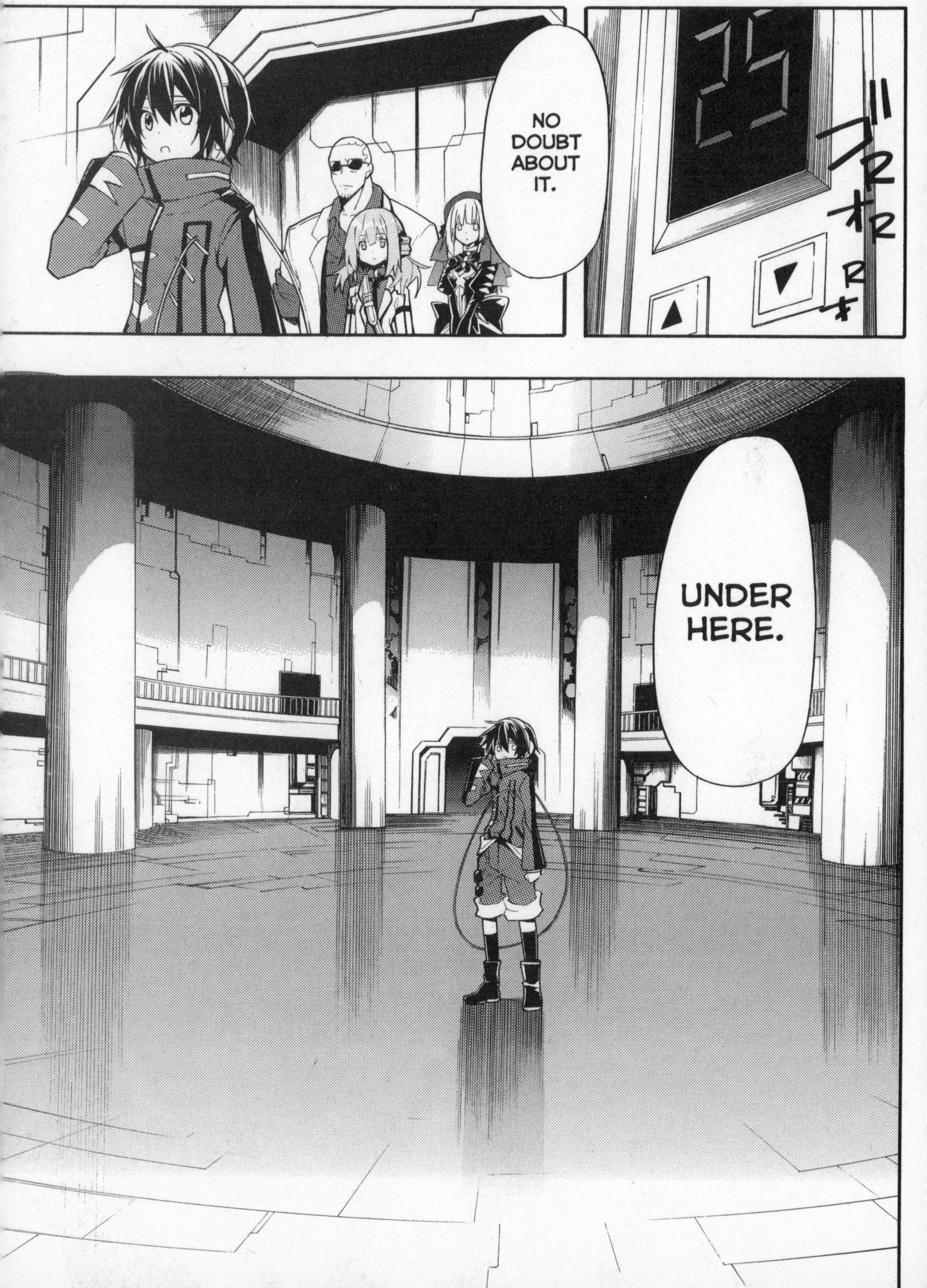
25
NO DOUBT ABOUT IT.
UNDER HERE.

Clock 15: Destroyer

GRID KYOTO

GRID SHIGA

「Purged」

GRID MIE

FACTORY ZONE

PLATE 25 [UNDERGROUND]

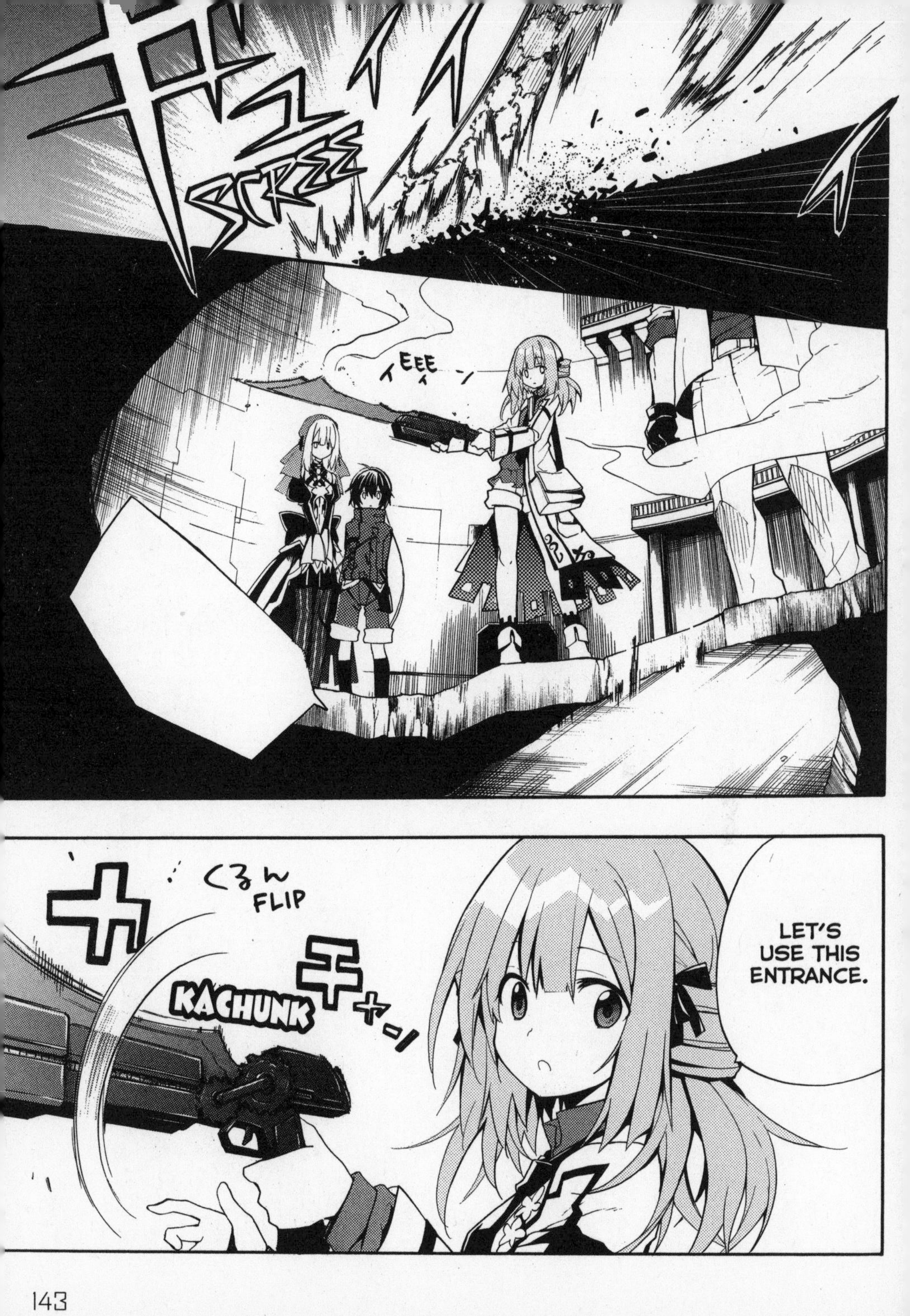
SCREE
EEE
LET'S USE THIS ENTRANCE.
くるん
FLIP
KACHUNK

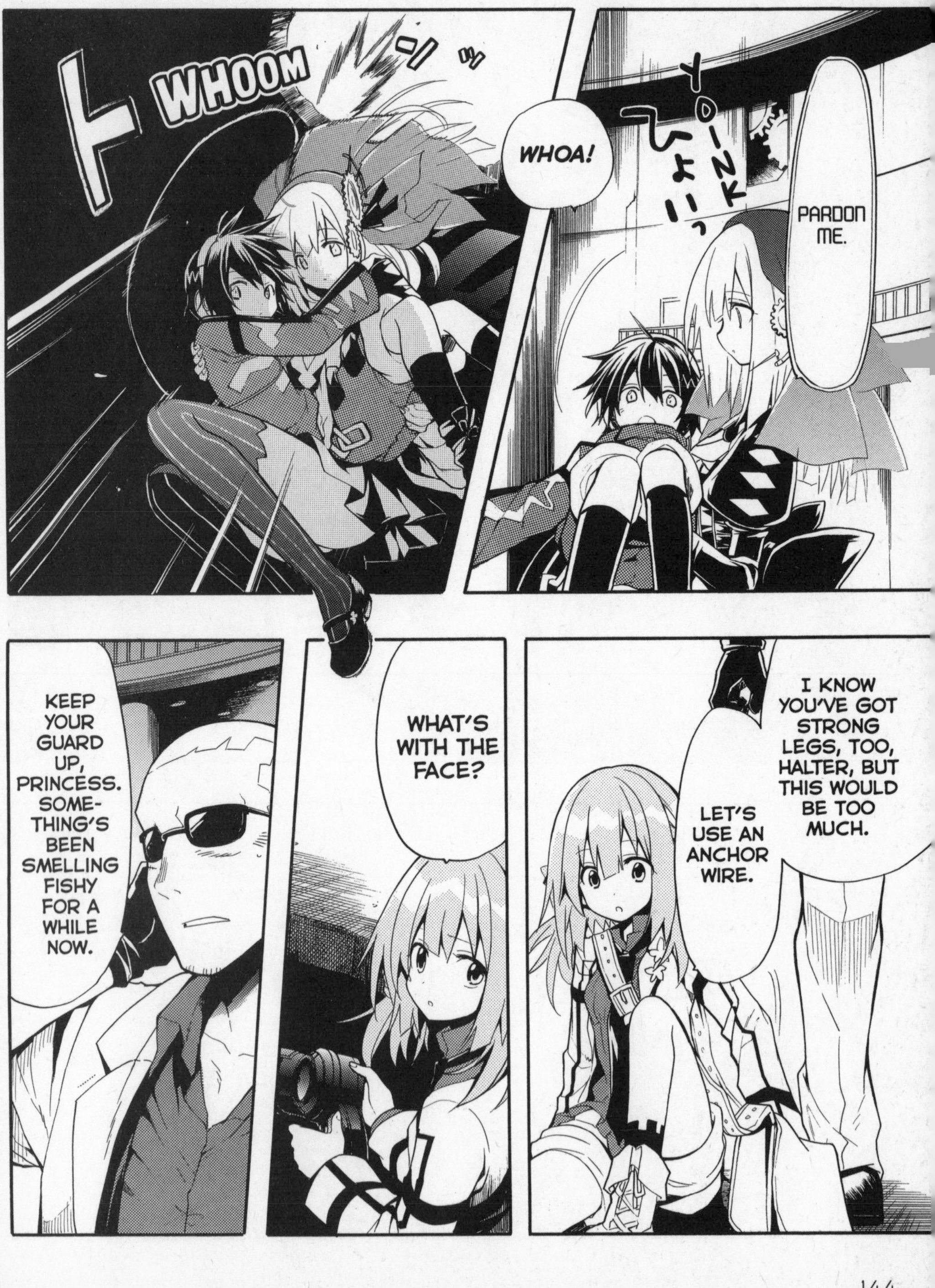
PARDON ME.
YOINK
ひょいっ
WHOA!
WHOOM
I KNOW YOU'VE GOT STRONG LEGS, TOO, HALTER, BUT THIS WOULD BE TOO MUCH.
LET'S USE AN ANCHOR WIRE.
WHAT'S WITH THE FACE?
KEEP YOUR GUARD UP, PRINCESS. SOME-THING'S BEEN SMELLING FISHY FOR A WHILE NOW.

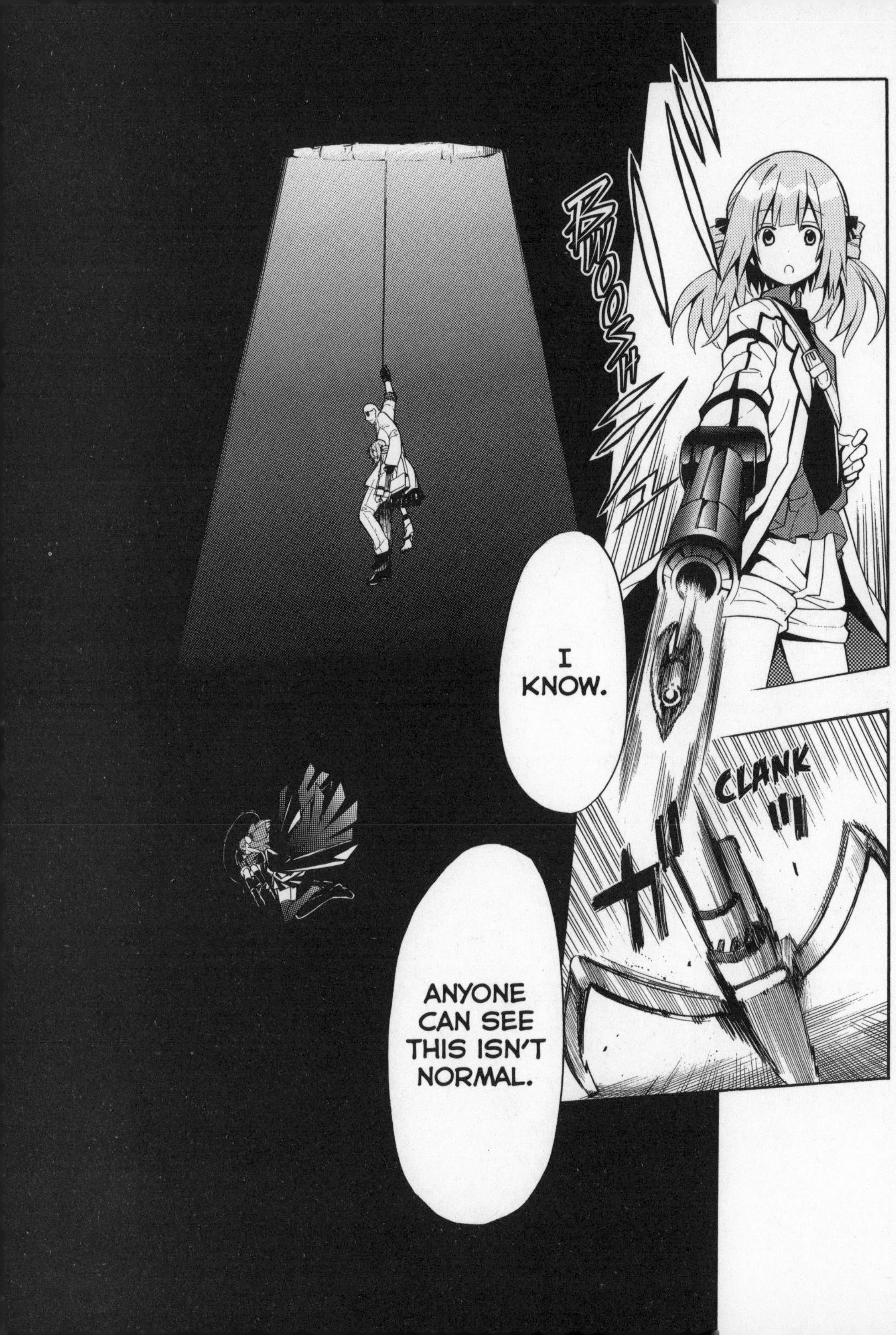
BWOOSH
I KNOW.
CLANK
ANYONE CAN SEE THIS ISN'T NORMAL.

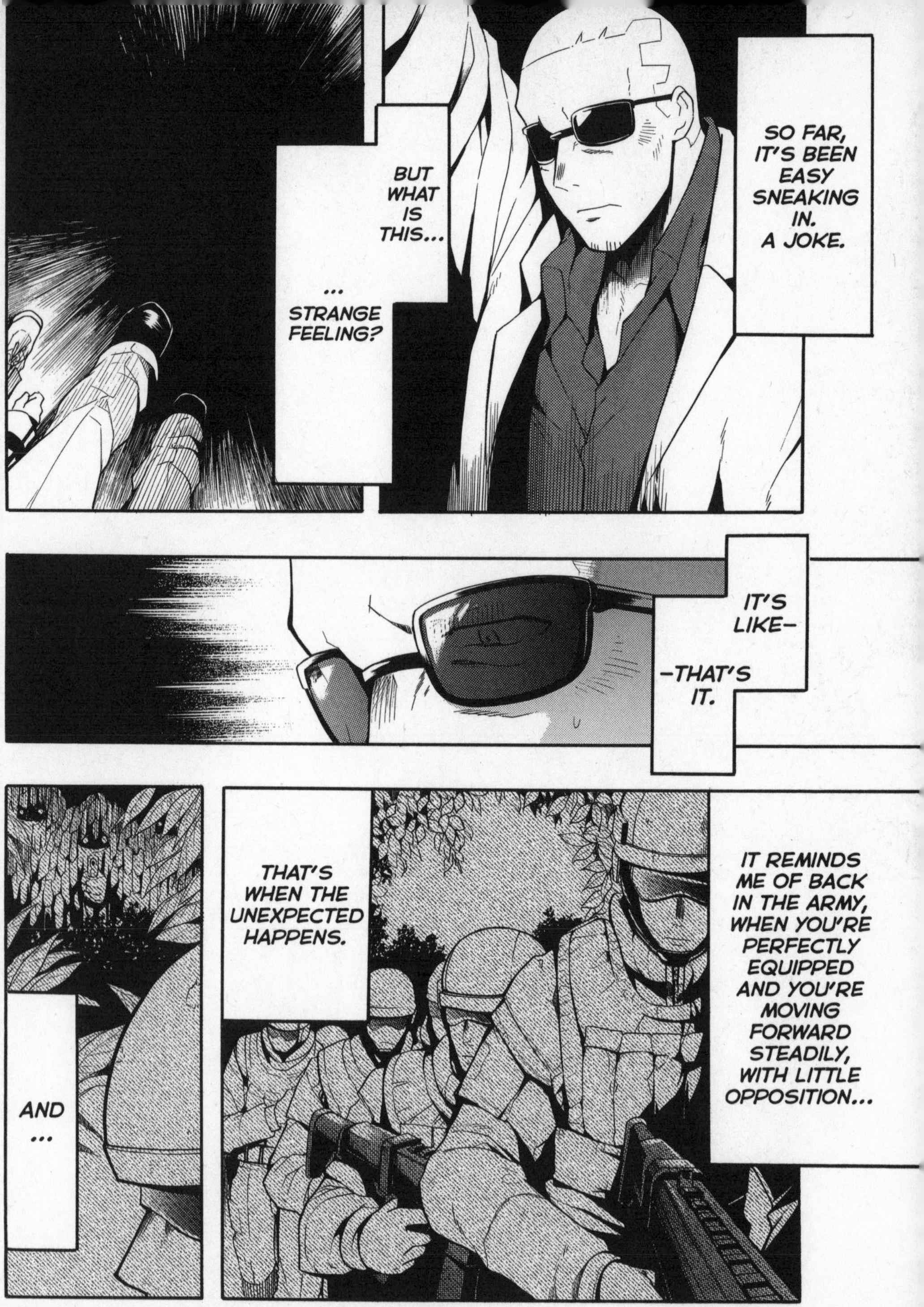
SO FAR, IT'S BEEN EASY SNEAKING IN. A JOKE.
BUT WHAT IS THIS...
...STRANGE FEELING?
IT'S LIKE—
—THAT'S IT.
IT REMINDS ME OF BACK IN THE ARMY, WHEN YOU'RE PERFECTLY EQUIPPED AND YOU'RE MOVING FORWARD STEADILY, WITH LITTLE OPPOSITION...
THAT'S WHEN THE UNEXPECTED HAPPENS.
AND ...

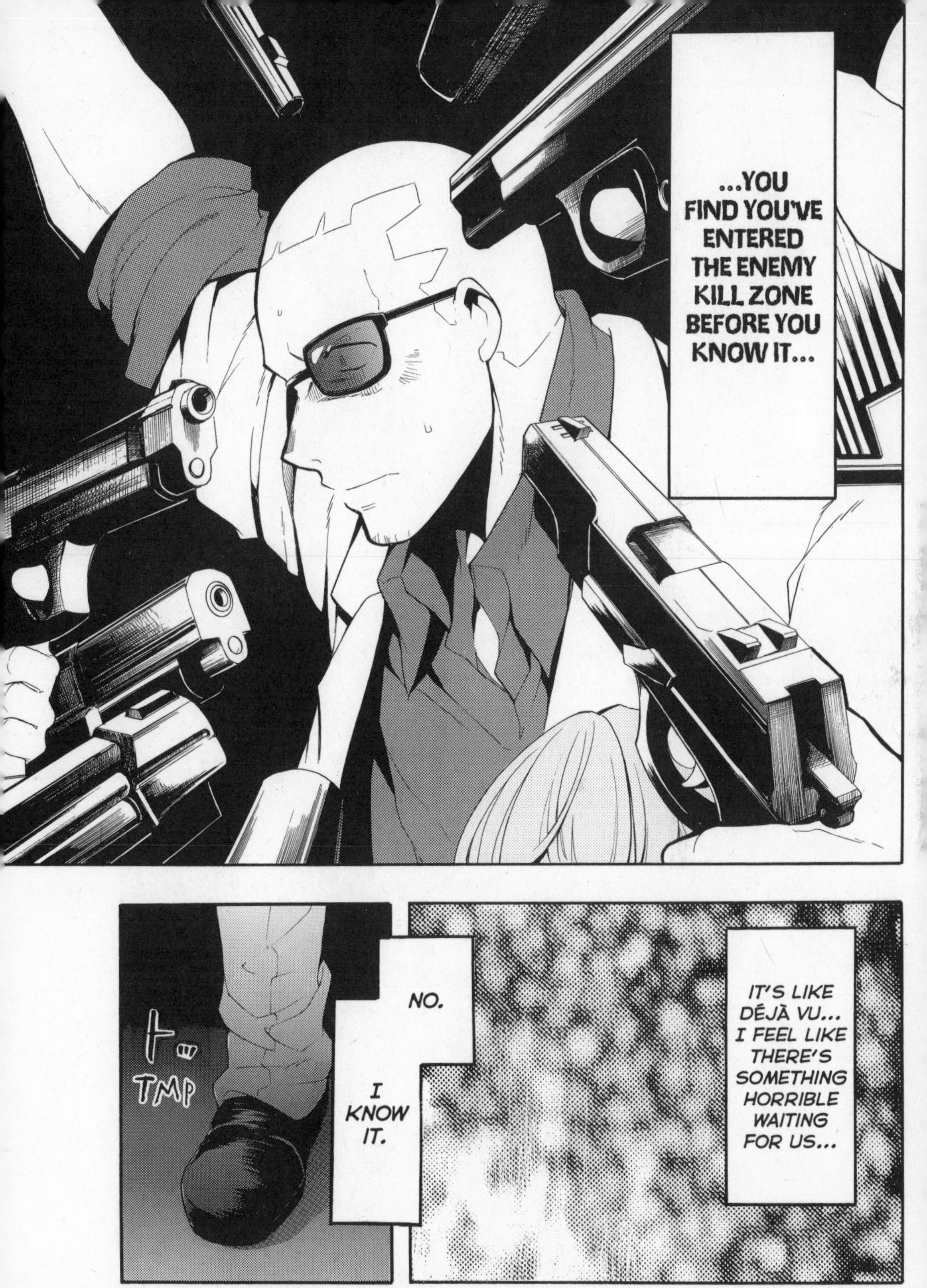
...YOU FIND YOU'VE ENTERED THE ENEMY KILL ZONE BEFORE YOU KNOW IT...
IT'S LIKE DÉJÀ VU... I FEEL LIKE THERE'S SOMETHING HORRIBLE WAITING FOR US...
NO.
I KNOW IT.
ト…
TMP

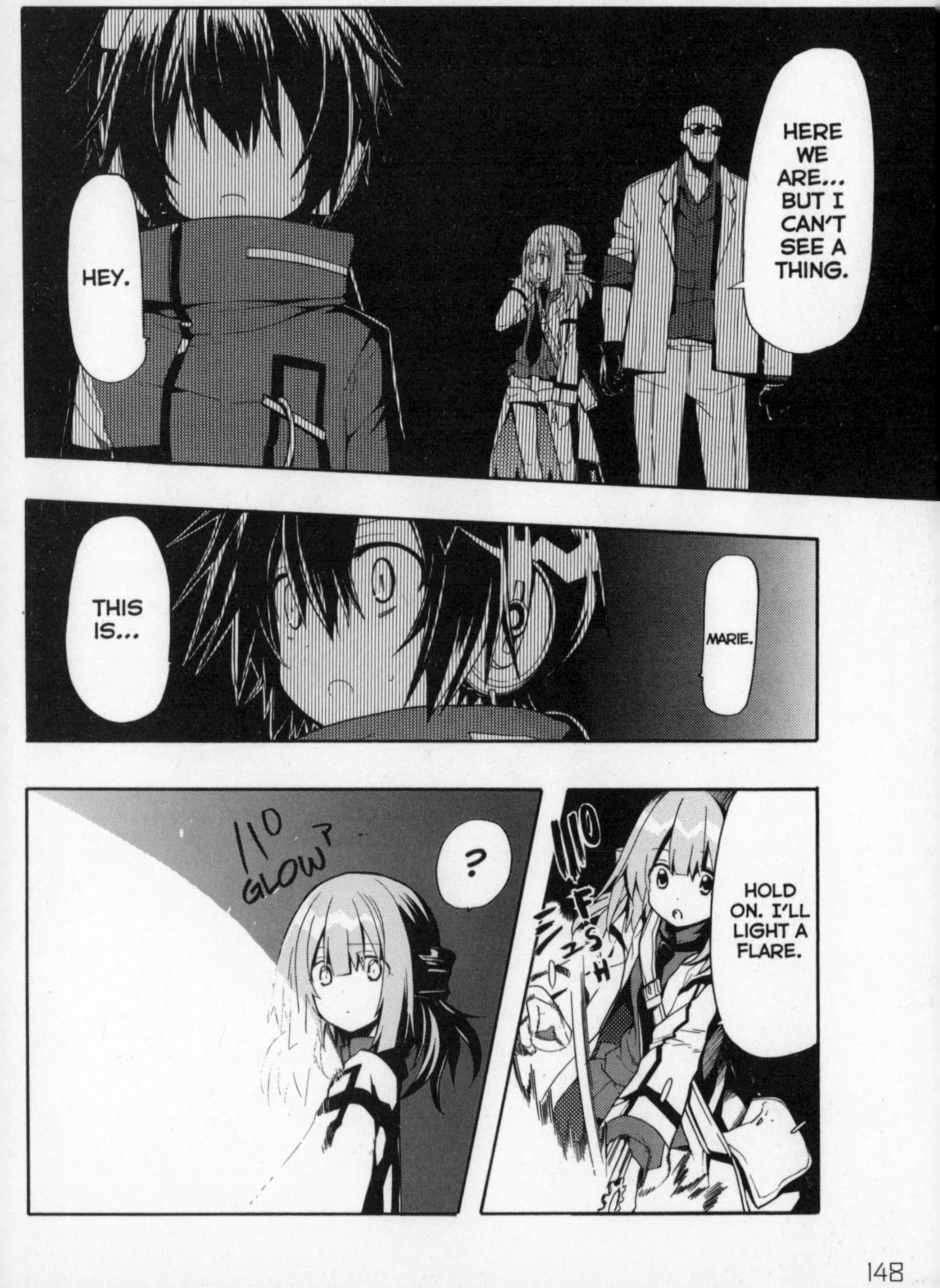
HERE WE ARE... BUT I CAN'T SEE A THING.
HEY.
MARIE.
THIS IS...
HOLD ON. I'LL LIGHT A FLARE.
FSSH
?
GLOW

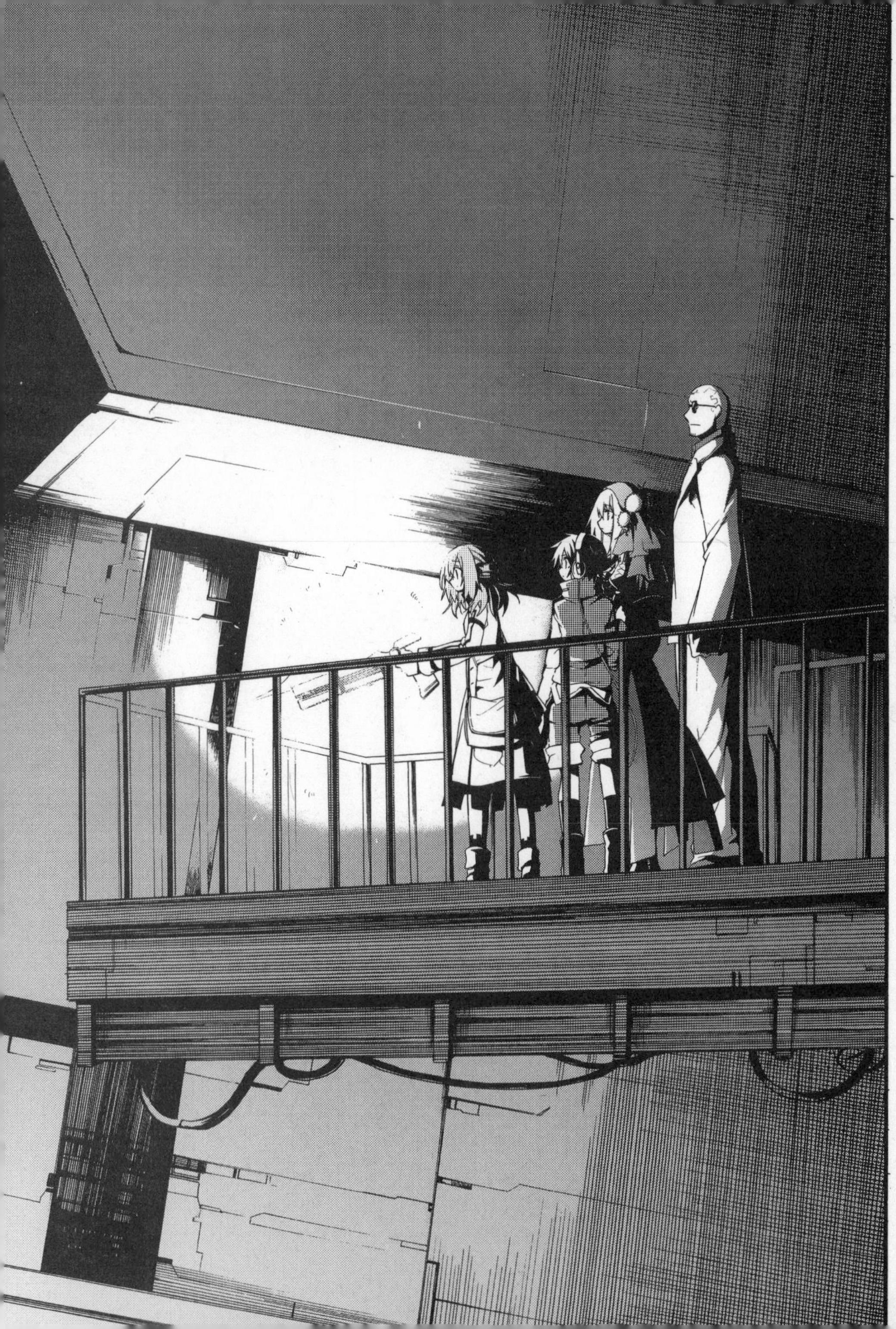

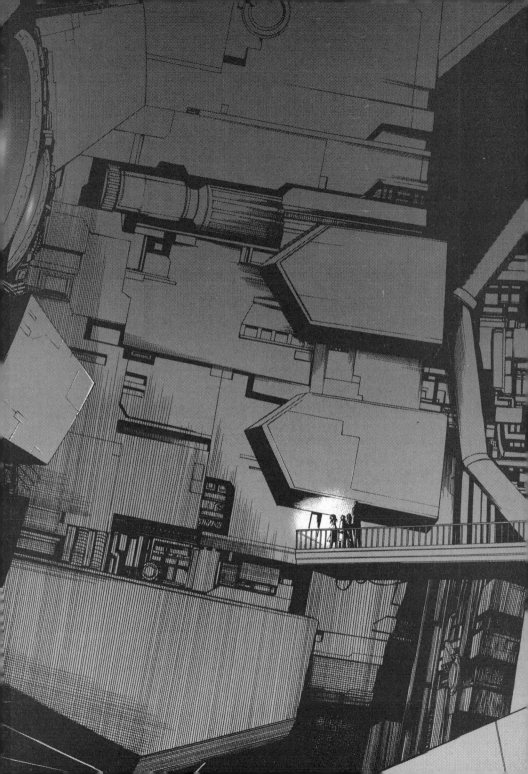

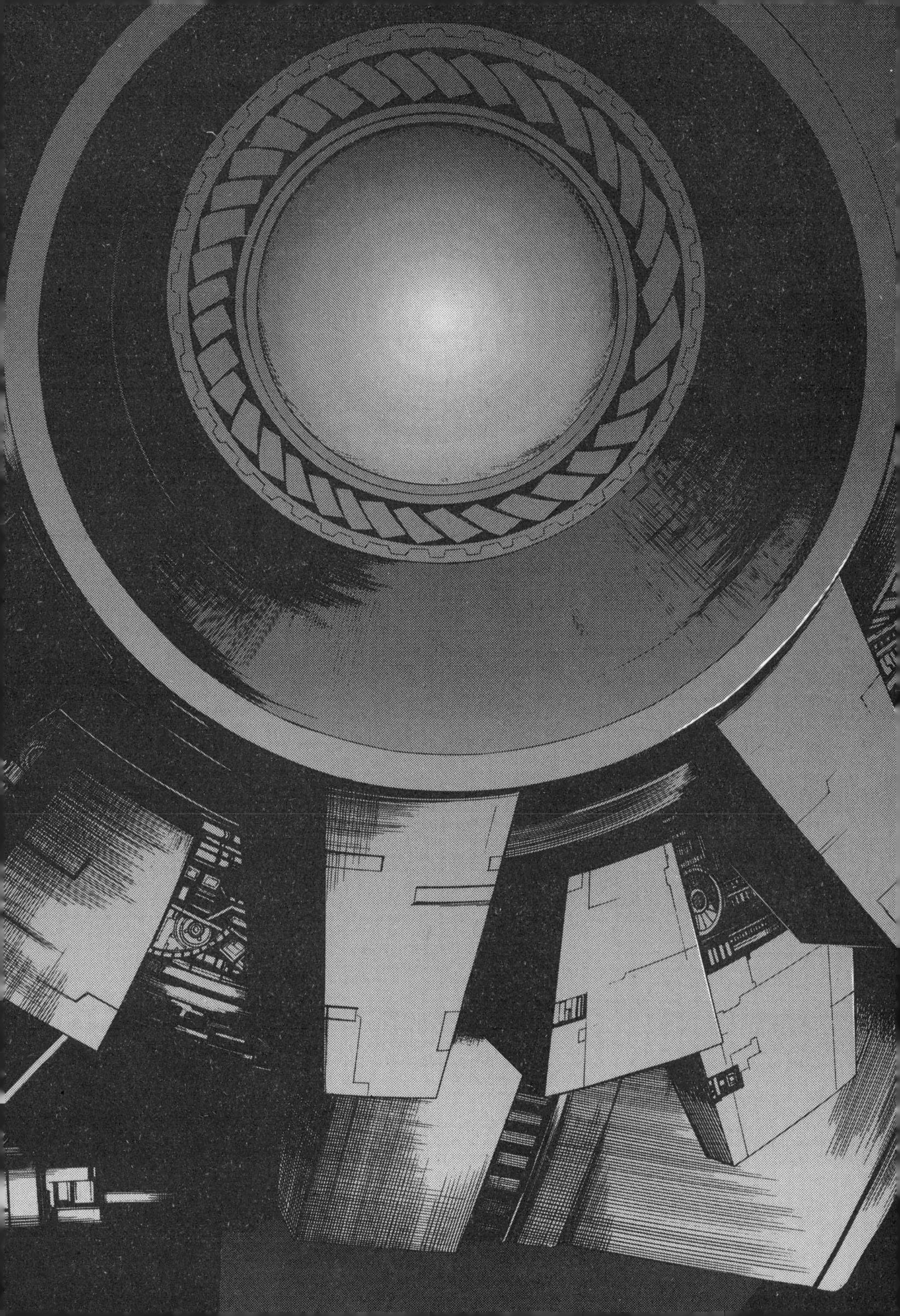

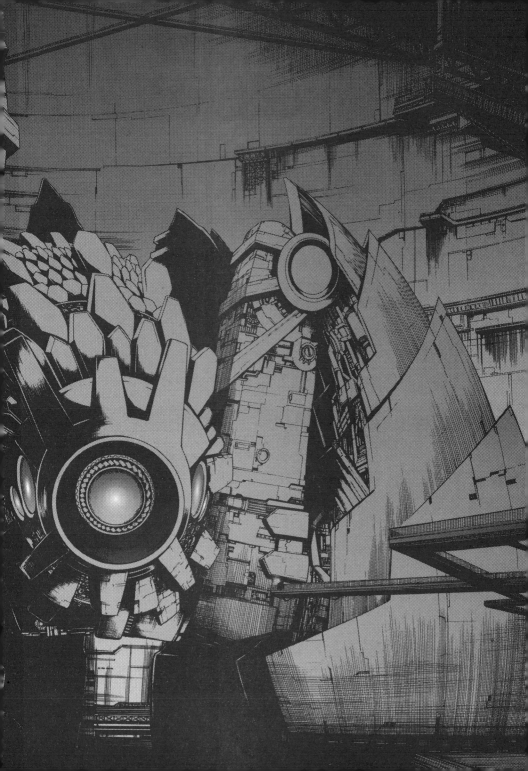

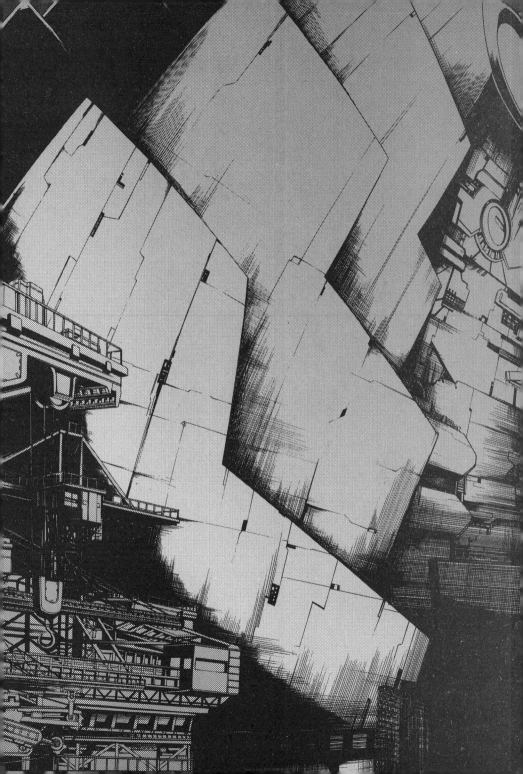

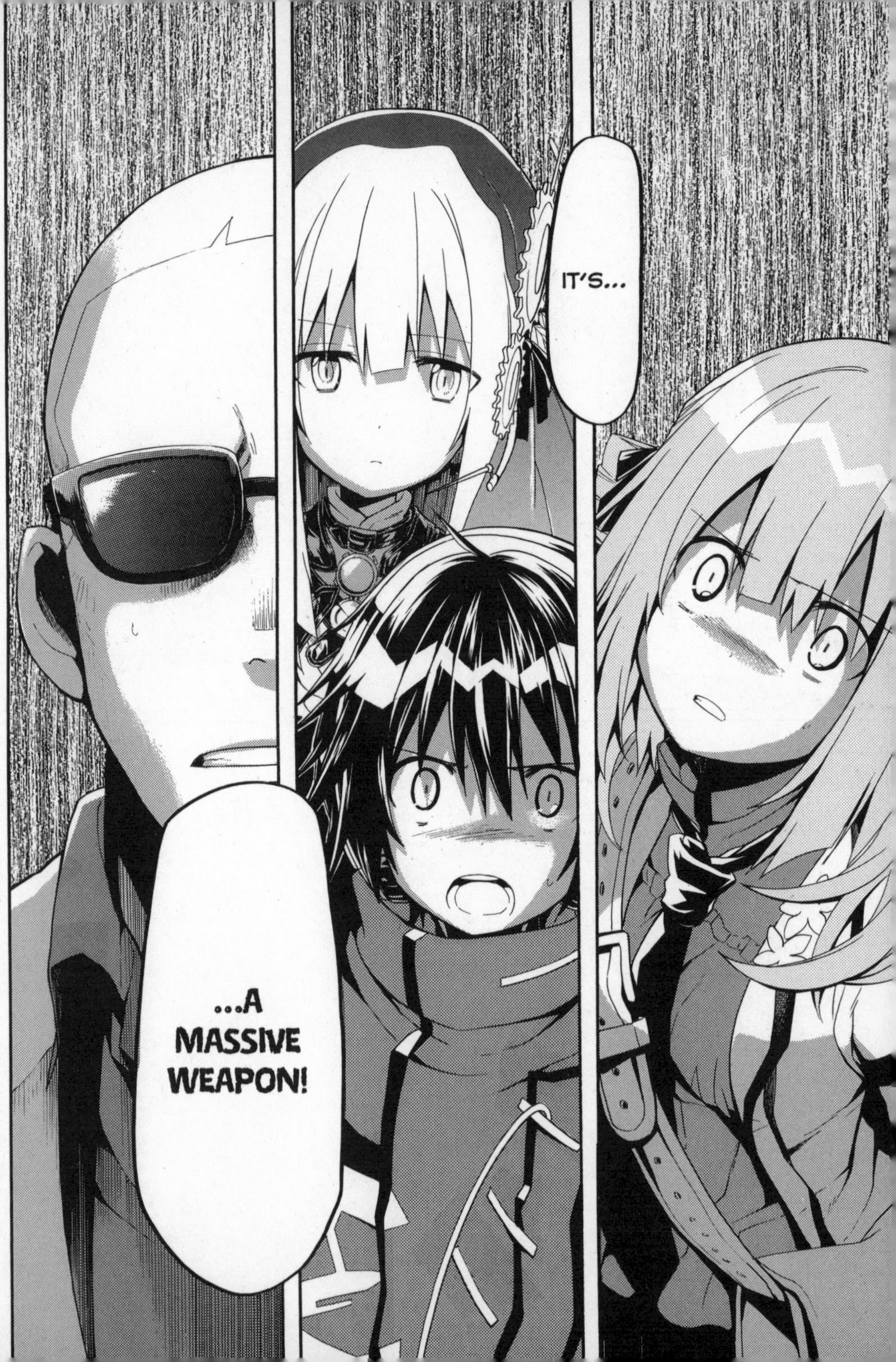
IT'S...
...A MASSIVE WEAPON!

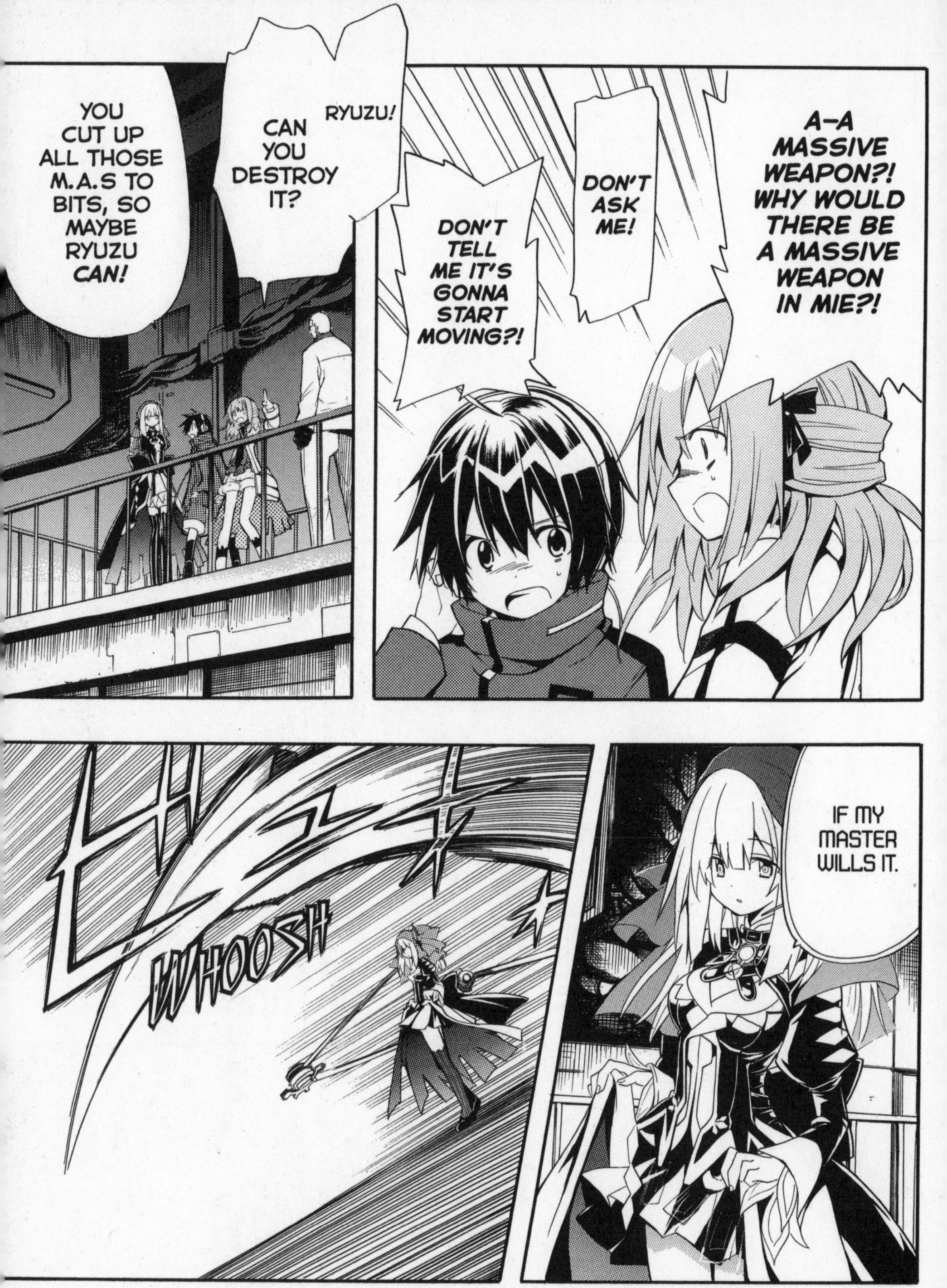
A-A MASSIVE WEAPON?! WHY WOULD THERE BE A MASSIVE WEAPON IN MIE?!
DON'T ASK ME!
DON'T TELL ME IT'S GONNA START MOVING?!
RYUZU! CAN YOU DESTROY IT?
YOU CUT UP ALL THOSE M.A.S TO BITS, SO MAYBE RYUZU CAN!
IF MY MASTER WILLS IT.
WHOOSH

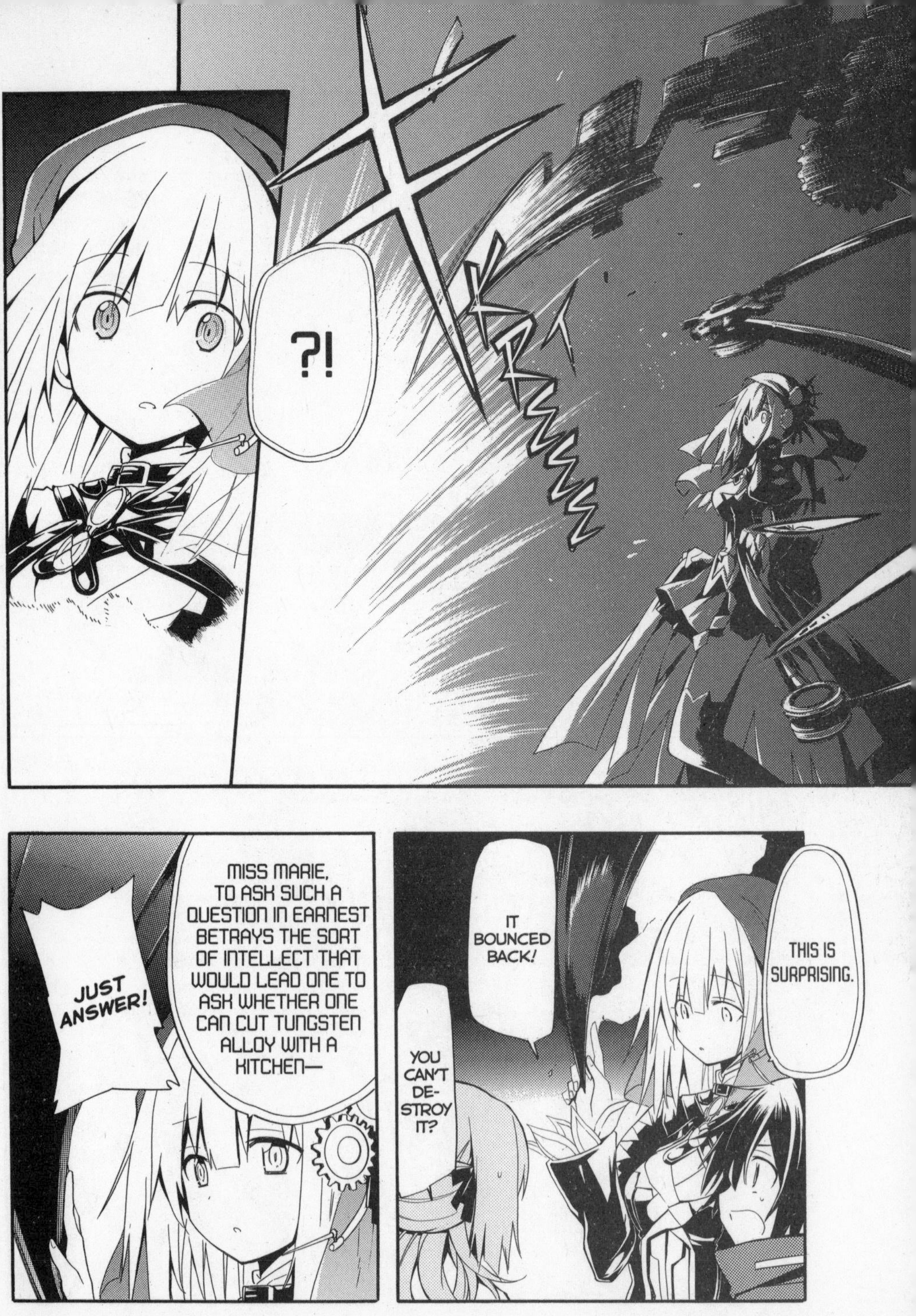
KRAWWWW
?!
THIS IS SURPRISING.
IT BOUNCED BACK!
YOU CAN'T DE-STROY IT?
MISS MARIE, TO ASK SUCH A QUESTION IN EARNEST BETRAYS THE SORT OF INTELLECT THAT WOULD LEAD ONE TO ASK WHETHER ONE CAN CUT TUNGSTEN ALLOY WITH A KITCHEN—
JUST ANSWER!

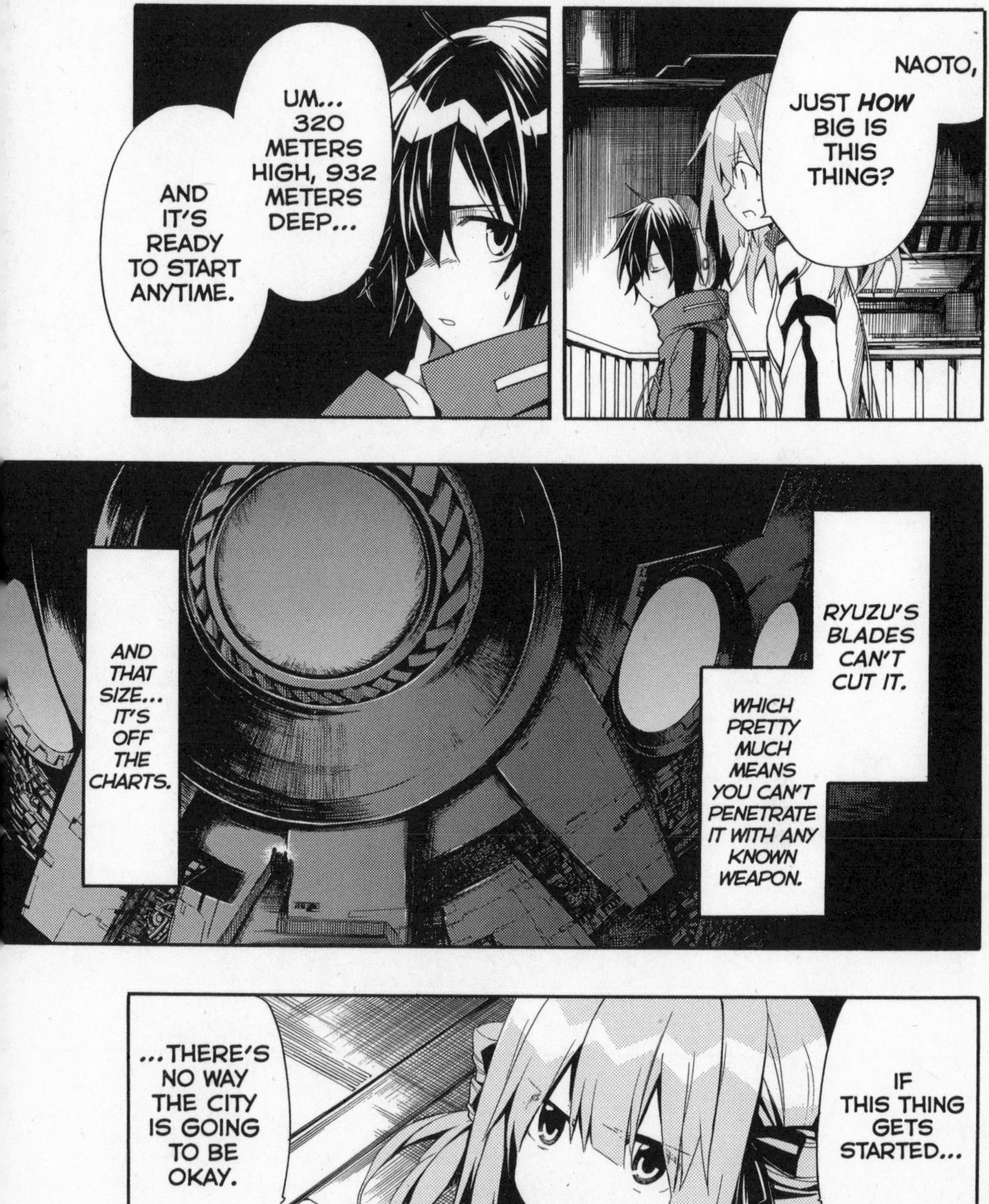
NAOTO, JUST HOW BIG IS THIS THING?
UM... 320 METERS HIGH, 932 METERS DEEP...
AND IT'S READY TO START ANYTIME.
RYUZU'S BLADES CAN'T CUT IT.
WHICH PRETTY MUCH MEANS YOU CAN'T PENETRATE IT WITH ANY KNOWN WEAPON.
AND THAT SIZE... IT'S OFF THE CHARTS.
IF THIS THING GETS STARTED...
...THERE'S NO WAY THE CITY IS GOING TO BE OKAY.

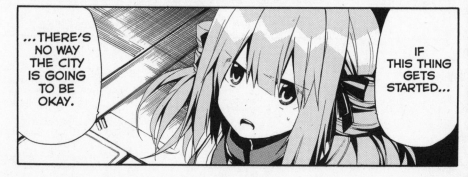

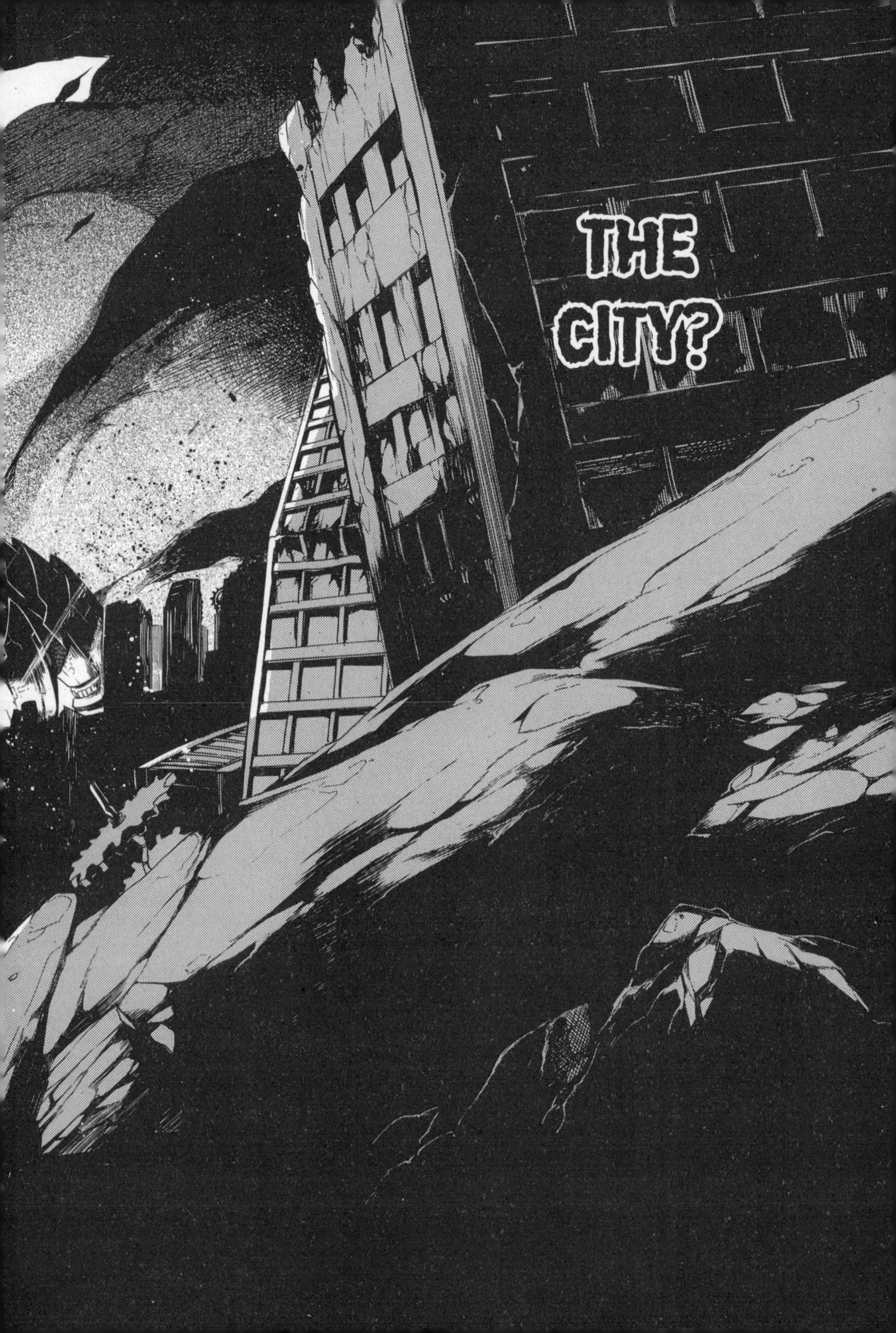
THE CITY?

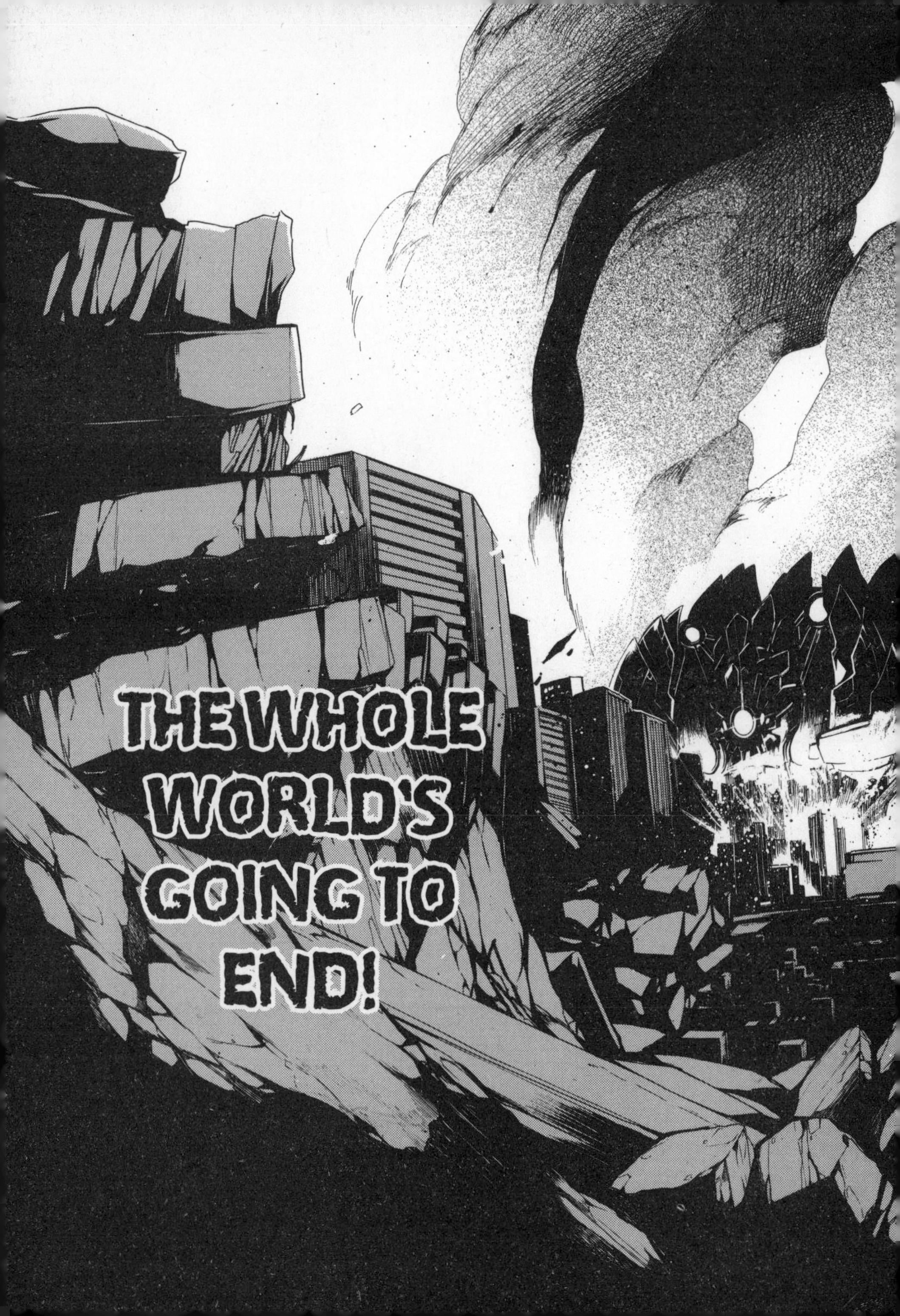
THE WHOLE WORLD'S GOING TO END!

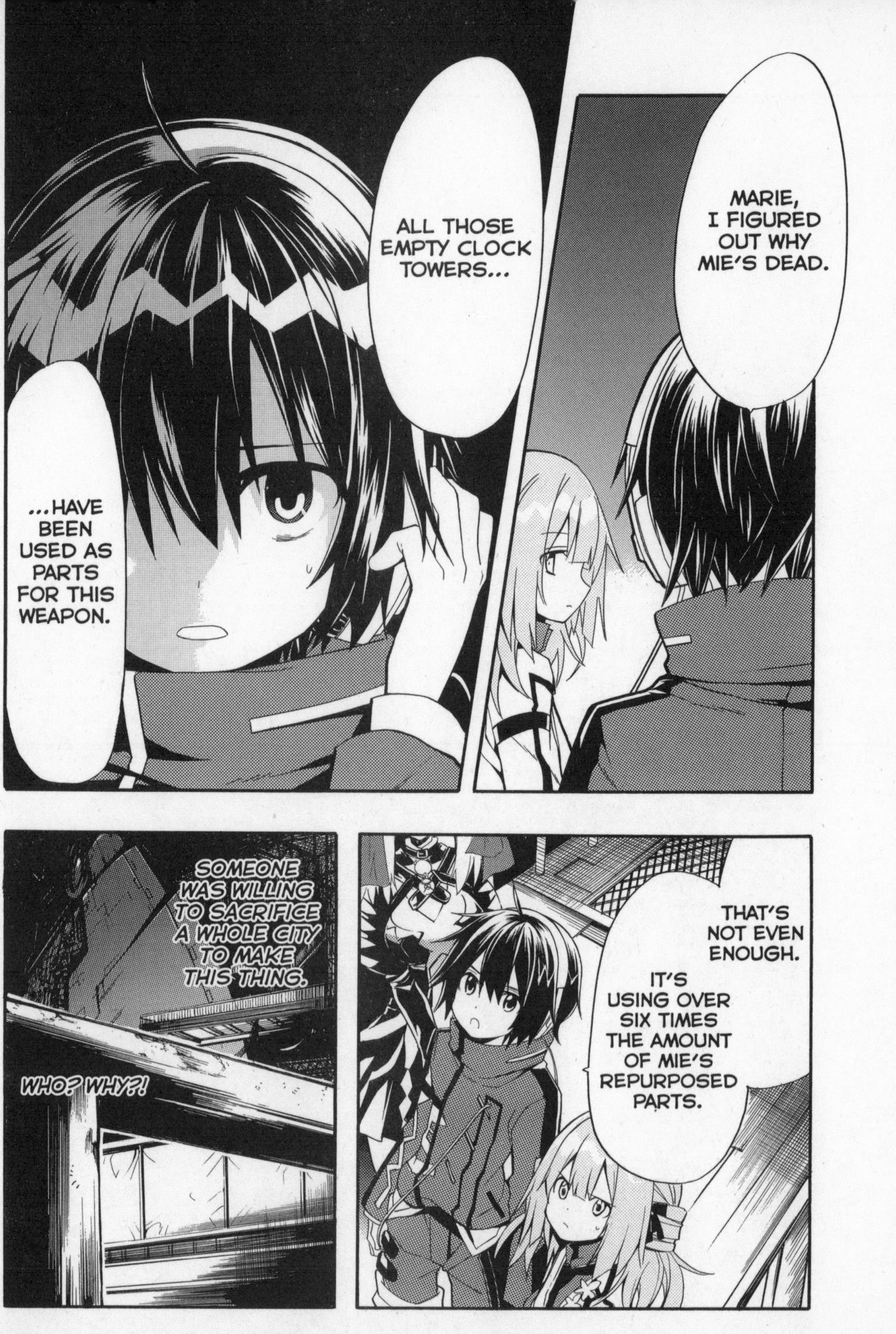
MARIE, I FIGURED OUT WHY MIE'S DEAD.
ALL THOSE EMPTY CLOCK TOWERS...
...HAVE BEEN USED AS PARTS FOR THIS WEAPON.
THAT'S NOT EVEN ENOUGH.
IT'S USING OVER SIX TIMES THE AMOUNT OF MIE'S REPURPOSED PARTS.
SOMEONE WAS WILLING TO SACRIFICE A WHOLE CITY TO MAKE THIS THING.
WHO? WHY?!

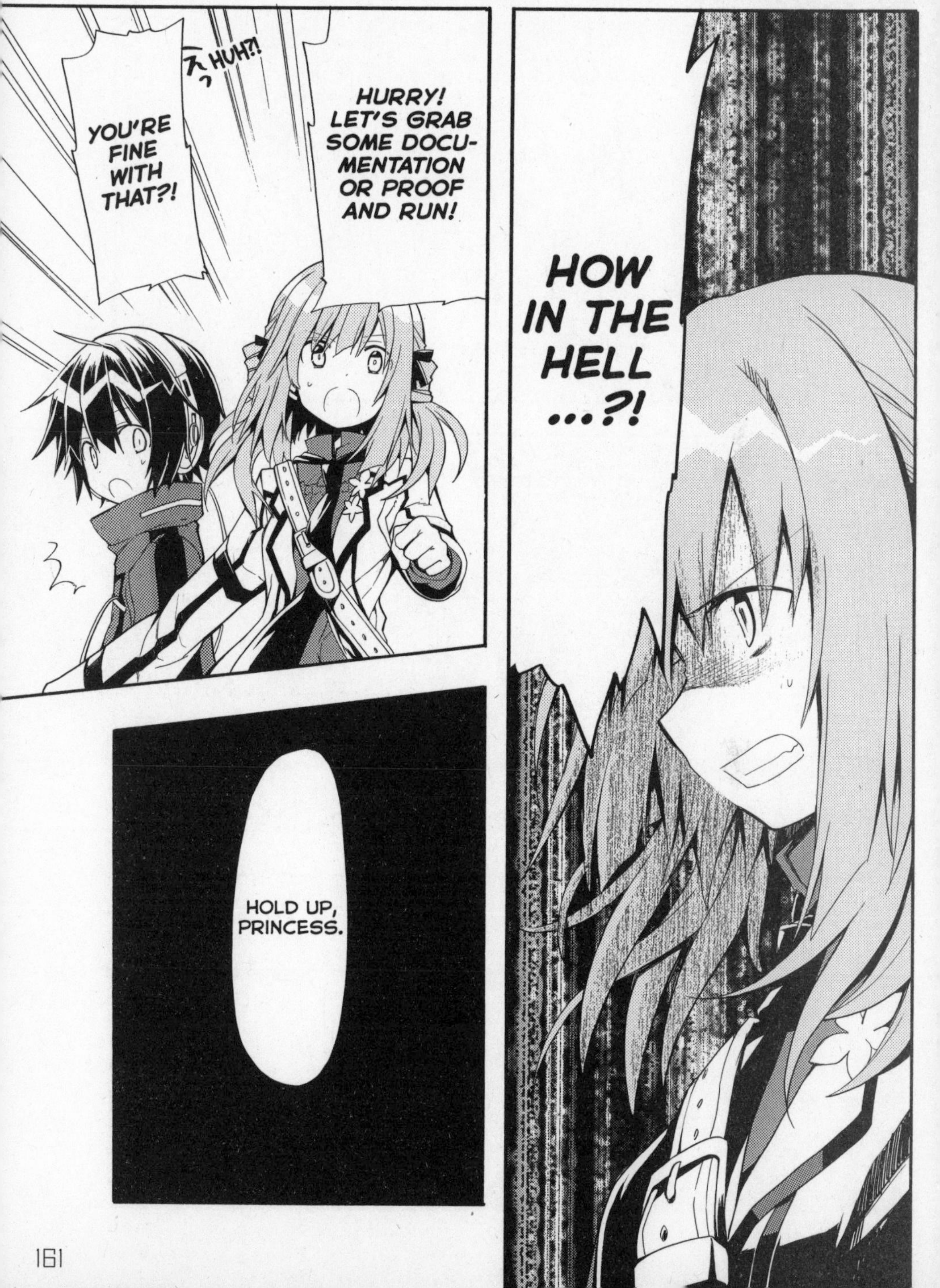
HOW IN THE HELL ...?!
HURRY! LET'S GRAB SOME DOCU-MENTATION OR PROOF AND RUN!
HUH?!
YOU'RE FINE WITH THAT?!
HOLD UP, PRINCESS.

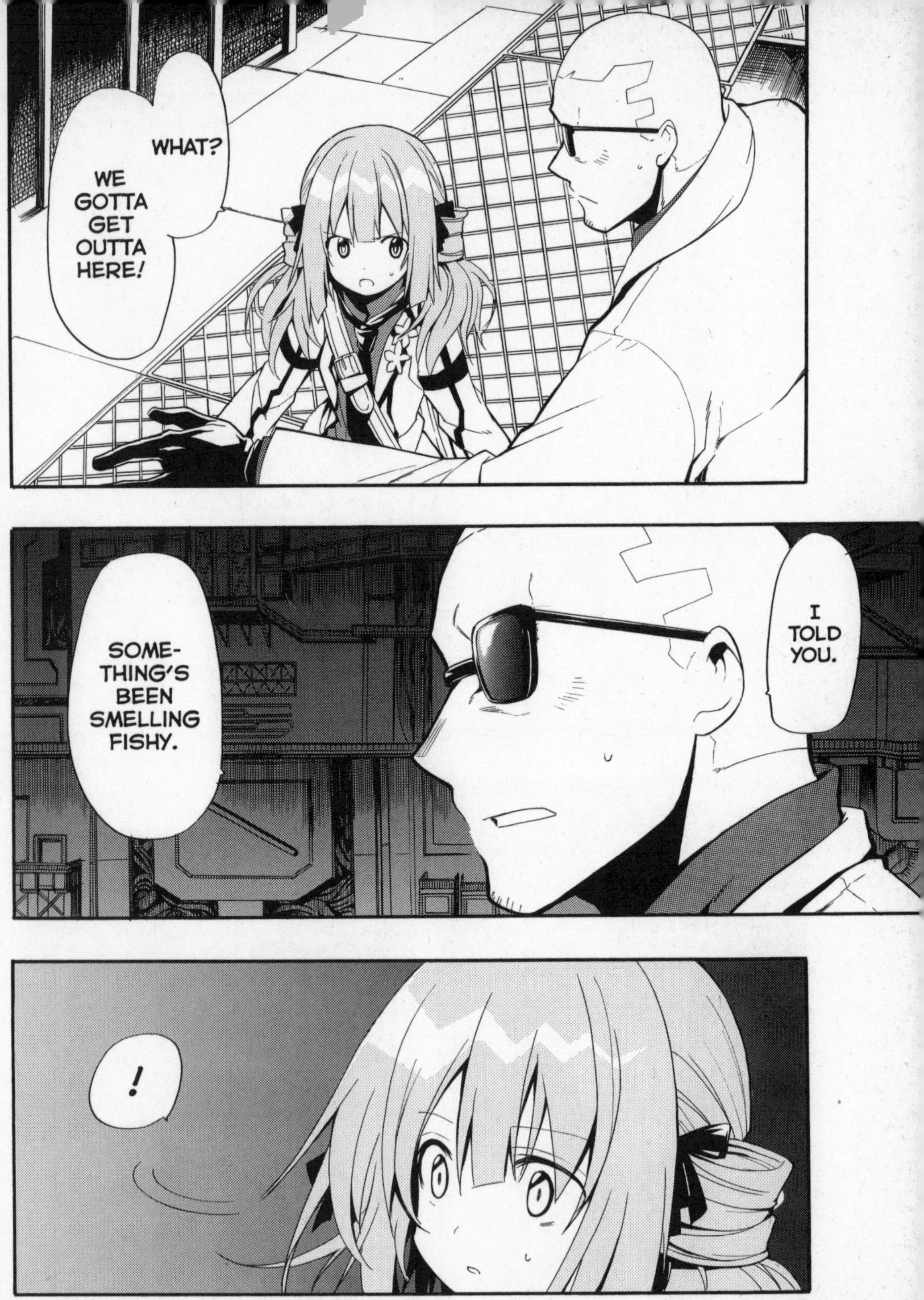
WHAT? WE GOTTA GET OUTTA HERE!
I TOLD YOU.
SOME-THING'S BEEN SMELLING FISHY.
!

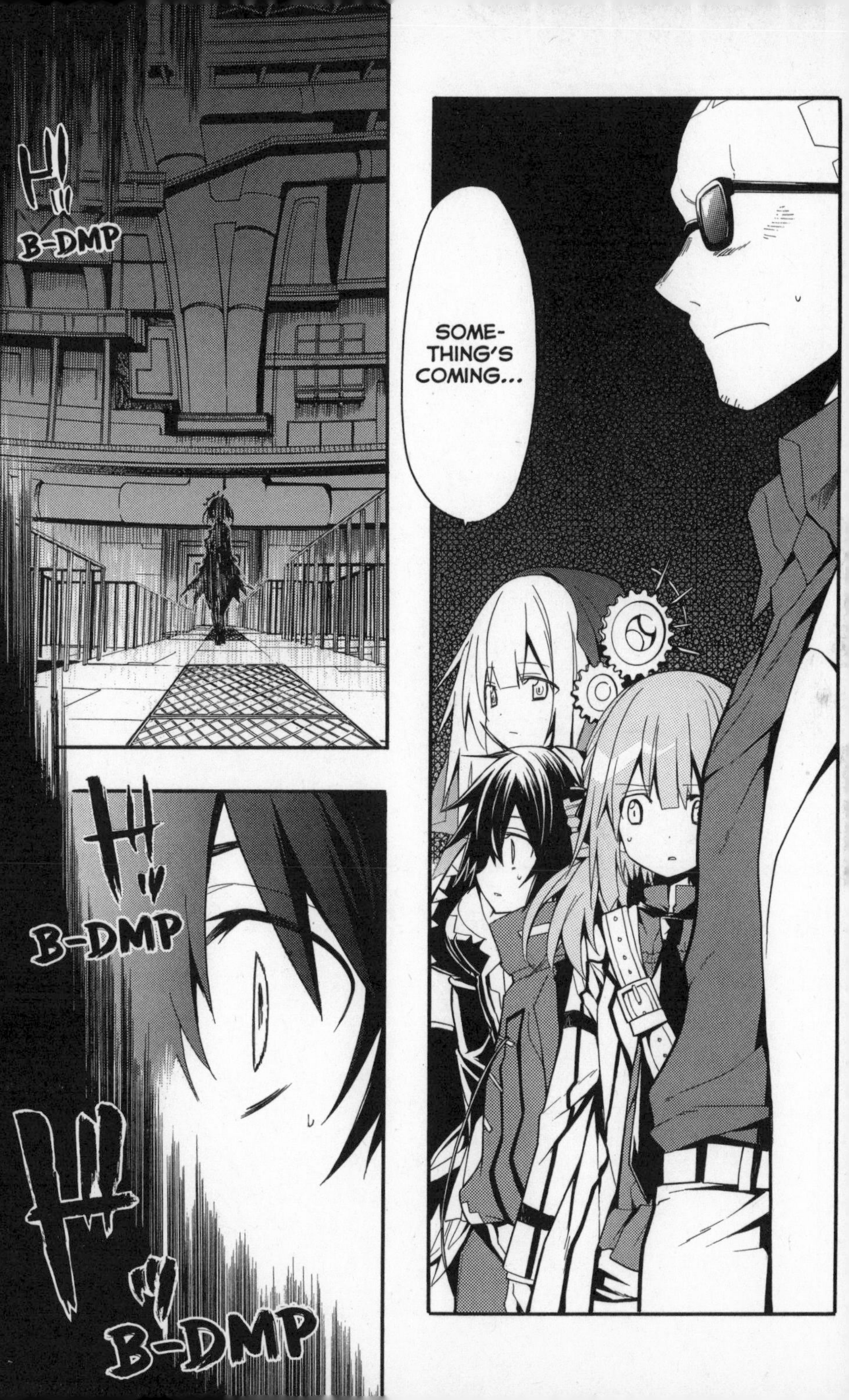
SOME-THING'S COMING...
B-DMP
B-DMP
B-DMP

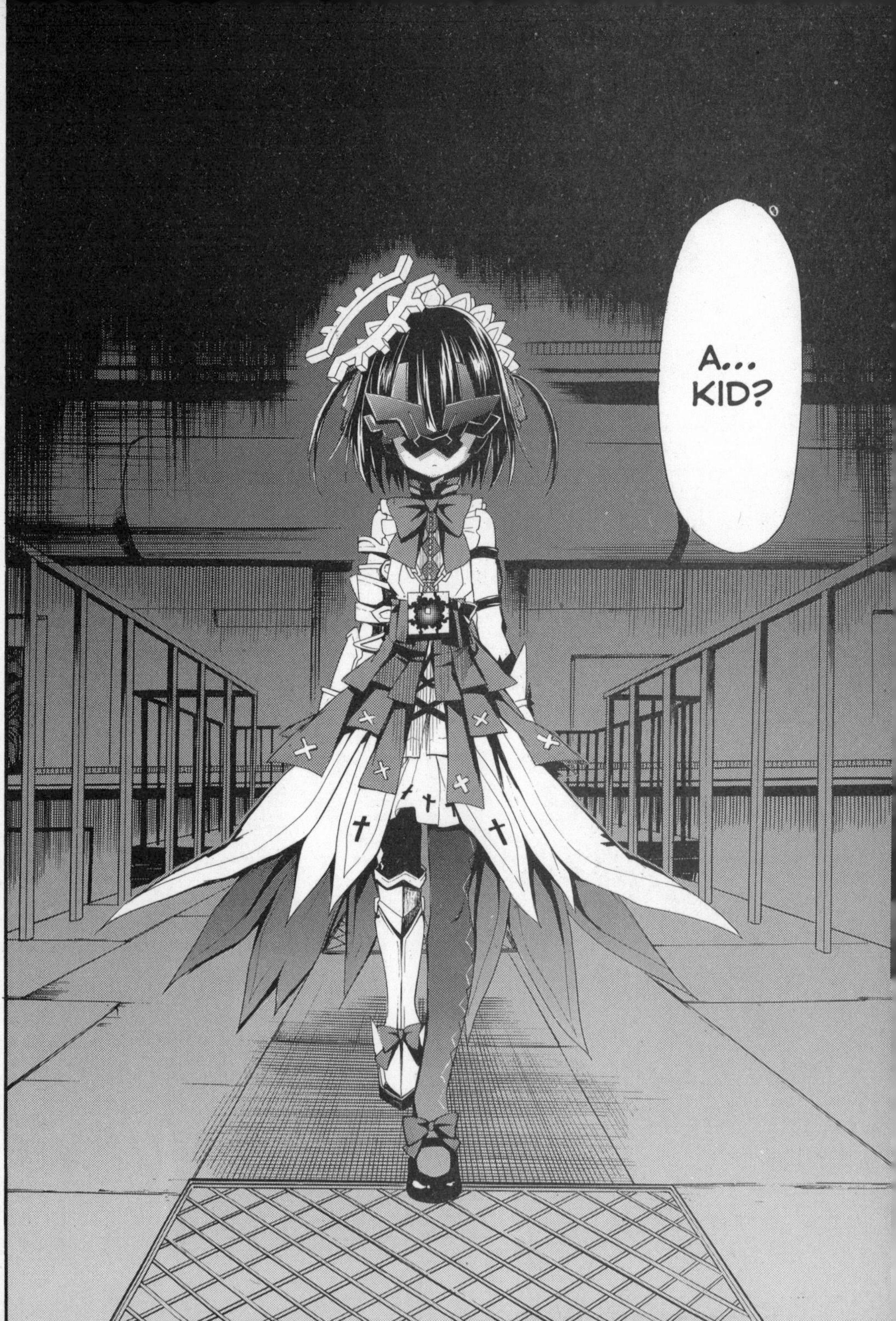
A... KID?

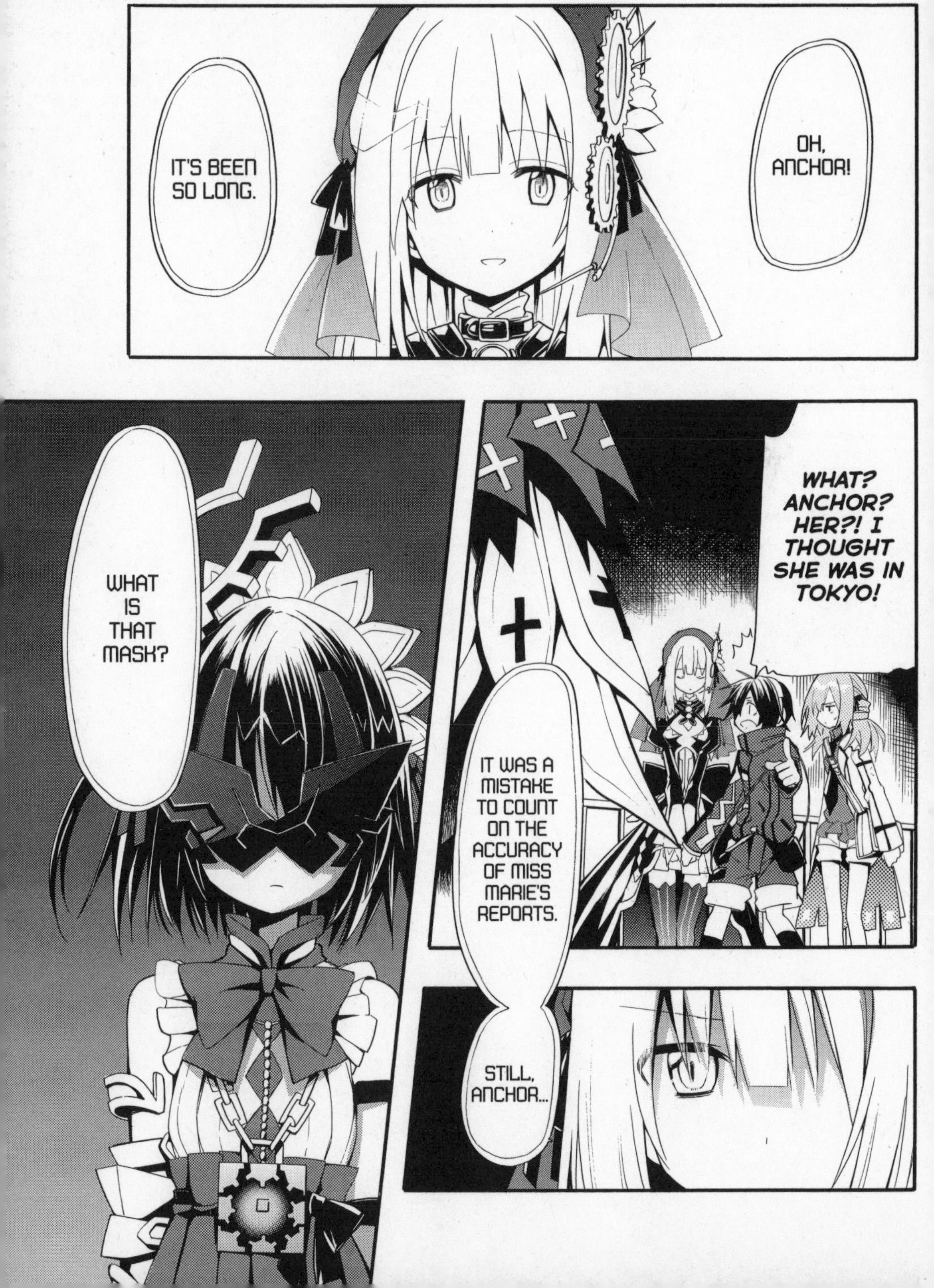
OH, ANCHOR!
IT'S BEEN SO LONG.
WHAT? ANCHOR? HER?! I THOUGHT SHE WAS IN TOKYO!
IT WAS A MISTAKE TO COUNT ON THE ACCURACY OF MISS MARIE'S REPORTS.
STILL, ANCHOR...
WHAT IS THAT MASK?

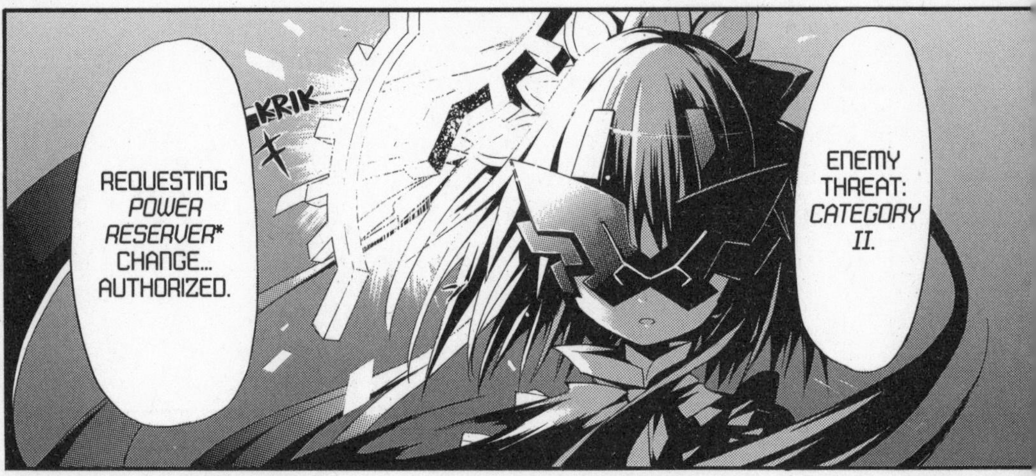
ENEMY THREAT: CATEGORY II.
KRIK
REQUESTING POWER RESERVER* CHANGE... AUTHORIZED.

*Kaleidoscopic incense box

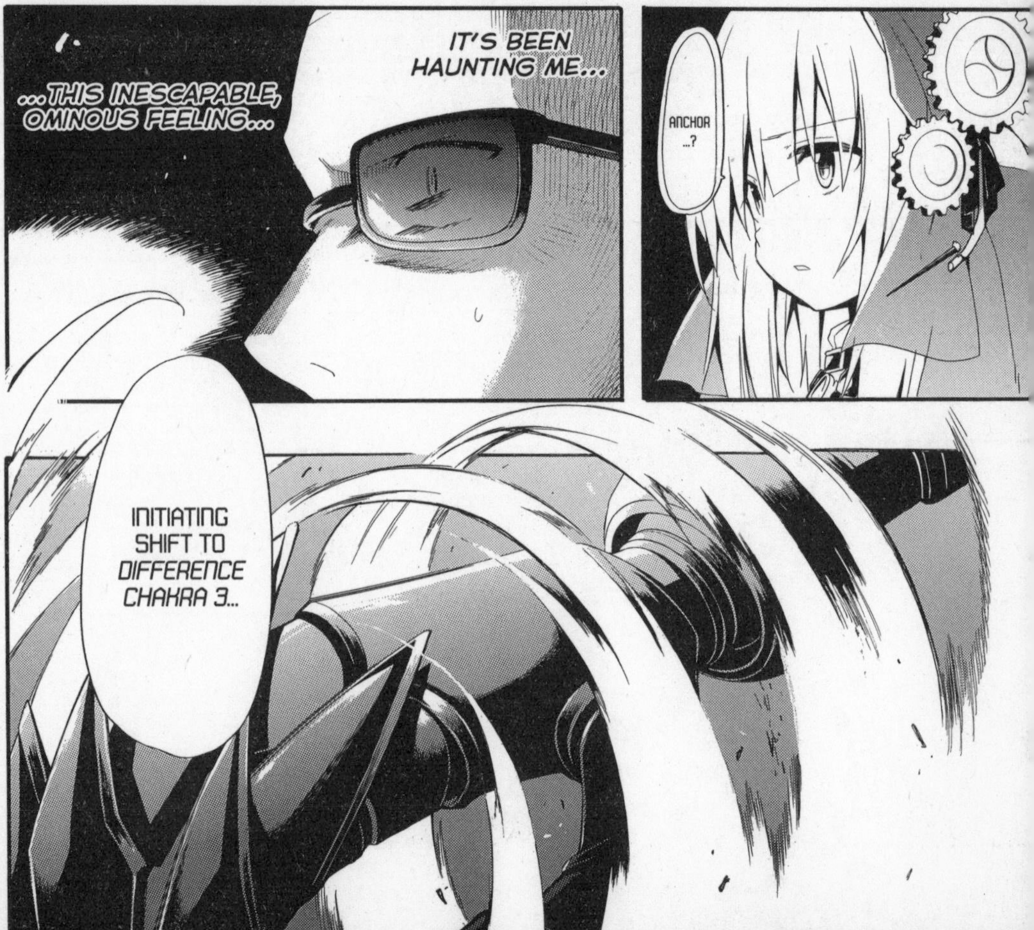
ANCHOR ...?
IT'S BEEN HAUNTING ME...
...THIS INESCAPABLE, OMINOUS FEELING...
INITIATING SHIFT TO DIFFERENCE CHAKRA 3...

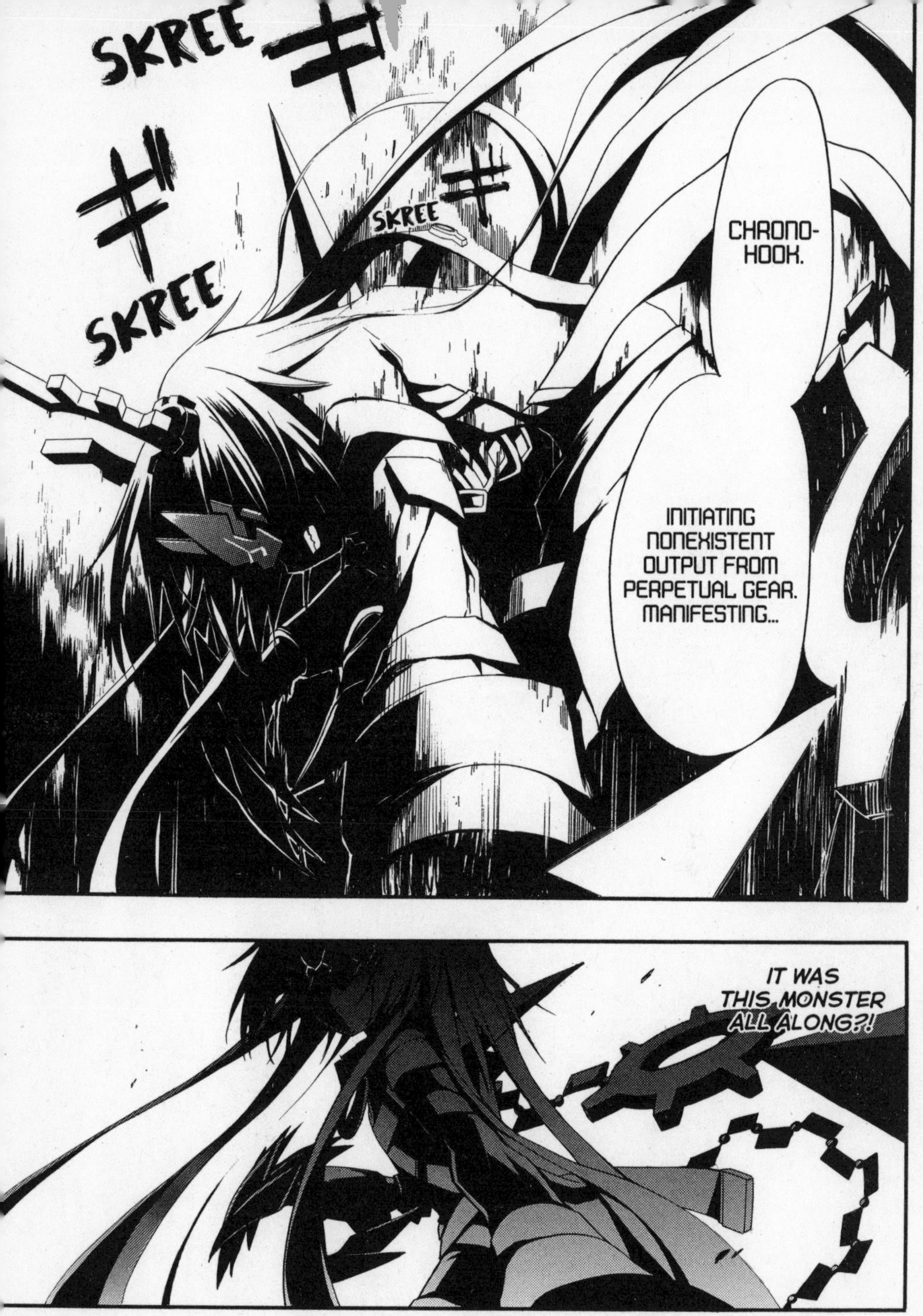
CHRONO-HOOK.
INITIATING NONEXISTENT OUTPUT FROM PERPETUAL GEAR. MANIFESTING...
SKREE
SKREE
SKREE
IT WAS THIS MONSTER ALL ALONG?!

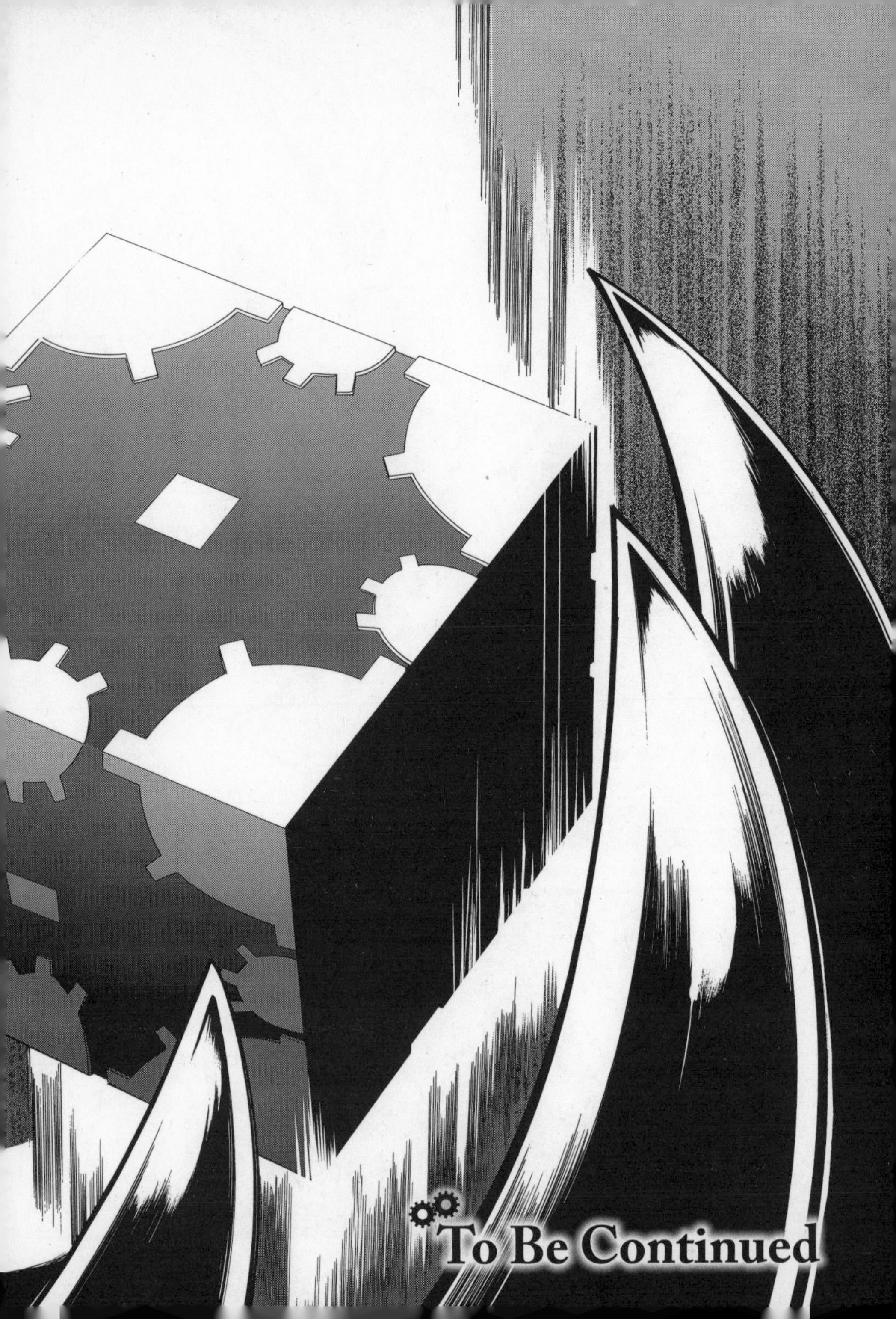
To Be Continued

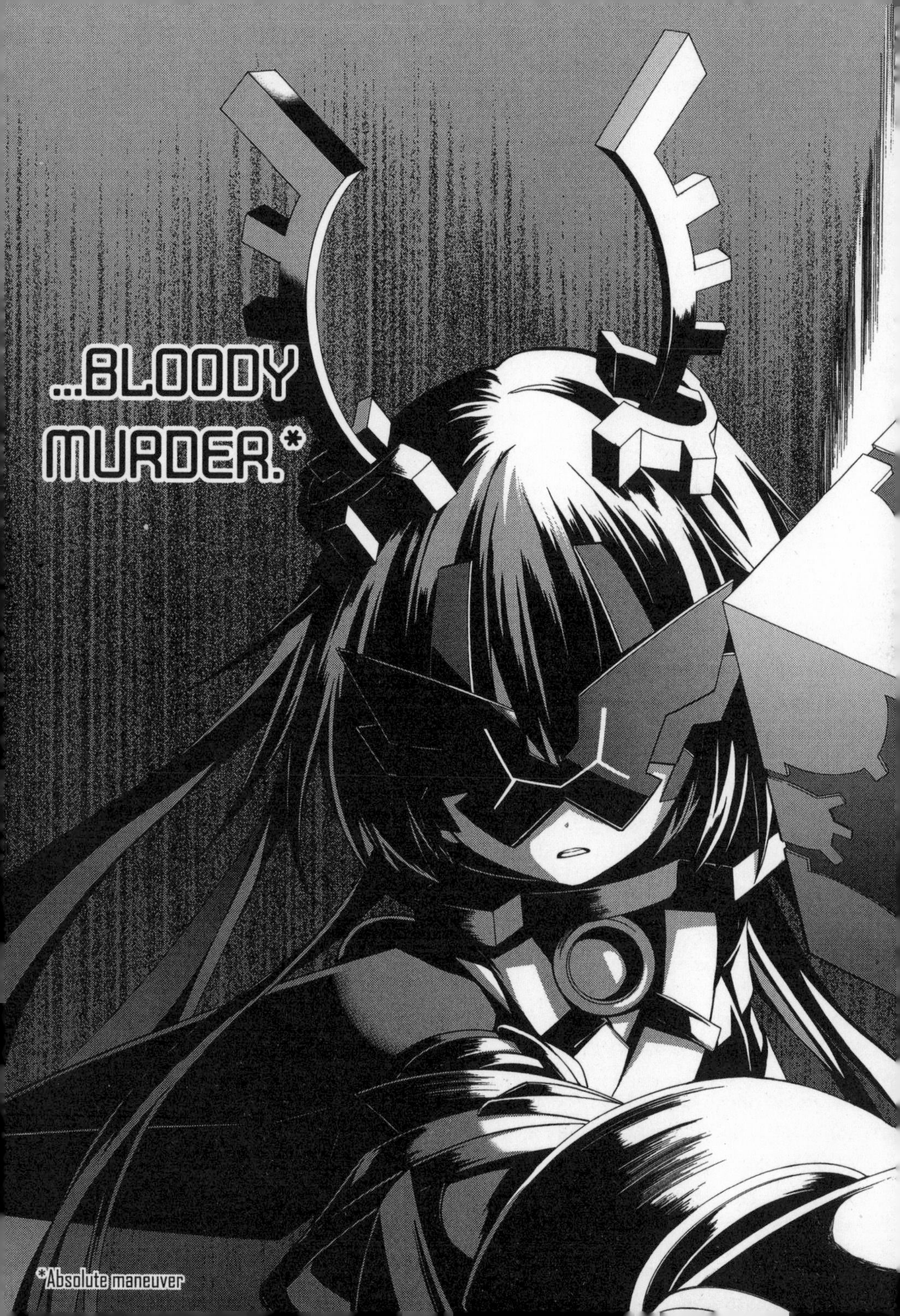
...BLOODY MURDER.*

*Absolute maneuver

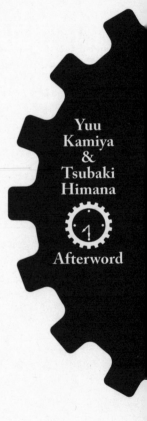

Yuu Kamiya & Tsubaki Himana

Afterword

YK: So, uh, here's Volume 3 of the manga version of *Clockwork Planet*. Woot.

TH: A big thank you to everyone who's purchased it! Dum da da dum, yay.

YK: So, they were like, "Your afterwords for the first two volumes were funny, so give us another one of those for the third one, lol." In other words, "Say something funny." So here we are, totally murdered by the MC.

TH: Come on. You don't have any problem being funny. The very fact you're alive is hilarious.

YK: Look, you want me to write all about how lately I've been running from the taxman and the editor and the doctor in connection with another work and I ran to the other side of the world and they still caught me? Who wants to read about that?

TH: I kind of do, actually, but oh well—can I ask you a question? About the hidden mysteries of *Clockwork Planet* you have not explained to me?

YK: What? I made you your bible, dude.

YK: Well, now that my friend has been reduced to a writing automaton, I'll proceed... Wow, this is something, isn't it? I cannot conceal my wonder and admiration that that novel of ours has been successfully adapted into a manga. You actually can visualize it!

TH: It's about "resonance communication." You write, "System for transmitting information by non-contact interlocking drive. Different from radio." And that's it. You call these crappy notes a bible? Look, if it's just the novels, I can bash out some kind of hand-waving B.S. perfectly in your spirit of "Hey, it's not like we have to draw it, so it's like, yeah, you know, probably like that," but what are we supposed to do if they need details for the manga?

YK: HA HA HA! Don't sweat it, Johnny. This is a clockwork planet, for God's sake. You start worrying about imaginary and perpetual motion systems and it's over for you!

TH: OKAY, Michael, then let me ask you about something that comes up pretty often, "resonance gear communication." What is the logic?

YK: Oh, that? *Ahem*. You ready? Resonance mechanisms in clockwork go back to the 18th century. You know how if you put two metronomes on a table and swing them out of sync, they'll get in sync with each other by themselves? The resonance gears in *Clockwork Planet* just take that a step further. You put resonant frequencies at a distance from each other—for instance, integrating them with the vibration of the air or the city itself—and you synchronize it all into a system that applies the principle by which separate movements can interlock without contact. While we're on the subject, the *resonance cannon* is an even further application of this, which uses resonant frequencies for crystal destruction! How about that?!

TH: Thank you for your painstaking elucidation, but isn't that the technology where you were talking to a real clocksmith and they told you, "That actually exists," and you were like, "What? I thought it was a figment of my imagination!"

YK: How did you know?!

TH: That would be because I was there.

YK: Uh, well—see, it's a good example of how modern technology is already catching up with sci-fi! Look at the 3-D printer; we might have replicators like in *Star Tr*k* soon! "The future is now"—

TH: (*laughing*) You and your 18th-century "modern technology"—

YK: Character limit! We're running up to the character limit! Wrap up pls!

TH: Uhh, Kuro, I'm sorry you have to burdened by Kamiya's B.S., but I think by having to draw this his luck has just about run—

YK: Dood, I am taking this seriously! Look, for instance, they don't have fossil fuels on Clockwork Planet, so for explosives— (*bvt*)

AFTERWORD
あとがき

As ever, Marie eats candy nonstop, Halter won't fit in the frame because of his height, and Naoto and Ryuzu are always flirting and frolicking. I want this to continue forever! It's Volume 3, yay! Thank you for picking it up.♪

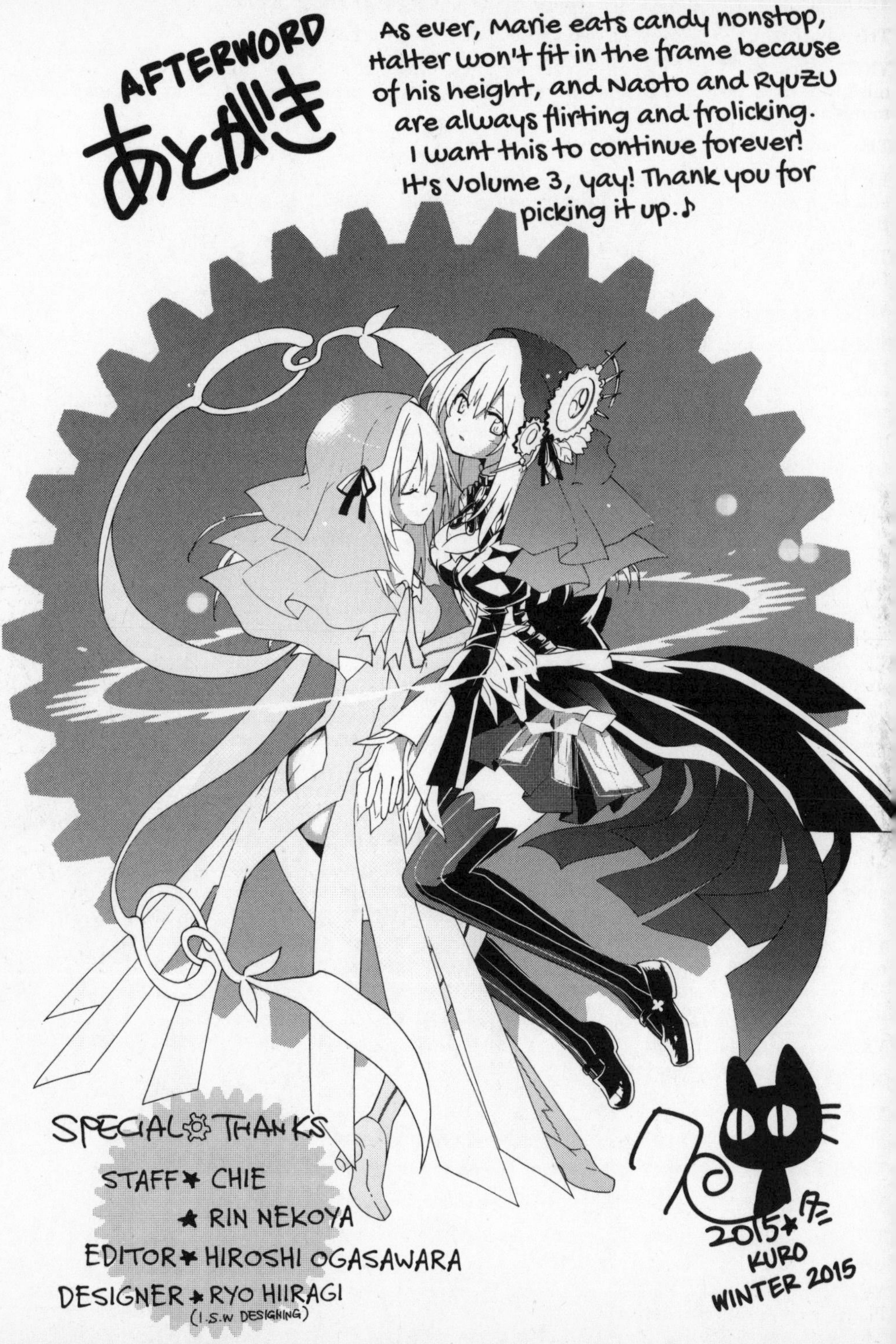

SPECIAL THANKS

STAFF ★ CHIE
★ RIN NEKOYA

EDITOR ★ HIROSHI OGASAWARA

DESIGNER ★ RYO HIIRAGI
(I.S.W DESIGNING)

2015★冬
KURO
WINTER 2015

Sino Afterword

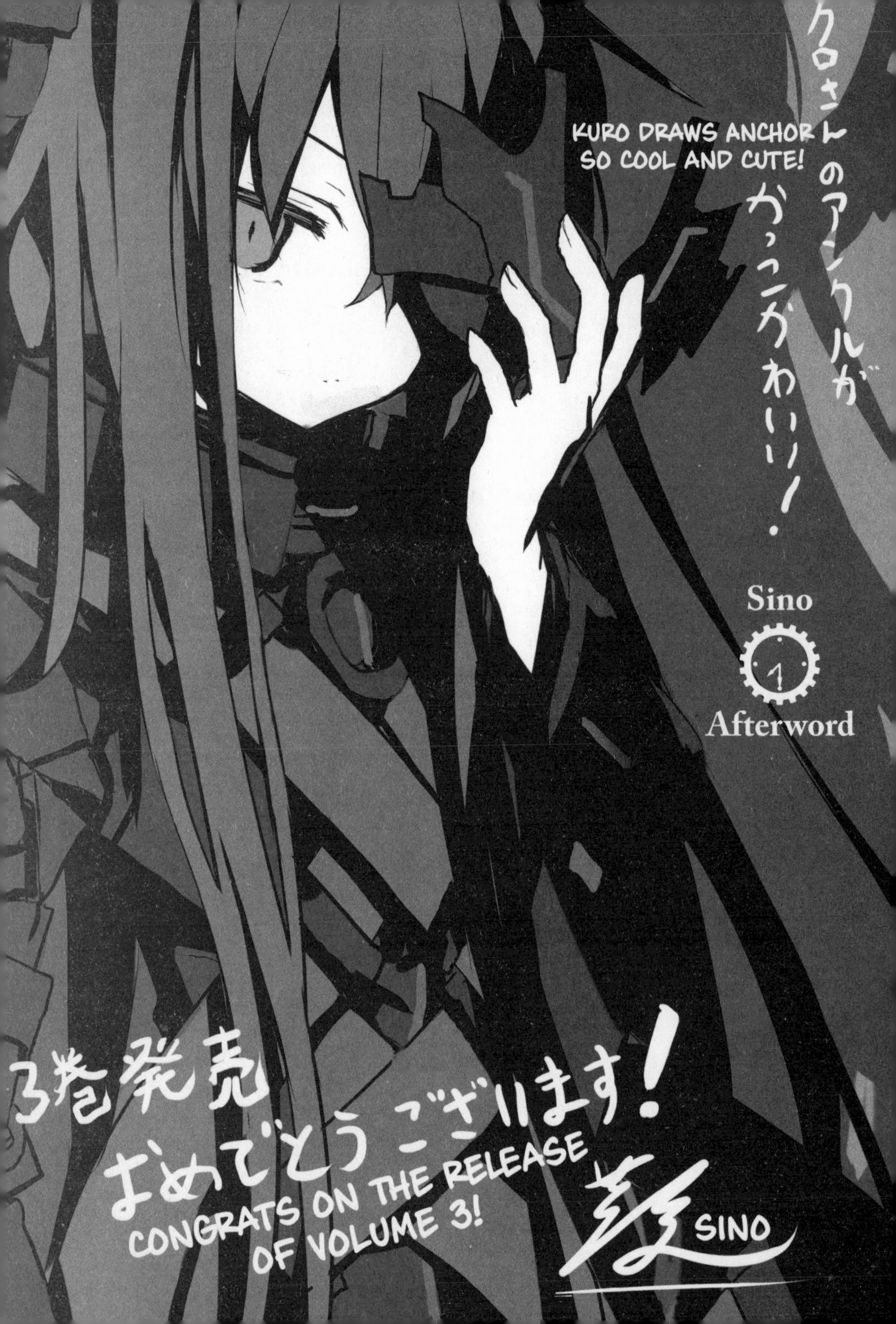

クロさんのアンクルがかっこかわいい!!
KURO DRAWS ANCHOR SO COOL AND CUTE!
3巻発売おめでとうございます!
CONGRATS ON THE RELEASE OF VOLUME 3!
SINO

Translation Notes

Jirai onna, page 10
Naoto uses this term to refer to Marie as "unpredictable." In Japanese, *jirai onna* is made up of the words "land mine" and "woman." A *jirai onna* is a negative label for women who appear pleasant on the surface, but have "land mines" hidden beneath the surface, which can go off at any time. They may act unpredictably, lash out, or cause trouble for the people around them. Women also use the term *jirai otoko/danshi* for men in the same way.

Izu disu a...pen?, page 13
"This is a pen" is a famous stock phrase from Japanese English textbooks.

Oideyasu, page 70
Oideyasu is an iconic bit of Kyoto dialect. It means welcome.

How's yours, page 80
The people in the background appear to be checking out fortunes like those sold by Japanese shrines and temples.

Oshiruko, page 81
Oshiruko, or *shiruko*, is hot, sweet red bean porridge, very similar to Chinese red bean soup.

Dango, page 82
Dango is a traditional Japanese snack or dessert made from rolled-up rice flour. The gelatinous balls of rice flour are skewered on a stick. Sometimes it is grilled, and has sauces and toppings.

IN THIS FANTASY WORLD, EVERYTHING'S A GAME—AND THESE SIBLINGS PLAY TO WIN!

No Game No Life © YUU KAMIYA
KADOKAWA CORPORATION

A genius but socially inept brother and sister duo is offered the chance to compete in a fantasy world where games decide everything. Sora and Shiro will take on the world and, while they're at it, create a harem of nonhuman companions!

No Game No Life, Please! © Kazuya Yuizaki 2016 © Yuu Kamiya 2016
KADOKAWA CORPORATION

LIGHT NOVELS 1–6 AVAILABLE NOW

LIKE THE NOVELS?

Check out the spin-off manga for even more out-of-control adventures with the Werebeast girl, Izuna!

Japan's most powerful spirit medium delves into the ghost world's greatest mysteries!

Story by Kyo Shirodaira, famed author of mystery fiction and creator of *Spiral*, *Blast of Tempest*, and *The Record of a Fallen Vampire*.

Both touched by spirits called yôkai, Kotoko and Kurô have gained unique superhuman powers. But to gain her powers Kotoko has given up an eye and a leg, and Kurô's personal life is in shambles. So when Kotoko suggests they team up to deal with renegades from the spirit world, Kurô doesn't have many other choices, but Kotoko might just have a few ulterior motives...

IN/SPECTRE

STORY BY KYO SHIRODAIRA
ART BY CHASHIBA KATASE

The award-winning manga about what happens inside you!

"Far more entertaining than it ought to be... what kid doesn't want to think that every time they sneeze a torpedo shoots out their nose?"
—Anime News Network

Strep throat! Hay fever! Influenza! The world is a dangerous place for a red blood cell just trying to get her deliveries finished. Fortunately, she's not alone...she's got a whole human body's worth of cells ready to help out! The mysterious white blood cells, the buff and brash killer T cells, even the cute little platelets— everyone's got to come together if they want to keep you healthy!

Cells at Work!

By Akane Shimizu

Having lost his wife, high school teacher Kōhei Inuzuka is doing his best to raise his young daughter Tsumugi as a single father. He's pretty bad at cooking and doesn't have a huge appetite to begin with, but chance brings his little family together with one of his students, the lonely Kotori. The three of them are anything but comfortable in the kitchen, but the healing power of home cooking might just work on their grieving hearts.

"This season's number-one feel-good anime!" —Anime News Network

"A beautifully-drawn story about comfort food and family and grief. Recommended." —Otaku USA Magazine

sweetness & lightning

By Gido Amagakure

New action series from Hiroyuki Takei, creator of the classic shonen franchise Shaman King!

In medieval Japan, a bell hanging on the collar is a sign that a cat has a master. Norachiyo's bell hangs from his katana sheath, but he is nonetheless a stray — a ronin. This one-eyed cat samurai travels across a dishonest world, cutting through pretense and deception with his blade.

By
Hiroyuki Takei

H A P · P I N E S S

—— ハピネス ——

By **Shuzo Oshimi**

From the creator of *The Flowers of Evil*

Nothing interesting is happening in Makoto Ozaki's first year of high school. His life is a series of quiet humiliations: low-grade bullies, unreliable friends, and the constant frustration of his adolescent lust. But one night, a pale, thin girl knocks him to the ground in an alley and offers him a choice. Now everything is different. Daylight is searingly bright. Food tastes awful. And worse than anything is the terrible, consuming thirst...

Praise for Shuzo Oshimi's *The Flowers of Evil*

"A shockingly readable story that vividly—one might even say queasily—evokes the fear and confusion of discovering one's own sexuality. Recommended." —The Manga Critic

"A page-turning tale of sordid middle school blackmail." —Otaku USA Magazine

"A stunning new horror manga." —Third Eye Comics

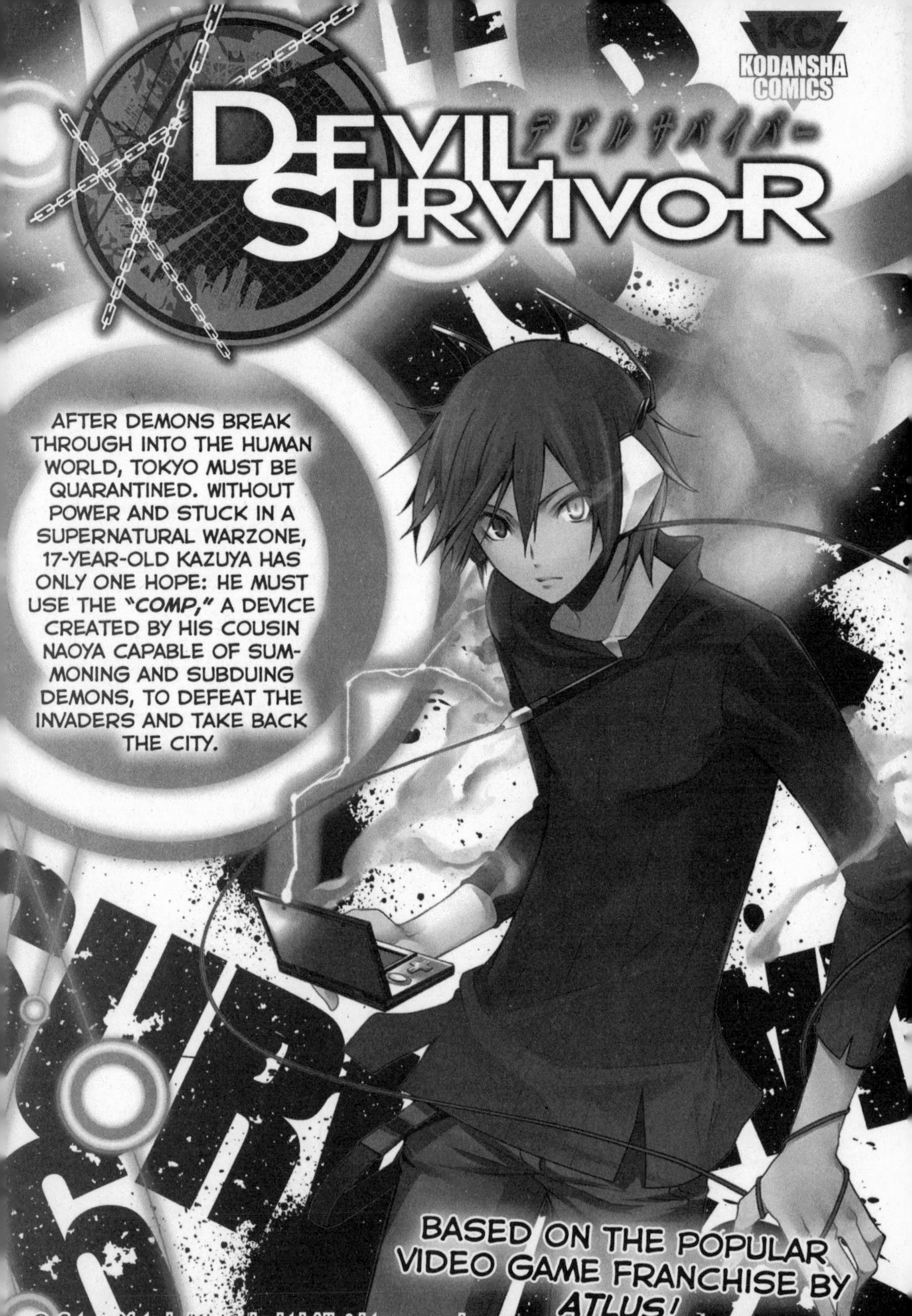
KC
KODANSHA COMICS
DEVIL SURVIVOR
デビルサバイバー
AFTER DEMONS BREAK THROUGH INTO THE HUMAN WORLD, TOKYO MUST BE QUARANTINED. WITHOUT POWER AND STUCK IN A SUPERNATURAL WARZONE, 17-YEAR-OLD KAZUYA HAS ONLY ONE HOPE: HE MUST USE THE "COMP," A DEVICE CREATED BY HIS COUSIN NAOYA CAPABLE OF SUMMONING AND SUBDUING DEMONS, TO DEFEAT THE INVADERS AND TAKE BACK THE CITY.
BASED ON THE POPULAR VIDEO GAME FRANCHISE BY ATLUS!

Based on the critically acclaimed classic horror manga

The first new *Parasyte* manga in over 20 years!

NEO Parasyte f

BY ASUMIKO NAKAMURA, EMA TOYAMA, MIKI RINNO, LALAKO KOJIMA, KAORI YUKI, BANKO KUZE, YUUKI OBATA, KASHIO, YUI KUROE, ASIA WATANABE, MIKIMAKI, HIKARU SURUGA, HAJIME SHINJO, RENJURO KINDAICHI, AND YURI NARUSHIMA

A collection of chilling new *Parasyte* stories from Japan's top shojo artists!

Parasites: shape-shifting aliens whose only purpose is to assimilate with and consume the human race... but do these monsters have a different side? A parasite becomes a prince to save his romance-obsessed female host from a dangerous stalker. Another hosts a cooking show, in which the real monsters are revealed. These and 13 more stories, from some of the greatest shojo manga artists alive today, together make up a chilling, funny, and entertaining tribute to one of manga's horror classics!

Clockwork Planet volume 3 is a work of fiction. Names, characters, places, and incidents are the products of the author's imagination or are used fictitiously. Any resemblance to actual events, locales, or persons, living or dead, is entirely coincidental.

A Kodansha Comics Trade Paperback Original

Published in the United States by Kodansha Comics, an imprint of Kodansha USA Publishing, LLC, New York.

Publication rights for this English edition arranged through Kodansha Ltd, Tokyo.

First published in Japan in 2015 by Kodansha Ltd., Tokyo

ISBN 978-1-63236-449-4

Printed in the United States of America.

www.kodanshacomics.com

9 8 7 6 5 4 3 2 1
Translation: Daniel Komen
Lettering: David Yoo
Editing: Haruko Hashimoto
Kodansha Comics edition cover design by Phil Balsman